CW01024344

THE JEWISH
Book of Days

The publication of this book was made possible through the generous support of

Board of Trustees and National Council

2005 JPS "Class" Gift

THE JEWISH Book of Days

A Companion for All Seasons

Jill Hammer

2006 | 5766
The Jewish Publication Society
Philadelphia

The Jewish Publication Society
2100 Arch Street
Philadelphia, PA 19103

www.jewishpub.org

Composition and Design by Masters Group Design, Inc. • Philadelphia, PA

Manufactured in the United States of America

06 07 08 09 10 10 9 8 7 6 5 4 3 2 1

Library of Congress Cataloging-in-Publication Data

Hammer, Jill.
The Jewish book of days : a companion for all seasons / Jill Hammer.
p. cm.
Includes bibliographical references and index.
ISBN 0-8276-0831-4
1. Spiritual life—Judaism. 2. Seasons—Religious aspects—Judaism. 3. Nature—Religious aspects—Judaism. 4. Calendar, Jewish. 5. Midrash. 6. Presence of God. 7. Days. I. Title.
BM724.H36 2006
296.7'2—dc22
2006005241

As long as the days of the earth endure,
seedtime and harvest,
cold and heat,
summer and winter,
day and night
shall not cease.

—Genesis 8:22

They shall build houses and dwell in them.
They shall plant vineyards and enjoy their fruits,
and like the days of a tree
shall be the days of my people.

—Isaiah 65:21–22

Acknowledgments

I would like to thank the staff of the Jewish Publication Society, particularly Janet Liss, Carol Hupping, Rena Potok, Arielle Levites, and editor-in-chief Ellen Frankel, for their work to produce *The Jewish Book of Days,* and to express gratitude to Harriet Goren for producing a beautiful Wheel of the Year so quickly. My thanks also to the library staff of the Jewish Theological Seminary for their help in locating midrashic works and also to the modern authors of midrash who enthusiastically agreed to be quoted in this book.

I would like to express my gratitude to my wonderful friends and colleagues: Joy Rosenberg, Rabbi Melissa Weintraub, Dr. Alicia Ostriker, Rabbi Rona Shapiro, and the rest of the staff of Ma'yan. A special thanks to The Jewish Women's Project, Rabbi Justin Lewis, Dr. Elizabeth Denlinger, Holly Taya Shere, Susie Kessler, Rabbi Shir Yaakov Feinstein-Feit, David Schildkret, Jay Michaelson, and Caroline Kohles, and my many other friends and well-wishers for their feedback and support during the thinking and writing process. Peter Pitzele is particularly to be thanked for offering the thought-kernel that grew into this book. The Tel Shemesh community also helped bring this writing into being through their sustained commitment to Judaism and to the earth. And I am most grateful to my parents, Dr. Leonard and Erna Hammer, for their warm support of my writing and their good advice (often at the last minute), and to my brother Marcus Hammer for taking an interest.

Last but by no means least, I want to thank Shoshana Jedwab for her love, compassion, and wisdom during the laborious, messy, and often joyous process of researching, writing, and editing this book.

For Shoshana Jedwab

with drums and with dances

— Exodus 15:20

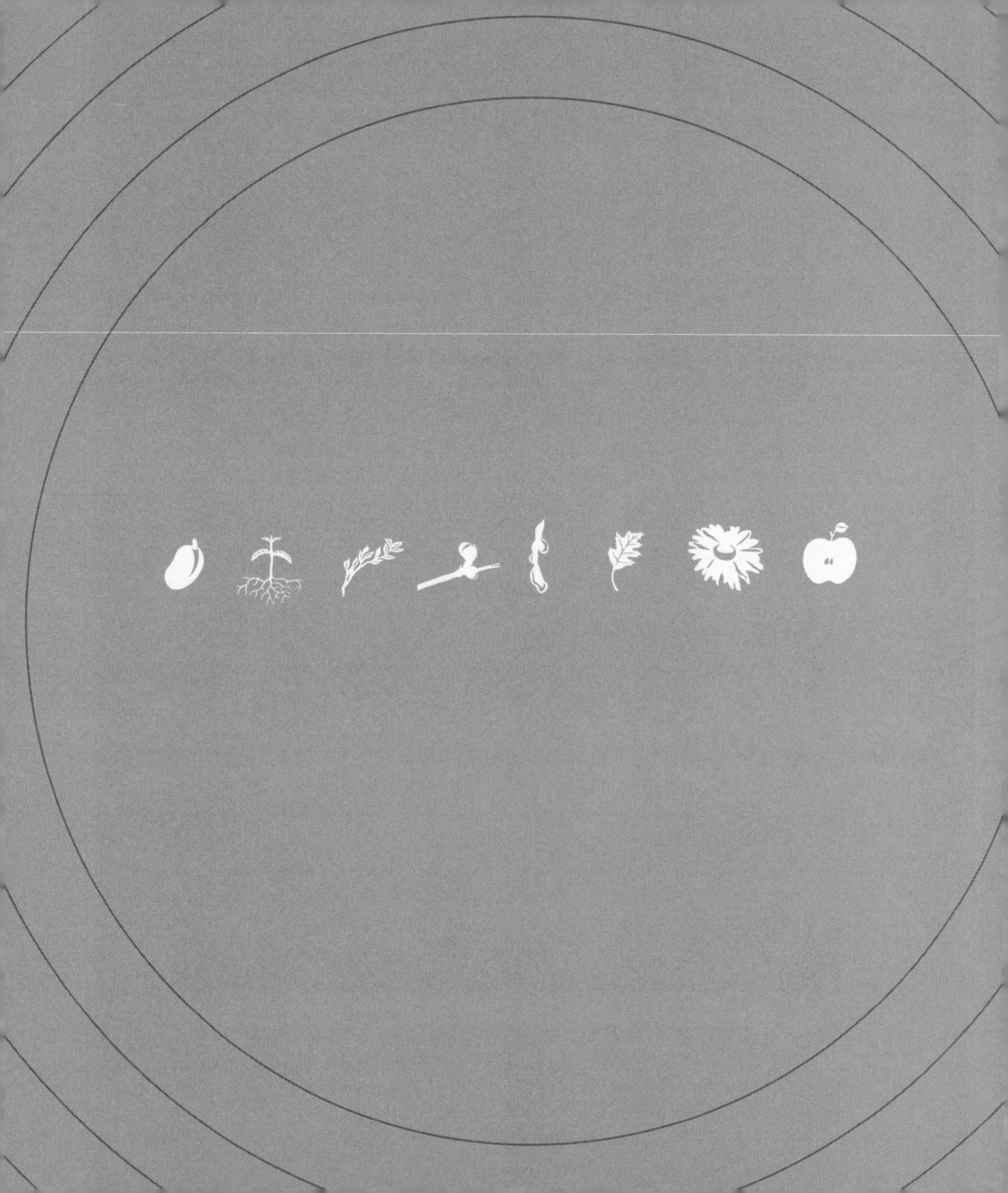

Contents

INTRODUCTION

THE DAYS OF THE YEAR

APPENDICES

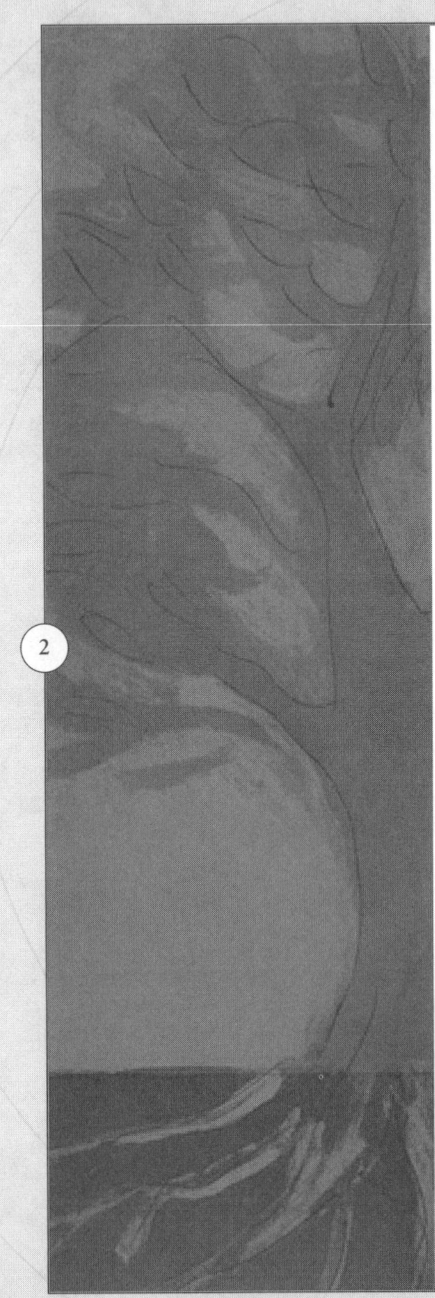

The Limbs of the Year

*Months and days and nights and solstices and seasons and cycles and passages of the year were before the Holy One of Blessing. The Holy One passed through the year, and then passed these teachings on to Adam in the garden of Eden, as it is written—This is the book of the generations of Adam. . . . Eve taught these things to Enoch, and he entered into every limb and passage of the year. . . . It is written: There will never cease from the earth planting (*zera*) and harvest (*katzir*), heat (*chom*) and cold (*kor*), summer (*kayitz*) and winter (*choref*). "Seedtime" is the season of Tishrei. "Harvest" is the season of Nisan. "Cold" is the season of Tevet, and "heat" is the season of Tammuz. "Summer" in its time and "winter" in its time.*

—Pirkei de-Rabbi Eliezer 7

In a midrash in *Pirkei de-Rabbi Eliezer,* based on the story of Adam and Eve, the first sacred book is called the *Sefer Toldot Adam,* the book of the generations of Adam. In this book are the secrets of the months and the days and the summers and the winters, secrets even the Holy One had to learn to enter Creation. This book of days, like that vanished one, seeks to uncover the secrets of days and seasons so that we, like Adam and Eve, may enter into every limb of the year.

We often experience the Jewish year as a reliving of myth and history: In Jewish time, the Exodus, Sinai, the destruction of the Temple, the victory of the Maccabees all become part of our experience as the months pass. This way of viewing the Jewish calendar connects us with the line of past and future. Yet the Jewish year is also a circle reflecting the cycles of the natural world. Throughout this yearly circle, planting and harvest, cold and heat, become our spiritual teachers and guides. They lead us through moments of joy and celebration and through times of mourning and destruction. The voice of the Divine comes to us not only from text and history but also from trees, the sky, the waxing and waning moon, and the wondrous and fragile functioning of our own bodies.

The generations of architects of the Jewish calendar deeply understood this. They instructed us to mark the trees as one year older in late winter on Tu b'Shevat (Babylonian Talmud, Rosh Hashanah 2a), count the sheaves of grain in the spring before the wheat harvest of Shavuot (Leviticus 23:15–16), and pray for rain in the autumn as part of Shemini Atzeret, the last day of the autumn holiday season (Babylonian Talmud, Sukkah 28b). As we smell the *etrog,* the fragrant yellow citron, on the harvest festival of Sukkot, we are meant to experience the mysteries of growth and decay that come with autumn; and as we tell the story of the Exodus at the spring festival of Passover, we are meant to think of the seedlings escaping the ground to burst into the air. We have the human gifts of intellect, spirit, and history, and the Jewish gifts of text, law, and tradition; yet we are still part of the natural world, dependent on its bounty and subject to its tides. The deep wisdom of the Jewish year invites us to understand ourselves as embodied beings, rooted in the earth and in our own sensory experience and rooted in the truths of our people. When legend and nature are combined, they weave a powerful web of meaning and connection.

Nature also offers us the gift of gratitude. Genesis Rabbah 1:4 states that the world was created for the sake of challah (the dough offering), tithes of the crops, and first fruits of the harvest. All of these offerings represent the bounty of the earth. Why should the rabbis teach that the Divine created the world so that we should give a tithe of the harvest? What is so valuable about the practice of offering part of the earth's produce? Perhaps this teaching emphasizes that gratitude for what we have been given is the core meaning in our lives. In that sense, the natural leads to the ethical, for gratitude compels us to acknowledge what we have and to give back what we have received.

Many of us have come to believe our sympathy with nature and our affection for Jewish tradition are two separate entities. This book, building on the wisdom of Sages, mystics, and moderns, seeks to bring together these two spiritual sources into a whole. The sacred stories of Torah can combine with the sacred teachings of the earth into a new book we read with the body, the mind, and the heart.

The kabbalists, both medieval and contemporary, tell us the *Shekhinah,* the feminine Divine Presence, the immanent face of God, is an intrinsic part of the physical world (Zohar I:49a). We experience Her through the falling leaves of autumn and through the birth of children. Yet we also find the *Shekhinah* in the Torah. She is the element of mystery in the text, asking us to keep looking for new interpretations, to keep adding to the Tree of Life. *The Jewish Book of Days* honors both houses of the *Shekhinah:* Torah and world, heaven and earth.

Space, Time, and Soul: What This Book Seeks to Do

The Divine is revealed in the world through
three dimensions: world, year, and soul.
—Mei haShiloach on Genesis 28:12

The *Sefer Yetzirah,* an ancient work of mystical lore, is often cited in this book because of its focus on the secrets of the months. *Sefer Yetzirah* 3:3 identifies three dimensions of human experience: space, time, and soul. Later commentaries, like Rabbi Mordechai Yosef of Izbitza's *Mei haShiloach* (19th century), use this principle to analyze stories in the Torah, imagining that certain moments in the text bring together all three of these dimensions, so that physical space, the flow of time, and the depths of the individual spirit are all sanctified at once. The entries in *The Jewish Book of Days* seek to bring together these three dimensions every day: the physical space of nature, the times of the year, and the spiritual movements of the days and seasons within each of us.

Many days of the Jewish calendar, holidays and mundane days, have biblical stories associated with them: the day Noah released the dove, the day Miriam died, the day trees were created. Each day is also a part of a larger season. Every day of the Jewish year has an entry in *The Jewish Book of Days.* Each entry has three components:

- A biblical quote.
- A midrash commenting on the biblical quote and/ or a Jewish tradition related to that day.
- A comment relating the text to the months, seasons, and cycles of the year.

Through these three components, the reader may engage daily in study, interpretation, observation of the natural world, and contemplation of spirit.

Each of the chapters of *The Jewish Book of Days* tells the story of one part of the Jewish year, using as a metaphor the life of a tree: seed, root, branch, sap, bud, leaf, flower, and fruit. Each chapter has a brief introduction to place it in the larger context of the

Jewish cycles of time (the cycles are explained in "Understanding the Larger Picture.") The appendix offers legends of the solstices and equinoxes and new rituals for the changing of the seasons.

For the most part, *The Jewish Book of Days* does not provide historical dates (important events, death dates of famous Jews, and so on) or biographies of talmudic Sages. This book also does not provide comprehensive details on how to observe holidays or perform Jewish rituals, though it frequently refers to rituals, customs, blessings, and the like. *The Jewish Book of Days* seeks to reveal and interpret biblical texts and legends about biblical texts that contribute to our sense of space, time, and soul so that we may reclaim the Jewish spiritual connection to the earth and its seasons.

Notes on the Language of *The Jewish Book of Days*

As the midrash in *Pirkei de-Rabbi Eliezer* says, the Divine too enters into the limbs of the year. We encounter divinity, and divinity encounters us, in different ways throughout the changing seasons. To this end, this book approaches God using a variety of names.

Readers will note that the biblical four-letter divine name *Yud-Heh-Vav-Heh* usually identified as *Adonai* (Lord) has been rendered in this book as "the Eternal" or sometimes "the Holy One." These names have been chosen because *Yud-Heh-Vav-Heh* comes from a word meaning "to be or become" and can be understood to mean "Eternal Being." "Holy One of Blessing" is a common Rabbinic appellation for this Eternal Being. In mysticism, this name of God is connected with the attribute of compassion.

The Hebrew name *Elohim,* usually rendered "God," has been translated as "the Divine," a meaning closer to the original term. *Elohim* (divinities) is a plural functioning as a singular noun, conveying a sense of multiple divine faces within a single deity. In some Jewish traditions, this name of God is connected with the attribute of justice and with the process of Creation.

Hebrew phrases usually translated as "the presence of God" or "the glory of God" here appear as "the *Shekhinah,*" the Indwelling One, a name for the feminine Divine. *Shekhinah* is a talmudic word for the tangible presence of God. The kabbalistic work called the Zohar, I:8a, 48a, 223a–b and II:65b transforms the *Shekhinah* into a mother, bride, and defender of the Jewish people, and the word becomes a name for the sparks of divinity within the earth and all creation. It is crucial, in reclaiming an embodied Jewish experience, to reclaim the feminine face of the Divine as a guide on our year's journey.

These unusual renditions shake up traditional notions of God as gendered solely as a male, as a lord or master, as a particular form or appearance of deity. Instead, readers are encouraged to be open to the ways the Divine appears to them within these legends and interpretations and to value their own perceptions. Biblical names of people and places have been rendered somewhat idiosyncratically, either in the traditional English form or in a Hebrew transliteration.

Roots and Seedlings: Beginning the Journey

If you are reading this book, it may be because you have experienced, at one time in your life or many times, a spiritual awakening in nature—in a garden, at the sea, on a hike, near a willow—and are looking for a Jewish voice to speak to your experiences: a midrash on moths, a Torah of trees. Or it may be that you deeply relate to cycles of time and have been moved by the yearly Passover seder, the outdoor celebration of Sukkot, or the solemn legends of Yom Kippur. You may love midrash and want to know more about the creative sacred stories of the Jewish people. Or you may be looking for a soul-journey, a new way of discovering your spirit every day. If these are your interests, this book will help you renew them as the days pass.

The Jewish Book of Days covers a wide range of environments, recognizing that humans live in every place on earth. However, if you are living in the Southern Hemisphere or in a climate significantly dissimilar from that of the Middle Eastern or temperate North American regions, this book will offer you some challenges. As you read it, consider what your own climate is doing at each season and how your experience of nature might connect to the sacred times and stories of the Jewish people.

This book is not an isolated work. It is woven from the learning of others: the Sages of the Talmud and later midrashic works, the medieval commentators, the mystics of the Zohar, the kabbalists and dreamers of Tzfat, the Hasidic masters, and the modern masters of time and earth like Gershon Winkler, Arthur Waskow, Marcia Falk, and Melinda Ribner. While many Jewish traditions about nature and cyclical time have been de-emphasized in the modern era, a new generation is reclaiming and reinventing those traditions to meet the pressing needs of today's Jews and of the world.

The need is great at this moment to rediscover these secrets. Humans daily destroy natural resources and whole species, ignoring the fragile balance of life across the globe. Meanwhile, we often have become distant from our soulful selves and our ancient traditions. To return to the wheel of the year as a spiritual discipline is to make a commitment to learn our place in the world and to respect the blessings we have received. To return to the cycle of the seasons is to walk in the ways of our ancestors and to tell their sacred stories while listening to the rhythms of our unique lives. The gifts of the seasons and the days are many; we have only to open the book of days given to us at the dawn of Creation and read it once more.

May you be guided by light and lore, by texts and trees, by stories and seasons.

—Jill Hammer

Understanding the Larger Picture

As long as the days of the earth endure,
seedtime and harvest,
cold and heat,
summer and winter,
day and night
shall not cease.

—Genesis 8:22

Genesis tells us that the year has different, interlocking parts: summer and winter, day and night. We learn in *Pirkei de-Rabbi Eliezer* that there are many layers to the year: seasons and times and cycles and passages. The wheel of the year is complex, wealthy with distinctions and characteristics added over time by a variety of interpreters. Understanding the cycle's different elements requires an overview of Jewish traditions related to the division of time. Following are a number of traditions related to the seasons of the year along with some new interpretations.

The Months

The 12 months of the Hebrew year are given in the table here.

LOCATING THE MONTHS IN SACRED AND SECULAR TIME

Month	*Falls During*	*Important Holidays*
Tishrei	September–October	High Holy Days, Sukkot
Heshvan	October–November	Rachel's yahrzeit
Kislev	November–December	Hanukkah
Tevet	December–January	Hanukkah, Fast of 10 Tevet
Shevat	January–February	Tu b'Shevat
Adar	February–March	Purim
(Adar II)*	March	Purim
Nisan	March–April	Passover
Iyar	April–May	Lag b'Omer
Sivan	May–June	Shavuot
Tammuz	June–July	Fast of 17 Tammuz
Av	July–August	Tisha b'Av/Tu b' Av
Elul	August–September	Preparation for New Year

*Appears only in leap years.

Tishrei, Heshvan, and Kislev are autumn months; Tevet, Shevat, and Adar are winter months; Nisan, Iyar, and Sivan are spring months; and Tammuz, Av, and Elul are summer months (*Pirkei de-Rabbi Eliezer* 7; Babylonian Talmud, Pesachim 94b). Most months contain a holiday or some form of sacred time (even Heshvan, the most notable exception to this rule, has significant days within it).

In *Sefer Yetzirah* and other mystical traditions, each month has an Israelite tribe associated with it as well as a sensory experience of the body, as shown in the table here.[1]

TRIBES AND SENSES OF THE HEBREW MONTHS

Month	*Tribe*	*Sense*
Tishrei	Ephraim	Sexuality
Heshvan	Manasseh	Smell
Kislev	Benjamin	Sleep
Tevet	Dan	Anger
Shevat	Asher	Taste
Adar	Naphtali	Laughter
(Adar II)	Dinah	Intuition
Nisan	Judah	Speech
Iyar	Issachar	Thought
Sivan	Zebulun	Movement
Tammuz	Reuben	Sight
Av	Simeon	Hearing
Elul	Gad	Action

*Appears only in leap years.

The Halves of the Year

The most basic division of the year is into halves: the six months from Tishrei to Adar (autumn and winter) and the six months from Nisan to Elul (spring and summer). The Talmud refers to the autumn and winter months as *yemot hageshamim*, "days of rain," and the spring and summer months as *yemot hachamah*, "days of sun" (cf. Babylonian Talmud, Gittin 70b, Bava Metzi'a 101b). These phrases are used in regard to calendrical dating and even in regard to laws of renting homes. Aside from the practical consideration that the Middle Eastern summer months are sunny and winter months are rainy, we could read these halves of the year as two modes of human spiritual action. In the days of rain, when the days are shorter and the outward holidays fewer and when we spend more time inside, we turn inward to work on our spiritual growth. In the days of sun, when the festivals and the weather draw us outside, we turn outward to use that spiritual growth in the world, for repair and celebration. In the days of rain, which correspond to the planting season in the Land of Israel, we plant new seeds within ourselves. In the days of sun, we harvest the fruit of those seeds.

The days of rain contain the festivals of the inner life: Rosh Hashanah and Yom Kippur are holidays of introspection; Sukkot and Shemini Atzeret, holidays of gratitude for the harvest; Hanukkah and Purim, holidays of individual faith and courage. The days of sun contain the festivals of communal life: Passover, holiday of national freedom; Shavuot, holiday of revelation to the whole people at Sinai; and Tisha b'Av, holiday of national mourning. The holidays of each half of the year remind us of that half cycle's innate qualities.

The Three Gates of the World

The Jewish year is punctuated by three pilgrimage festivals: Passover or Pesach (the spring freedom festival and barley harvest), Shavuot (first fruits, covenant, and the giving of the Torah), and Sukkot (the final harvest festival). Each one of these lends its character to the seasons. Arthur Waskow,[2] for example, notes that Passover, Shavuot, and Sukkot are a kind of national life cycle in which Passover represents birth, Shavuot represents marriage and commitment, and Sukkot represents maturity.

Another way to look at these three festivals is as symbols of Creation. The Torah teaches us that God made three realms in the world: sky, earth, and sea: "In seven days the Eternal made the sky, the earth, and the sea with everything in it, and rested on the seventh day" (Exodus 20:11). These three realms manifest through the three pilgrimage festivals—Passover, Shavuot, and Sukkot—and the days that follow them.

Shavuot is connected to the sky. The sky is the source of the Torah and the wedding canopy of Israel. The holiday of the giving of the Torah, Shavuot, has a beautiful legend associated with it, taught to me by my teacher Rabbi Ilyse Kramer in the name of her teachers: On Shavuot at midnight, the sky opens and all prayers rise straight to heaven. Shavuot, when we study all night to do honor to the Torah, holds the key to the gate of heaven.

We may imagine that this gate of heaven is open from Shavuot, in spring, all the way to Sukkot, when the harvest is completed. While the sky-gate is open, we receive the Torah from the heavenly realms. We pray for the harvest to be successful and for rain to fall. On Tisha b'Av, when the keys of the Temple rose up to heaven, we pray for the afflicted and the martyred (Babylonian Talmud, Ta'anit 29a). On Rosh Hashanah, we contemplate the past year and consider our deeds. On Yom Kippur, we wear white like the angels, the legendary residents of heaven. The heavens correspond to the dimension of the soul, and this is the season when we do the most soul work.

Sukkot is connected to the earth. On Sukkot, the fields open to give us their bounty. This harvest festival, when we dwell outside in booths, holds the key to the gate of the earth, which is open from Sukkot until Passover. During these six months, we plant crops (particularly in the Middle East, when, according to the Talmud, planting begins in the fall). We celebrate the holidays of Hanukkah and Purim, when earthly actions by human beings saved the Jewish people. We honor the trees on Tu b'Shevat, the trees' new year.

The gate of the earth corresponds to the dimension of space. Hanukkah celebrates the rededication of the Temple, the most holy space of the people. On the 1st of Nisan, just before Passover, we mark the anniversary of the building of the Tabernacle, the portable sanctuary that brought the *Shekhinah* the Divine Presence, down to earth.

Passover is connected to the realm of the ocean. On Passover, the Sea of Reeds parts to allow the Israelites to pass from slavery to freedom. Passover opens up the gate of the sea, which is open the shortest time of the three gates: only 49 days. The sea represents birth; and at this season, the Jewish people are born. During this time, Miriam's well, the well of water that was said to accompany the wandering Israelites on all their journeys, appears in the desert. The sea, which ebbs and flows in patterns of days and months, corresponds to the dimension of time; and it is at this season that we pay the most attention to time, counting every day between Passover and Shavuot.

These three realms exert a subtle influence on the year, directing us toward particular energies at particular moments in time. They also remind us that "up" is not the only direction in which to pray. All realms of the world can open to reveal the Divine to us.

The Four Elements and the Four Directions

In cultures around the world, the four seasons are often associated with four directions and four elements, the four elements being the fundamental mythic components of existence. This is also true in the Jewish tradition.

In *Sefer Yetzirah* 3:4, it is written:

> Three mothers in the year are fire, water, and breath. Fire is for the hot season, water for the cold season, and air, for the season of abundance, balances between them.

That is, fire is associated with summer, water with winter, and air with spring and autumn. Gershon Winkler, author of *Magic of the Ordinary*, uses this general approach to suggest that we look at summer as a fire season, winter as a water season, spring as an air season, and autumn as an earth season.

However, in the Zohar II:24a, we learn:

> Fire, air, earth, and water are the sources and roots of all things above and below, and on them are all things grounded. In each of the four winds these elements are found: fire in the North, air in the East, water in the South, earth in the West.

Because Judaism is a Northern Hemisphere tradition, we would expect winter to be associated with north and summer with south. In some midrashic traditions the tribes associated with south (Reuben, Simeon, Gad) are also associated with summer, and the tribes associated with north (Dan, Asher, Naphtali) are associated with winter (*Otzar ha-Midrashim: Konen* 13). This suggests winter is the fire season, spring is the air season, summer is the water season, and autumn is the earth season.

Using the creative tension between these two systems and considering that each time of year has both physical and spiritual dimensions, we may imagine that each season has an inner and an outer element. Nature teaches us both about what is most present in the world at each season and about what we lack and need to seek. This secret of the seasons allows us to discover our blessings, revealing our deepest desires at each moment of the year.

Autumn's outer element is earth, reflecting the harvest and, in the Middle East, planting. The holiday of Sukkot, with its four plant species, honors this physical dimension of autumn. Autumn's inner element is air, or breath. The shofar blown on Rosh Hashanah and Yom Kippur reflects this inner element of air, which is embodied in the prayer and song of the High Holy Day season. The twin holidays of Shemini Atzeret and Simchat Torah also reflect these elements: On Shemini Atzeret, we pray for rain to bless the earth, whereas on Simchat Torah we concentrate on the blessings of air—the words of the Torah. The *Shekhinah,* who the Talmud teaches is always in the west, presides at this season.

Winter's outer, physical element is water, reflecting the rain and snow of the winter season. Its inner, spiritual element is fire, and this is reflected in the candles of Hanukkah lit at this time, and in the hearth fires of our homes, which we may seek more often in these days. At this season, we celebrate Tu b'Shevat, the new year of the trees. In some areas, the sap begins to run inside the trees at this season. The Hebrew word for "sap" *(saraf),* comes from the word for "fire." The sap within the trees embodies both the nourishing water and the inner fire of these days.

Spring's outer element is air or wind. The buds bursting into the breeze reflect this outer element. Spring's inner element is earth: the seeds still inside the ground, waiting to be released. Passover celebrates both these elements. The slaves' passage through the Sea of Reeds is like a birth into the wilderness—we enter the uncertain, airy freedom of the desert, seeking a new land, a new earth, in which to plant ourselves. Shavuot is also a celebration of air and earth: The Israelites gather at a mountain (the earth) to receive sacred words (air, or breath).

Summer's physical, external element is fire. The bright sun that warms us and even burns us at this time is a reflection of the season's more obvious element. Summer's inner element is water, the water we use to quench our thirst and the inner juices of the ripening fruits. The tears we shed during the fast days of Tammuz and Av are a sign of this secret element of summer.

These four elements can help us understand the spiritual energies of the seasons as we move through them. According to Isaac Luria, the 16th-century mystic, earth represents the world of action, water the world of emotion, air the world of the intellect, and fire the world of the spirit.[3] The pinnacles of each season reveal these four energies.

Around the month of Tishrei, we examine our deeds (earth), and through this examination we alter the ways we think and remember (air). We gather in the physical blessing of harvest (earth); yet within, we empty ourselves of pretense and self-deception and make space to act in new ways (air).

Around Tevet, we celebrate the victories of Hanukkah and look beyond the emotions of fear and anger toward the flame of spirit, faith, and hope (fire within water). We rekindle the fire even when that seems impossible, just as the Prophet Elijah once kindled fire from water.

Around Nisan, we celebrate Passover and allow the words and stories of the Passover seder to inspire our earthly actions (earth within air). In Tishrei we empty ourselves; but in Nisan, we fill ourselves with the blessings of the Divine.

Around Tammuz, at the sad time of the Jewish year when we remember exile and destruction, we consider the burning of the Temple and allow our tears and emotions to flow (water within fire). We attempt to put out the fires of our own destructive hatred, using the flowing compassion of our hearts.

Contemplation of the year's inner and outer elements helps us balance those same forces in ourselves. Spirit and body, intellect and emotion are all necessary to the health of our deepest selves, and each needs to be nurtured. By following the path of the seasons, we meet spirit, body, intellect, and emotion in their various combinations, and learn to integrate them in everything we do.

Eight Phases of Growth

As long as the days of the earth endure,
seedtime and harvest,
cold and heat,
summer and winter,
day and night
shall not cease.
—Genesis 8:22

This verse from Genesis promises the eternal renewal of the seasons as part of the divine covenant with Noah. The Sages of the Talmud comment on the passage above, which seems to indicate the various seasons of the year, by claiming that there are not four seasons but six. They explain each phrase in the passage in Genesis as a two-month period of time.

> Rabbi Shimon ben Menashya would say: Half of Tishrei, Marcheshvan, and half of Kislev, this is "seedtime." Half of Kislev, Tevet, and half of Shevat, this is "winter." Half of Shevat, Adar, and half of Nisan, this is "cold." Half of Nisan, Iyar, and half of Sivan, this is "harvest." Half of Sivan, Tammuz, and half of Av, this is summer. Half of Av, Elul, half of Tishrei: this is heat. Rabbi Yehudah counts [the six seasons] from Tishrei, and Rabban Shimon ben Gamliel counts [the six seasons] from Marcheshvan.
> —Babylonian Talmud, Bava Metzi'a 106b

This passage is interesting for two reasons: first, because Rabbi Shimon ben Menashya is willing to divide months to make his seasons correspond to the changes he perceives in nature and, second, because the Sages cannot agree on exactly what the six seasons are. Each Sage begins "seedtime" in a different place, depending on his own tradition or experience.

If we look carefully at the Jewish calendar, another possible interpretation of Genesis 8:22 appears—another midrash on Jewish time. In fact, the words the Divine speaks to Noah contain eight phrases: seedtime, harvest, cold, heat, summer, winter, day, and night. The Sages ignore day and night as irrelevant; but what if we interpreted those phrases more metaphorically and saw them also as seasons?

The idea that there are eight phases to the Jewish year immediately finds resonance in the calendar itself because there are eight natural dividing points in the calendar. One set of four corresponds to the new moon of Tishrei (Rosh Hashanah), the new moon of Tevet (Hanukkah), the new moon of Nisan (just before Passover), and the new moon of Tammuz. These four days begin the seasons of autumn, winter, spring, and summer (*Pirkei de-Rabbi Eliezer* 7). In fact, an ancient Jewish source, the book of Jubilees 6:23 claims these four days as the "days of remembrance and days of the transitions of the seasons" declared by Noah, leading us to believe that those four days (which may once have corresponded to the equinoxes and solstices) are significant transition points in the calendar.

The second set of transition points corresponds to four minor holidays on the Jewish calendar: the 11th (or 15th) of Heshvan, Tu b'Shevat, Lag b'Omer and Tu b'Av. In Heshvan, on the 11th or sometimes the 15th, Jews honor the anniversary of the death of the matriarch Rachel with pilgrimages to her tomb (*Yalkut Shimoni, Shemot* 162; Jubilees 32:33). Tu b'Shevat, as we have said, is the new year of the trees, mentioned by the Babylonian Talmud (Rosh Hashanah 2a) and celebrated by mystics (*Pri Etz Hadar*). Lag b'Omer, the 33rd day of the counting of the Omer and the 18th of Iyar, is a minor outdoor celebration, marking events such as the fall of the manna and the death of the Sage Shimon bar Yohai (Babylonian Talmud, Yevamot 63a; Zohar III:296b). Tu b'Av is an ancient celebration, recorded by the Talmud, in which women would dress in white and go out to the vineyards to dance and seek husbands from among the gathered men (Babylonian Talmud, Ta'anit 31a).

These four holidays are small in themselves, but they are what the Celtic calendar, which also has eight sections, calls "cross-quarter days." These four days form approximate midpoints to each season, coming at the center of autumn, winter, spring, and summer. (The Talmud even notes this on one occasion, saying that after Tu b'Av, "the sun's strength wanes" [Babylonian Talmud, Ta'anit 30b].) Each of these minor dates separates a season into two parts, making eight half seasons in all.

So, one possible new midrash on the verse in Genesis is:

> Tishrei and half of Heshvan: This is called seedtime.
> Half of Heshvan and Kislev: This is called night.
> Tevet and half of Shevat: This is called winter.
> Half of Shevat and Adar: This is called cold.
> Nisan and half of Iyar: This is called harvest.
> Half of Iyar and Sivan: This is called day.
> Tammuz and half of Av: This is called summer.
> Half of Av and Elul: This is called heat.

The eight stages of the year correspond to eight parts of the tree:

> The seed, corresponding to seedtime.
> The root, buried in the darkness of the soil.
> The branch, laid bare in winter.
> The sap, beginning to run in the cold season.
> The bud, emerging to be harvested in its time.
> The leaf, drawing in light during the long days.
> The flower, beginning to fade in the summer sun.
> The fruit, ripening in the heat of summer.

The Jewish Book of Days is structured around these eight stages of growth, honoring the words of Isaiah 65:22: "Like the days of a tree shall be the days of my people." The introduction to each stage will reveal its particular characteristics and mysteries.

This book is only one of many midrashim on the Jewish calendar. The reader is encouraged, on his or her walk through Jewish time, to discover and invent others. For we learn in Ecclesiastes 3:1: "Everything has its own time, and there is a season for everything under the sky."

Wheel of the Year

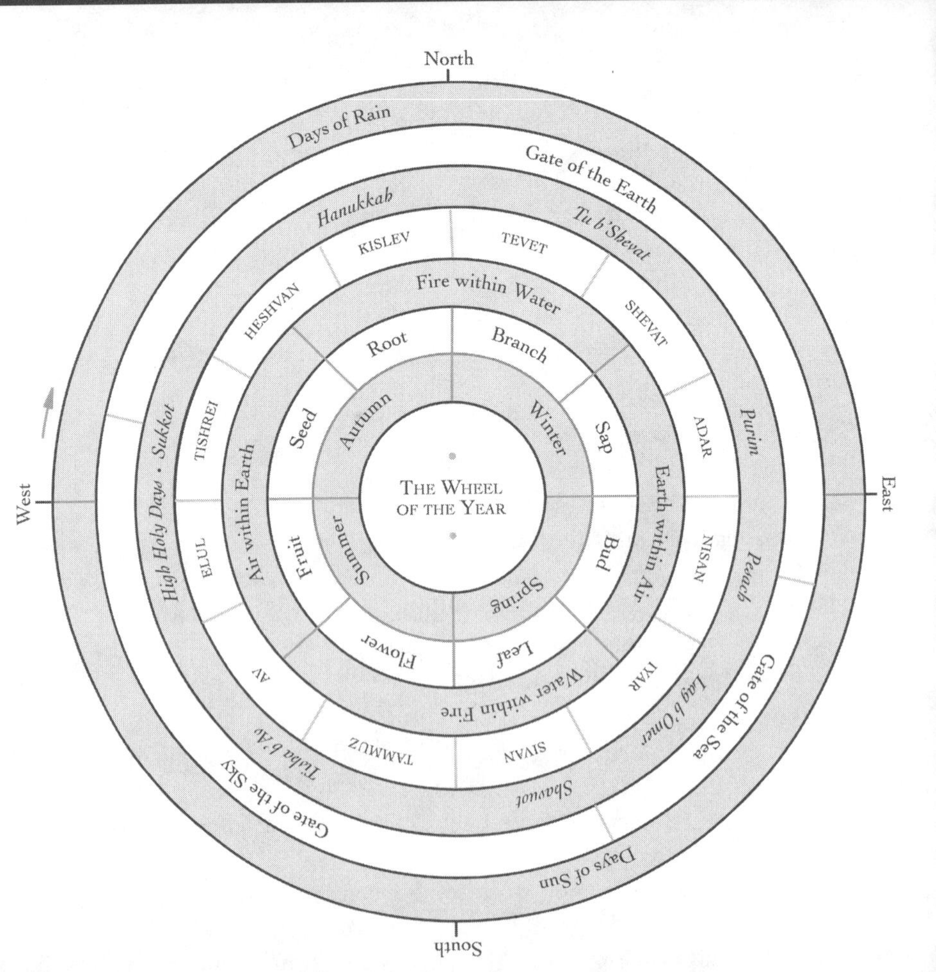

KEY TO WHEEL OF THE YEAR

Outermost ring:
The halves of the year—days of sun and rain

Second ring:
The three gates of the year—earth, sea, and sky

Third ring:
The major holidays

Fourth ring:
The Hebrew months

Fifth ring:
The four quarters of the year: outer and inner elements

Sixth ring:
The tree-stages of the year

Seventh ring:
The four seasons

Note that the four quarters of the year begin and end with the minor holidays of Rachel's yahrzeit (mid-Heshvan; see p. 77), Tu b'Shevat (mid-Shevat; see p. 175), Lag b'Omer (mid-Iyar; see p. 276), and Tu b'Av (mid-Av; see p. 371). The four seasons, in contrast, start at the new moon in the months of Tishrei, Tevet, Nisan, and Tammuz.

A Note on the Legends

The legends and stories that appear in *The Jewish Book of Days* are drawn from a variety of sources spanning more than two thousand years. All of these sources are part of the literary project known as *midrash*: creative interpretation of sacred text. And many of these works have a particular perspective on the flow of Jewish time.

Some interpretive works, like those from the books of Jubilees or Judith, were written after the Bible but before the time of the Talmud. Others, like *Genesis Rabbah, Pirkei deRabbi Eliezer,* or *Seder Olam,* were written around the time of the Talmud, while others are from medieval times, like *Yalkut Shimoni, Midrash Tanhuma,* or the commentaries of Rashi or Ibn Ezra. Still others, like the Zohar, are from the 13th century kabbalists of Spain, and other commentaries, like the *Sefat Emet* or the *Mei haShiloach*, are Hasidic in origin, written in the 18th and 19th centuries. And there are modern sources as well, written by poets and scholars of our own age.

These sources are attempts to understand the Torah, but they also add their own imagination. This is why many of the biblical events you will read about in *The Jewish Book of Days* have dates ascribed to them, not by the Bible itself, but by later tradition. These writings allow us to see how Jews might have viewed months, holidays, and seasons in various times and places. They also allow us to connect legends like Abraham's birth, the death of Sarah, or the creation of light to a particular day and season. This invention allows us to live our days in tune with the stories of our tradition—and teaches us real wisdom about the truths of each part of the year.

The Seed

1 TISHREI TO 14 HESHVAN

SEASON
Autumn

WIND
The west

HALF OF THE YEAR
The rains

ELEMENT
Air within earth

GATE
The heavens/the earth

ANGEL
Raphael (healing)

DIVINE FACE
The *Shekhinah*

And the earth brought forth grass,
and herb-yielding seed after its
own kind, and trees yielding fruit
with the seed in it, after its own kind,
and God saw that it was good.

—Genesis 1:12

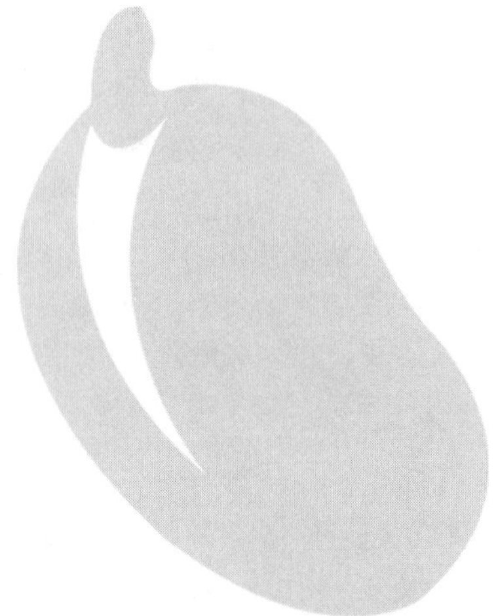

The first motion of the year is stillness: the stillness of a seed preparing to grow. The beginning of autumn is both the gathering in of harvest and the gathering of the seeds we will soon plant. Within the silence of this pause, we encounter gratitude for what is, regret for what has been, hope and anxiety about what will be. If we do not harvest well, within and without, the circle of life cannot begin again.

This is our goal in every time and season: to further the circle of life. We do this in the most real and concrete of ways, by seeding the ground with food for ourselves and our descendants. We also do this in inner ways, by engaging in the spiritual journey our Sages called *teshuvah*, "return." The Jewish year begins at the moment of return, when the fruit of harvest becomes the seed. Our deepest spiritual truth we learn from a garden: New seed must be planted.

In nature, this is the season of earth. The Zohar I:49a teaches: "The *Shekhinah*, the Divine Presence, resides in the altar of earth." During these days we build an altar of festival and renewal to welcome the immanent Divine. Yet, in the spiritual realm, this is the world of air, the opposite of earth: the call of the shofar, the breath of prayer, and the insubstantial call within the spirit to change for the better.

The days of rain, which begin at this season, symbolize the reflection and growth we must do within ourselves. This is the time of healing, when we look at our wounds so we may recover from them. On Rosh Hashanah, the new year, we reflect on the meaning and purpose of human life: How are we to act this year? What seeds are we meant to plant? As we reflect on the birth of the world, we reflect on the importance of letting our inner seed reach its potential in the limited time it has. On Yom Kippur, we fast, to focus ourselves on the more difficult inner harvest. Wearing white, the color of the ever-changing moon, we try to find and discard all within us that keeps us from necessary change. Rosh Hashanah and Yom Kippur are the poles of the season: earth and air, physicality and spirit.

The holiday of Sukkot—with its roofless festive booths, rain, sun, and wind—celebrates the earth and teaches us the fragility of our existence. On Sukkot we wave the ritual bundle of palm, citron, myrtle, and willow to represent the blessings of harvest, and we pray for the gifts of the Divine Presence: abundance, health, and rain.

The holidays of Shemini Atzeret and Simchat Torah celebrate circles. Shemini Atzeret, with its prayers for rain, honors the cycle of water. Simchat Torah, when Jews finish the yearly cycle of Torah readings and begin again with Genesis, honors the ever-renewed circle of Torah. One festival marks an earthly circle, the second a spiritual one.

The remaining days of this season encompass the end of the month of Tishrei and the month of Heshvan. The Talmud calls these days "seedtime," when in Israel seeds are planted for the coming year (Babylonian Talmud, Bava Metzi'a 106b). This time also contains the 11th of Heshvan, the death date of the biblical matriarch Rachel, who represents the return to the land after long exile.

Jews are not alone in celebrating the harvest at this season. Many cultures hold harvest festivals in autumn. The Celtic festival of Mabon and the Catholic festival of Michaelmas, both falling near the autumn equinox, welcome the harvest and so does the mid-autumn festival celebrated in China.[1] In India, Hindus celebrate Lakshmi, the goddess of prosperity.[2] The Hawaiian new year celebrates creation at this season, as does the Jewish calendar.[3] The whole Northern Hemisphere is welcoming harvest at this time, while in the Southern Hemisphere, spring arrives. The Jewish calendar marks natural events honored by all people, yet the first commandment given to the Israelites in the Torah is that they must make their own calendar. This first phase of our calendar connects us to the Divine Presence within the earth, by turning the days into a journey of the spirit.

Conceiving Seed

Rosh Hashanah

Then one [angel] said, "I will return to you next year, and your wife Sarah shall have a son." . . . And Sarah laughed to herself, saying, "Now that I am withered, am I to have enjoyment, with my husband so old?" Then the Divine said to Abraham, "Why did Sarah laugh, saying, 'Shall I in truth bear a child, old as I am?' Is anything too wondrous for the Source of Life? I shall return to you at this same season next year, and Sarah shall have a son."
—GENESIS 18:12–14

Many barren women were remembered with her and many sick people were healed on that same day, many prayers were answered with hers, and great was laughter in the world.
—RASHI ON GENESIS 21:2

In autumn, as leaves are withering, it is hard to believe life will ever grow again. Yet beneath the earth, the cycle of life is beginning. The wrinkled seed, buried after harvest, waits to sprout. On Rosh Hashanah we discover that we too can blossom even after we have withered.

A legend tells that on Rosh Hashanah the Divine made the barren matriarch Sarah fertile, and she conceived from her husband Abraham (Babylonian Talmud, Rosh Hashanah 10b). We read the story of Isaac's birth on the new year to celebrate this seeding of life. Sarah, 90 years old, is like the soil of autumn: outwardly dry and barren, yet inwardly fecund.

Rashi adds to this story of growth, telling us that many women around the world conceived when Sarah conceived, and many sick people were healed. The 1st of Tishrei is a day of healing and creating, a day we conceive ourselves anew through self-reflection. The word *teshuvah* (repentance) signals not only regret but turning. As the rains of autumn ready the earth for spring, we too return to the cycle of life and growth. If we do not turn back to the cycle of life, do not grow, we become stagnant and hold life back. If we do turn, we become part of the earth's renewal.

The First Return

Rosh Hashanah

In the seventh month, on the first day of the month, you shall observe a sacred occasion: you shall not work at your occupations. You shall observe it as a day when the horn is sounded. … You shall present a burnt offering of pleasing odor to the Eternal: one bull of the herd.
—NUMBERS 29:1–2

On the day Adam was created, he saw the sun setting above him and cried, "Woe! Because I sinned, the world is darkening … the Divine will return the world to chaos and void. This is the death heaven has decreed for me." So … he sat and wept the whole night. … But when the dawn arose, he said, "This is the way of the world. Then he offered a bull as a sacrifice."
—BABYLONIAN TALMUD, AVODAH ZARAH 8A

The path of return is not only joyous but also frightening. In a midrash from the Talmud, the first night Adam and Eve spend outside Eden fills them with fear that the world will return to darkness and void. They reflect on their actions, regretting they ate the fruit of knowledge of good and evil. When dawn arrives, they come to understand night is not a punishment: It is the way of the night to fall and the way of the day to come again. Adam offers a sacrifice in thanksgiving for the dawn. His sacrifice perhaps also indicates that his soul-searching has drawn him closer to God.

Rosh Hashanah falls as the days grow perceptibly shorter. It is a re-creation of the first humans' long night. In this mythic darkness, we move through anxiety about our future toward a sense of gratitude and understanding. Adam and Eve discover darkness is not permanent but part of a larger cycle of life. On Rosh Hashanah, we too pass through a dark night of the soul so we may renew ourselves.

The End Is Found in the Beginning

The Fast of Gedaliah • Third Day of Repentance

King Nebuchadnezzar of Babylon put Gedaliah son of Ahikam son of Shaphan in charge of the people whom he left in the land of Judah. In the seventh month, Ishmael son of Nethanyia son of Elishama, who was of royal descent, came with ten men, and they struck down Gedaliah and he died.
—2 KINGS 25:22,25

On the third of Tishrei Gedaliah son of Ahikam was killed by Ishmael son of Nethanyia. A fast was proclaimed because the death of a righteous person is like the burning of the Temple.
—BABYLONIAN TALMUD, ROSH HASHANAH 18B

The *Sefer Yetzirah* 1:7 teaches: "The end is contained in the beginning." Each new thing unfolds from the seed of its origin. At the new year, we must be aware not only of our intentions but of how we do what we do.

The day after Rosh Hashanah is a minor fast day: the Fast of Gedaliah, commemorating the first exile of the Jews. When the conqueror Nebuchadnezzar takes the aristocracy of Judea into exile, he leaves behind some farmers in the charge of a governor, Gedaliah. A Judean rebel, Ishmael, assassinates Gedaliah. The poor residents of the land, terrified Nebuchadnezzar will punish them, flee to Egypt. Thus the whole Jewish people goes into exile, not just the leadership. The people most connected to the land are forced to leave it.

Why mark this event with a fast day? In the season of seedtime, we remember the exiled farmers and know nothing good can grow from a bad seed. The murder of Gedaliah, a righteous man, did not end the rule of Nebuchadnezzar; rather, it solidified his rule. As we consider our deeds during the 10 days of repentance stretching from Rosh Hashanah to Yom Kippur, we consider Ishmael and what came of his actions. Each of our deeds is a seed determining the path of the future. As we plant our deeds in the world, we pray that we will have the wisdom to make them righteous ones.

The Birth of Abraham

Fourth Day of Repentance

Now this is the line of Terah: Terah begot Abram, Nahor, and Haran.
—Genesis 11:27

Nimrod [the king] sent a message to Terah, "Last night your wife gave birth to a son. Give him to me, that I may kill him, and I will fill your house with silver and gold." . . . What did Terah do? He hid away his son in a cave for three years, and the Holy One provided for the child two nipples—out of one came oil, out of the other, flour.
—Beit ha-Midrash 2:118–196[4]

Every infant represents a harvest of the past and a seed of the future. It is said that the patriarch Abraham (Abram, as a child) is born in the month of Tishrei (Babylonian Talmud, Rosh Hashanah 10b). Nimrod, a powerful king in Abraham's city, hears a prophecy that a child will be born who will defeat him, and so he examines all pregnant women, including Abraham's mother, Emtelai. When Abraham is born, Terach hides him in a cave, and the cave breast-feeds Abraham with oil and milk.

This story reminds us of the earth's abundance in autumn: The child Abraham is fed by the earth itself, just as we eat the summer's harvest at this season. Abraham later trusts divine providence because he has felt it in his own life. And the story has a deeper meaning as well.

In the *Zohar* I:96a,137a, Abraham represents *hesed*: "love and generosity." The child Abraham symbolizes our own desire to love and be loved. Yet there are forces within us and outside us, forces of selfishness and fear, seeking to crush the love and vulnerability within us. The days between Rosh Hashanah and Yom Kippur are a time to strengthen our spirit of kindness. During these days, we shelter and feed love within us, just as the cave shelters and feeds the tiny Abram and helps him grow.

The Deer Sent Forth

Fifth Day of Repentance

Naphtali is a hind let loose, which yields goodly fawns.
—Genesis 49:21

Naphtali is a hind let loose—this means that Naphtali leaped back to Egypt to get the document of ownership for the cave of Machpelah, so that his father could be buried there.
—Midrash Bereshit 97:20

Naphtali, son of Jacob and Bilhah, is the swift runner of Israel. His father, Jacob, calls him "a deer let loose," and the Talmud teaches that he is as fast as a deer (Babylonian Talmud, Sotah 13a). According to *Midrash Tadshe*, Naphtali was born on the 5th of Tishrei. At this season, Naphtali teaches us the importance of rushing to do good.

There are many legends of Naphtali's zeal to bring good news. When Joseph's brothers want to kill him, Naphtali runs to get Judah, who intervenes so that Joseph's life is spared (*Midrash Aggadah, Genesis* 49:21).[5] In one midrash, it is Naphtali who races to tell Jacob that Joseph is alive, putting an end to Jacob's agony and loneliness (*Targum Yonatan, Genesis* 49:21).

Naphtali teaches us the secret of the deer running in the forest, the secret of swiftness. Many of us have good intentions but are slow to carry them out. We put off writing a check to a charity, visiting a bereaved person, or making a phone call to an elected official on behalf of the oppressed. Naphtali reminds us of the importance of speed and zeal in following our good impulses. Seeds in the ground, if they wait too long to sprout, lose their chance to grow. The same is true of us.

The Well of the Wanderer

Sixth Day of Repentance

The Eternal heard the cry of the boy, and an angel of the Divine called to Hagar from heaven and said to her, "Fear not, for the Eternal has heeded the cry of the boy. … Come, lift up the boy and hold him by the hand, for I will make a great nation of him." Then the Eternal opened her eyes and she saw a well of water. She went and filled the skin with water, and let the boy drink.

—Genesis 21:17–19

Why … hadn't Hagar seen the well before God pointed it out to her? Because her eyes were filled with tears. It was only after God had assured her Ishmael would be saved that she dried her tears and saw the well.

—David Curzon, *The View from Jacob's Ladder*[6]

On Rosh Hashanah, we read the story of Hagar, concubine of Abraham. Hagar's son, Ishmael, is playing, and the matriarch Sarah, Hagar's rival, sees him. Sarah does not want Ishmael to inherit along with her son, Isaac. She demands Hagar and Ishmael be exiled into the desert.

Hagar and Ishmael soon lose their way. When Ishmael can no longer walk, Hagar leaves him under a bush and sits weeping. An angel calls to Hagar, comforting her. Hagar's eyes are opened, and she finds a well of water. The modern poet David Curzon imagines the well has sprung from Hagar's tears.

In *Pirkei de-Rabbi Eliezer* 30, the well of Hagar is none other than the healing well the Divine made at the dawn of Creation. This well later accompanies the Israelites through the desert and becomes known as Miriam's well. Perhaps this well too comes from the tears of those who grieve.

During these days of turning, our hearts may suffer from memories of exile and betrayal. The Divine opens to us a well of living waters to revive and rebirth our spirits. Our task is to open our eyes and let the tears flow so we may find the well we seek.

Soul Candles

Seventh Day of Repentance

Then they took Joseph's tunic, slaughtered a kid, and dipped the tunic in the blood. They had the ornamented tunic taken to their father, and they said, "We found this. Please examine it: is it your son's tunic or not?" He recognized it, and said, "My son's tunic! A savage beast devoured him!" Jacob rent his clothes ….
—Genesis 37:31–35

The sons of Jacob slaughtered a kid, and dipped the coat of Joseph in the blood, and sent [it] to Jacob … on the tenth of the seventh month. Bilhah heard that Joseph had perished … and Dinah also died …. For this reason it is ordained for the children of Israel that they should afflict themselves on the tenth of the seventh month.
—Jubilees 34:12–15

As life around us hibernates, we approach Yom Kippur, when we consider our frailty as mortals. The book of Jubilees relates that on Yom Kippur Joseph's brothers betray him by selling him into Egypt; then they convince their father, Jacob, that Joseph is dead. Jacob's concubine Bilhah and his daughter, Dinah, die of sorrow over Joseph's apparent demise. According to the book of Jubilees, Yom Kippur honors the betrayal of Joseph and the memory of Bilhah and Dinah.

On Yom Kippur we will recite *Yizkor,* the memorial prayer. At this season, those who have died are close to us; and we mourn, as Jacob mourned for Joseph, Bilhah, and Dinah. Some Jews visit the graves of their beloved dead at this season. Some Eastern European Jews have the custom of making "soul candles" between Rosh Hashanah and Yom Kippur; these candles have many wicks to represent family members and friends, both living and dead.[7] These are only some of the ways we honor departed souls at this season. As we move into the new year, we weave into its fabric the threads of love and memory.

The Dedication of the Temple

Eighth Day of Repentance

When Solomon finished praying, fire descended from heaven and consumed the burnt offering and the sacrifice, and the glory of the Divine filled the House. The priests could not enter the House of the Divine, for the glory of the Divine filled the House of the Divine. … On the eighth day … they observed the dedication of the altar seven days, and the Feast [Sukkot] seven days.
—2 CHRONICLES 7:1,9

God drove out the man. … He went out of the garden of Eden to Mount Moriah. From that place the Divine took him, and there he returned, to the place from which he was taken, as it is written, "to work the earth from which he was taken" (Gen. 2:15).
—PIRKEI DE-RABBI ELIEZER 20

According to 2 Chronicles, King Solomon begins his dedication of the Temple on this day. In one midrash, the Temple marks the spot where the Divine took dust from the earth to make the first human, and breathed into us the breath of life. Tishrei begins the season of air within earth, when the outer world harvests from the soil and the inner world harvests from the soul. At this season, we remember the creation of breath from earth.

The autumn month of Tishrei was once the season of cleansing the shrine of Israel. Yom Kippur washed away any impurity that had arisen in the holy sanctuary as a result of the people's sins. In our day, we have no temple to purify. Yet by repenting on Yom Kippur and renewing our spirits, we re-enact the first creation of humans. By doing so, we rededicate the temple of the earth from which we were taken. We return to a place of purity, renewing ourselves as our ancestors did before us.

Jephthah's Daughter

Kol Nidrei

"His god says I must die …
My god would have no
country, need no armies,
and any promise would
be negotiable."
—Enid Dane, "Jephthah's Daugher"[8]

" … When Jephthah arrived at his home in Mizpeh, there was his daughter coming out to meet him with timbrel and dance. … On seeing her, he rent his clothes and said, "Alas, daughter, you have … become my troubler, for I have uttered a vow to the Divine and I cannot retract."
—Judges 11:30–35

On the evening of Yom Kippur, Jews perform the ceremony of *Kol Nidrei.* Three times the community recites a formula annulling all vows to the Holy One between one year and the next. The ritual is a reminder that nothing we say can be regarded as absolute.

Jephthah promises if he is granted victory in war he will sacrifice the first creature to greet him. When his daughter dances out from his door, he sacrifices her. Rabbinic Sages excoriate Jephthah for his cruelty (*Midrash Tanhuma, Be-hukkotai* 5). Why, they ask, did Jephthah not annul his vow? Enid Dame, a modern poet, also asks why promises to the Divine cannot be negotiable, why a loving deity would need Jephthah to kill his daughter just because he made a promise. Both ancient and modern midrashim remind us that the ceremony of *Kol Nidrei* could have saved Jephthah's daughter from her fate. As we remember her, we question our own rigid assumptions.

The Holy of Holies

Yom Kippur

[The high priest] shall purge the Shrine of the uncleanness and transgression of the Israelites, whatever their sins, and he shall do the same for the Tent of Meeting. … When he goes in to make expiation in the Shrine, nobody else shall be in the Tent of Meeting until he comes out.
—LEVITICUS 16:16-17

He walked through the sanctuary until he came to the place between the two curtains that separate … the Holy Shrine and the Holy of Holies. … He placed the fire-pan between the two poles. He mounded the incense on the coals, and the whole room filled with smoke. He came out by the way he entered, and he prayed … in the outer room, but did not prolong his prayer so as not to frighten Israel.
—MISHNAH YOMA 5:1

Nothing could be more mysterious than the image of the high priest entering the holiest chamber of the Temple on Yom Kippur. As the high priest utters the secret name of the Divine within a cloud of incense, it is as if he planted the sacred word like a seed, creating the cosmos anew. Emerging from the shrine, the high priest renews the land and inspires the people to awe and repentance.

On Yom Kippur, many Jews fast and pray the whole day. The words of the Yom Kippur prayers are like the winding journey of the high priest toward the Holy of Holies. Each prayer takes us a little closer to the innermost depths of ourselves. On this day, we are all high priests meeting the Divine in privacy and intimacy. Surrounded by clouds of song and petition, we are able to look into our hearts more deeply than on any other day of the year.

The high priest does not overly prolong his prayer so as not to worry those who wait for him. We too do not prolong our prayers more than necessary. We finish the service at the moment of darkness, and emerge from the fast into our daily lives.

Building the Tabernacle

All citizens in Israel shall live in booths, so that future generations may know I made the Israelite people live in booths when I brought them out of the land of Egypt, I the Eternal your God.
—Leviticus 23:42–43

And Moses gathered them [to build the Tabernacle] the day after Yom Kippur, when he came down from the mountain.
—Rashi on Exodus 35:1

Sukkot, the joyful festival of the harvest, opens the gate of the earth. It begins the part of the year when we are most connected to the soil and to the sacred dimension of space. By tradition, Jews start building their sukkah, the ritual booth for the festival of Sukkot, on the day after Yom Kippur. This booth reminds us of the roving *mishkan*, "the Tabernacle," which is the portable shrine of the Israelites in the wilderness. In this shrine, the *Shekhinah,* the indwelling presence of the Divine, makes Her earthly home.

The *mishkan* is a portable structure of curtains, rods, and ornaments, a resting place for the Divine Presence while the Israelites wander in the wilderness. Today, according to Rashi, is the day the Israelites begin to gather materials for the holy sanctuary. The Tabernacle artists take the cloth, gold, spices, and wood they collect and make it into a place for the Divine.

The building of the sukkah and the building of the Tabernacle both come in the autumn, at the time when nature is rebuilding in preparation for winter and spring. Building the sukkah after Yom Kippur reminds us of this year-long process of tearing down and building up. By creating this temporary shelter after Yom Kippur, we remind ourselves that we always have the opportunity to build a home for holiness.

The Boards of the Tabernacle

You shall make the planks for the Tabernacle of acacia wood, upright.
—Exodus 26:15

Where did the trees come from? The patriarch Jacob planted them. When his children went down to Egypt, he said to them, "My children, it has been decreed that you will be redeemed from here. Then the Holy One will command you to make a Tabernacle. Plant cedars now, so when the Divine asks you for a Tabernacle, the cedars will be ready." So Jacob's children planted cedars, doing as he had commanded them. This is why the Torah says: "the boards"—the boards Jacob had prepared.
—Midrash Tanhuma, Terumah 9

The sukkah, as we have discovered, is related to the Tabernacle (*mishkan*) of the Divine. Where, one midrash asks, do our ancestors get fine cedar wood for the *mishkan?* Jacob, we are told, plans ahead. He instructs his children to plant trees so that one day they can use them to make the boards of the Tabernacle. When the Israelites leave Egypt, they cut down the trees and use them to build the walls and roof of the *mishkan.*

So too for us to have tree branches for the tops of our sukkah booths, we must protect the trees that grow in our world. And we must plant trees so that our children will be able to build leafy booths to celebrate the harvest. Building a fragile and holy space once a year reminds us to conserve the ecosystem, which is itself a fragile and holy space.

We build the sukkah so that we can look at the stars at night. Its branches have gaps to let in the sky. Observing the wonder of creation is one of the delights of the sukkah; and so, as we build the shelter, we pledge to preserve those wonders for generations to come.

The Goats' Hair

And all the skilled [lit. wise-hearted] women spun with their own hands, and brought what they had spun, in blue, purple, and crimson yarns, and fine linen. And all the women who excelled in that skill [lit. whose hearts stirred them up in wisdom] spun the goats' hair.
—Exodus 35:25

It was an extraordinary artistry: they spun the hair from the backs of the goats.
—Rashi on Exodus 35:25

The Torah tells that every wise person among the Israelites brings his or her special talent to building the house where the *Shekhinah* will dwell. According to the commentator Rashi, the women of Israel are zealous in bringing gifts to the Tabernacle, and this is one of the reasons they are given the holiday of Rosh Hodesh (the new moon) as a special celebration for women (Rashi on Babylonian Talmud, Megillah 22b).

The wise women of the wilderness have a special talent for spinning. The literal translation of Exodus 35:25 says: "the women spun the goats." One legend claims that is exactly what they do: They spin the hair right off the goats' bodies, without having to shear or card it first! This is what it feels like when humans and nature work in concert, without conflict or exploitation. In this story, the women and the goats are not masters and servants but partners.

Before Sukkot, we hang the sukkah with bright fabrics. We think of those wondrous Tabernacle tapestries, made by humans and nature in complete concert, without destruction or exploitation. We hope, through our actions, to create a world in which such partnerships will be possible.

Artist in the Shadow of God

The Divine spoke to Moses, "See, I have singled out by name Bezalel son of Uri son of Hur, of the tribe of Judah. I have endowed him with a Divine spirit of skill, ability, and knowledge in every kind of craft, to make designs for work in gold, silver, and copper, to cut stones for setting and to carve wood, to work in every kind of craft."
—EXODUS 31:1–5

If you compare the curtain Bezalel made to one made by another, you will see that the one made by Bezalel has more grace and balance than any other, even if the two curtains are fashioned in the same manner.
—MEI HASHILOACH ON EXODUS 36:30

On Sukkot, we decorate the festive booths with art, flowers, lights, and fruit. The Tabernacle in the wilderness also was filled with art, and the artist chosen to design all this art was named Bezalel, "in the shadow of God." Bezalel is so wise in the ways of building the Tabernacle that Moses thinks Bezalel had been sitting in the shadow of God while Moses was receiving the Revelation of Torah (*Midrash Tanhuma, Be-ha'alotekha* 6). This midrash implies Bezalel designs everything in the Tabernacle as he thinks it should look, yet his vision miraculously corresponds to the words of the Holy One.

What made Bezalel such a great artist? Bezalel could make exactly the same curtain as someone else but the curtain would somehow look different: It would be airier, more balanced. So too anyone could have followed Moses' instructions on how to build the Tabernacle, but Bezalel was able to fill his artwork with light and spirit.

We are close to the autumn equinox at this season: a time representing balance and the reconciliation of opposites. As the finishing touches are put on Sukkot decorations, right before the holiday begins, we emulate the balancing art of Bezalel. The gifts of our hearts add grace to our spiritual observances.

Willow, Myrtle, Citron, Palm

First Day of Sukkot

On the first day you shall take the product of hadar *trees, branches of palm trees, boughs of leafy trees, and willows of the brook, and you shall rejoice before the Eternal your God seven days.*
—Leviticus 23:40

The fruit of the hadar *tree* [etrog] *is Abraham, whom the Holy One glorified with a good old age. . . . Branches of palm trees is Isaac, who was spread and bound on the altar. . . . Boughs of thick trees is Jacob . . . just as the myrtle is gifted with leaves so was Jacob gifted with children. Willows of the brook is Joseph: as the willow wilts before the other species, so Joseph died before his brothers.*
—Leviticus Rabbah 30:10

As we welcome the first day of Sukkot, the full moon rises overhead. The gate of the earth opens to welcome us into abundance. We enter the leafy tabernacle of the sukkah and invite the first of seven pairs of mythical guests: Abraham and Sarah, a biblical couple known for hospitality. In the morning, we chant psalms and wave the *lulav,* a bundle consisting of the good-smelling fruit called the *etrog* (citron), a palm branch, two willow branches, and three myrtle branches.

Some say the *lulav* represents four parts of the body: the palm branch is the spine, the willow leaves are the mouth, the myrtle leaves are the eyes, and the yellow, round citron is the heart (*Midrash Tanhuma,* Emor 19. Or the willows might represent water, the myrtle, air, the palm, fire, and the *etrog,* the fertile earth. Or the four species represent Abraham, Isaac, Jacob, and Joseph; Sarah, Rebekah, Rachel, and Leah (*Leviticus Rabbah* 30:10). The *lulav* is the offering we wave to honor the oneness of all things.

The Joy of the Water Drawing

Second Day of Sukkot

You shall rejoice in your festival … and have nothing but joy.
—Deuteronomy 16:14–15

One who never saw the joy of the Water Libation never saw joy in life. Rabbi Shimon ben Gamliel used to juggle eight torches during the Ceremony of the Water Libation . . . and when he bowed . . . he kissed the temple floor. . . . At the going-out of the first festival day they went down to the Court of the Women and set up four lamps of gold and golden bowls on top. … There was not a courtyard in Jerusalem that did not shine in the light of the water-drawing. Pious folk used to dance before the lamps with burning torches in their hands, singing songs.
—Babylonian Talmud, Sukkah 53a, 54a

Sukkot is the Jewish earth holiday par excellence. Yet our modern rituals are tame compared to the water pouring of the temple festival of Sukkot. The celebration of the earth's abundance in Jerusalem ran wild with joy at seeing the harvest completed. The celebration of water, which was an extended ritual to bring the rain, was the happiest of all Jewish rituals, full of fire and dance and song. The four lamps lit during the ritual perhaps represented the four seasons of the year or the four directions; and the eight torches of Shimon ben Gamliel hint at the year's eight phases. At dawn, after this dancing and singing and torchlit procession, the people would go out of the Temple through the Gate of the Dawn and see the sun and moon together in the sky. They would draw water from a sacred spring and bring it to the altar and then pour it on the altar to cleanse it. Thus they would inaugurate a new season of rain.

On this day, we invite into the sukkah Isaac and Rebekah, both of whom are associated with the drawing of water. Jewish mystics say that the Divine dwells within everything we consume, so whenever we drink water, we touch sparks of the Divine.

Dwelling in Clouds of Glory

Third Day of Sukkot

You shall live in booths . . . in order that future generations may know that I made the children of Israel live in booths when I brought them out of Egypt.
—Leviticus 23:42

How many clouds of glory surrounded Israel in the wilderness? Rabbi Hoshaya and Rabbi Josiah disagreed. Rabbi Josiah said: "Five, four toward the four winds of the world, and one that went in front of them." Rabbi Hoshaya said: "Seven, four toward the four winds of the world, one above them, one below them, and one that went ahead of them three days' distance and destroyed the snakes and scorpions and boulders."
—Numbers Rabbah 1:2

We celebrate Sukkot, legend tells, because the Holy One caused the Israelites to dwell in booths while they wandered in the wilderness. One ancient rabbi, Akiva, says these sukkot were actual booths. Another, Eliezer, claims they were clouds of glory: spiritual mists of protection that kept the wanderers from harm (Babylonian Talmud, Sukkah 11b). On Sukkot, as we enter our ritual booths to eat and sleep, we feel the truth of both rabbis' statements. Our sukkot give us the experience of living as temporary wanderers, yet they also give us a feeling of protection from the *Shekhinah,* the Divine Presence. On this day we invite Jacob and Leah into the sukkah, a patriarch and matriarch in whose tent the *Shekhinah* dwelled.

On Sukkot, we wave the *lulav*, the festival bundle of four plant species, in six directions: south, west, north, east, up, and down. Some people wave the *lulav* a seventh time, inward toward the self. This ritual calls to mind the six (or seven) directions of the clouds of glory. On Sukkot, by greeting the directions of the earth, we remember we are frail, earthly creatures, yet we also hope for shelter from the Divine. We hold these two realities in tension, just as we hold in tension the real booths of Sukkot and the intangible clouds of glory.

The Peace of the Nations

Fourth Day of Sukkot

Fourth day: ten bulls, two rams, fourteen yearling lambs, without blemish; the meal offerings and libations for the bulls, rams, and lambs, in the quantities prescribed; and one goat for a sin offering.
—NUMBERS 29:23–25

My children, I know that on all the seven days of the Sukkot festival, you are busy with offerings on behalf of the peoples of the world.
—PESIKTA RABBATI 4:7

The Sukkot sacrificial offerings are among the most complex of any biblical festival. According to one interpretation, the many sacrifices occur because Sukkot is the holiday of universal peace. The Babylonian Talmud, Sukkah 55b, records that on this day, the priests would sacrifice 70 bulls in the Temple on behalf of the 70 nations of the world. Sukkot is a time for Jews to pray for all nations, remembering that the fate of one people is interwoven with the fates of all peoples.

Sukkot is a time for Jews to examine their relationships with other peoples to see whether we are truly practicing righteousness toward others. By taking on this act of introspection, we draw closer to the world we want to build. In Zechariah 14:16, the prophet imagines that in messianic times all peoples will celebrate the festival of Sukkot. We may not expect others to begin celebrating Jewish holidays, but perhaps one day nations will celebrate the harvest together in peace, as a sign of our commitment to the earth and one another. Each nation and individual has a responsibility to work toward that day.

The Sea Is Never Full

Fifth Day of Sukkot

One generation goes,
another comes,
But the earth remains
the same forever.
The sun rises and the sun sets—
And glides back to where it rises.
Southward blowing,
Turning northward,
Ever turning blows the wind,
On its rounds the wind returns.
All streams flow into the sea,
Yet the sea is never full.
To the place [from] which
they flow,
The streams flow back again.
—ECCLESIASTES 1:4–7

All the streams flow into the sea—the wisdom of a person comes from the heart. But the sea is never full—but the heart can never be filled.
—ECCLESIASTES RABBAH 1:4

On the Sabbath that falls during Sukkot, it is customary to read the book of Ecclesiastes. Ecclesiastes is a mournful work about the futility of possessions, wisdom, and ambition in the face of death. Yet Ecclesiastes is also about the acceptance of time and the poignant beauty of the ephemeral. Enjoy life, the author of the book says, and do good deeds and know that your stay on earth will not last forever. This seems the right message for Sukkot. The harvest is itself the beginning of a journey into winter and an uncertain future.

The writer of Ecclesiastes is called Kohelet, "the gatherer." A king in Jerusalem, he has reaped a harvest of wisdom, wealth, and love; and yet he cannot hold onto these gifts forever. He struggles with this reality and finally accepts it. On Sukkot, we too know that the harvest will soon be eaten. Our hearts are full only for a moment. Then we must be willing to move on. This is the wisdom of the heart: We are like the sea, always filling, yet never entirely full. On this day of Sukkot, we invite into our sukkah Moses and Miriam, redeemers who crossed the sea toward an unknown future.

The Mother Bird

Sixth Day of Sukkot

You have seen … how I bore you on eagles' wings, and brought you to me.
—EXODUS 19:4

We ask the sukkah to spread itself over us and rest upon us and protect us as a mother protects her children, so that we will feel safe on every side. When Israel . . . welcomes this sukkah of peace to their homes as a holy guest, the holy Divine Presence comes down and spreads Her wings over Israel like a mother embracing her children. . . . This sukkah of peace grants new souls to Her children, for all souls have their home in Her.
—ZOHAR I:48A

On Friday night, the evening liturgy contains a prayer: "Spread over us the sukkah of your peace." At that moment, we imagine the Divine as a hovering presence, sheltering us from violence and sorrow—a mother shielding her children. The once-a-year sukkah of Sukkot reminds us that we experience a sukkah every week on *Shabbat.*

Many Jews think of God as a stern judge and warrior. Those who are uncomfortable with these images may think Judaism has no room for them. Yet the faces of the Divine that appear throughout the Bible are varied. The mother eagle, for example, is a picture of divine love and human independence: The eagle carries her young on her strong wings until they are able to fly on their own (Deuteronomy 32:11).

In the Zohar I:48a, the *Shekhinah* is the mother of souls and the source of rest and comfort. We invoke Her name when we long for a deity who is feminine as well as masculine, who fights for justice yet also seeks peace, who represents all the faces of good in the world. When we dwell in the sukkah, we dwell in the shadow of the *Shekhinah*'s wings.

The Circle of Rain

Seventh Day of Sukkot • Hoshanah Rabbah

"I found that water was issuing from below the platform of the Temple. . . . It was a stream I could not cross, for the water had swollen into a stream that could not be crossed except by swimming. . . . When [these waters] come into the sea . . . the waters will become wholesome. . . . Everything shall live wherever that stream goes."
—EZEKIEL 47:1,5,8,9

Save human and beast, flesh and spirit and soul, sinew and bones and flesh, image of the Divine and corporeal matter, this glory that is a fleeting breath . . . renew the face of the earth, let flowers bloom, let grasses grow, let rivers flow, let dew fall, here is the earth suspended in space, save us!
—HOSHANAH RABBAH LITURGY

Hoshanah Rabbah, or "great praise," is the seventh day of Sukkot. It is not a holiday but a "festival weekday," when work is permitted; yet it has some of the most elaborate ritual of the Jewish year. Celebrants walk behind one another in a circle seven times, holding palm branches, willows, myrtle, and citrons while reciting ancient poetry to ask the Divine for rain. Each circuit has its own poem asking for a different kind of fertility, and each circuit represents a mystical attribute of God. At the end of the ceremony, celebrants beat willow branches on the floor until the leaves fly off, as a sign of their desire to be free of sin and perhaps also to awaken the earth to its task of growth.[9]

Water moves in a cycle. The circles we make on Hoshanah Rabbah represent the circle of water from sky to earth. Ezekiel's vision of a stream of water that bursts from beneath the temple altar to heal the world is a poetic version of the life-giving water cycle.

Hoshanah Rabbah also begins a new cycle for us: It is the last day of the season of repentance, the last day when one's fate decreed on Yom Kippur can be "appealed" before the heavenly court. As our new cycle begins, we connect to the cycle of water and its mystery.

The Circle of Love

Eighth Day of Assembly: Shemini Atzeret

Solomon and all Israel with him . . . observed the Feast [of Sukkot] at that time before the Eternal our God, seven days and again seven days, fourteen days in all. On the eighth day he let the people go. They bade the king goodbye and went to their homes, joyful and glad of heart over all the goodness that the Divine had shown.
—1 KINGS 8:63–66

"On the eighth day you shall have a solemn assembly." This is like a king who said to his servants: "Make me a great feast." On the eighth day, he said to one he loved, "Make me a small meal so I may enjoy your company."
—BABYLONIAN TALMUD, SUKKAH 55B

"Shemini what?" is a common question for those not familiar with the Jewish calendar. "Shemini Atzeret" means "eighth day of assembly." In Israel, Shemini Atzeret is the day Jews finish the last chapter of Torah and begin the circle of Torah again (also known as Simchat Torah). Jews in the Diaspora celebrate the days of Shemini Atzeret and Simchat Torah (the rejoicing in the Torah) separately. For those Jews, what is the meaning of Shemini Atzeret?

One explanation is that Shemini Atzeret is a day for the Divine to say good-bye. The Jewish people have been celebrating with festivals for weeks now. At this moment, we are about to return to our mundane lives. On Shemini Atzeret, the eighth day of assembly, the Holy One asks us to stay one more day and have a small meal, out of love. The holiday, in this telling, has no specific historical meaning; it is simply an opportunity for affection.

Like the cycle of rain, the cycle of love has no beginning and no end. It fertilizes us and changes us. Shemini Atzeret is a time to celebrate love itself, and to say good-bye to the festival season. Tishrei will soon be over, and the seed of our love must carry us into the coming year.

The Circle of Torah

Simchat Torah

Moses the servant of the Eternal died there in the land of Moab, at the command of the Eternal. . . . Never again did there arise in Israel a prophet like Moses.
—DEUTERONOMY 34:5,10

In the night, on the twenty-third of Tishrei, Deborah Rebecca's nurse died, and they buried her . . . under the oak of the river, and he called the name of the place, "the river of Deborah," and the oak, "the oak of the mourning of Deborah."
—JUBILEES 32:25–30

On Simchat Torah, the Torah scrolls are taken from the ark. People dance with them through seven rounds of circle dancing. Everyone, including children, has an aliyah, an "ascent to the Torah." A member of the congregation, called the *hatan* or *kallahTorah* (the groom or bride of the Torah), is honored with reading the final verses of the Torah. Then another person is called up as the *hatan* or *kallah Bereshit*, the groom or bride of the Beginning, and the first verses of the Torah are read. Simchat Torah is the solstice of the Torah: The circle of Torah comes around to its beginning and then spins onward.

The book of Jubilees claims Deborah, the nurse of the matriarch Rebekah, died on this day. Little is known about Deborah other than that she was buried under *Alon Bakhut*, "the oak of weeping." Deborah may have been a person of some importance, a prophet and healer perhaps, as Rabbi Lynn Gottlieb suggests in her book *She Who Dwells Within.*[10]

Deborah's death is intertwined with the symbolic death of the Torah, and her burial under a tree represents the Torah's rebirth. This is the message of Simchat Torah; the Torah is reborn again and again, year after year. The oak of weeping becomes the oak of rejoicing. As we dance the seven circles of Simchat Torah, we dance the Torah back to its place of beginning.

The Feast of Wisdom

Another Interpretation of Simchat Torah

At Gibeon the Eternal appeared to Solomon in a dream by night, and the Divine said, "Ask, what shall I grant you?"
—1 KINGS 3:5

Solomon said, "If I ask for silver and gold … the Divine will give them to me. But if I ask for wisdom, everything will come along with it." … The Holy One said to him, … "Wisdom and knowledge are granted to you, and through them I will give you wealth." Immediately Solomon awoke and it was a dream. … Rabbi Isaac said: "The dream became real. … Solomon … made a feast for all his servants." Rabbi Eliezer said: "From here we learn that one makes a feast to celebrate the conclusion of the Torah."
—SONG OF SONGS RABBAH 1:9

One midrash teaches that the holiday of Simchat Torah derives from the celebration of Solomon. In a dream, the Holy One asks Solomon his dearest wish. Solomon prays for wisdom, not wealth, knowing wisdom will bring him all good things. His prayer is granted, so he makes a feast. So too, each year as we reread the Torah, we ask for new wisdom to come to us, and we celebrate it when it comes.

This legend hints wisdom derives not only from the Torah but from the earth. Solomon's gift is not that he is a scholar, but that he can understand the language of birds and animals. As we celebrate the completion of the circle of Torah, we ask to be part of the greater circle of wisdom: the wisdom of life. In this way, we draw closer to all our fellow creatures. As the holiday season ends, we re-enter the world to learn what it can teach us.

Becoming Fruitful

Israel stretched out his right hand and laid it on Ephraim's head, though he was the younger, and his left hand on Manasseh's head. … "May the angel who has redeemed me from all harm bless the lads. In them may my name be recalled, and the names of my fathers, Abraham and Isaac, and may they be teeming multitudes upon the earth."
—GENESIS 48:14,16

Teeming multitudes: like fish that are fruitful and multiply, and the Evil Eye does not rest on them.
—RASHI ON GENESIS 48:16

In the *Sefer Yetzirah* 8:3, we learn Tishrei is a month when we focus on sexuality or intimacy. Why is this the month of sexuality? Perhaps because this is the time when Israel celebrates its festivals, which are acts of intimacy with the Divine. Or perhaps it is because not only plants need seeds to grow. Humans too grow from a seed. More than that, humans benefit and grow from acts of love and pleasure. Meditating on sexuality at this season reminds us how much a part we are of the cycle of growth. As the holiday season ends, we enter our most intimate lives with renewed joy.

The tribe of Ephraim, meaning "fruitful," is the tribe of this month. Early in his life, Ephraim is blessed to be more numerous than his brother. Yet unlike all other brothers in Genesis, Ephraim and Manasseh do not quarrel. Instead, both tribes are fruitful, and neither tribe quarrels with the other. Ephraim teaches us not only about reproduction but about how to create families in which there is love and respect.

This half of the year is known in the Talmud as "the days of rain" (Babylonian Talmud, Berakhot 29a)—it is a time when we focus inward, on our internal lives. As we enter the days of the rains, we hope for our houses and our most intimate relationships to be places of sanctity, gentleness, and compassion.

Naming Our Cities

The men of Gath, born in the land, killed [Ephraim's sons] because they had gone down to take their cattle. Ephraim their father mourned many days, and his brothers came to comfort him. He cohabited with his wife, who conceived and bore a son, and she named him Beriah, because it occurred when there was misfortune in the house. His daughter was Sheerah, who built both Lower and Upper Beit-horon, and Uzzen-sheerah.
—1 CHRONICLES 7:21–24

She gave her own name to the city that she built.
—*MEFARESH*

It is time to take down the sukkah. In biblical times, pilgrims would be on the road this day, hiking their way home. As the autumn equinox passes, we move into the dark season of the year. The seed we have planted, in the earth and in the spirit, is beginning to unfold itself.

In the *Sefer Yetzirah*, the month of Tishrei is connected with the tribe of Ephraim, younger son of Joseph. A story in 1 Chronicles tells of Ephraim's sons and his daughter Sheerah (her name means "sustenance"). Sheerah is a builder. Her first two cities are called Lower and Upper Beth-horon. Her third city is Uzzen-sheerah, "the strength of Sheerah."

The names that Sheerah gives to her cities teach about work and daily life. Her first two cities are called "Lower" and "Upper," reminding us our lives are both physical and spiritual. They are also called "Beth-horon," or "house of freedom," for we are free to choose our path. Sheerah's third city, Uzzen-sheerah, she names after her own strength. We too must find our own strength as we try to keep the promises we made at the new year. Like Sheerah, we are our own building project.

The Giant Bird

I know every bird of the mountains, the ziz of the field is with me.
—Psalms 50:11

Rabbah bar bar Chana said: "Once we traveled on a ship and we saw a bird standing up to its ankles in the water, yet its head touched the sky. We imagined the water was not deep and were about to descend into it to cool ourselves, when a divine voice called out: "Do not descend, for a carpenter's axe fell into this water seven years ago and it has never reached bottom." . . . Rabbi Ashi said: "That bird was Ziz of the field, for it is written, 'The ziz of the field.'"
—Babylonian Talmud, Bava Batra 73b

The *ziz* is a bird of Jewish legend, similar to the roc in the tales of Sinbad. It is so large that its wings darken the sun, and it protects the earth from the harsh south winds with its great bulk. Once an egg of the *ziz* fell and broke and flooded 60 cities.[11] The *ziz* is connected to the season of Tishrei. On the autumn equinox, the *ziz* makes order among the creatures of the sky. It rises up and cries out, frightening all the birds so that the great birds of prey do not devour the small birds (*Otzar Midrashim: Hashem Behohmah, Yasad Aretz* 6).

In a tale from the Talmud, the Rabbis see the *ziz* bathing in the sea and decide to bathe there too. A divine voice warns that the water is too deep for them. If they bathe where the *ziz* bathes, they will drown. The *ziz* reminds us to tread carefully among the forces of the earth. Humans are used to being masters of nature, yet like the Rabbis, we can get into water too deep for us. When we build houses on fragile coastlines or cut down the mangroves that protect seashores from erosion with their thick roots, the sea will harm us—and there are many other ways in which nature can prove mightier than we are. We must act in ways that respect the power of the earth.

Ivory Houses

The king also made a large throne of ivory, and he overlaid it with refined gold.
—1 KINGS 10:18

In Tevet, Shevat, and Adar, the Israelites in the wilderness would cover their houses with cedar wood. In Nisan, Iyar, and Sivan they would cover their houses with panes of glass. In Tammuz, Av, and Elul they would cover them with marble, and in Tishrei, Heshvan, and Kislev they would cover them with ivory.
—OTZAR MIDRASHIM: ARAKHIM 6

A Jewish legend tells that the Israelites who wandered in the wilderness built different homes in each season of the year. The Israelites, gifted with all kinds of wonderful materials by the Divine, would roof each of their temporary homes with a different substance. In Tishrei, Heshvan, and Kislev, the Israelites covered their houses with ivory.

Why ivory? Ivory was used for the throne of King Solomon. In Tishrei, when we accept the Divine as ruler over the universe, ivory reminds us of the divine throne. Ivory lets light through, reminding us of the spiritual light of the new year.

Ivory is also a substance for which animals are cruelly and unnecessarily killed. While our ancestors in the desert may have had an abundance of ivory, we must work to keep animals like elephants and walruses safe from ivory hunters lest these species become extinct. This too is the message of ivory in Tishrei; as we go out to sow the seeds of righteousness in the world, we must preserve all creatures as an inheritance for the generations to come.

Asenath's Journey

Pharaoh then gave Joseph the name of Zaphenath-paneah, and he gave him for a wife Asenath, daughter of Poti-phera, priest of On.
—GENESIS 41:45

Imagine that Asenath was Joseph's wife because she was his true soul mate, his bashert. *Imagine that she was able to dream and remember the dreams, interpret them for herself and for others, and act on them to bring about blessing, reconciliation, and transformation.*
—DEBRA JUDITH ROBBINS, "IN SEARCH OF DREAMERS" [12]

According to legend, Pharaoh freed Joseph from prison on Rosh Hashanah (Babylonian Talmud, Rosh Hashanah 10b) and appointed him leader over all Egypt. At that time, Pharaoh also offered Joseph a wife: Asenath, daughter of the priest Poti-phera. Today, four weeks after the 1st of Tishrei, could be the anniversary of the wedding of Joseph and Asenath.

Many legends tell of Asenath's wisdom and her love for Joseph. It is she who reveals to her father, Potiphar (or Poti-phera), that Joseph is innocent of the rape of Potiphar's wife (*Yalkut Shimoni, Va-yeshev* 146). It is she who suggests that Joseph take his sons to be blessed by Jacob the Patriarch, and it is she who leads the women in wailing at Jacob's funeral (*Pesikta Rabbati* 3:2).

A modern midrash written by Debra Judith Robbins imagines that Asenath is a dreamer like Joseph. She is an equal spouse to him, with equal prophetic power. Asenath, an Egyptian, reminds us of how strangers in our midst may have the most to teach us. In Tishrei, month of intimacy and love, we remember Asenath as a loyal spouse to Joseph and a welcome addition to his family.

The Closing of the Circle

How lovely are your feet in sandals [or, in closings].
—Song of Songs 7:2

There are two closings: the closing of Passover and the closing of Sukkot. The Holy One of Blessing said to Israel, "You close before me on Sukkot, and I close before you on Passover. You end the work of the harvest before Me at Sukkot, and at that time I open the skies and bring the rain and the sunshine, and make the plants sprout, and ripen the fruits . . . and give to all of you your needs. I close before you at Passover, and you go out to reap and thresh and winnow, and do what you must in the field—and you find it abundant in blessing."
—Song of Songs Rabbah 7:2

In an extraordinary midrash in *Song of Songs Rabbah*, the year is a cycle. In the winter half of the year, the Divine works in the fields, bringing rain and sun and opening the fruits and vegetables. In the summer half of the year, human beings go out to harvest, doing their share of the work to make the world flourish. The human half of the year begins at Passover. The divine half of the year begins at Sukkot. It is interesting that the letters of the word "Tishrei" can be rearranged to form *reishit* (beginning).

So at this season we can imagine the Divine going off to work, whistling, to make the fields fertile. We, on the other hand, are freed to do our own inner work at this time. In spring, we will focus more deeply on our work in the world, while the Holy One will engage in an inner drama of covenant and redemption during the festivals of Passover and Shavuot. The circle of the year teaches that both human and divine, both inner and outer focus, have a role to play in turning the seasons.

As Tishrei ends, we close our work of harvest. We pray for nature to bring us abundance and not disaster. We take well-needed rest and reflection time. And we begin to prepare ourselves for the work we will do come spring to till the fields of the world.

The Birth of Noah

New Moon of Heshvan

When Lamech had lived 182 years, he begot a son. And he named him Noah, saying, "This one will provide us relief from our work and from the toil of our hands, out of the very soil that the Divine placed under a curse."
—Genesis 5:28

Before Noah's birth, when people sowed, they reaped something other than what they had sown. If they sowed wheat, thorns and thistles grew. But after Noah was born, the earth returned to its normal ways. People reaped what they sowed. If they sowed wheat, they reaped wheat. … Also, until Noah was born, people worked the earth with their hands. … At the birth of Noah, they received plows, scythes, hoes, and other tools for working the earth.
—Midrash Tanhuma, Bereshit 11

The month of Heshvan, corresponding to September and October, is primarily associated with water. During this month, the rains of autumn fall (Babylonian Talmud, Ta'anit 5a). In the Middle East, according to the Talmud and Rashi, Heshvan was planting season for some crops, and this is one reason we call this time of year "seedtime."

In the first week of Heshvan, we read of the birth of Noah. As Adam and Eve leave the garden, the Divine tells them the ground will yield thorns and thistles for them. This punishment goes on for generations. Yet *Midrash Tanhuma, Bereshit* 11 explains that when Noah is born, this curse is lifted. Noah's birthday gift is a plow and a scythe, tools that make farming possible. This is why the child is named Noah, meaning "rest." His birth makes life easier for other human beings. So too when we farm the earth, we are grateful for those who are able to learn its secrets and make life easier for all who get their food from the ground.

The Falling of the Rain

Let the heavens rain down
victory;
Let the earth open up and
triumph sprout.
Yes, let vindication spring up.
I the Eternal have created it.
—Isaiah 45:8–9

Rabbi Levi said: "The upper waters are male while the lower are female, and they say one to the other: 'Receive us; you have been created by the Holy One, and we are messengers of the Holy One.'"
—Genesis Rabbah 13:13

Heshvan, the planting season, is also the rainy season. Some Jewish myths imagine the rain and the waters under the earth as lovers who long for one another. Though rain falls from the sky and ground water rises from the earth, both come from the same sacred source. When they meet, they greet one another with a shared purpose: to nurture creation.

The meeting of these two bodies of water is a metaphor for the two parts of us. Part of us comes from the earth, and the other is soul. They both long to be joined, so that body and spirit act, grieve, and rejoice together. We often do not allow the two parts of ourselves to communicate, but body has much to tell us about spirit, and the soul has wisdom to teach about body.

This season of air within earth reminds us to bring together sky and earth within ourselves. As we read the story of the rain and the earth waters, we too remember our longing to be one in body and spirit. Heshvan, month of rain, helps us achieve this union.

The Seeding of the Land

I will give the rain for your land, autumn rain and spring rain in its season.
—DEUTERONOMY 11:14

They sow . . . in Marcheshvan, and reap in Nisan.
—RASHI ON LEVITICUS 25:21

Every day in the traditional Jewish liturgy we recall our need for rain in autumn and rain in spring so that the planting cycle can continue. The Hebrew word for "autumn rain" is "*yoreh,*" which comes from the word meaning "to shoot an arrow." The autumn rains plummet like arrows to their destination in the earth, soaking the soil and giving drink to the seeds. These rains are also teachers, showing us the wisdom of going straight to our destination. While it is the spring rains that fall on the crops as they grow, it is the autumn rains that prepare the seeds for spring. The *yoreh,* the autumn rain of Heshvan, teaches us to nurture seeds at the very beginning so that they will bear fruit as time passes.

"*Yoreh*" can also mean "teacher." The autumn rains remind us how to be good teachers. When the rain falls too heavily and strongly, it can cause floods. When the rain falls too sparsely, seeds die. Rain must be neither too overwhelming nor too spare to successfully water the land. So it is with teachers: They must give information in a gentle yet persistent way to succeed in transmitting their wisdom.

Isaac in *Yeshivah*

According to the *Machzor Vitry*, the *Akedah*, the binding of Isaac, happens on the autumn equinox.[13] After that troubling event, Abraham returns from the mountain alone, and he and his servants go home. Where does the traumatized Isaac go that autumn? A legend from *Genesis Rabbah* claims he travels to a place known in Jewish myth as the *yeshivah*—the study hall—of Noah's son Shem and Noah's grandson Ever. Isaac remains there, learning, until the time of his wedding to Rebekah.

[After the Akedah*] Abraham then returned to his servants, and they departed together for Beer-sheba, and Abraham stayed in Beer-sheba.*
—Genesis 22:19

Where did Isaac go? He went to Shem to study Torah from him.
—Genesis Rabbah 56:11

Isaac lives in a time long before the Talmud, before the giving of the Torah. What do the Sages mean by saying that Isaac studies in a talmudic *yeshivah*? Perhaps the Rabbis of the Talmud imagine the patriarchs as being like themselves, immersed in the study of text. By saying that Isaac studies Torah, the Rabbis tie him to their own vision of the Jewish people.

The Rabbis may also be offering a teaching about the heart. Isaac, nearly sacrificed by his father, can no longer make sense of the world. He enters a school headed by the prophet Shem to heal from his terrifying experience and acquire wisdom. So too each of us must study Torah in his or her own way, not just through the eyes of the preceding generation. Torah holds seeds that we must gather and plant.

Naamah Brings Seeds onto the Ark

As for Zillah, she bore Tubal-cain, who forged all implements of copper and iron. And the sister of Tubal-Cain was Naamah.
—Genesis 4:22

Then God called out to Naamah: "Walk across the land and gather the seeds of all the flowers and all the trees. Take two of every kind of living plant and bring them on the ark. They shall not be for your food but they shall be your garden, to tend and to keep."
—Sandy Eisenberg Sasso, *A Prayer for the Earth* [14]

The month of Heshvan, the time of heavy rains, is associated with the biblical Flood. Its ancient name is Bul which may mean "flood." The tale of the Flood reveals our anxiety that the small and fragile seeds we plant, whether physical or spiritual, will be washed away by disaster. At this season of the seed, we invoke preservers of seed as our role models.

One modern midrash connects the Flood and its destruction with the preservation of seed. In her children's book *A Prayer for the Earth,* Sandy Eisenberg Sasso creates a tale based on the ancient legend that a woman called Naamah was the wife of Noah (*Genesis Rabbah* 23:3). Although the Holy One asks Noah to collect food for the animals, we never see him gathering plants and seeds to save aboard the ark. Sasso innovates another chapter to the story. She imagines the Divine calling to Naamah to gather and preserve the seeds of all the plant life on earth.

The task of gathering seed still remains. There are all kinds of seeds that need to be saved: actual seeds and seeds of imagination and truth. Part of our task as individuals is to learn what seeds we are meant to preserve.

Seeds in the Granary

I will give you treasures concealed in the dark.
—ISAIAH 45:2

When all the fruits are being gathered in, come in yourself also to seek a more weatherproof mode of life and hope for rest in place of the toils that you endured when laboring on the land.
—PHILO OF ALEXANDRIA[15]

The seasons turn toward autumn. There has been a profound change around us and within us. As physical seeds are gathered up, we are gathered into a kind of spiritual granary. Perhaps the new year brought us into connection with community, inspired new ideas about an old story or ritual, or planted in us the will to do a good deed. Now, in the rest after the holiday, is the time to let those ideas percolate.

Philo, the ancient Jewish philosopher, claims we too are like grain in the storehouse. We are resting, waiting to see what will become of us. We are the treasure of the *Shekhinah*, the vast storehouse of seeds saved for the needs of the future. In the storehouse it is dark. We may not necessarily see where or how we will be planted. Yet we have potential in us that will grow in the coming season. Heshvan reminds us that we ourselves are seeds, resting after the harvest and waiting for the right soil and season.

Praying for Rain

I will give you rain in its season, rain in autumn and rain in spring.
—Deuteronomy 11:14

Amemar said in the name of Rabbi Chisda: "On the third day of Marcheshvan we begin to pray for rain." Rabban Gamliel says: "On the seventh of Heshvan." Rabbi Chisda said: "The law is according to Rabban Gamliel."
—Babylonian Talmud, Ta'anit 6a

According to Rabban Gamliel's opinion in the Talmud, today is the first day Jews in Israel add the prayer for rain to the daily liturgy. The 7th of Heshvan is far enough into the rainy season that it is likely to rain. If the rain holds off much longer, the Talmud's advice is to fast and pray because lack of rain after this date may lead to drought.

The Talmud teaches: "We do not depend on miracles" (Babylonian Talmud, Kiddushin 39b). We pray for rain only once it becomes likely that rain will come. Prayer must be accompanied by practical wisdom and action. When we pray for loved ones to be healed of disease, we also attempt to heal them by natural means. We know that for our prayers to be efficacious the bodies of the sick must fight off the illness. By praying for rain in the rainy season, we remind ourselves of divine power but also of all we must do to sustain our crops while maintaining work, health, and growth.

Noah and the Phoenix

From birds of every kind, cattle of every kind, every kind of creeping thing on earth, two of each shall come to you to stay alive.
—Genesis 6:20

Eliezer, Abraham's servant, asked Shem, Noah's son, "How did you keep alive all those families of animals?" Shem said, "We had a lot of trouble in the ark! … My father found a phoenix lying in a corner of the ark and asked, 'Don't you want something to eat?'" The phoenix said, 'I saw your work was difficult, and did not want to cause you any trouble.'" Noah said, "May it be the divine will that you never die. This is why the Bible says, 'I shall multiply my days like the phoenix' (Job 29:18)."
—Babylonian Talmud, Sanhedrin 108b

The phoenix, according to one Jewish legend, is the only creature that never dies. Every 1,000 years, it is reborn out of its own ashes. The phoenix represents life itself and the possibility of rebirth after destruction.

Of all the animals that come onto Noah's ark, the phoenix is the only one that does not ask for food. It restrains its hunger so as not to trouble the exhausted Noah, who has been feeding every animal on the ark. Noah rewards the phoenix for its compassion by bestowing eternal life. The phoenix also learns through this gift; it realizes that its needs are important.

The phoenix teaches that we can attain renewal, as individuals and as a society, only through thoughtfulness and moderation of our needs. However, being modest does not mean having no needs. We are always called to investigate the needs and feelings of those around us and to value our own needs, even when that requires asking help from others. The phoenix, which is mortal and immortal at the same time, teaches us to be humble and to value ourselves.

How Demons Got onto the Ark

They came to Noah into the ark, two each of all flesh in which there was breath of life.
—Genesis 7:15

From all flesh in which there was breath of life: Even spirits entered with Noah onto the ark.
—Genesis Rabbah 31:13

Genesis Rabbah tells that when the Flood came, the demons did not want to drown. They crowded around Noah, pleading to be taken aboard the ark. Imagine little creatures with forked tails and terrible habits leaping up and down and making a case for why Noah should save them from destruction. This fantastical scene, fit for a Japanese anime film, reminds us how our own demons—our doubts, fears, and angers—though challenging and difficult, may be good for something. In the Talmud, sometimes a Sage repeats a piece of Torah he has heard from a wise demon (Babylonian Talmud, Pesachim 115a). Demons, in Jewish thought, are there to provoke us and determine our true character: If they trouble us, they are doing their God-given job of getting us to question ourselves.

A folk legend tells how King Solomon once asked some demons to heat water for him so that people might bathe in it and be healed. The hot baths of Tiberias are the waters heated up by those very demons, and they are still warm and healing for those who bathe in them. Those same waters, the legend continues, roil forth from the place in the earth where God released the waters of the Flood of Noah. The demons saved from the Flood now use the water to heal others.[16] So too may we transform our demons into forces for good.

The Birth of Luck

When Leah's maid Zilpah bore Jacob a second son, Leah declared, "What fortune!" … So she named him Gad [luck].
—Genesis 30:11

Gad was born on the 10th of Heshvan, and died at one hundred and twenty-five years.
—Yalkut Shimoni 162

The 10th of Heshvan, in one Jewish legend, is the birthday of Gad, first son of the patriarch Jacob and Zilpah, the maid of Leah. Leah gives the boy the name Gad, meaning "luck." This is a rather odd choice for a matriarch who has been praying for children for many years. If Leah believes the Holy One grants children, what does she mean by luck?

When seeds are planted, we know some of them will grow and some will not. Does a divine force determine which will grow? Some of us may believe so. Others among us may believe that scientific factors like the nutrients in the soil, the warmth or cold of the weather, and the amount of rainfall are what determine the eventual yield of the harvest. Sometimes events feel as if they were meant to be, and sometimes we experience them as utterly random. This is why Leah can say of one child, "God has heard my affliction," and of another, "Luck has come."

In Heshvan, we pray for the earth to be fruitful. We also know that the harvest differs from year to year and that human prayers are not to blame if the harvest is sometimes blighted. Many of us live in two emotional worlds: the world of providence and the world of luck. So now that we have prayed for rain, we also wish the new seeds good luck on their journey.

The Death of Rachel

When her labor was at its hardest, the midwife said to her, "Have no fear, for it is another boy for you." But as she breathed her last, for she was dying, she named him Ben-Oni; but his father called him Benjamin.
—GENESIS 35:17–18

Jacob buried her on the path, and did not bring her to the city of Bethlehem, for he saw by prophecy that Bethlehem would belong to Judah, and he did not want to bury her outside the borders of her son Benjamin's portion.
—NACHMANIDES ON GENESIS 35:20

On the 11th of Heshvan Rachel dies in childbirth (*Midrash Tadshe*, *Jubilees*). On this date Jews go on pilgrimage to the shrine near Bethlehem where legend holds Rachel is buried. Those who have no children pray to Rachel to intercede for them, winding a red thread, representing fertility, around the stone that marks her burial site. A midrash claims Rachel intercedes with the Holy One to end the exile for the Jewish people. In Jewish mysticism, Rachel is the embodiment of the *Shekhinah* and the earth (Zohar I:153b–154a).

Some plants die in releasing seed, giving their lives so their offspring may live. Thus Rachel the matriarch dies bearing her second child. She names her son Ben-Oni, which means "son of my strength" and also "son of my sorrow." Rachel holds two truths in tension: the joy of a healthy child and the pain of leaving the world. A grieving Jacob renames the child Benjamin, "son of my strong right hand," and buries Rachel by the side of the road outside Bethlehem.

Today we honor Rachel as a sacred ancestor. Many other cultures, from Ireland to Scandinavia to Mexico, honor ancestors at this time of year, visiting their graves and remembering their lives.[17] In Heshvan, as the light fades, we mourn the loss of Rachel, and celebrate her legacy.

Methuselah's Sword

All the days of Methuselah
came to 969 years,
then he died.
—Genesis 5:27

"After seven days, the Flood came on the earth." (Genesis 6:10) What is the reason for the seven days? Rav said: This was the mourning for Methuselah, and this teaches that the death of the righteous delays punishment in the world.
—Babylonian Talmud, Sanhedrin 108b

The 11th of Heshvan, the day Rachel dies, is also the day on which Methuselah dies, and today is one of the seven days of mourning for Methuselah (*Genesis Rabbah* 3:6). The Bible relates that Methuselah, the ancestor of Noah, lives the longest of any human being (969 years!). The Holy One esteems Methuselah so much that the Flood waits until after Methuselah's death and burial are completed.

One Jewish legend about Methuselah is that he was the first to learn how to fight demons. By fasting for three days while standing in a river, Methuselah obtains the power to write God's name on his sword. He then uses the sword to smite the demons who afflict humankind. The eldest demon, Agrimus, comes to Methuselah and asks him to desist killing the demons; in return, Agrimus gives Methuselah the name of every demon. Using the names, Methuselah banishes the demons to the far recesses of the ocean ("Midrash Avkir").[18]

The darkening autumn is a time of reflection and, for some, of depression or regret. Yet when we learn the names of our demons, they no longer have power over us. It is interesting that Methuselah uses a body of water as a place to send the demons. Water, a symbol of the unconscious, represents the place we must go at this time of year to discover ourselves.

Entering the Ark

Of the clean animals, of the animals that are not clean, of the birds, and of everything that creeps on the ground, two of each, male and female, came to Noah in the ark, as the Divine had commanded Noah. And on the seventh day the waters of the Flood came upon the earth.
—Genesis 7:8–10

Noah saw the Angel of Death coming toward him, and he entered the ark to hide.
—Zohar Hadash I:68b

How does Noah know it is time to enter the ark? One tale says Noah sees the Angel of Death coming toward him. He becomes aware of the presence of death in the world and takes steps to protect his family and the animals he has saved.

Whenever we are aware of death's presence, life seems smaller and more fragile, just as life seemed fragile when the ark was tossed on the waves. A period of grieving is necessary to re-emerge into a world of joy and openness. That is why Jewish tradition recommends a period of seven days, called shivah, when mourners remain inside the house and tell stories of the dead. Afterward, they emerge from the house and walk in the sunlight, just as Noah emerges from the ark after the Flood. It is the responsibility of the community to help mourners exit their "ark" and rejoin the world.

The darkness of autumn and winter, followed by the brightness of spring, teaches us a great deal about the progression of human emotion. Like shivah, the dark months are a period of retreat, allowing us later to emerge whole. The seasonal retreat must take its allotted length of time so that healing can be complete.

The Seed of Sarah

Sarah died in Kiriath-arba, which is Hebron, in the land of Canaan, and Abraham came to mourn for Sarah and to weep for her. . . . Isaac brought Rebekah into the tent of Sarah's mother and found comfort after his mother's death.
—GENESIS 23:2;24:67

While Sarah was alive, a cloud of glory hung over the entrance to her tent. When she died, the cloud vanished. When Rebekah came, the cloud returned. All the days Sarah was alive, her doors were open to the outside. When she died, the openness stopped. When Rebekah came, openness returned. As long as Sarah lived, her lamp burned from one Sabbath to the next. When she died, the light went out. When Rebekah came, the light returned.
—GENESIS RABBAH 60:16

We began the season of the seed, with Sarah and we end it with Rebekah. The autumn season is the time of the *Akedah*, the binding of Isaac. A midrash tells that Sarah dies after Abraham nearly sacrifices Isaac. She is slain by the grief of knowing how her son was almost lost (*Leviticus Rabbah* 20:2). One story claims Sarah lingers after she learns of the *Akedah* and dies in Heshvan (*Esther Rabbah* 3:7).

Rebekah, the woman who will marry Isaac, is born on the same day Sarah dies (*Genesis Rabbah* 58:2). When Rebekah is grown, she travels to a new land to marry Isaac. She comes to Sarah's tent, and performs all the sacred tasks and miracles Sarah performed during her lifetime. The cloud of the *Shekhinah,* the lamp, and the blessed bread all return when Rebekah takes up Sarah's mantle (*Genesis Rabbah* 60:16). If Sarah is the dry milkweed pod, Rebekah is the floating seed.

As the new seed burrows into the ground to become the root, we remember the hope of all generations: that the next generation will carry on its ancient legacy. The autumn brings a time of quiet and darkness in nature, yet in this season of seeds, we renew our belief that life will go on.

NOTES

1 Carole Angell, *Celebrations Around the World: A Multicultural Handbook* (Fulcrum, 1996).

2 Patricia Telesco, *365 Goddesses* (HarperSanFrancisco, 1998).

3 Page Two, Inc., "2003 Native American-Meso American-Hispanic Holidays." http://www.wheeloftheyear.com/2003/nativeamerican.htm

4 A. Jellinek, *Beit ha-Midrash* .(Bamberger and Wahrman, 1938), 2:118–196.

5 Cited in Yisrael Yitzchak Chasida, *Otzar Ishi haTanakh* (Ya'ir Giat, 1995), p. 309.

6 David Curzon, *The View from Jacob's Ladder: One Hundred Midrashim* (The Jewish Publication Society, 1996), p. 35.

7 Jane Enkin, "Soul Candles," unpublished article, available at http://www.telshemesh.org/tishrei/soul _candles.htm.

8 Enid Dane, "Jephthah's Daughter," in *Living Text: The Journal of Contemporary Midrash* 5 (1999).

9 See Jules Harlow, ed. *Siddur Sim Shalom* (Rabbinical Assembly, 1989), p. 538–547.

10 Lynn Gottlieb, *She Who Dwells Within: A Feminist Vision of a Renewed Judaism* (Harper SanFrancisco, 1995), p. 94.

11 Louis Ginzberg, *Legends of the Jews* (Jewish Publication Society, 1938), vol.1, pp. 30–31.

12 Debra Judith Robbins, "In Search of Dreamers," in *The Women's Torah Commentary* (Jewish Lights Publishing, 2000), p. 101.

13 *Machzor Vitry,* supplement 14, cited in Louis Ginzberg, *Legends of the Jews* (The Jewish Publication Society, 1938), 6: 204, n.109.

14 Sandy Eisenberg Sasso, *A Prayer for the Earth: The Story of Naamah, Noah's Wife* (Jewish Lights Publishing, 1996), p. 8.

15 Philip Goodman, *The Sukkot/Simchat Torah Anthology* (Jewish Publication Society, 1973), pp. 14–15.

16 Ze'ev Vilnay, *Kol Agadot Eretz Yisrael* (Hotzaat haSefer, 1929), p. 180.

17 John Greenleigh and Rosalind Rosoff Beimler, *The Days of the Dead: Mexico's Communion with the Departed* (Pomegranate Communications, 1998). See also Starhawk, *The Spiral Dance: A Rebirth of the Ancient Religion of the Great Goddess* (HarperSanFrancisco, 1999), pp. 209–212.

18 Translated from the fragmentary Hebrew text published by A. Marmorstein, "Midrash Avkir," *Devir* 1 (1923), pp. 137–139. See also Ronald Hutton, *The Stations of the Sun: A History of the Ritual Year in Britain* (Oxford University Press, 1996), p. 360–370.

SEASON
Autumn shading into winter

WIND
The north

HALF OF THE YEAR
The rains

ELEMENT
Fire within water

GATE
The earth

ANGEL
Gabriel (strength)

DIVINE FACE
Gevurah (strength and limits)

The Root

15 HESHVAN TO 30 KISLEV

There is hope for a tree:
if she is cut down, she will renew herself
and her new shoots shall not cease,
for her roots are old in the earth,
even though her stump dies in the ground.

—JOB 14:7–8

The second motion of the year is descent: the descent of the roots into darkness. Within the earth, the seed spins a thread. This thread, the root, will take sustenance from the soil and hold the seed secure. The tail end of autumn is rainy in many parts of the world and may be fiery with bright leaves. As the earth takes in the descending mulch and water, the roots will feed from rain and leaves alike. So too at this season we nourish our own deep places.

The root is the core and foundation of the plant; and in this second phase of the year, we seek out our core selves, trying to discover who we are. Heshvan and Kislev, which may span the months of October, November, and December, are a time of decreasing light, the dark months of the year. They encourage us to look inward for understanding, into our roots and the roots of our people. According to the mystical *Sefer Yetzirah* 8:3, the month of Heshvan connects to the sense of smell, whereas the month of Kislev connects to the activity of sleep. Smell is evocative of intensely personal and individual memories. Sleep brings dreams, which may hold imagery meaningful only to us or may tap into the collective unconscious.

Roots symbolize our ancestors. On the Sabbaths of Heshvan and Kislev we read the book of Genesis, the most ancient record of our forebears. Like a collective dream, the stories of Genesis draw us together, raising critical questions of identity and selfhood. Jews are not alone in remembering ancestors at this time. A number of other cultures do the same—for example, during the Day of the Dead in Mexico and during All Souls' Day and Halloween in Europe and America.[1]

We are still in the half year designated as the days of rain—in the Middle East and elsewhere, it rains or snows heavily at this time. In Heshvan and Kislev, we remember the story of Noah and the Flood, for in Jewish tradition it is in Heshvan that the Flood begins and in Kislev that it ends (Rashi on Genesis 7–8). We also begin to recite prayers for rain to bless the earth.[2] In the physical realm, this is the season of water. Like dreams, water is a symbol of the unconscious. We may be lifted by it or swept away.

The divine face of this season, *gevurah,* means "power, justice, or strength." In this meaning, *gevurah* refers to the strength of standing on our roots. *Gevurah* can also mean "severity or limitation"—the pain of our personal and national histories. The divine aspect of *gevurah* is connected to *binah* (understanding, order, and creativity). When we understand our roots, we are able to give meaning to our lives.

Gevurah and *binah* are represented by fire, and within the sweeping waters of the season is a spark of fire: the Festival of Lights, or Hanukkah. At the end of Kislev, close to the winter solstice, we light candles for eight days: one on the first night and an additional candle on each successive night. The increasing light reminds us of the sun's light, which grows as the winter passes. Hanukkah reflects both faces of *gevurah:* the strength of the Jewish people in the time of the Maccabees and the harshness of civil war, which we also remember during Hanukkah. On Hanukkah, the roots of the season become branches, torches of fire to light our way into the next season, when the light will grow and we will begin the ascent into spring.

Joseph at Rachel's Tomb

Thus Rachel died. She was buried on the road to Ephrath, now Bethlehem. Over her grave Jacob set up a pillar; it is the pillar at Rachel's grave to this day.
—GENESIS 35:19–20

They passed by Ephrath and came near the grave of [Rachel] his mother. . . . Joseph fell on his mother's tomb and cried and wailed. He heard a voice speaking to him, saying, "Do not be afraid, for God is with you. Go down to Egypt."
—SEFER HA-YASHAR, VA-YESHEV

According to a medieval work *Sefer ha-Yashar*, after Joseph's brothers sell him into slavery, Joseph has an encounter with the spirit of his mother, Rachel. Part of a slave caravan bound for Egypt, Joseph has no home, nothing to comfort him, nothing to remind him of who he is. When the slave caravan passes his mother's tomb, he breaks away from his captors and weeps on Rachel's grave, pleading for her help. Rachel's spirit tells Joseph he is on the right path, even though he is suffering. After this encounter, Joseph is able to accept his circumstances with courage.

Though Jews commemorate Rachel's death on 11 Heshvan, some make pilgrimage to her tomb near Bethlehem on 15 Heshvan, the full moon of the month.[3] There they pray for Rachel to intercede with the Divine on their behalf. This pilgrimage calls to mind the legend of Joseph's unintended yet passionate pilgrimage to his mother's tomb.

The plant's roots, deep in the ground, nourish it in difficult seasons. So too sometimes we allow the love and faith of our families and ancestors to carry us through. In this season of roots, we seek out those who came before us so that we have a better sense of who we are.

The Cave of Machpelah

Abraham bowed low to the people of the land, the Hittites, and he said to them, "If it is your wish that I removed my dead for burial, you must agree to intercede for me with Ephron son of Zohar. Let him sell me the cave of Machpelah he owns."
—GENESIS 23:7–9

Rabbi Banaah used to mark the caves where the dead were buried, so that people should not walk there without realizing it. When he came to the cave of Abraham, he found Eliezer, the servant of Abraham, standing at the entrance. "What is Abraham doing?" Rabbi Banaah asked. Eliezer replied, "He is sleeping in the arms of Sarah, and she is looking with devotion at his head."
—BABYLONIAN TALMUD, BAVA BATRA 58A

In Genesis, Machpelah is the *Ur*-grave, the first Israelite tomb. Abraham buys it as a place to bury Sarah. According to Jewish tradition, Adam and Eve, Abraham and Sarah, Isaac and Rebekah, and Jacob and Leah are all buried in the cave of Machpelah (Genesis 50:31). The meaning of the name of the cave is "double," because of the cave's lower chamber and also because four pairs of husbands and wives lie there. Jews, Muslims, and Christians go to Machpelah on pilgrimage to pray at the tombs of their ancestors.

In a talmudic story, the Sage Rabbi Banaah honors the dead by watching over their graves. When he arrives at Machpelah, Abraham's servant Eliezer stands at the entrance of the cave. Abraham and Sarah are embracing within. The embrace of Abraham and Sarah is a joining of spirit. This joining symbolizes the union of the souls of our first ancestors. We learn from this tale how to link our spirits with our ancestors even though they have left the world.

The Roots of Courage

The king took … the two sons that Rizpah daughter of Aiah bore to Saul … and he handed them over to the Gibeonites… They impaled them on the mountain before the Lord…. They were put to death in the first days of the harvest, the beginning of the barley harvest. Then Rizpah … took sackcloth and spread it on a rock for herself, and she stayed there from the beginning of the harvest until rain from the sky fell on the bodies.
—2 Samuel 21:8–11

They were put to death on the sixteenth of Nisan. … "From the beginning of the harvest until rain from the sky fell on their bodies." … they remained suspended from the sixteenth of Nisan until the seventeenth of Marcheshvan.
—Numbers Rabbah 8:4

According to the book of 2 Samuel, after King Saul dies, King David hands over seven of Saul's relatives to be executed by a local tribe to solve a political crisis. The executioners leave the bodies of the dead to be torn by animals. Rizpah, mother of two of the dead men, spreads out sackcloth and spends her days and nights chasing away birds and beasts so that the bodies of her sons and their comrades will not be defiled. Impressed by Rizpah's actions, King David buries the bodies of the men on the 17th of Heshvan.

Like the Greek Antigone, who risks her life to bury her brothers, Rizpah defies a royal order to preserve her loved ones' honor. Her tears over her sons express her inner fire of love and heroism. Rizpah's strength embodies the *gevurah,* the power of this darkening season. Rizpah is not afraid to do what she knows is right. David responds to this fire of strength by returning to the path of integrity. We too respond to the inner heat of Heshvan by seeking justice for others.

The Flood Begins

Noah, with his sons, his wife, and his sons' wives, went into the ark because of the waters of the Flood.
—GENESIS 7:7

Noah and his sons by themselves; his wife and the daughters-in-law by themselves.
—RASHI ON GENESIS 7:7

The *gevurah,* the severity of this season, finds its full expression in the Flood of Noah, which legend says came about because of human misdeeds. In Jewish tradition, it is on the 17th of Heshvan that Noah and his family enter the ark (Rashi on Genesis 7:7). By the 18th, today, the rain is well under way. Noah must shut the door and wait for the waters to lift the ark from its resting place. The notion that the Flood begins at this season perhaps comes from the fear that the heavy rains of autumn will flood the earth and the crops will be ruined. By telling the story of the Flood and its end, we share our fears and find hope again.

In the midrash cited by Rashi, Noah and his family refrain from sexual activity while they are on the ark. Perhaps this is out of guilt: They do not want to enjoy themselves while others are suffering. This "survivor's guilt" is a natural response to tragedy. However, when the Flood ends, Noah and his wife come out of the ark together, and the sons come out together with their wives. Now that their lives are beginning anew, they are willing to enjoy the world even though others have perished. They rejoin with one another to create relationships and rebuild the world. So too we try to be willing to go on in the face of personal and national tragedies.

The Mystery of the Sea

Have you penetrated to
the sources of the sea,
or walked in the recesses
of the deep?
—Job 38:1

Our Sages taught: It happened that Rabbi Eliezer and Rabbi Joshua were traveling on a ship. Rabbi Eliezer was sleeping and Rabbi Joshua was awake. But then Rabbi Joshua shuddered, and Rabbi Eliezer, waking up with a start, asked, "What happened?" Rabbi Joshua said, "I have seen a great light in the sea." Rabbi Eliezer said: "You may have seen the eyes of Leviathan, for it is written: 'His eyelids are like the glimmerings of dawn.' (Job 41:10)"
—Babylonian Talmud, Bava Batra 74b

The story of Noah's Flood is a reminder of how mysterious, dangerous, and ubiquitous is the sea. Life first moved within the sea, and our origins lie there. It is like another world, a place of strange creatures and vast power. Many Jewish stories, including those in Psalm 104:9 and Job 38:8–11, tell of the commands God issued to the sea so that it would not engulf the earth.

The sea represents the unconscious. In this season, the season of roots, we delve into our collective memory. In the cycle of Torah readings, we read Genesis at this time, the stories of the patriarchs and matriarchs, stories that, like dreams, reveal our own needs and desires. In Heshvan, we allow the sea of stories to rise within us. Within it is the fire of spirit, lighting our way through the autumn.

In Heshvan, Noah, Naamah, and their children begin their journey through the sea. We voyage with them, learning what there is to learn in the mysterious deeps. The truths we find will help us begin a year of discovery.

The Scent of Abraham

Go forth from your native land and from your ancestral house to the land that I will show you. I will make of you a great nation, and I will bless you; I will make your name great.
—Genesis 12:1

Rabbi Berekiah said: What was Abraham like? He was like a closed jar of fragrant myrrh, lying in a corner so that its fragrance did not travel. As soon as it was picked up and opened, though, the scent came out. In the same way, the Holy One said to Abraham, "Move from place to place, and I will make your name great in the world."
—Genesis Rabbah 39:2

The *Sefer Yetzirah* tells us that Heshvan is the month of scent, when we experience our sense of smell in a deep way. The tale of Abraham and Sarah, which we read at this season, is also about scent. The Holy One "uncorks" Abraham like a vial and spreads his fragrance around the world for all to experience. In a later midrash (*Genesis Rabbah* 40:5), Sarah too is hidden—Abraham hides her in a box, for fear someone will kidnap her. When the box is opened, the whole land lights up from Sarah's radiance. Both Abraham and Sarah have to be opened up in order to fulfill their task on earth.

In their home country, Abraham and Sarah are not known—the people around them do not realize their true gifts, beliefs, and talents. Once they travel, their true nature reveals itself. Heshvan, reminds us not to hide our own scent, or light, under a bushel. As the nights grow longer, we need to stir up our own radiance and fragrance. If there are brightly colored leaves around at this time, as there are in some places, they should inspire us to make our own colors brighter as well.

The Keys of the Hidden Realms

Isaac pleaded with the Eternal on behalf of his wife, because she was barren, and the Eternal responded to his plea, and his wife Rebekah conceived.
—GENESIS 25:21–22

Three keys are in the hands of the Holy One: the key of the grave, the key of the rains, and the key of the womb. Others say: the key of sustenance.
—GENESIS RABBAH 73:4

Many of the stories read in the Torah during this season relate to the opening of the womb. Abraham and Sarah, Isaac and Rebekah, Jacob and Rachel all struggle with infertility. We relate to their longings for birth. In Heshvan, as we pray for rain, we hope for openings of the sky and of the self.

A midrash teaches the Divine holds three keys: the key of the womb, the key of the grave (which is also the key of rebirth), and the key of rain. Some add a fourth key: the key of livelihood or sustenance. The key of sustenance allows Abraham to gather wealth and Sarah to receive gifts from Pharaoh. The key of rain blesses the wells of Isaac and the flocks of Rachel and Jacob. The key of birth opens the wombs of Sarah, Rebekah, Rachel, and Leah. The key of the grave saves Isaac from sacrifice.

The four keys also relate to the four seasons. The key of birth refers to the spring, the season of Passover (Pesach), when the Israelite nation is born. The key of the grave refers to the summer, the time of Tisha b'Av, when the Jewish people is nearly destroyed but rises from its ashes. The key of sustenance refers to the autumn, when we gather in the harvest. The winter season holds the key of the rain. In Heshvan, we ask that as winter approaches, the treasury of rain be opened to us.

The Task of Manasseh

Joseph named his first-born Manasseh, meaning, "The Divine has made me forget completely my hardship and my parental home."
—Genesis 41:51

[Joseph decreed] that no person could enter the royal palace until he had written his name and the name of his father and grandfather. Manasseh would stand at the door and receive these writings.
—Genesis Rabbah 91:4

In the *Sefer Yetzirah,* Manasseh is the tribe of Heshvan. Manasseh is the son of Joseph, the son of Jacob and Rachel who was sold into Egypt by his brothers and has become the vizier of Egypt. When Joseph's wife, Asenath, gives birth to her first son, Joseph names him Manasseh *(Menashe)* or "forgetful," because he wishes to forget how much he misses his family and how angry he is at his misfortunes. Yet in midrash, Manasseh is the one who helps Joseph remember how important his roots are.

One rabbinic legend holds that when a famine begins and people come to Egypt to buy food, Joseph starts to look for his brothers. One of the ways he does this is to make travelers sign in by writing their ancestry. This ruse allows him to locate his brothers when they come. Manasseh, Joseph's eldest son, helps him in this task by collecting the lineages of all the visitors to Egypt. Eventually, through this method, Joseph finds his brothers and is finally able to confess who he really is.

In Heshvan, the spirit of Manasseh helps us find our brothers and sisters. We read the stories of Abraham and Sarah, Isaac and Rebekah, and find new links to the sacred stories of our people. We enter ourselves in the geneaology of Torah by acknowledging our link to previous generations.

The Five Daughters of Zelophehad

The daughters of Zelophehad, of Manassite family … came forward. The names of the daughters were Mahlah, Noah, Hoglah, Milcah, and Tirzah. They stood before Moses, Eleazar the priest, the chieftains and the whole assembly at the entrance to the Tent of Meeting, and they said, "Our father died in the wilderness . . . and he has left no son. Let not our father's name be lost to his clan just because he had no son! Give us a holding among our father's kinsmen."

—Numbers 27:1–4

Why do we find the names of the daughters of Zelophehad listed not once, but four times? This is to teach us that when we speak up for ourselves, we claim the right to name the world as we see it.

—Naomi Hyman, "Davar Acher"[4]

According to the *Sefer Yetzirah* 5:1–2, the month of Heshvan is the month of Manasseh. The five daughters of Zelophehad, descended from Manasseh and Joseph, are symbols of the roots of Heshvan, drawing sustenance from the waters of Torah and from their own inner fire. In this season, when the gate of the earth is open, we remember how these five daughters asked to live and work on the earth.

The daughters of Zelophehad journey through the wilderness with the Israelites. When the people approach Israel, Moses does not assign land to women. The daughters of Zelophehad complain to Moses that their father will have no heirs. Moses brings their case before the Holy One and returns with an answer: If a man has no sons, his daughters may inherit.

The daughters of Zelophehad stand up for *gevurah,* justice and self-definition. Naomi Hyman notes how unusual it is that the five women are each named four times. She suggests this emphasis contains the teaching that by standing up for ourselves, we name the world as we see it.

The Smell of the Messiah

He shall smell the truth by his reverence for the Divine. He shall not judge by what his eyes behold, nor decide by what his ears hear.
—Isaiah 11:3

Rava said: The Messiah smells and judges.
—Babylonian Talmud, Sanhedrin 93b

According to the *Sefer Yetzirah* 5:9, the month of Heshvan is related to the sense of smell. Our sense of smell is a gift, allowing us to enjoy food, detect when something has gone rotten, or sniff out a coming rain or snowfall. Animals rely even more deeply on their sense of smell to find sustenance and avoid danger. In the rabbinic tradition, smell is also a metaphor for perfect perception. One legend claims that human beings derive the most pleasure from the sense of smell (Babylonian Talmud, Berakhot 43b). Smell leads us back to our origins, bringing back our most powerful childhood memories with a single whiff.

Legend holds that our generations will one day lead to a redeemer, the Messiah. Heshvan, according to some legends, is the month when the Messiah is destined to arrive. Some Jews believe the Messiah is a person, and some believe the Messiah is a symbol of the future, an ideal of justice and compassion we strive to reach. The Messiah is said to judge, not by sight or hearing, but by smell. He or she uses the most basic of instincts to determine what is healthy or rotten in the world. Heshvan, a month of scenting, is a time to remember how to trust our gut, how to listen to the inner wisdom that tells us what is right and wrong.

The Future Holiday

In the eleventh year, in the month of Bul [Heshvan]—that is, the eighth month—the House was completed according to all its details and all its specifications. . . . All the people of Israel gathered before King Solomon at the Feast [of Sukkot], in the month of Ethanim [Tishrei]—that is, the seventh month.
—1 KINGS 6:38, 8:2

Heshvan will be repaid in messianic times, because the Temple was finished during Heshvan but not dedicated in Heshvan.
—YALKUT MELACHIM 184

Autumn is a time of loss, and Heshvan reflects this subtle grief. It is, according to the *Yalkut Melachim*, the month when Solomon finished the First Temple. It receives no celebration or festival because of this; therefore, it is a sad sort of month. Yet there is a midrashic principle that nothing is ever lost. The Babylonian Talmud (Sanhedrin 107a) tells us that when the letter *yud* is taken out of Sarai's name so that the Holy One can change her name to Sarah, the *yud* complains. It is put into Hosea ben Nun's name, and his name becomes Joshua, assistant of Moses. So Heshvan too must be repaid for its loss.

The legend arises that one day, in the world to come, Heshvan will be paid back because of King Solomon's oversight. Heshvan will become the month when the Third Temple, the temple of peace among all peoples, is built. Like the Messiah, the Third Temple is the legendary culmination of all legends and all generations. Heshvan, though apparently without holidays, holds the promise of a future holiday: the dedication of a new and universal sacred space. This reflects the truth of nature—the decay of autumn will be paid back a hundredfold with growth in the spring.

The North Wind

The north wind gives birth to rain, thunderous faces, secret words.
—Proverbs 25:23

From the north wind darkness comes to the world. The wind of the north the Divine made but did not finish, and said, "Anyone who claims to be a god, come and finish the north wind, and we will know you are a god." And from there come the spirits and demons.
—Pirkei de-Rabbi Eliezer 3

As Heshvan moves to its conclusion, we enter the realm of the north wind, blowing its chill air into fields and streets. The north wind is the source of mystery, bringing us secrets and darkness. Heshvan leads from the ancestors through the messianic future into the space of mystery. What are we meant to do on earth? Why is the circle of life the way it is? Where were we before we were born? What happens when we die? When the north wind blows, it brings us these questions.

A midrash in *Pirkei de-Rabbi Eliezer* tells us that the north wind is a place of incompletion. The Divine left it incomplete to remind anyone with pretensions of godhood that some things in the world are beyond understanding. The season of late autumn brings with it a sense of awe before the secrets of Creation.

Learning from Our Roots

The sayings of the wise are as goads, like nails fixed in prodding sticks.
—ECCLESIASTES 12:11

Why are the words of the wise compared to a planting? Because just as the roots of a tree travel and root in all places, so the words of the wise enter and root themselves throughout the body.
—NUMBERS RABBAH 14:4

Heshvan holds the mysteries of water and fire, of rain and of Torah. To learn these mysteries of the season, we must learn how to learn. Roots, our companion throughout Heshvan and Kislev, can teach us how to absorb what we need from the Torah and from the world.

A root may dive deep to drink groundwater or send out tendrils to sip from the cracks in rock. It may thread its hairs near the surface of the earth to catch rain, or it may do all three. Roots remind us that we too have different ways of learning. Some of us are divers who plunge into one great passion, whereas others of us divide our attention among many kinds of knowledge. Some of us love a challenge and send our roots to pry into stone, while others need to rest by still waters. All of us are able to learn if we honor our own needs and interests.

The wisdom of our tradition, like a root system, is a support beneath us: We draw on it in body and spirit as we move through our lives. Yet we also must let our roots move in the direction of what is fresh and flowing. In this season of secrets and storytelling, we too have teachings to share.

Buried Coals

A warrior's sharp arrows, with hot coals of broomwood.
—Psalms 120:4

All other coals, when they go out, go out completely. But coals of broom, even when they appear to go out, are still burning on the inside. … A story of the broom tree: Someone extinguished a broom coal, and it burned a whole year, winter into summer into winter.
—Genesis Rabbah 98:19

Between Sukkot and Passover, there are no major holidays. In Heshvan, there are no minor festivals either. The sun seems to retreat and grow small. Yet the spirit of the year continues to inspire us, burning from Sukkot to Passover and welcoming us back to the pageantry of festivals when the spring arrives.

The patience of life is one of nature's great mysteries. In 2005, a scientist reported he had found frozen bacteria that had survived over 30,000 years.[5] When he thawed out the bacteria, they began swimming and moving around. The fire of life is long lasting, even when it has been dormant a long time.

The burning bush of the Exodus may have been a broom tree, a tree that, when burned, can smolder for months and months. Perhaps, the midrashic legend hints, the burning bush that Moses saw in the spring had been burning throughout the autumn and winter, waiting for Moses to arrive—just as plant life burns in hiding until it is time to emerge, sprout, and flower. We too may be burning inside, only needing the right moment to bring our fire out into the world.

The Waning Moon

The Eternal made the two great lights: the greater light to dominate the day, and the lesser light to dominate night.
—GENESIS 1:16

The moon said to the Divine, "…can two kings share one crown?" The Divine replied, "Go and make yourself smaller." "Sovereign of the Universe," she said to him, "because I made a proper claim before you, am I to make myself smaller?" He said to her, "Go, and you will rule over both the day and the night." She said, "What good is a lamp in broad daylight?" He said, "Go! Israel shall use you to count the days and years." On seeing that the moon would not be consoled, the Holy One … said, "Bring an atonement for me for making the moon smaller."
—BABYLONIAN TALMUD, HULLIN 60B

The last mystery of Heshvan is the disappearing moon. On this date, the moon is waning or already dark, and the season too is darkening. Yet the moon continues to be a teacher of renewal, a symbol of the power of darkness and dreams.

According to midrash, the moon complains that two rulers cannot wear a single crown. In response, the Holy One makes the moon smaller than the sun. The moon points out that this is not a fair response. Why should it be smaller? The Holy One tries to appease the moon by promising she will shine night and day; but the moon is still unhappy. Finally, the Divine ordains a special new moon sacrifice to atone for God's mistake.

The moon has gotten to the root of a thorny problem: Why is it fair that some are leaders and others are followers? One answer is that we lead in different ways: The moon may not provide heat and light, but it shows us how to measure time. Another answer is that the moon can participate in the sun's leadership by shining during the day. But the moon isn't completely satisfied. So too we shouldn't be satisfied when we see unfair leadership or wrongful authority. The moon, a symbol of the *Shekhinah*'s renewal, reminds us to keep changing our world.

Yom Kippur Katan

New Moon of Kislev

Just as we began Heshvan with the matriarch Rachel, we also end with Rachel: the secret Rachel of the kabbalists. Mystics saw Rachel as a manifestation of the *Shekhinah* and identified her with the moon, waxing into radiance and waning into darkness. The kabbalists of Tzfat in the 16th century created the custom of *Yom Kippur Katan* (Little Yom Kippur), fasting at the dark of the moon as a kind of lesser Day of Atonement. They saw the decrease in the moon's light as a symbol of exile from God's presence and prayed for the moon's restoration to brightness. They hoped to bring a day when the world would be perfected and the sun and moon would be equally bright.

The first *Yom Kippur Katan* of the year is observed in Heshvan, to welcome the beginning of the month of Kislev. This darkness is powerful, drawing us into the core of ourselves. The coming month of Kislev is close to the winter solstice, a month of deep darkness. Shefa Gold, chanter and mystic, reminds us that this darkness evokes in us a longing for the *Shekhinah*'s light. It is our task to learn from the winter, yet also draw down the spring light into the world through our deeds and sacred intentions. As *Yom Kippur Katan* passes, we press deeper into the year, bearing both fragments of darkness and shards of light.

And the light of the moon shall become like the light of the sun, and the light of the sun shall become sevenfold, like the light of the seven days.
—Isaiah 30:26

With the exile of the Shekhinah, *darkness enters into our existence, and with that darkness comes a longing for Her return.* Yom Kippur Katan *comes at a point in the cycle when that longing is at its peak. . . . It is a call to recreate ourselves in God's image.*
—Shefa Gold, "The Dark Rays of the Moon"[6]

The New Moon Fires

New Moon of Kislev

And on your joyous occasions—your fixed festivals and new moon days—you shall sound the trumpets over your burnt offerings and your sacrifices of well-being. They shall be a reminder of you before your God.
—Numbers 10:10

On six new moons messengers ride forth: Nisan because of Passover, Av because of the fast, Elul because of the new year, Kislev because of Hanukkah, and Adar because of Purim. At first, they would light bonfires. After the Samaritans confused the calendar, they would send messengers.
—Mishnah Rosh Hashanah 1:3, 2:2

In Kislev, the darkest month, a sliver of moon appears like a dusting of snow. In ancient times, the Rabbinic court of Jerusalem would send messengers to announce the coming of the new moon on six months of the year: Kislev, Adar, Nisan, Av, Elul, and Iyar, to remind the people of upcoming holidays. The new moon of Kislev was the first of these occasions, and it heralded the coming of Hanukkah.

Once the new moon was announced, bonfires were lit in the hills above Jerusalem. Far-flung communities would see the bonfires and light their own, until all the Jewish communities knew that the new moon had come. As stars help a ship locate itself on the sea, the bonfires helped Jews locate themselves in time, joining them to the root consciousness of their people.

According to Rabbi Judah, the 1st of Kislev is the first day of winter in Israel (Babylonian Talmud, Bava Metzi'a 106b). We are close now to the darkest days of the year, and the new moon bonfires remind us of the Hanukkah candles growing each night. The flames teach that when the moon is dark, we can expect its face to shine again, and when the sunlight is dimming, soon it will begin to grow again. This is true also for us: The quiet of introspection can and should lead to outward action in the world.

The Month of Dreams

Then Pharaoh awoke: it was a dream. Next morning … he sent for all the magicians of Egypt … and Pharaoh told them his dreams, but none could interpret them …. The chief cup-bearer … said to Pharaoh, "I must make mention … of my offenses. Once Pharaoh was angry … and placed me in custody … with the chief baker. We had dreams the same night … each of us a dream with a meaning of its own. A Hebrew youth was there … and when we told him our dreams, he interpreted them for us."
—GENESIS 41:7–12

If one has had a disturbing dream, that one should go and have it interpreted in the presence of three. . . . [L]et that person bring three others and say to them, "I have seen a good dream."
—BABYLONIAN TALMUD, BERAKHOT 55B

Kislev, *Sefer Yetzirah* 5:9 tells us, is the month of sleep, a month when the sun seems asleep in the sky, when roots sleep in the earth. We too may be drawn to sleep and dream more than usual. The Rabbis of the Talmud say that a dream is one sixtieth of prophecy (Babylonian Talmud, Berakhot 57b) and add that an uninterpreted dream is like an unread letter (Babylonian Talmud, Berakhot 55a).

The Talmud provides a ceremony to interpret one's dreams and turn a bad dream into a good one. The dreamer convenes a *beit din*, "a court of three," and this improvised court declares that the dream is a good dream, thus nullifying any of its ill effects. The Talmud's vision of dreams teaches us how to approach Kislev. As we delve into our inner selves, we may find painful images and words. If we acknowledge these difficult truths, and interpret them, we can use them for good.

3 KISLEV

The Month of the Rainbow

"I have set my bow in the clouds, and it shall serve as a sign of covenant between Me and the earth. When I bring clouds on the earth and the bow appears in the clouds, I will remember My covenant between Me and you and every living creature among all flesh, so that the waters shall never again become a flood to destroy all flesh."
—GENESIS 9:13–15

It is forbidden to look at the rainbow when it is seen in the skies, because this shows disrespect to the Shekhinah. *The colors of the rainbow in the lower world are a reflection of the radiance in the upper world, and not for the eyes of humans.*
—ZOHAR I:72A

Kislev brings us the mystery of the rainbow. The sign for Kislev is the bow (*keshet*), an appropriate sign for a month in the rainy season. In the Torah, the Holy One offers the rainbow to Noah as a sign that the world will never again be destroyed by flood. The rainbow, light reflected through water droplets, is a sign of the fire concealed in the moisture of winter and a promise of God's compassion toward human beings.

In the Zohar, the rainbow is a manifestation of the immanence of the Divine. The Zohar (somewhat unreasonably) asks us not to look at a rainbow out of respect for the *Shekhinah,* whose radiance appears in its colors. The rainbow is a glimpse of sacred mystery. By looking at it, we catch a glimpse of the radiance at the root of existence.

Kislev, the month of the bow, is also a month to pursue *gevurah* (justice), for equity, like the rainbow, is a reflection of the *Shekhinah.* Hanukkah, the upcoming holiday, teaches the importance of defending freedom. The bow of Kislev is a reminder to be vigilant against those who seek to harm the world and its inhabitants.

Rebuilding the Temple

In the fourth year of King Darius, on the fourth day of the ninth month, Kislev, the word of the Eternal came to Zechariah—when Bethel-sharezer and Regem-melech and his men sent to entreat the favor of the Divine, and to address this inquiry to the priests of the House of the Eternal and to the prophets: "Shall I weep and fast in the fifth month, as I have been doing all these years?" . . . The word of the Eternal came to Zechariah: "Thus said the Holy One of Hosts: Execute true justice, deal loyally and compassionately with one another."
—ZECHARIAH 7:1–2,8–9

For the Tabernacle, the Holy One of Blessing wanted sincere donations from the deepest root of the heart of the people, because the Tabernacle is an eternal structure.
—MEI HASHILOACH ON EXODUS 36:5

In Kislev, the Israelites of the Torah brought and made gifts for the *mishkan* (the Tabernacle). This day of Kislev recalls Zechariah's prophecy centuries later concerning the rebuilding of the Temple after the first exile. A number of Jews come to Zechariah and ask him if they should continue to observe the fast of Tisha b'Av to mourn the First Temple's loss, now that the building of the Second Temple is under way. His response to them is that they should take care of widows and orphans and be kind to one another. Zechariah doesn't answer the technical question. Instead, he points the people toward just behavior. This, Zechariah prophesies, is the way to honor both the old Temple and the new one.

The *Mei haShiloach,* a Hasidic commentary, suggests that gifts to a sacred shrine must come from the root of the heart: They must not only be outward gifts, but inward ones, coming from the depths of the person. Zechariah makes the same point with his words about justice: Just acts that come from the soul can lead to sacredness in the world.

Jacob's Ladder

He had a dream; a stairway was set on the ground, and its top reached to the sky, and angels of the Divine were going up and down on it. And the Divine was standing beside him and said, "I am the Eternal, the God of your father Abraham and the God of Isaac. The ground on which you are lying I give to you and your offspring."
—GENESIS 28:12–14

One interpretation: the angels were going up and down on the ladder. Another interpretation: the angels were going up and down in him.
—GENESIS RABBAH 68:12

As animals in cold climates sink into dreaming, we read the sections of the Torah telling of Jacob, son of Isaac and Rebekah, and of Joseph, son of Jacob and Rachel. During the weeks of Kislev, we study the mythic dreams of our ancestors and use them to burrow into our own thoughts and memories.

Jacob's first dream is of a ladder to heaven, with angels going up and down on it. An ancient midrash, drawing on the Jewish tradition of dream interpretation, tells that the ladder was really not a ladder at all but Jacob himself. Like a root in the earth, Jacob draws the energy of the heavens into him, and the angels move up and down his spine as if through the trunk of a tree.

In Kislev, in the cold, we are aware of the warm energy flowing in our bodies. Dreams and visions rise up and sink down in us, helping us understand the past and shape the future. Our spines, and our dreams, are a way for us to travel between sky and earth.

Dreaming of Bread

And Pharaoh said to Joseph, "I have had a dream, but no one can interpret it. I have heard it said of you that for you to hear a dream is to tell its meaning."
—GENESIS 41:15

All the things of the world are like a dream that needs interpretation. . . . "Bread, lechem, *is a word made of the same letters as dream,* chalom. *Even bread must be interpreted, as must all things from which we derive benefit."*
—MEI HASHILOACH ON GENESIS 41:15

On the 6th of Kislev, in winter, we are exactly half a year away from Shavuot, the spring holiday when we offer bread as a sacrifice. Kislev is the season of the dream (*chalom*), and Shavuot is the season of bread (*lechem*). The roots now dreaming in the earth are a sign that the harvest of spring will come.

The Pharaoh chooses a young slave to help rule over Egypt because he is a good interpreter of dreams. What do dreams have to do with governing the real world? Joseph's ability to interpret the signs that appear to him has practical value: It allows him to prepare for the future, to store bread for a famine that will come. The biblical texts about Joseph teach us that our own dreams can prepare us to act wisely in the world.

On the 6th of Kislev, we honor the buried seeds and roots that will become the produce of spring. We remember Joseph, who turned vision into reality. We promise we too will use our dreams to transform the world into a place of sustenance.

The Burning of the Scroll

This word came to Jeremiah from the Divine: Get a scroll and write upon it the words I have spoken to you.... The king sent Jehudi to get the scroll.... Jehudi read it to the king.... Since it was the ninth month [Kislev], the king was sitting ... with a fire burning in the brazier before him. And every time Jehudi read three or four columns, [the king] would cut it up with a ... knife and throw it into the fire....
—JEREMIAH 36:1–2,21–23,26

Jeremiah said, "When I went up to Jerusalem, I saw a woman sitting on the mountain top, dressed in black with disheveled hair, and she was weeping and wailing, 'Who will comfort me?' She said to me, 'I am your mother Zion.'"
—PESIKTA DE-RAV KAHANA 166

The snows of winter highlight the beauties of the world. But sometimes the snows have an erasing effect, as if what is beneath them were gone forever. King Jehoiakim tries for a similar effect when the prophet Jeremiah indicts his behavior in a written scroll. In Kislev, the king burns the scroll. It is ironic that this burning of a scroll takes place half the year away from Shavuot, season of the giving of the Torah. This vile action is reminiscent of all leaders who decline to hear the truth.

Mother Zion is the opposite of King Jehoiachim; she seeks to bring out the truth by telling her story to Jeremiah and asking for help. Her grief is very great, yet like the scorched root of a tree, she will grow again. Mother Zion represents truth, and she also represents all those we must comfort and protect. She and Jeremiah are our allies as we seek to be honest.

Dreaming of the Well

Jacob resumed his journey…. There before his eyes was a well in the open. Three flocks of sheep were lying there beside it, for the flocks were watered from that well. The stone on the mouth of the well was large…. Rachel came with her father's flock, for she was a shepherdess. And when Jacob saw Rachel, the daughter of his uncle Laban, and the flocks of his uncle Laban, Jacob went up and rolled the stone off the mouth of the well, and watered the flock of his uncle Laban. Then Jacob kissed Rachel.

—GENESIS 29:1–2,9–11

A well of water I have discovered. And have rolled the great stone off the rock, and drunk from it. And still I was thirsty.

—REBEKAH TIKTINER, MENEKES RIVKA[7]

At this season of water, in many lands, the wells and cisterns of the world refill with rain and snow. Wells are also a source of blessing in the Torah portions of these weeks. We first meet Rebekah by a well, and Jacob meets his beloved, Rachel, by a well. A midrash suggests this well represents Sinai, mountain of the covenant (*Genesis Rabba*h 70:9). Halfway around the year from the Revelation at Sinai, we recall the mountain of Torah through the image of a cistern.

This scene by the well is also dreamlike for Rachel. When Jacob meets her, he rolls a stone off the well, which perhaps represents an opening of possibility for her. Through meeting Jacob, Rachel starts down a path that will lead away from her home and family. Rachel and Jacob link their lives together by a well, a symbol of life, and in so doing create the nation that will come to Sinai.

Rebekah Tiktiner, a 16th-century Yiddish writer, imagines herself as Jacob rolling the stone from the well. The poet drinks, yet still she is thirsty. Our lives, like dreams, hold questions we have not answered. On Shavuot we will receive the black letters of the communal sacred text. Now, in winter, we receive the white spaces, the dreams and dark waters, the inner symbols and silences.

Joseph's First Dream

Once Joseph had a dream which he told to his brothers, and they hated him even more. He said to them, "Hear this dream which I have dreamed. We were binding sheaves in the field, when suddenly my sheaf stood up and remained upright. Then your sheaves gathered around and bowed low to my sheaf." His brothers answered, "Do you mean to reign over us? Do you mean to rule over us?" And they hated him even more for his talk about his dreams.
—Genesis 37:5–8

Rabbi Chiyya bar Abba said: If one sees wheat in a dream, one will see peace, as it is written: "The Divine will endow your realm with peace and will satisfy you with choice wheat" (Ps. 147:14).
—Babylonian Talmud, Berakhot 57a

Joseph is the favorite child of his father, and his brothers hate him for this favored position. When the young Joseph has a dream implying he wants to be lord over his brothers, his brothers hate him still more for his pride. Yet Joseph's dream is vindicated: Joseph's brothers end up bowing down to him after Joseph becomes a great lord in Egypt.

Joseph's dream has an additional meaning. The Talmud tells us wheat is a symbol for peace and prosperity. This dream reveals that one day Joseph will provide food for his family when they are hungry. The brothers fail to discern this meaning, and so they hate Joseph. Neither Joseph nor Jacob sees the dream's meaning until later, after it comes to pass.

If we live in a cold climate, we may hate the cold, or if it rains at this season, we may dislike the rain. Yet the rain and the roots it waters promise us food, just as Joseph fed his brothers when there was famine. So too there are people in our lives who annoy us, yet we may find that they have gifts to offer. The message of Joseph's dream is that everyone can have value at the right time and season.

Joseph's Second Dream

(Joseph) dreamed another dream and told it to his brothers, saying, "Behold I have had another dream. This time, the sun, moon, and eleven stars were bowing down to me." And when he told it to his father and brothers, his father berated him. … "Are we to come, I and your mother and your brothers, and bow low to you to the ground?"
—GENESIS 37:9–10

Rabbi Yochanan said in the name of Rabbi Shimon bar Yochai: …you cannot have a dream without some meaningless things in it. Rabbi Berekiah said: A dream, even if part of it comes true, all of it never comes true. How do we know this? From Joseph, as it is written: "The sun and the moon … were bowing down to me."
—BABYLONIAN TALMUD, BERAKHOT 55A

In Joseph's second dream, the sun, moon, and 11 stars bow down to him, representing his father, mother, and 11 brothers. His father and brothers chastise him for the dream. In one Rabbinic tradition, Joseph's father, Jacob, is disturbed not by Joseph's wish for domination but by the dream's inaccuracy (*Genesis Rabbah* 84:11). Joseph's mother, Rachel, is dead; she can never bow down before Joseph. We may imagine that Joseph's dream contains not only premonition but also wish fulfillment. It is only natural he would dream of seeing his mother again and making her proud of him.

Some seeds will sprout and some will not. This is the reality of the world. Like Joseph, we have dreams and aspirations that can come true, and we also have wishes and desires that cannot be fulfilled. Part of the work of Kislev is to sort the wheat from the chaff, the nourishing parts of our dreams from the parts that must be left behind. Knowing what can and cannot be helps us root ourselves in reality.

Miriam's Dream

The Eternal came down in a pillar of cloud, stopped at the entrance of the Tent, and called out, "Aaron and Miriam!" The two of them came forward; and the Divine said, "Hear these My words: When a prophet of the Holy One arises among you, I make Myself known to him in a vision, I speak with him in a dream."
—NUMBERS 12:5–6

When the tribes went out with their banners, they would not travel until Miriam walked before them.
—YALKUT SHIMONI, TAZRIA 937

The Bible does not report the dreams of women. However, the Torah hints at a woman prophet who dreams. In Numbers, the Divine mentions (while chastising Miriam for criticizing Moses) that most prophets receive their prophecy by dreaming. So, like Jacob and Joseph, Miriam dreams. What dreams does Miriam have? What makes her so important that the tribes will not travel unless Miriam goes before them?

Melinda Ribner offers this interpretation of Miriam's name: Miriam means "*mar yam*," "bitter" and "sea."[8] Even in the days when her life is bitter from slavery, Miriam knows one day she will stand at the shore of the Sea of Reeds and feel that she is free, and she will dance. This dream makes her a pillar of fire, guiding us to pass through the waters to freedom. Miriam is like the sun, leading the people through the dark waters of the sea into the bright wilderness.

It is striking to think that as a girl, Miriam dreams of the Sea of Reeds and sees the waters part. Perhaps this is why, at the time of the Exodus, Miriam brings musical instruments with her, so that the women will have timbrels to play when they celebrate their freedom. In Kislev, as we approach Hanukkah, season of renewed sun and renewed freedom, we remember Miriam's dream.

The Fire and the Flame

The house of Jacob shall be fire, and the house of Joseph flame, and the house of Esau shall be straw.
—Obadiah 1:18

"Israel is called fire, as it is written: 'The house of Jacob shall be fire.'"
—Exodus Rabbah 15:6

We are now two weeks away from Hanukkah. It may still be wet outdoors, but in the sacred calendar, the season's inner aspect of fire begins to reveal itself. We prepare to kindle flames, but the mystery of the season is that we are flames, burning with a spirit that transcends weather.

Hayyim Vital and Rachel Aberlin were both great mystics of the early 18th century. Aberlin had a dream in which she saw Vital and, behind him, she saw burning straw and hay. Vital suggested her dream was a midrash on a verse in Obadiah: "The house of Jacob shall be fire." Aberlin replied to him that he was able to quote the verse, but she was able to see the spiritual fire Obadiah saw. Her midrash was not textual but visceral—she actually had the experience of prophecy.[9]

At this season, Aberlin teaches us not only to study the stories of Hanukkah but to live as if we too could see the flame at the heart of existence. Light is not only outside us but inside us as well. We ourselves are the fires of the winter season.

Benjamin Dreams of His Brother

Benjamin's sons: Bela, Becher, Ashbel, Gera, Naaman, Ehi, Rosh, Muppim, Huppim, and Ard.
—GENESIS 46:21

"I named my children for my brother: Bela, for Joseph was swallowed (balah) *among the nations; Becher, for he was firstborn* (bachor) *of his mother; Ashbel, for God nourished him* (savo el)*; Gera, for he dwelled* (gar) *in temporary places; Naaman, for he was very handsome* (na'im)*; Ehi veRosh, for he is my brother and leader* (achi veroshi)*; Muppim and Huppim, for he did not see my wedding canopy* (huppah) *and I did not see his; and Ard, for he went down* (yarad) *among the peoples of the world."*
—BABYLONIAN TALMUD, SOTAH 36B

The month of Kislev, the month of dreams and of roots, is also the month of the tribe of Benjamin. This is partly because Jerusalem, the city of dreams and the root of the Land of Israel, is in Benjamin's territory. Yet Benjamin also has a deeper connection to dreams.

When Benjamin's half brothers sell his full brother, Joseph, into slavery, Benjamin is silent about the matter. Yet as Benjamin grows older, he names his children after Joseph's disappearance. Each name he gives to a child hints at the fact that he knows what happened to his brother. He gestures, almost unconsciously, that Joseph is in a foreign land, that he has married, that he is still his mother's firstborn and Benjamin's elder brother. The more Joseph's existence is hidden, the more Benjamin's namings strive to reveal it.

In this dark half of the year, we may think things are more concealed, but it is often in darkness that we allow the truth to slip out. Particularly in dreams, we become aware of things we have not allowed ourselves to know. The tribe of Benjamin teaches us to be aware of the ways we reveal truth to ourselves.

The Birthday of Reuben

The Eternal saw that Leah was unloved, and opened her womb, but Rachel was barren. Leah conceived and bore a son, and named him Reuben, for she declared: "The Eternal has seen my affliction. Now my husband will love me."
—Genesis 29:31–33

Rabbi Levi said: The Holy One saw the sorrow of Leah, and gave her pregnancy for the belly and comfort for the spirit. She gave birth to a good-looking and wise boy, and said: "Look at the child the Holy One gave me!"
—Pirkei de-Rabbi Eliezer 36

Winter is, for some of us, a season when the growing darkness may have an effect on our mood. On the 14th of Kislev, which in *Midrash Tadshe* is the birth date of Reuben, we can look to Leah, wife of Jacob, as a model for a person who finds renewed joy in life in spite of her sadness.

Leah, forced into a loveless marriage with Jacob by her father, Laban, bears many children. With each child, she continues to hope Jacob will love her, but this longed-for love never seems to materialize. Leah's sister, Rachel, on the other hand, is Jacob's true love. Leah is the more tragic of the two women, yet in the mystical tradition, Leah symbolizes wisdom and wholeness.

In *Pirkei de-Rabbi Eliezer,* the Holy One seeks to comfort Leah in her sorrow by giving her a son, Reuben. This son seems to lift Leah's mood, even as she still expresses pain that Jacob does not love her. Leah not only receives "pregnancy of the body" but consolation for the soul as well. Perhaps it is Leah's increasing sense of joy and gratitude that comforts her.

Benjamin's Blessing

Of Benjamin he said:
Beloved of the Eternal,
he rests securely beside
the Holy One.
Ever does the Divine
protect him,
as he rests between the
shoulders of the Infinite.
—DEUTERONOMY 33:12

This blessing is placed next to the blessing of Levi because the blessing of Levi deals with the temple offerings and the blessing of Benjamin is that the Temple will be built in the territory of the tribe of Benjamin.
—RASHI ON DEUTERONOMY 33:12

In these 10 days before Hanukkah, our task is to dedicate a space of light within ourselves. Part of dedicating this space is examining the physical spaces around us. We learn this task from the tribe of Benjamin, whom the Torah says "dwells between God's shoulders," at the place of the sacred central shrine. Like earth holding a root, the tribe of Benjamin "holds" the Temple.

Benjamin is not noted as a farmer or builder or sculptor. How does he create sacred space? He is the one brother of Joseph who loves him fully and is concerned for him throughout all the years of Joseph's absence. Benjamin reminds us we create holy spaces not only through ritual and beautiful objects but also through love.

Kislev prepares us for the renewal of the sacred. We recall the ways we can be containers for holy space in our daily lives—as keepers of our homes, workplaces, synagogues, and public places. We keep in mind the lesson of Benjamin, who shows us how love and memory can make our dwellings holy.

The Foundation Stone

Do you know who fixed its (the world's) dimensions, or who measured it with a line? Onto what were its bases sunk, who set its cornerstone while the morning stars sang together and all the divine beings shouted for joy?
—Job 38:5–6

The Holy One created the world by taking a stone, the "foundation stone," and casting it into the abyss so that it stayed there, and from it the world grew. This is the center of the universe, and atop it stands the Holy of Holies. . . . The stone is made of fire, water, and air, and rests on the abyss. At times water flows out of it and fills the deeps.
—Zohar I:231a

In this season of the gate of earth, as we meditate on sacred space, we begin to wonder what lies beneath our existence. Jewish mysticism imagines that at the heart of the universe is a foundation stone, a single point on which every other thing is built. This foundation stone, or *even shtiyah,* is the reason the world does not fall back into chaos. It is made of fire, water, and air, which *Sefer Yetzirah* (3:3) teaches are the three building blocks of Creation. The *even shtiyah* is a foothold, a floor over the abyss, atop of which reality can come into being. It is the root holding the world in place.

In Jewish lore, this stone rests beneath the Holy of Holies, the most sacred chamber in the Temple (*Midrash Tanhuma, Kiddushin* 10). Yet the stone could really rest anywhere. All places are above the foundation stone; all moments touch both the wonder of creation and the threat of chaos. As we prepare to rededicate sacred space during Hanukkah, we remember this truth.

Playing with Leviathan

There is the sea, vast and wide, with its creatures beyond number, living things, small and great. There go the ships, and Leviathan that You made to play with.
—PSALMS 104:25–26

There are twelve hours in the day. In the first three hours, the Holy One sits and studies Torah. In the second quarter … , the Holy One sits and judges the whole world, and when the Holy One sees the world is guilty, the Holy One rises from the throne of judgment and sits on the throne of mercy. In the third quarter of the day, the Holy One sits and feeds all the creatures … . In the fourth quarter of the day, the Holy One sits and plays with Leviathan.
—BABYLONIAN TALMUD, AVODAH ZARAH 3B

In medieval Jewish lore, each season of the year is associated with a particular mythical animal. The winter is the season of Leviathan, the great sea serpent of the deeps (*Otzar Midrashim: Hashem Behohmah, Yasad Aretz* 6). Leviathan, ruler of the sea, represents myth and the unconscious: all that is outside our awareness and outside time. The Zohar (II:20a) teaches us that just as we humans have counterparts in the spiritual world, the angels, so too we have a counterpart in the underworld, Leviathan. An ancient story tells that Leviathan is the Holy One's playmate.

This legend is a reminder to us that we too require play. Our most sacred holidays and rituals are a form of play, where we are allowed to dream, imagine, and transform ourselves into Maccabees or Jews leaving Egypt. Play is necessary to our spirits and brings us light even in dark times. As we move through the last days of Kislev toward Hanukkah, may we remember to play, to imagine, and to experience wonder.

The Power of Snow

To snow, God said,
"Become earth!"
—Job 37:6

From where was the earth made? From snow under the divine throne, as it is written: "The Divine said to the snow: 'Become earth'" (Job 37). The Holy One took snow and cast it on the water. The water froze into ice, and the ice turned into the dust of the earth.
—Otzar Midrashim: Moshe 25

Rabbi Judah Loew of Prague (the Maharal) believed that half of the Jewish year is dedicated to light and half is dedicated to darkness. Rabbi Boruch Leff writes that the Maharal teaches about the purpose of each half of the year.[10] The summer half is dedicated to spiritual growth, while the winter half of the year is the dark half, dedicated to spiritual maintenance and rest rather than growth. The snow that falls in winter (at least in Prague, where the Maharal lived) is a vessel of spiritual light helping us in this time, reminding us of God's "colorless" presence in the world at this season.

Snow is physically as well as spiritually helpful, providing a warm blanket for the ground so that plants do not die and giving water to thirsty roots. A midrash even tells us that snow lies under God's throne and helps create the world. But how did the snow get under God's throne? Perhaps the midrash sees snow as some kind of concrete manifestation of divine light. It is both fire and water, both heavenly and earthly. Snow, falling from sky to earth, reminds us of our own need to shine our spiritual light on earth during this dark part of the year.

The Windows of the Temple

For the House he made windows, broad and narrow.
—1 Kings 6:4

When one builds a house, one makes the windows narrow on the outside and wide on the inside, so the light will enter from outside. When Solomon built the Temple, he did differently. He made the windows narrow on the inside and wide on the outside, so that the light would shine out from the Temple and light up the outer world.
—Midrash Tanhuma, Be-ha'alotekha 2

The layout of a sacred space teaches us something about the way the makers of that space view the world. If one goes into a synagogue one will see an ark with the Torah in a central place and an eternal light lit somewhere in the sanctuary. These carefully placed items teach the centrality of the Torah for Jews as well as the concept of eternal service and witness to the Divine. So too the ritual objects and spaces in the Tabernacle and the Temple teach us how to order our spirits at this season of rededication.

Rabbi Avin tells us that the windows of the Temple were wide on the outside and narrow on the inside so that light would flow, not inward, but outward. The Temple dwellers were concerned, not with getting enough sunlight from the outside world, but with letting the spiritual blessing of the Temple shine through its windows. At this season we not only receive light from the world but we give light as well, just as the root of a tree takes in moisture and sends it upward and outward to the whole tree. The darkness of the winter, which turns us inward, reminds us to open our own windows.

The Burning Castle

For love is strong as death,
passion as mighty as life's
end, its flames are flames
of fire, a blaze of God.
—SONG OF SONGS 8:6

Rabbi Isaac told the story of a man who was journeying from place to place and saw a burning castle. He said: "Is it possible that the castle has no owner?" At that moment the owner of the castle looked out at him and said: "I am the owner of the castle." So too, Abraham said: "Is it possible the world should be without someone to care for it?" The Holy One looked out at him and said: "I am the owner of the world!"
—GENESIS RABBAH 39:1

This is the season of contemplation, but we must not be naive about contemplation. Meditating on the world can bring light, but it can also bring us sorrow and even cynicism. Sometimes we look at our planet and see a world where chaos reigns and pain, grief, and anger rage around us.

The Sages imagine Abraham has the same problem we do. He observes reality and sees a burning castle: a beautiful place, perhaps, but in flames and about to be destroyed. Only when the Holy One looks at him from within the flames does he become convinced that the castle has someone to guide it. The sense that the Divine Presence also endures the flames convinces Abraham the world is a sacred place in spite of its sorrows.

The lights of Hanukkah we will kindle in a few days represent not only our joy but also the troubles of the world. The candles are witnesses to the creation and destruction that marks our mortal existence. Yet through our communal celebration of light, we assert that life has meaning and power, that it is a castle of light, not only a building in flames.

The Sacred Space of the Womb

The lifebreath of the human being is the lamp of the Eternal.
—Proverbs 20:27

Before an embryo is formed in the womb … the Holy One says to the soul: "Enter into that sperm and that egg. …I have created you for this purpose."… The Holy One sends the soul off and the angels bring it to the womb. Two angels feed it and care for it. A candle burns over its head…. By the light of the candle they teach the embryo Torah. After nine months … the angels say: "… when the time comes to leave, you will not want to go." The child enters the air of the world. The angel taps it on the upper lip … and it forgets all its Torah and all it has seen and known.
—Midrash Tanhuma, Pekudei 3

A midrash tells how the womb is a sacred space. When we enter a sacred place, or a sacred time like *Shabbat*, we are fed by Torah and by our community. It is as if a special light burns within us. We are happy and feel our holiness. Why would we want to depart from that place? Yet we must leave. The protective holy space prepares us to enter the world. The world in which we enact daily holiness is even better than the carefully prepared sacred space, for it is the place in which we make our real lives.

The Hanukkah nights invite us into a flickering temple of warmth and holiness. When Hanukkah ends, we may not want it to be over, but the womb of Hanukkah is only a preparation for the planting and harvest that will come. The rededication of the Temple does not happen so that we can stay in the Temple but so that we can leave it.

The Lights of Fire

There shall be light at eventide.
—Zechariah 14:7

At the end of the Sabbath, the Holy One gave Adam knowledge of the heavenly patterns. He brought two stones and struck them against one another, and fire came forth from them . . . and over the flame Adam spoke the blessing: "who creates the lights of fire."
—Babylonian Talmud, Pesachim 54a

For those of us who live in a cold climate, the depth of winter is the time when we are most aware of what fire does for us. Fire warms us, cooks our food, and fuels our machines. We use it as a weapon and as a source of light. Fire is infinitely entrancing. Watching a flame mesmerizes us.

Fire creates sacred space and human community. It is the perfect ritual implement: We use it to welcome the Sabbath and honor its departure, we use it to symbolically purify the house before Passover, and we use it to celebrate Hanukkah. It is no surprise that fire is a metaphor for the soul and the Divine.

The ritual of *Havdalah*, of ending the Sabbath, recalls the gift of fire to the first humans on earth. At the end of the Sabbath, the blessing over the light of fire reminds us of the transforming power this divine gift has for humankind. We are particularly grateful for it in the depths of Kislev.

The Rising of Fire

You set the rafters of
Your lofts in the waters,
make the clouds your chariot,
move on the wings of the wind.
You make the winds Your
messengers, fiery flames
Your servants.
—Psalms 104:3–4

The Holy One created four natural substances in the world. . . . The water is above the earth; the air, from which the wind is made, is above the water, and the fire is above the air, for fire is lighter than the others, ascending up to the sky. A sign of this thing is that when the flame emerges from the burning coal it flowers upward. It is said that the fire surrounds the whole world up to the sky.
—Numbers Rabbah 14:11

Jewish tradition imagines that the different "elements" of the world have different weights and that fire is the lightest element, the closest to heaven. It soars upward by its nature, the Rabbis say, yearning to return to the sky. We send fire up to heaven as part of the Hanukkah celebration. The candles we light represent our own yearning to surge upward.

"Up" represents spirit and mystery in much of our tradition. "Down" represents the groundedness and sustaining power of the earth. In mystical lore, the roots of the Tree of Life are upward, in heaven. The flames burning upward signal our wish to achieve our spiritual aspirations. By lighting lights at Hanukkah, we become messengers of radiance, helping ourselves and others rise up like sparks from a flame.

Wrestling with the Angel

Jacob was left alone. And a man wrestled with him until the break of dawn. When he saw that he had not prevailed against him, he wrenched Jacob's hip at its socket. . . . Then he said, "Let me go, for dawn is breaking." But he answered, "I will not let you go unless you bless me."
—GENESIS 32:25

He forgot some small jars and returned for them.
—RASHI ON GENESIS 32:25

Jacob is on his way home to confront his angry brother, Esau, and see his aging parents before they die. One night, he sends his wives and children onward and remains behind; and a man comes to wrestle with Jacob all night until the dawn. Then, finally, the man asks Jacob to let go, saying that dawn is breaking. Jacob demands, and receives, a blessing. The blessing takes the form of a new name.

The being that Jacob wrestles may be an angel, or it may be Jacob's brother, Esau (or Jacob's inner image of Esau), come to confront Jacob after years of bitterness. Whoever the mysterious wrestler is, he brings light to Jacob by giving him a knowledge of himself he did not have before. So too, by lighting the lights of Hanukkah, we shed light on our memories and our inner selves.

Rashi comments on Genesis 32:25 that Jacob meets the angel because he has gone back to retrieve some small jars (*pachim ketanim*) he has forgotten. According to Nachman of Bratzlav, one of these small jars is handed down through history and becomes the small jar of oil found in the Temple, the one that miraculously lasts for eight nights.[11] So Jacob's wrestle with darkness is deeply connected to the festival of Hanukkah, which begins tonight.

2022

Harvest of Fire

First Day of Hanukkah

Mark, on the fifteenth day of the seventh month, when you have gathered in the yield of your land, you shall observe the festival of the Lord seven days, a complete rest on the first day, and a complete rest on the eighth day.
—Leviticus 23:39

Since we are about to celebrate the purification of the Temple on the twenty-fifth day of the month of Kislev, we think it necessary to inform you [the Jews of the Diaspora] so you too may observe this delayed Sukkot festival—also the festival of the kindling of the fire.
—2 Maccabees 1:18–19

Hanukkah celebrates the military victory of one segment of the Jewish people. Maccabees, Jews loyal to Jewish law, rebelled against the Syrian Greeks and their Jewish allies, who wanted the Jews to assimilate to the Greek religion and way of life. During this civil war, the Temple was in the hands of the Syrian empire. After the victory of the rebels, the Jews rededicated the Temple and relit the sacred lamps. The Talmud records that although there was only enough pure oil left for a single day's light, the oil burned for eight days, long enough to prepare new oil.

The holiday of Hanukkah, meaning "dedication," has eight days for another reason. During the civil war, the people could not celebrate Sukkot—a seven-day festival with an eighth holy day added on at the end. The Maccabees ordered a "delayed" eight-day Sukkot festival, which became Hanukkah. Sukkot celebrates the harvest of the earth; Hanukkah, the second Sukkot, celebrates the harvest of fire.

The Invisible Tabernacle

Second Day of Hanukkah

Thus was completed all the work of the Tabernacle of the Tent of Meeting. The Israelites did [the work]; just as the Eternal had commanded Moses, so they did. Then they brought the Tabernacle to Moses, with the Tent and all its furnishings.

—Exodus 39:32–33

The work of the Tabernacle was completed on the 25th of Kislev, but the Tabernacle stayed rolled up until the new moon of Nisan. Israel kept on saying: "Look, we have made a Tabernacle! When will the Shekhinah *come and dwell in what our hands have made?"*

—Numbers Rabbah 13:2

In one Jewish legend, Hanukkah celebrates the day the Israelites of the wilderness completed the dwelling place of the Divine. This is why, during Hanukkah, we read the Torah portion that tells of the gifts to the Tabernacle. Yet even though the holy shrine was completed, the Holy One wanted the *mishkan* dedicated in springtime, on the new moon of the month of Nisan, at the season of new life. From the 25th of Kislev through the 29th of Adar, the Israelites waited for the spring.

What did they do while they waited? *Numbers Rabbah* tells that they prayed for the Divine Presence to enter the beautiful things they had made. The gifts some Jews give on Hanukkah recall the gifts of artistry, generosity, and spirit in the days of the Tabernacle.

By rededicating the *Shekhinah*'s home during Hanukkah, we question the violence of the Maccabees as well as that of the Syrian Greeks. We are no better than our enemies if we do not pursue holiness and justice, just as the furniture of the Temple is not holy until the Divine Presence enters it. Knowing this can help us mediate conflicts and respect every person as a reflection of the Divine.

Fire within Water

Third Day of Hanukkah

The sons of Aaron the priest shall put fire on the altar.
—LEVITICUS 1:7

It is also the festival of the kindling of the fire. . . . For when our ancestors were being taken [into exile], the pious priests of that day took some of the fire on the altar and hid it, so that the place remained unknown to anyone. Many years later . . . Nehemiah sent the descendants of the priests who had hidden the fire to get it. . . . They could … find … only muddy water. He ordered them to draw some water … [and] sprinkle the water on the wood and offerings.… The sun, which had been clouded over, came out and shone on it, and a great blaze was kindled.
—2 MACCABEES 1:19–22

According to a little-known legend, when the Jews went into exile for the first time, the priests hid the Temple's sacred fire in a cistern. When the Jews returned from exile, the flame had gone out. The people took water from the cistern and poured it on the altar, and the sun kindled the water into flame. Hanukkah celebrates this miracle.

The sacred fire is a theme throughout the world, from India to Greece to Ireland. The renewal of the hearth fire is a sacred act. In this legend, the hearth fire of the Jewish people—the eternal flame of the Temple—is hidden inside water. When the altar is rededicated, the fire leaps forth from the water, rededicating the nation's hearth.

Hanukkah is a home holiday because it is the renewal of the Jewish hearth. Holidays are often stressful and quarrelsome precisely because we want our home to live up to this mythic ideal of warmth and renewal, but it does not always do that! Yet the fire hidden in the water teaches that with goodwill, we often can rekindle our hearths.

The Miracle of the Oil

Fourth Day of Hanukkah

You shall further instruct the Israelites to bring you clear oil of beaten olives for lighting, for kindling lamps regularly.
—Exodus 27:20

When the Greeks entered the Temple, they defiled the oil there. When the Hasmonean clan defeated the Greeks, they searched and found only one cruse of oil that still retained the seal of the high priest. There was only enough oil for one day's lighting. A miracle happened, and they kindled the lamps for eight days from that cruse of oil. The next year, they declared those days festival days to be celebrated with praise and thanksgiving.
—Babylonian Talmud, *Shabbat* 21b

Many of us grew up with the story of the Hanukkah miracle: The Greeks defiled the eternal light of the Temple; and when the Jews returned, they used the one remaining cruse of sacred oil to light the eternal lamp. The oil lasted eight days, long enough for new oil to be prepared. How does this miracle story reflect the winter season?

The candle we use to light the other candles of the menorah is called *shammash*, or "sun." The eternal lamp is a sign of the ever-renewed sun. The light seems to die at this winter season, yet it always comes back. The Divine provides a daily miracle: The light of a star burns for millennia and warms the earth so life can survive here.

According to this view, the eight days of Hanukkah represent eight segments of the year: early and late spring, early and late summer, early and late fall, and early and late winter (the same eight segments on which this book is based). The Hanukkah light, which is the light of the sun, burns through all the seasons, reminding us of the beauty and distinctiveness of each one.

Spears of Light

Fifth Day of Hanukkah

They shall beat their swords into plowshares and their spears into pruning hooks.
—Isaiah 2:4

When the sons of the Hasmonean high priest (Mattathias) defeated the Greeks, they entered the Temple and found there eight iron spears. They stuck candles in these spears and kindled them.
—Megillat Ta'anit

The menorah was a major fixture in the Temple in Jerusalem, but it had six branches plus a seventh middle branch. Where does the *hanukkiah*, the eight-branched Hanukkah menorah, originate? One legend tells that when the Jews who had been fighting the Syrian Greeks entered the temple courtyard, they found eight iron spears, left over from the enemy. The Jews took up these spears and used them to build a makeshift lamp of celebration.

The Maccabees use leftover weapons, perhaps weapons that killed others, to build a sacred lamp. Does this defile the Temple? Perhaps, but perhaps not. As Isaiah says, even weapons can be beaten into tools to sow and plant. By turning their spears into vessels for light, the Jews signal their readiness to put aside war and begin to rebuild.

These two texts teach us the power of recycling—recycling objects and recycling emotions. To recycle means not only to use again but to use in a new way. Hanukkah is a festival of freedom, and it is important to remember that while at times we may need to fight for freedom, at other times we are more likely to win true freedom by becoming peacemakers.

Feast of Double Life

Sixth Day of Hanukkah (in years where there are 30 days in Kislev)

When Jacob came home from the field in the evening, Leah went out to meet him and said, "You are to sleep with me, for I have hired you with my son's mandrakes." And he lay with her that night. The Divine heeded Leah, and she conceived and bore him a fifth son. . . . She named him Issachar.
—GENESIS 30:16–18

Leah hesitates, then reaches into the bosom of her gown. "My son found mandrakes, said to lure desire, or cause fecundity." . . . Leah holds out a fistful of white-fleshed, man-shaped roots. Rachel takes one of the mandrakes, flourishes it through the air . . ., then stirs it into the wine and drinks. "Henceforth we will speak only of our sons. We will share in creation."
—NORMA ROSEN, "RACHEL AND LEAH"[12]

According to the commentary known as the *B'nei Yissachar,* the matriarch Leah conceives Issachar during Hanukkah. In Genesis, Leah's son Reuben brings her some mandrakes (an aphrodisiac and fertility aid) and her sister, Rachel, wants them because she has never been able to conceive. Leah trades Rachel the mandrakes for a night with Jacob, their husband.

Leah, the mother of six sons and one daughter, is intimately linked to Hanukkah. Leah plus all her children equals 8. Furthermore, the Hebrew word "Leah" adds up (in the Jewish numerology known as *gematria*) to 36, the number of Hanukkah candles we light. The Hebrew word for "life," *chai*, equals 18; and 36, in *gematria*, is double *chai*, or twice life.

This double *chai* of Hanukkah could refer to Rachel and Leah, the sisters who battle over their husband, Jacob. In the midrash by Norma Rosen, Leah and Rachel conspire to pour their life forces together. Each acknowledges the other's share in creating the tribes of Israel.

On Hanukkah, as we light the 36 candles, we remember Leah—whose name equals double *chai*—and Rachel, who helped Leah give life. We too ask for double life: life for us and for the world.

NOTES

1 John Greenleigh and Rosalind Rosoff Beimler, *Days of the Dead: Mexico's Communion with the Departed* (Pomegranate Communications, 1998). See also Starhawk, *Spiral Dance: a Rebirth of the Ancient Religion of the Great Goddess* (Harper SanFrancisco, 1999), pp. 209–212. See also Ronald Hutton, *The Stations of the Sun* (Oxford, 1996), p. 360–370.

2 Jules Harlow, *Siddur Sim Shalom* (Rabbinical Assembly, 1989), p. 214.

3 Goddard Deutsch, Judah David Eisenstein, and M. France, "Pilgrimage," in *Encyclopaedia Judaica* (Keter Publishing House, 1971).

4 Naomi Hyman, ed., *Biblical Women in the Midrash: A Sourcebook* (Jason Aronson, 1997), p. 99.

5 Reuters, "Frozen Organism's Survival Suggests Life Could Be Found on Mars," *Boston Globe*, March 1, 2005.

6 Susan Berrin, ed., *Celebrating the New Moon: A Rosh Chodesh Anthology* (Jason Aronson, 1996), p. 126.

7 Wendy Zierler, *And Rachel Stole the Idols: The Emergence of Modern Hebrew Women's Writing* (Wayne State University Press, 2004), p. 19.

8 Melinda Ribner, lecture at Camp Isabella Freedman (Sukkot 2003).

9 Tirzah Firestone, *The Receiving: Reclaiming Jewish Women's Wisdom* (HarperCollins, 2003), p. 227.

10 Rabbi Boruch Leff, "The Mystical White Snow," http://www.aish.com/spirituality/kabbala101/The_Mystical_White_Snow.asp.

11 Rabbi David Ingber, *Shabbat* lecture, December 2005.

12 Norma Rosen, "Rachel and Leah: A Thousand and One Nights of Love," in *Biblical Women Unbound* (The Jewish Publication Society, 1996), p. 91.

The Branch

1 TEVET TO 14 SHEVAT

SEASON
Winter

WIND
The north

HALF OF THE YEAR
The rains

ELEMENT
Fire within water

GATE
The earth

ANGEL
Gabriel (strength)

DIVINE FACE
Gevurah (strength and limits)

Behold, I am bringing my servant the Branch

—Zechariah 3:9

The third movement of the year is waiting. Bare branches wait for sun to touch them, and trees wait for sap to begin to rise. Animals and humans dream, waiting for the sun's power to increase. The seedling waits in the earth for the nourishment of light. In time the shoot will develop branches and buds; birds and insects will live in it and feed from it. Yet for now, it is warmed by a blanket of earth or a blanket of snow. It sleeps, and wakes slowly.

In midwinter, we journey through the month of Tevet and the first weeks of Shevat. These are months when, according to legend, the Israelites were waiting for the Tabernacle to be set up (*Numbers Rabbah* 13:2). Each year, as we learn the lessons of winter, we wait for a different holy space: the tabernacle of spring. The Torah portions we read at this time of year tell the story of Joseph, who was freed from slavery, and of the Exodus, when the Israelites escaped to freedom. These tales give us the courage of the shoot that works its way out of the earth and the branch that pokes out of the snow.

In nature, this is the season of rains, snow, ice, or hail, depending on where you live. According to the *Sefer Yetzirah* (3:5), water is the element of winter, and this fits with our experience at this time. Yet according to the Zohar, north, the direction of the glaciers for those of us in the Northern Hemisphere, is the direction of fire. Fire, with its liveliness and warmth, is our inner role model at this time. It is the warmth beneath the snow, the heat at the roots of the tree. As the days grow longer, we awaken to the warmth of the coming spring. The *Shekhinah* washes us with increasing light, and we hold still, allowing all that is within us to rise to the surface, to become vulnerable and real.

We begin this season of waiting with the tail end of Hanukkah, which itself marks a time of awaiting freedom and redemption. After Hanukkah, there are no holidays during this period. Only a minor fast day, the 10th of Tevet, punctuates the season. This day too is a time of waiting; it marks the beginning of the siege of Jerusalem, the beginning of a long wait. Yet as soon as the six weeks of the branch end, the holiday of the trees, Tu b'Shevat arrives, to let us know that our waiting has borne fruit.

In many cultures, the period during and after the winter solstice is a season of waiting for the sun to grow in strength, a season of expectation. Our own secular new year falls during this time, as does Christmas and the modern African American festival of Kwanzaa. The Romans celebrated Saturnalia during the winter solstice period, a fact recorded in the Talmud (Babylonian Talmud, Avodah Zarah 8a). The Hindu Diwali, a festival of lights, also comes during this season.[1] This period of the Jewish calendar teaches us patience and courage: skills we will need to tend and harvest the seeds we have planted. For now, we are like the branches of the trees—strong enough to weather whatever comes, until the season of buds is on us again.

Woman of Fire

Seventh Day of Hanukkah/New Moon of Tevet

In the tenth moon, the month of Tevet.
—ESTHER 2:16

Judith . . . went to the pillar that was at his bed's head, and loosed his sword. . . . She took him by the hair …, and said: "Strengthen me, O Lord God, at this hour." She … cut off his head …, delivered the head of Holofernes to her maid, and told her to put it into her purse. The two went out of the camp to pray. … Judith cried to the watchmen upon the walls: "Open the gates for God is with us." . . . And all ran to meet her from the least to the greatest…. Lighting up lights, they all gathered about … to see her and bless her, and some … performed a dance in her honor.
—JUDITH 13:3–16

The book of Judith tells that Holofernes, a general of Nebuchadnezzar, besieges Judith's city, Bethulia. The city elders want to surrender. Judith, a wise, beautiful, and pious widow, promises to save the city. She goes to the enemy camp and convinces Holofernes that she believes in his victory. Flattered, he plans to seduce her. While he sleeps, she cuts off his head. The enemy flees, the city is saved, and Judith leads a procession to the Temple. Though Judith's story is not a Hanukkah story, many medieval menorahs bear Judith's image. Judith is a flaming branch, a symbol of the light chasing away the darkness of winter. When she returns from her brave deed, the people light candles to welcome her. We remember Judith's story at the season of inner fire.

Jews of Morocco, Algeria, and Tunisia celebrated 1 Tevet as the Festival of the Daughters, a time to honor Judith and all heroines. Mothers would give their daughters gifts on that day and pass inheritances to them. Old women and young women would come together to dance. Another tradition was for women to pray for the health of their daughters.[2] 1 Tevet, the darkest night of winter, is a time to draw the generations together, letting the root of one generation grow into a new cluster of strong branches.

Eight Days of Sorrow, Eight Days of Joy

Eighth Day of Hanukkah

God sent the human forth from the Garden of Eden, to till the soil from which humans were taken.
—GENESIS 3:23

When Adam saw the days beginning to get shorter, he said, "Woe is me! Perhaps because I sinned, the world is growing darker because of me, and is returning to chaos and confusion, and this is the death heaven has decreed for me." So he sat eight days in fasting and prayer. But when the winter solstice arrived, and he saw the days getting longer, he said, "This is the way of the world," and went and celebrated eight festival days. The following years he made the eight days preceding and the eight days following the solstice festivals.
—BABYLONIAN TALMUD, AVODAH ZARAH 8A

The tales of Genesis imagine the first humans being driven forth from an ideal existence in a lush and abundant garden into a life of uncertainty. The Talmud tells us that when Adam and Eve experience winter and the shortening of the days, they are terrified. If God is gradually diminishing the light, surely this is a sign that the world will be destroyed. Adam fasts and prays and waits. Only after the light begins to grow again does he learn the cycle of light and dark is a part of the world, not a punishment but a daily miracle.

The eight days of Hanukkah remind us of the eight days that Adam sat in fear and the eight days on which he celebrated. This story helps us realize Hanukkah celebrates not only the victory of a faction of pious Jews over assimilationists and foreign governments but also light itself. We celebrate midwinter because of the knowledge that the sun will return to bring light and warmth. At the end of Hanukkah, as eight candles blaze upward, we recall the eight phases of the year, from seed to fruit, and are grateful for winter, the messenger of spring.

Winter Solstice

In the Divine hand are the depths of the earth; the peaks of the mountains are His.
—PSALMS 95:4

On the new moon of the first month he was told to make an ark, and the earth became dry, and he opened the ark and saw the earth. On the new moon of the fourth month the mouths of the depths of the abyss were closed. On the new moon of the seventh month all the mouths of the abysses of the earth were opened, and the waters began to descend into them. On the new moon of the tenth month the tops of the mountains were seen, and Noah was glad … he ordained them for himself as feasts for a memorial forever, and so are they ordained.
—JUBILEES 6:23–28

The book of Jubilees, an ancient Jewish text, marks the first days of Nisan, Tammuz, Tishrei, and Tevet as the beginnings of the seasons. These four days may have corresponded at one time to the solstices and equinoxes. At this time of the winter solstice, we learn from Jubilees about the spiritual nature of winter.

Jubilees tells us Tevet, the middle of winter, is the time when Noah, Naamah, and their children, trapped in the ark with floodwaters all around, see the peaks of the mountains appear above the waters. The text informs us that Noah rejoices at this sight. Even though Noah still has to wait until spring for the ark to come to rest, the peaks of the mountains bring him and his loved ones hope. So too we rejoice in the depths of Tevet, because the appearance of Tevet is a promise of the renewal of spring. Perhaps this is the reason the root of the word "Tevet" is "*tov*," meaning "goodness, abundance, and beauty." Though the fires of Hanukkah have now ended, Tevet shows us there is still a spark of life within the deep waters.

4 TEVET

Leviathan in Winter

There is the sea, vast and wide, with its creatures beyond number, its living things small and great. There go the ships; and Leviathan that You created as a playmate.
—Psalms 104:25–26

The Divine made in the sea big fish and little fish. . . . If it were not for the compassionate actions of the Holy One, the big fish would have swallowed up the little fish. What action did the Holy One take to rectify the situation? The Divine created the Leviathan. On every winter solstice, Leviathan raises his head … and snorts in the water …, and the fear of him falls on all the fishes in the ocean. If it were not so, the small could not stand before the great.
—Otzar Midrashim: Hashem Behohmah, Yasad Aretz 6

A Jewish legend of the equinoxes and solstices tells that at each point of seasonal transition, a great creature rises up to maintain order in the world. At the winter solstice, it is Leviathan, the giant sea serpent of the deep, who fulfills this task. The large fish in the sea attack and eat the small fish without mercy, yet Leviathan's roar frightens the large fish and restrains them from destroying all marine life. Because of this roar, the small fish come to praise and honor the Divine.

The *Sefer Yetzirah* teaches Tevet is the month of anger. A season of waiting is an ideal time to examine our inner anger and frustration and learn to temper it. Leviathan, the dragon of the deep, reminds us to restrain our anger lest it harm others. Yet Leviathan, a symbol of the unconscious and of mythic strength and power, also teaches us not to repress the roar of our spirit, for in it is the Divine Presence. In Tevet, the month of patience, we learn to take time, to reflect, to balance between listening to our inner voice and honoring the voice of peace. We learn to cool our fire with the waters of Leviathan.

Midnight Transitions

In the twelfth year of our exile, on the fifth day of the tenth month, a fugitive came to me from Jerusalem and reported: "The city has fallen." Now the hand of the Lord had come upon me the evening before the fugitive arrived, and the Divine opened my mouth before he came to me in the morning . . . and I was no longer speechless.
—Ezekiel 33:21–22

A harp hung above King David's bed, and when midnight came, a north wind would blow upon the harp and it would play by itself. David would arise and study Torah until dawn.
—Babylonian Talmud, Berakhot 3b

On the 5th of Tevet, in the heart of winter, Ezekiel, a priest and prophet in exile, learns Jerusalem has fallen. The Babylonian Talmud (Rosh Hashanah 18b) regards the 5th of Tevet as a fast day. Yet in the dark night before the bad news arrives, Ezekiel receives a revelation. In the morning, he is able to speak.

This story is somewhat reminiscent of the tale of King David's harp. The north wind, symbol of winter and mystery, comes at midnight, the darkest moment of the night, and plays a song for David. At an hour when most sleep, David rises to study. He too is not without words, in spite of the darkness around him. The harp brings him inspiration.

Winter is often a time of telling stories. Ezekiel, when faced with the most devastating event of his generation, responds by beginning to speak. David, in the darkness of night, finds words to express wisdom and song. Both tale-tellers teach us how to find words at this season.

The Coming of Lilith

The Divine created the human in the Divine image, in the image of the Divine It created it, male and female the Divine created them.
—GENESIS 1:27

When the first man, Adam, saw that he was alone, God instantly made for him a woman like himself, from the earth. God called her name Lilith and brought her to Adam. They immediately began to quarrel. Adam said: "You lie beneath me." And Lilith said: "You lie beneath me! We are both equal, for both of us are from the earth." And they would not listen to one another. As soon as Lilith saw this, she uttered the divine name and flew up into the air and fled.
—ALPHABET OF BEN SIRA 23A

In Jewish lore, the darkness has long been the realm of Lilith. Lilith, a night demon, is responsible for the death of babies, for nocturnal emissions, and for giving birth to demons.[3] The Zohar teaches she is the dark shadow of the *Shekhinah*.[4] Yet a story in the *Alphabet of Ben Sira* says that Lilith is the first woman. The Divine creates her as an equal partner to Adam, but they quarrel because Lilith will not agree to be sexually subservient to her mate. She utters the divine name and flies away to the Sea of Reeds. When angels go to bring her back, Lilith declares she would rather be a demon than return. So the Divine creates Eve in her place.

This is the season of the north, and the north is the place of mystery, and also the place of spirits. During this season, we honor the mystery of our inner selves. We seek to discover the part of us that remains untamed and free, that can fly, no matter what constraints our lives place on us. This part of us is frightening, but also necessary, for without it we become weary and lifeless. In Tevet, month of darkness, we remember the spirit of Lilith, waiting in the blackness of night for us to discover.

The Door Opens for Esther

Esther was taken to the … royal palace in the tenth month, which is the month of Tevet, in the seventh year of his reign.
—ESTHER 2:16

Why did she enter the king's house in Tevet? Tevet is a season when one body benefits from the warmth of another.
—BABYLONIAN TALMUD, MEGILLAH 13A

The Bible mentions Tevet explicitly only once: in the book of Esther. Esther, a Jewish woman who enters the king's harem after winning a royal beauty contest, prepares for months with the other harem residents to become a royal concubine. In Tevet, she goes to King Ahasuerus. The king is taken with her and makes her the new queen. Because of her influence with the king, Esther is later able to save her people, the Jews, from destruction at the hands of the king's adviser, Haman.

There is no explicit divine intervention in the book of Esther. Yet the Talmud comments that there is a hidden reason for the date of Esther's arrival in the palace: Tevet is a cold month, when everyone appreciates someone warm to cuddle! Timing, the Talmud suggests, is everything. Esther's entry to the palace in Tevet is not a coincidence.

Yet the potential goodness of Esther's new position is not immediately apparent, just as the buds are not yet apparent on the trees. Esther must wait to learn what the outcome of her high position will be. For now, she only enters a door, and as the poet Adrienne Rich writes, "the door itself makes no promises. It is only a door."[5] As we seek out human warmth in Tevet, we wait to know what unexpected doors the winter has opened to us.

The Goats of Tevet

They took Joseph's tunic, slaughtered a kid, and dipped the tunic in the blood.
—GENESIS 37:31

The Holy One said to Judah: "You deceived your father with a kid. By your life, Tamar will deceive you with a kid!"
—GENESIS RABBAH 85:10

According to the *Sefer Yetzirah,* the sign of the month of Tevet is the *g'di,* or "goat." Not long before Tevet, several goats appear in the Torah. Joseph's brothers, guided by Judah, dip his coat in the blood of a goat to convince their father, Jacob, that Joseph is dead.

Afterward, we meet the goat of Tamar. Tamar is Judah's daughter-in-law. After her first husband dies, Judah gives Tamar his second son as a husband, as is the custom. When his second son dies, Judah refuses to give Tamar his third son, Shelah, as he is obligated to do. Tamar conceives a plan. She dresses up as a harlot and seduces Judah, who offers her a goat as payment. Judah gives Tamar his staff and seal and ring as a sign he will pay. Tamar becomes pregnant and Judah wants her burned as an adulteress. She reveals to him his staff, seal, and ring, proving she is the woman he made pregnant. Ashamed, Judah declares her innocent. Like his father, he has been tricked by a goat.

The goat of Tevet teaches us to wait for the end of the story. Tevet offers us the patience to learn from our painful experiences and believe our lives will have a new chapter. This month, like the branches of trees, we patiently work our way upward into the sun.

The Death of Ezra

Ezra the priest, scholar in the law of the God of heaven . . . you are commissioned by the king and his seven advisers to regulate Judah and Jerusalem according to the law of your God, which is in your care.
—Ezra 7:12,14

Ezra decreed ten things: [Among them] were that the people should read Torah on the afternoon of Shabbat, *that they should read Torah on Mondays and Thursdays, and that the Sages should hold court on Mondays and Thursdays.*
—Babylonian Talmud, Bava Kamma 82b

The 9th of Tevet is traditionally observed as the yahrzeit, or "death anniversary," of Ezra, a scribe who led the Jews who returned from exile to build the Second Temple. Ezra is known for leading the people to Jerusalem, and also for re-establishing many of the laws of the Torah that had fallen away during the people's exile. Ezra is, first and foremost, a guardian of the Torah in difficult times.

The Talmud attributes several traditional Jewish practices to Ezra's decrees. One of them is the reading of Torah on Mondays and Thursdays and the meeting of rabbinic courts on the same days. Monday and Thursday were market days. This decree, which added two weekday Torah readings to the weekly *Shabbat* reading, permitted those who came to market to hear the Torah and to conduct religious affairs. Ezra's decrees were a way to involve ordinary Jews in spiritual life.

Tevet is the month when the days are shortest. Physically and spiritually we turn inward at this season, staying close to home. Ezra teaches us to come together as a community even during these inward days, sharing sacred stories and acts of kindness with one another. Just as the branches of a tree all grow from one trunk, we are all part of the Tree of Life.

The Siege of Jerusalem

In the ninth year, on the tenth day of the tenth month, the word of the Eternal came to me: O mortal, record this date, this exact day, for this very day the king of Babylonia has laid siege to Jerusalem.
—EZEKIEL 24:1–2

It is written: "The fast of the fourth month, the fast of the fifth month, the fast of the seventh month, and the fast of the tenth month shall become occasions for joy and gladness (Zech. 8:18)." In time of peace they shall be for joy and gladness, and when there is no peace, they shall be fasts.
—ROSH HASHANAH 18B

Hanukkah is closely followed by the fast of the 10th of Tevet, the day Babylonia began its siege of Jerusalem in 587 B.C.E. Jews observe this day with dawn-to-dusk fasting, Torah reading, poetic laments, and other forms of mourning. In Israel, this is the Yom ha-Kaddish ha-Klali, the day to recite the mourners' kaddish for all those whose death date is unknown.[6]

The fast of the 10th of Tevet carries many of the themes of Tevet. It commemorates a siege, a time of waiting, just as Tevet is a month of waiting. This is a fast of winter, the season of darkness, and we remember those whose death dates are hidden by darkness. The bare branches of winter remind us of the deprivations of the siege. Tevet is, according to the *Sefer Yetzirah,* the month of anger, and in Tevet we remember the feeling of helplessness before our enemies. Yet some say 10 Tevet is also the day Jeremiah (32:9–15) bought a piece of land in Israel and buried the deed in a jar, as a sign the people would be redeemed one day and reclaim their homes.[7]

The Talmud tells us fast days like the one today will someday be transformed to joyful days. Why? Perhaps because we will no longer fear the darkness of Tevet. Instead of a time to fight one another, Tevet will be a time to enter the darkness together and be reborn.

Joseph's Anger

When Joseph saw his brothers, he recognized them, but he acted like a stranger to them and spoke harshly to them. He asked them: "Where do you come from?"
—Genesis 42:7

Rabbi Joshua ben Nechemya said: He made himself become like a stranger to them.
—Genesis Rabbah 91:7

Tevet is the month of anger (*Sefer Yetzirah* 5:10). During Tevet, we tell the story of how Joseph and his brothers meet one another in Egypt after decades apart. Joseph is now a ruler in Egypt, responsible for distributing food to those afflicted by famine. Joseph's brothers come to ask for grain. When Joseph sees his brothers, he knows who they are, but he pretends to be a stranger. A Rabbinic midrash suggests that Joseph makes himself foreign to his brothers, as if they had never known each other.

This is what anger does to Joseph: It covers him, like a veil, and makes him into a stranger. Instead of revealing himself, Joseph waits. He tricks his brothers to punish them for selling him into slavery. He wants to learn whether their hearts have changed. Only months later, when Joseph's brothers approach him with honesty and vulnerability, can he finally say, "I am Joseph."

In some parts of the world, the winter makes the land look utterly different. Trees hang with icicles and snow covers familiar features of the ground. Even in parts of the world where winter is a green and warm season, the land appears to be different from the way it is in spring or summer. Yet beneath its outward appearance, the land is still the same. We learn this lesson from the winter: Our inner spirit remains steadfast.

Pharaoh's Anger

On the twelfth day of the tenth month, the word of the Eternal came to me: O mortal, turn your face against Pharaoh king of Egypt, and prophesy against him and against all Egypt.
—Ezekiel 29:1

A new king arose in Egypt who did not know Joseph: "He acted as if he did not know Joseph."
—Rashi on Exodus 1:8

The prophet Ezekiel tells that on this day of Tevet he received a prophecy condemning the kings of Egypt. This is in sync with the season, as during Tevet we read the Torah story of Joseph and then of the Hebrews' enslavement.

The first pharaoh mentioned in Exodus, we are told, does not know Joseph. Traditional commentators read this to mean Pharaoh does not want to remember Joseph's story. Maybe this is because Pharaoh feels an annoying debt of gratitude to Joseph's family since Joseph saved Egypt from famine while he was vizier of Egypt. Maybe Pharaoh feels uneasy about Joseph's foreign identity. Like many human beings, Pharaoh chooses not to think about something that bothers him.

Yet what gets covered up must get uncovered. The more Pharaoh hides his feelings about Joseph, the more they come out in other ways: Pharaoh's anger at Joseph spills over into hatred for the Hebrew people. Pharaoh enslaves Joseph's tribe and brutally oppresses them, setting the stage for the Divine to redeem the people and free them from Egypt. Tevet, month of anger, teaches us that what is covered up must eventually be revealed, just as the ground, covered with dry brush, leaves, or snow, will soon show itself again.

Jacob's Blessing

And Jacob called his sons and said, "Come together that I may tell you what is to befall you in days to come. Assemble and hearken, O sons of Jacob, hearken to Israel your father."
—GENESIS 49:1–2

Promise me, my children, that you will put the past to rest and build together for our future. Tell me that you will love one another and cherish the ties that bind our family as one—one people covenanted with the God who created heaven and earth.
—NORMAN COHEN, *VOICES FROM GENESIS*[8]

In Tevet, just before we move to the book of Exodus, we read the deathbed blessing of Jacob. Jacob, now old and living in Egypt, blesses his 12 sons and offers them his hopes for their futures as individuals and as a group. In Jacob's imagination, each son becomes a tribe, as if they were 12 branches growing from a single tree.

Sometimes, though, Jacob expresses anger at his children. He takes this moment to chastise his eldest son, Reuben, for having sex with Jacob's concubine Bilhah. He also condemns Simeon and Levi for murdering a whole town to avenge the rape of their sister, Dinah.

Norman Cohen, in a midrash, imagines that what Jacob really wants is to bring his family together in love. To do this, he must ask them to reconcile with one another in spite of their justifiable anger. Jacob is really trying to teach them how to be honest with one another.

Winter, in many cold climates, is a time when the trees have no leaves. We notice the tree limbs much more when they are bare, when they have a unique kind of beauty. The bareness and frankness with which Jacob offers his blessing also has a unique beauty, one we hope to inherit.

Waiting for Deliverance

There is an odd moment during Jacob's final blessing. He pauses between the blessing of Dan and the blessing of Gad and recites: "I wait for Your deliverance, Eternal!" Bible scholars suggest this phrase is a comma marking the halfway point of the blessing. One traditional explanation for the phrase is that Jacob, while prophesying, sees a disturbing moment in the future and prays to avoid it (*Midrash Tanhuma, Va-yechi* 12).

"I wait for Your deliverance, Eternal!"
—GENESIS 49:18

Was [Dinah] not the sister of all the tribes?
—MIDRASH TANHUMA, BE-SHALLAH 1

One other possibility is that this brief, staccato sentence is the blessing of Dinah, daughter of Jacob. Dinah is the one child of Jacob whom he does not mention during his deathbed speech. She is the forgotten branch on the tree. Yet perhaps Dinah's blessing is hidden in Jacob's words. "I wait for Your deliverance" is an indication that Dinah, too, waits to be blessed.

These words invite us to have patience as we wait for new growth. They remind us that this moment of winter, whether freezing cold or balmy, contains a unique kind of deliverance, if we can open ourselves to it. Like Dinah, we too can seek out the blessings of strength, patience, and courage.

Jochebed Waiting

Then Pharaoh charged all his people, saying, "Every boy that is born you shall throw into the Nile, but let every girl live." A certain man of the house of Levi went and married a daughter of Levi. The woman conceived and bore a son, and when she saw how beautiful he was, she hid him for three months.
—Exodus 1:22, 2:1

Yocheved stands on the threshold between two worlds: freedom in Canaan and slavery in Egypt. She looks backward and forward at once. She carries within her the seeds of freedom that the Children of Israel brought from Canaan. She also bears the dreadful responsibility of birthing children into slavery.
—Penina Adelman, *Praise Her Works*[9]

At the beginning of Exodus, Jochebed becomes pregnant. She already has two children, Miriam and Aaron. This pregnancy is different, though, because Pharaoh plans to kill all male children born to Hebrew women. On this date, according to the Talmud, Jochebed would be three weeks away from giving birth to her son Moses (*Exodus Rabba*h 1:24).

Jochebed herself is born as her people enter Egypt. Trapped in an oppressive realm and hardened by slave labor, Jochebed waits for the birth of Moses, not knowing whether her child is male and subject to the decree of death or female and safe. As Penina Adelman tells us, Jochebed is caught between her hope of freedom and her knowledge that her child will be subject to the whims of Pharaoh. What these months of waiting are like is hard for us to imagine. When Moses is born, perhaps delivered by his sister, Miriam (both Miriam and Jochebed are midwives according to Jewish legend), Jochebed hides her infant for three months. Once again Jochebed waits, hoping something new will present itself. In Tevet, we learn from Jochebed how to exist in the present even when we have fears for the future.

The Winter Mother

There was a certain man from Zorah, of the stock of Dan, whose name was Manoah. His wife was barren and had borne no children. An angel of the Eternal appeared to the woman and said to her, "You are barren and have borne no children, but you shall conceive and bear a son. Now be careful not to drink wine or other intoxicant, or to eat anything unclean. For you are going to conceive and bear a son; let no razor touch his head."
—JUDGES 13:1–5

Hatzlelponit was the mother of Samson. She would sit and spin and sell in the market, and bring up her son, and not only that, but she would sit and teach Torah until the Torah rang out in clarity (hitzlilah haTorah).
—BATEI MIDRASHOT II:16:15

In the *Sefer Yetzirah,* Tevet is the month of the tribe of Dan. Dan is associated with the north and with darkness, both symbols of winter. This tribe raised up one judge: Samson, or *Shimshon*, the man of great strength who never cut his hair. Samson observed this restriction because an angel had spoken to his mother before he was born, telling her that her son must never drink wine or cut his hair.

Samson's mother, called Hatzlelponit in Rabbinic midrash, is an extraordinary woman in her own right. In the Bible, she is unafraid to speak to the angel; and when her husband shows fear because he has seen a divine being, Hazlelponi comforts him with wise words, saying: "Had the Eternal meant to take our lives, we would not have seen all these things" (Judges 13:23) Midrash tells us Hazlelponi is industrious and learned, studying Torah late into the night. No wonder her son is called Samson, which means "sun." He is like the dawn: the culmination of his mother's hopes and dreams. The hardworking, practical, wise Hazlelponi is akin to the bare branches of winter—she abstains from wine, symbol of the festivals, which do not occur in winter, and her words show a direct, simple approach to life. Yet it is she who brings forth the increasing brightness of the sun.

Samson's Anger

Samson and his mother and father went down to Timnah. When he came to the vineyards of Timnah, a full-grown lion came roaring at him. The spirit of the Eternal gripped him, and he tore him asunder with his bare hands as one might tear a kid asunder.
—JUDGES 14:5–6

The Shekhinah *rang before him like a bell.*
—BABYLONIAN TALMUD, SOTAH 9B

Samson, the judge from the tribe of Dan, has great courage—and great anger. He is able to fight lions and Philistines with equal vigor. The *Shekhinah* fills him with a holy spirit. The Talmud imagines Her running before Samson clanging a bell, as if to say: "Look out! Samson is coming!" Yet Samson's worst failing is that he goes into violent rages when he feels tricked or cheated. He also has a tendency to choose female companions who are not necessarily trustworthy. In the end, his passion for a woman named Delilah becomes his downfall when she betrays him to his enemies.

Samson, whose name means "sun," is associated with fire, and his being seems to reflect the fitful burning of a flame. He is like an unpredictable winter storm, flashing across the landscape and leaving wreckage in its path. While Samson is a prisoner, his fiery passion returns to him one last time and allows him to destroy his enemies—he knocks down the two pillars that hold up a Philistine temple and dies among those who have captured him.

Like fire itself, Samson's spirit can be used for good or ill. It can stir him up either to help his people or to destroy. In winter, when we use fire to warm ourselves, it is wise to remember that some forces, outside us and inside us, have a double edge. Tevet teaches us to use those strong forces with thoughtfulness and restraint.

The Sister of Anger

[Samson's] brothers and all his father's household came down and carried him up and buried him in the tomb of his father Manoah, between Zorah and Eshtaol. He had led Israel for twenty years.
—Judges 16:31

The mother of Samson was Hatzelponit, and his sister was Nashyan.
—Babylonian Talmud, Bava Batra 91a

When the judge Samson dies, his family comes to bury him in his father's tomb. Though he has lived much of his life as a lone wanderer, he is buried respectfully by his relatives after his violent death.

The Talmud records the name of Samson's mother, as do other midrashim. Strangely, the Talmud also mentions the name of Samson's sister: Nashyan. The Bible does not indicate that Samson has a sister, though perhaps she is among the people who bury him. Why does the Talmud indicate the name of Samson's sister when the Bible does not?

One answer may be that there were legends of Nashyan at the time of the Talmud that we no longer have. Another might be that the Talmud is teaching us two approaches to anger. "Nashyan" means "forgetful one." Samson never forgets a slight, but his sister's name implies the opposite trait: a readiness to let go of anger. Perhaps the two together make up one human person—prone to be angry yet also ready to forgive.

In Tevet, the month of anger, strength, and inner fire, we consider how to deal with the sparks of memory burning inside us. Samson and his sister, Nashyan, like two boughs balancing a tree, remind us when to remember and when to let ourselves forget.

Nourishing the Seeds

He then took some of the seed of the land and planted it in a fertile field; he planted and set it like a willow, beside abundant waters.
—EZEKIEL 17:5

In Tevet, Shevat, and Adar, the sun travels through the wilderness so as not to dry up the seeds.
—BABYLONIAN TALMUD, ERUVIN 56A

Tevet can be a wet month, both in parts of North America and in parts of Europe and Israel. In Israel and other warm climates, seeds are already busily growing. It is crucial that the sun not dry out the earth too much at this season. The Talmud imagines the sun as a benevolent force of nature, willfully absenting itself from the fields where seeds have been planted so that the sun's heat will not harm the buried seeds. The sun works in concert with the ground to bring about life. Winter, the text of Eruvin suggests, is part of the divine plan to help human beings cultivate the land.

In this season of wetness and buried seeds, we think back to the spiritual seeds we planted three months ago, in Tishrei. How are those seeds growing? Have they dried out in the heat of more pressing needs? Have we given them sufficient nourishment? The days of Tevet, when the sun travels in the wilderness, can be a time to re-examine our spirits and see how our own seeds are doing.

Blending Sky and Earth

The storm wind comes forth from its chamber, and the cold from the constellations. By the breath of the Divine ice is formed, and the expanse of the water becomes solid....
—JOB 37: 9–10

The colors correspond to the four seasons of the year. From Tishrei to Tevet (autumn), the days are like the color blue, so blue is worn. From Tevet to Nisan (winter), snow comes down, so white garments are worn.
—BEIT HA-MIDRASH 5:39

A legend tells that once, long ago, the Israelites wore colors representing the essence of the seasons. In the autumn, they wore blue to represent the beauty of the autumn skies. Beginning in the winter month of Tevet, the people wore white to honor the snow of the season. Why would they honor snow? Perhaps they chose to commemorate the snow because of its function as a protective covering for the land and a source of moisture for new growth. Snow can also represent the connection of heaven with earth.

Sometimes in winter, heaven seems to blend into earth. When it is cloudy or foggy and it rains or snows, the sky seems almost to touch the ground, as if the two were not very far apart. This is one of the messages of Tevet: Heaven and earth are not two separate realms; they are constantly feeding from and giving to one another. Whenever we act in the physical world, we act in the spiritual realm as well, and vice versa. White, the color of Tevet, reminds us of the souls that, like branches, connect heaven with earth.

The Birth of Simeon

Again [Leah] conceived and bore a son and declared: "This is because the Divine heard that I was unloved, and has given me this one also." Therefore she named him Simeon.
—GENESIS 29:33

Joseph then seized Simeon, bound him before their eyes, and said: "This one will stay in prison with me until you bring me the youngest." Why did he bind Simeon? Because it was Simeon who had pushed him into the pit.
—GENESIS RABBAH 91:6

According to *Midrash Tadshe*, the 21st of Tevet is the birthday of Simeon, second son of Jacob and Leah. Simeon has a personality that relates to Tevet: He is violent and full of anger. In Genesis 34, he and his brother Levi avenge the rape of their sister, Dinah, by massacring a whole village. A midrash suggests it is Simeon who most desires to kill Joseph out of jealousy, and this is why Joseph later imprisons Simeon as a hostage. The most tender moment in Simeon's life, according to another midrash in *Genesis Rabbah* (80:11), is when he, and he alone, sneaks out of Egypt to bury Dinah in Canaan.

Simeon reminds us of the violence of winter, when hungry animals seek to kill and eat other creatures. He reminds us of human beings who prey on others out of fear, hatred, and jealousy. Yet when we look back to his birth, his mother names him not for hatred, but for the feeling of being hated. Leah, in despair that her husband despises her, pours some of her frustration and fury into her son's name.

Simeon represents the pent-up grief of an oppressed soul. He channels the rage he has inherited into cruel actions. Simeon, who we all carry inside us, reminds us to bare our resentments before they spill out of us.

22 TEVET

Waiting for the Exodus

Joseph died, and all his brothers, and all that generation. But the Israelites were fertile and prolific; they multiplied and increased very greatly, so that the land was filled with them. . . . [The king of Egypt] said to his people, "Look, the Israelite people are much too numerous for us. Let us deal shrewdly with them, so that they may not increase."
—Exodus 1:6–10

The three patriarchs Abraham, Isaac, and Jacob were created to correspond to heaven, earth, and sea, for of them it is written: "I will multiply your seed as the stars in heaven," "I will make your seed as the soil of the earth," and "as the sands by the shore of the sea."
—Otzar Midrashim: Pinchas ben Yair 5

In Tevet we learn how, once Joseph and his brothers are dead, the Egyptians cease to be grateful to Joseph for saving them from famine. They turn on the family of Joseph, fearing their prosperity. Within a short time, the wealthy and powerful family has become a clan of slaves. Although weary and helpless, they manage to build families and multiply as they wait for redemption.

How does the battered house of Jacob cling to its identity? We see that the family continued to call their children by Hebrew names even though they lived in Egypt. Like branches in winter, they were able to keep their *gevurah,* their strength, courage, limits, and boundaries. They remembered their ancestors and stayed connected to them, drawing on their strength, just as branches of a tree draw on the tree's roots.

One midrash connects the three patriarchs, Abraham, Isaac, and Jacob, to the three realms of the world, heaven, earth, and sea: Abraham is blessed with the abundance of stars, Isaac with the abundance of earth, and Jacob with the abundance of the sands by the sea. In this season, we look for the blessings of heaven, earth, and sea, blessings that lie sleeping in the roots beneath our feet and shine in the stars of the winter nights.

Gabriel, Angel of Fire

The daughter of Pharaoh came along to bathe in the Nile, while her maidens walked along the Nile. She spied the basket among the reeds and sent her slave girl to fetch it. When she opened it, she saw that it was a child, a boy crying. She took pity on it and said, "This must be a Hebrew child."
—Exodus 2:5–6

The maids said to the daughter of Pharaoh: "Our lady, it is the way of the world that when a king gives an order, even if the whole world disobeys, his children and household members obey. Would you disobey your father's order?" And Gabriel came and struck them to the ground.
—Exodus Rabbah 1:23

In the Zohar, Gabriel is the angel of the north, of fire and of strength. Gabriel is also intimately involved in the events leading up to the Exodus, which we read about at this time. One might say Gabriel is the angel of winter.

Moses is three months old. His mother, Jochebed, and sister, Miriam, have put him in a basket on the Nile. When Pharaoh's daughter sees the basket, she asks that it be brought to her. Immediately, her handmaidens object. "Should not the princess obey her father's order?" they ask. The angel Gabriel comes and knocks these obedient women to the ground.

Pharaoh's daughter and her maidens represent parts of us—the part of us that knows how to confront power when it is wrong and the part that wants to be part of the crowd. In Tevet, Gabriel defends us from the inner voice of fear and helps us stand in our strength.

The Prophecy of Haggai

Take note, from this day forward—from the twenty-fourth day of the ninth month, from the day the foundation was laid for the Temple of the Eternal—take note: while the seed is still in the granary, and the vine, fig tree, pomegranate, and olive tree have not yet borne fruit. For from this day on I shall send blessings.
—HAGGAI 2:18–19

Rabbi Jacob ben Dostai said, … Once I arose early in the dawn and walked in fig honey up to my ankles.
—BABYLONIAN TALMUD, KETUBBOT 111B

According to the prophetic book of Haggai, Jews laid the foundation of the Second Temple on this day, millennia ago. On that same day, the prophet Haggai received a message from the Divine that the 24th of Tevet would mark an outpouring of blessing on the Jewish people.

In Tevet, we wait for the harvest that will come as the year turns. In winter, when no fruit is on the vine or the branches of the trees and when the only food is in the storehouses, Haggai reminds the people that the Divine brings the earth to fruition. Winter is the laying of the foundation, the preparation of the temple of the earth for the harvest to come. By extension, Haggai teaches that the Divine can bring the people's potential to joyful fruition as well.

Now, in the depths of Tevet, we dream of abundance, as did Jacob ben Dostai, who walked in fig honey up to his ankles because of the goodness of the harvest. Even in winter, the world conspires to ensure that life and abundance continue. According to the Bible, it is on this winter day that we are promised the richness of the new harvest.

Gabriel, Angel of Waiting

When the child grew up, she brought him to Pharaoh's daughter, who made him her son. She named him Moses.
—Exodus 2:10

Pharaoh used to … hug the child Moses, and Moses would grab Pharaoh's crown and put it on his head, … as he was destined to do to Pharaoh in the future. … They brought the child gold and coals in a bowl, saying: if he reaches for the gold, he has sense, and we will kill him. If he reaches for the coals, he has no awareness and is not deserving of death. Moses reached for the gold, but Gabriel … pushed his hand so that he took the coal. Moses pushed the burning coal into his mouth, and burned his tongue, and that is how be became slow of speech.
—Exodus Rabbah 1:26

The child Moses, growing up in Pharaoh's palace, is accustomed to taking his adopted grandfather's crown and placing it on his own head. The court magicians take this as a sign that Moses is destined to overthrow Pharaoh, and they want to kill him. Jethro, a Midianite priest who will one day be Moses' father-in-law, says this is ridiculous: The child wants only the shining gold. To test Moses, they bring him gold, and a coal even shinier than the gold. Moses reaches for the gold, but Gabriel pushes his hand toward the coal. Moses puts the coal in his mouth. This is how Moses comes to injure his tongue, so that he becomes slow of speech.

Moses is the destined redeemer, but Gabriel knows he is not yet ready to fight Pharaoh. Gabriel saves Moses so that he may grow up and fulfill his destiny. So too there are tasks for which we may not yet be prepared, just as there are seeds not yet ready to grow. The winter month of Tevet teaches us to wait and to learn, because sometimes our goals take time.

The Good Name

When Moses had grown up, he went out to his kinsfolk and witnessed their labors. He saw an Egyptian beating a Hebrew, one of his kinsmen. He turned this way and that, and seeing no one about, he struck down the Egyptian and hid him in the sand.
—Exodus 2:12

Some say: He killed him with a lump of mortar. The Sages said: He spoke to him the explicit Name and killed him with it.
—Exodus Rabbah 1:29

As a young Egyptian prince, Moses goes out to see the Hebrews as they work. Perhaps he has known of his secret identity as a Hebrew since childhood, perhaps he has recently found out, or maybe he feels the kinship of simple humanity. He relates to the slaves and their suffering. When he sees a taskmaster beating a Hebrew, he checks that there are no witnesses, then kills the oppressor.

Moses has not yet learned patience or strategy. He does not seek freedom for the slaves, only vents his anger on one man. Yet Moses does understand that injustice profanes divinity in the world. Some say Moses kills the taskmaster by speaking the name of the Divine. This is an act of poetic justice, as the taskmaster has unfairly and cruelly attacked the divine image within another human being. In time, Moses will be a vehicle of justice for his entire people.

The word "Tevet" comes from the word for "good," which is related to the goodness of Creation. As it says in Genesis (1:12), "the Divine saw that it was good." Tevet asks us to respect the divine image and the divine creative genius in one another and in the world. The tree branches we see in Tevet remind us we are branches on the Tree of Life, sharing in the essence of all things.

The Snake and the Branch

But Moses … said: "What if they do not believe me … ?" The Eternal said …: "What is that in your hand?" And he replied: "A rod." The Eternal said: "Cast it on the ground." He cast it … and it became a snake. … Then the Eternal said …: "Put out your hand and grasp it by the tail." He put out his hand and seized it, and it became a rod in his hand.
—Exodus 4:1–4

Rabbi Levi said: That staff was created … on the last day of Creation and given to Adam, the first human. Adam gave it to Enoch, Enoch gave it to Shem, Shem … to Abraham, Abraham … to Isaac, Isaac to Jacob, Jacob brought it to Egypt and gave it to his son Joseph.
—Pirkei de-Rabbi Eliezer 39

Dan, the tribe of Tevet, has as its emblem a snake. We also read about a snake at this season: the snake within Moses' staff. The snake, a reptile who sleeps in the cold and rouses when warm, teaches us some of the lessons of Tevet.

Moses fled Egypt because he has killed a taskmaster in his rage over the evils of slavery. One day he sees a bush in flames, and hears the voice of the Divine asking him to go back to Egypt. Moses expresses doubts about this mission. The Holy One gives Moses a sign, turning Moses' staff into a snake and then back into a staff. This staff is a symbol of *gevurah,* "strength." It is at the same time part of a tree, a symbol of the Tree of Life; and as a snake, which is able to put its tail in its mouth, it is a symbol of the circle of life.

Moses has been a staff: He has supported his wife and father-in-law and nurtured his flock. Now he is to become a snake and bite at the heel of Pharaoh. The Divine asks Moses to respect and nourish the circle of life. Moses must be willing to turn back into a staff, back into a nourisher and sustainer, when that is needed. According to *Pirkei de-Rabbi Eliezer,* the staff of Moses has been a gift to humanity since Creation. It teaches us to be gentle as well as fierce.

The Night Encampment

At a night encampment on the way, the Eternal encountered [Moses] and sought to kill him. So Zipporah took a flint and cut off her son's foreskin … saying: "You are truly a bridegroom of blood to me." And when the Divine let [Moses] alone, she added, "A bridegroom of blood because of the circumcision."
—Exodus 4:24–25

The story of Tziporah begins with her name, which translates into English as "bird." . . . The ancient texts make Tziporah's nameless mother the one who names her. … perhaps she named her for the goddess who came to her in a vision at the moment of Tziporah's birth. … Many of the ancient traditions worshipped goddesses in the forms of animals, particularly birds.
—Rebecca Alpert, "Rediscovering Tziporah"[10]

As Moses returns to Egypt, he and his wife, Zipporah, and their sons stop at an encampment. Inexplicably, the Divine attacks Moses in the night. A midrash tells that Zipporah deduces the reason for the Holy One's anger: Moses' sons are not circumcised (*Exodus Rabbah* 5:8). She grabs a stone from the floor of the desert and circumcises her son, and the Eternal desists from this bizarre murderous intent.

Perhaps this incident is a metaphor for the long night of the soul. In his heart, Moses feels both Hebrew and Egyptian. Part of him does not want to go back and engage in a struggle between his two peoples. This is the part of him that is under attack.

Rebecca Alpert , in her modern midrash, points out that Zipporah's name, "bird," may refer to her flight with Moses, or it may suggest that the Divine comes to her as a bird. Zipporah, guided by the bird voice within her, wisely understands that Moses must fly free of Egypt. Her bloody, yet necessary act toward her son frees Moses from his old assumptions and allows him to embrace a new identity. Zipporah teaches us to fly free of our certainties and be open to new visions.

The Darkness of Tevet

The Divine called the light Day, and the darkness the Divine called Night.
—Genesis 1:5

"The light" refers to Abraham, whose light is the light of day and whose radiance increases and strengthens like the light of day. . . . "The darkness" refers to Isaac, who represents darkness and night, and this is why when he was old his eyes became dim.
—Zohar II:141b–142a

We often think of light and darkness as "good" and "bad," yet at the beginning of Genesis the Holy One calls both day *and* night "good." Tevet, the dark month whose name means "goodness," reminds us of this truth: The darkness of Tevet teaches us about the nature of our spirits just as much as the brightness of the summer months. Dark and light, increase and restraint, clarity and mystery, are two branches of our experience, both valuable and necessary.

The Zohar teaches us this by naming two of our ancestors "light" and "darkness." Abraham, a master of lovingkindness, is called "light," whereas Isaac, a master of strength and faith, is called "darkness." Abraham and Isaac also represent water and fire, the two opposing energies of this season. Both of these patriarchs live within us. It is our task to unite them and balance their energies, so we can act with greater wisdom.

We began Tevet with Judith, a woman who exemplifies darkness and light together. Now we end Tevet by remembering Abraham and Isaac, who teach us the preciousness of light and darkness as separate gifts. As Tevet, month of branches, passes, we discover truths about the many branches of ourselves.

Teaching of the Trees

New Moon of Shevat

It was in the fortieth year, on the first day of the eleventh month, that Moses addressed the Israelites in accordance with the instructions that the Eternal had given him for them.
—DEUTERONOMY 1:3

The new moon of Shevat is the new year of the trees: these are the words of Beit Shammai. Beit Hillel says: the fifteenth of Shevat.
—BABYLONIAN TALMUD, ROSH HASHANAH 2A

On this day, in the final year of wandering in the wilderness, Moses began to teach the people a new book of the Torah: Devarim, or Deuteronomy. This is also the day, according to Shammai, that trees become a year older: it is the new year of the trees. Although, according to the majority opinion, Jews will not celebrate the trees' new year until the 15th of this month, the new moon of Shevat represents the first moment when we might consider the trees to be renewed after the winter.

Like the budding trees, Deuteronomy is a new flowering of the divine will. On the 1st of Shevat, as the people prepare to enter the land without him, Moses offers them the best of his wisdom to sustain them. So too the branches that have survived the winter sustain this new life, and the tree waits to burst into new buds. Indeed, in Israel and similar climates, trees may already be budding at this time.

Shevat is a month of renewed growth and vigor, and this first day of Shevat begins that renewal. As Moses begins to teach new Torah, the trees teach us their Torah by shaking off their slumber and awakening to growth. Deuteronomy (20:19) teaches that "a person is like a tree of the field." This is the message of Shevat as well.

Branches of the Tree of Life

And from the ground the Eternal Divine caused to grow every tree that was pleasing to the sight and good for food, with the Tree of Life in the middle of the garden.
—GENESIS 2:9

The tree of life has forty-eight branches, and each one is like a complete world.
—OTZAR MIDRASHIM: GAN EDEN GEHINNOM 4

In this month when trees are celebrated, we recall the Tree of Life, the legendary tree in the garden of Eden. The fruit of this tree can cause one to live forever. In some Jewish legends, this tree still exists in the hidden world of souls. It has 48 branches: 4 times 12, with 4 being the number of the directions of the world, and 12 being the number of the months of the year. Thus "48" represents the propagation of life through space and time.

A legend claims each of the branches of the Tree of Life is like a world in itself. This reminds us that, even as we contemplate the grandeur of the world, the smallest part of it is equally grand. One branch can be a source of fruit; a home to birds, insects, small mammals; and a unique and beautiful shape against the sky. We too are our own world, populated by unique people, ideas, relationships, and memories. Just as each branch of the Tree of Life contains a world, each branch in our own daily reality contains a world as well, if we know to look for it. In the season of branches, Shevat teaches us about the many, many worlds we walk through every day.

Sense of Taste

In *Sefer Yetzirah* (5:10), Shevat is the month of taste. Yet this is not the month of harvest but the month when trees begin their cycle of bearing fruit. Perhaps the *Sefer Yetzirah* means to teach us that taste is as much about the expectation of sweetness, about the waiting, as about actual eating.

In Genesis, Eve's desire to taste the fruit of the tree of knowledge propels humanity out of Eden and into history. Taste is a powerful motivator, inspiring us to seek out new experiences. Indeed, the Jerusalem Talmud (Kiddushin 66d) relates we are obligated to look for foods we have not tasted before and try them if possible. Human curiosity and desire for experience is part of the divine plan to help us fully discover our world.

Jewish tradition does not ask us to detach from the world. In fact, we are asked to invest in our attachment to the world's beauty and pleasure and be grateful for it. By recognizing the beauty and attraction the earth holds for us, we learn to value the physical world and treat it with care.

When the woman saw that the tree was good for eating and a delight to the eyes, and that the tree was desirable as a source of wisdom, she took of its fruit and ate.
—Genesis 3:6

The Rabbis said in Rav's name: a person will have to give an accounting for all the good food he saw and did not enjoy.
—Jerusalem Talmud, Kiddushin 4:9

Waiting for Good Earth

The trees of the Eternal drink their fill, the cedars of Lebanon, the Holy One's planting.
—Psalms 104:16

In the beginning, the trees were like locusts' horns, but the Holy One of Blessing dug them up and planted them in the garden of Eden.
—Genesis Rabbah 15:1

At this season the gate of the earth is open, and we pray for the needs of the earth. In Shevat, in the northeast of the United States, we wait for the sap to rise, for fiery sweetness to rise from the wet wood of winter. The trees may seem all but dead at this time, bare and lifeless. Yet, if all goes well, they will be green again in only a little while.

One midrash tells us that the very first trees the Holy One planted did not do so well. They were tiny, like the horns of an insect. They refused to thrive. Then He dug them up and planted them in rich new soil: the soil of Eden. Eden's soil nourished the trees, and they grew up into great cedars and oaks and cypresses. Perhaps because Eden had the Tree of Life at its center, it was a better place for trees than the original place the Eternal chose to plant them.

It is a wonderful image to think of the Divine digging in the dirt to uproot a tree that is stunted, and planting it in better earth so that it thrives. Sometimes we all need such replanting. We ask for the ability to sustain ourselves with richer spiritual and creative lives, just as the first trees needed richer soil to grow.

The Planting of the Barley

When you enter the land that I am giving to you and you reap its harvest, you shall bring the first sheaf of your harvest to the priest. He shall elevate the sheaf before the Eternal for its acceptance in your behalf.
—LEVITICUS 23:10–11

They sow the seed seventy days before Passover, and from it they make the fine flour for the offering.
—BABYLONIAN TALMUD, MENACHOT 85A

The spring season will mark Passover, the beginning of the grain festivals, when in ancient times a priest would elevate the first sheaf of barley in the Temple. Today, 70 days before Passover, is the day this offering is officially planted. The 5th of Shevat, which in the Middle East comes at the tail end of winter, represents the beginning of preparations for spring.

Even in a time of waiting, we do not wait without preparation. In Tevet and Shevat, we count the days so that we will know when to plant. The 5th of Shevat is a lesson in sacred anticipation. From today, even though many days and holidays will fall between now and the month of Nisan, we begin to wait for Passover, the festival of freedom, and for the taste of the new grain.

We are not told what ritual our ancestors used to plant the barley that would be offered in the Temple. However, the planting of the barley may remind us of the words of Rabbi Nachman of Bratzlav: "Every blade of grass has an angel that whispers to it: grow, grow!"

The Riches of Asher

Asher's bread shall be rich,
and he shall yield royal dainties.
—GENESIS 49:20

His bread shall be rich—
he shall have beautiful and
pleasant daughters, and they
shall be worthy of queendom.
—GENESIS RABBAH 99:12

In the text of the *Sefer Yetzirah,* the tribe of Shevat is Asher. Asher is the son of Jacob and Zilpah; his name means "happy" or "fortunate." Both Jacob and Moses bless the tribe of Asher with rich and tasty food—this is perhaps the reason why Asher is associated with Shevat, the month of taste.

One of the most repeated legends about the tribe of Asher is that its women were beautiful and regal. Many Asherites, this legend goes, marry priests and kings. Women like Serach bat Asher (Serach the daughter of Asher) make their mark as wise women who change the course of history (*Exodus Rabbah* 5:13, 20:19). Asher becomes an honorable tribe not through warfare but through the reputation of its members. The daughters of Asher are like the branches of a tree, spreading out through the tribes to offer their wealth of spirit.

As we begin to look forward to the harvesting of grain, we remember the necessity of bread. So too we remember the necessity of the kind and graceful people in our lives. Like the light of the sun, or the branches of trees, the daughters of Asher remind us of our own potential for grace and beauty—our own ability to be "sons and daughters of happiness."

The First Coal

Awake, O north wind! Come, O south wind! Blow upon my garden that its perfume may spread!
—Song of Songs 4:16

In the month of Shevat, God throws down three burning coals to warm the earth. On the seventh of Shevat the first coal falls, to warm the air. On the fourteenth of the month the second falls, to warm the water in the trees. On that day the Arabs say: "Today water has entered the trees." On the twenty-third of Shevat, the third coal is thrown, to warm the soil.
—Hai Gaon[8]

It is a sacred moment, a stirring of the *Shekhinah*, when the first warm breeze blows our way. Even without language, buds know when to form, and sleeping animals remember to uncurl. The return of life in plant and animal is a kind of signal fire, telling us the seasons are on the move once more.

Hai Gaon tells a story about how the Holy One throws coals into the wind to warm it. In Hai Gaon's legend of the three coals, today is the day God throws the first coal to warm the air. Though Hai Gaon's legend is not science but myth, the Sage teaches us that learning about the world and the way it works is one way to encounter the mystery some of us call God. To be a religious being is not to ignore the physical world but to study it and engage with it.

In this season of inner fire, fire begins to move outward. Something about the warmth in the wind makes us happy in our bones. The eternal light burns in the trees and the sky: During Shevat, if we go outside, we will see it and even smell it.

The Branches of Queen Tzimtzemai

The Eternal spoke to Moses, saying: "Next take choice spices: five hundred weight of solidified myrrh, half as much—two hundred and fifty—of fragrant cinnamon. … Make of this a sacred anointing oil."
—EXODUS 30:22,25

The trees of Jerusalem were of cinnamon, and when they were cut down their smell would waft through all the Land of Israel. When Jerusalem was destroyed they were hidden away. Only a few of them remain, and they can be found in the treasuries of Queen Tzimtzemai.
—BABYLONIAN TALMUD, SHABBAT 63A

The branches of this season recall a legend of the branches of Jerusalem. In one passage in the Talmud, the trees of Jerusalem smelled like cinnamon when their branches were cut down to make firewood for the Temple. These unusual trees did not fall into enemy hands when the Temple fell. Rather, they disappeared. The remaining fragrant branches are hidden in the treasuries of Queen Tzimtzemai.

Who is the mysterious Queen Tzimtzemai? In the Kabbalah, the word "*tzimtzum*" (making the self smaller) refers to the action the Divine took at the beginning of the universe, making the God-self smaller so that there would be room for a world. Queen Tzimtzemai, read in a mystical way, may refer to the Divine, who becomes smaller so there is room for us.

Where is the treasure house of the Queen Who Makes Herself Smaller? Is it the garden of Eden or the heavenly Jerusalem? Or is it the world itself? Maybe if we keep searching for the cinnamon trees, we will find out. In these days of Shevat, everything around us becomes a treasure box we prepare to open.

Dancing with Branches

Let them praise the Divine name in dance!
—PSALMS 149:3

They tell of Rabbi Judah bar Ilai that he used to grab a myrtle branch and dance before the bride at her wedding, singing: "O bride, fair and full of grace!"
—BABYLONIAN TALMUD, KETUBBOT 17A

As much as this season is about waiting for something new, it is also about rejoicing in what is: the sharp cold or the mild warmth or whatever the wind may bring. Rabbi Judah bar Ilai teaches us this gift of joy in the moment. He leaves his Torah study, the Talmud claims, for every wedding, and he rejoices in the joy of the couple by dancing for the bride with a myrtle branch in his hand. The myrtle branch represents joy, fertility, and eternity—all the things we would hope for a bride and groom.

Yet we do not need a wedding to dance with a myrtle branch. In a mystical sense, we can wed the world every day simply by being aware of our connection to all that is. When we greet *Shabbat*, the symbol of Creation, we also dance and sing. Our lives can become a dance before the Bride—the *Shekhinah*, the embodiment of holiness within the world. Today, seven days before Tu b'Shevat, we rejoice with the Tree of Life.

In the days of Shevat, the rabbi with the myrtle branch symbolizes our ability to find joy in whatever weather the season brings.

The Plague of Locusts

Locusts invaded all the land of Egypt and settled within all the territory of Egypt in a thick mass; never before had there been so many, nor will there ever be so many again. They hid all the land from view, and the land was darkened; and they ate up all the grasses of the field and all the fruit of the trees which the hail had left, so that nothing green was left of tree or grass of the field, in all the land of Egypt.
—Exodus 10:14–15

They devoured every green leaf.
—Rashi on Exodus 10:15

At this time we read in the Torah about the plague of locusts. Rabbi Tzadok ha-Cohen writes in his work *Pri Tzadik* that Shevat was the month the plague of locusts fell upon Egypt. As a punishment for Pharaoh's stubbornness in refusing to free the Hebrew slaves, a horde of insects devours all the green life in the land. The branches of the trees are left completely bare as the locusts devour every green leaf.

Shevat, the month of the trees' new year, is also the month when we recall the destruction of plant life in Egypt and commit to patience and care in dealing with nature and with one another. Our conflicts and wars and our enslavement to endless production can render us like Egypt, leaving us open to vast natural catastrophes. The days of Shevat that lead up to the new year of the trees call us to reflect on the plague of locusts, to remember how fragile our world is, and to renew our covenant with the earth.

Rachel Becomes Pregnant with Benjamin

The sons of Jacob's wife Rachel were Joseph and Benjamin.
—Genesis 46:19

When Jacob came to Rachel, they were like the sky and the earth to one another.
—Zohar II:153b

Today is nine months before the 11th of Heshvan, the birthday of Benjamin and the death date of Rachel. Sometime around now, Rachel becomes pregnant with her second son, Benjamin, youngest of Jacob's children. At the time when, in the Middle East, flowers are forming on the branches, Rachel and Jacob too sow their seeds.

Though it is customary for the Bible to announce the matriarchs' conceptions and when they give birth, we never hear about Rachel's conception of Benjamin. So too the trees quietly conceive around us, beginning their production of flower, fruit, and seed slowly and without fanfare—within twigs, branches, and tiny buds. Then, like Rachel, the trees burst forth unexpectedly into their fertile state.

The Zohar teaches that Jacob and Rachel are like the sky and the earth in union. In their long wait for conception, Jacob and Rachel represent the rain and sun falling on the earth for long seasons until new growth finally appears. As we prepare to celebrate Tu b'Shevat, which marks the end of deep winter, we honor Rachel and Jacob as they bring forth Benjamin. We remember, in Shevat, the slow ascendance of the sun and the long patience of the sleeping earth.

The Burning Branch

He further showed me Joshua, the high priest, standing before the angel of the Eternal, and the Accuser standing at his right to accuse him. But the Eternal said to the Accuser: "The Eternal rebuke you, O Accuser, may the Eternal who has chosen Jerusalem rebuke you! For this is a brand plucked out of the fire."
—ZECHARIAH 3:1–2

At the time of the burning of the Temple, eighty priests concealed themselves within its chambers. All were burned except Joshua . . . who remained alive.
—JERUSALEM TALMUD, TA'ANIT 4:5

On the 24th of Shevat, Zechariah, a prophet carried away in the Babylonian exile, has an extended vision of the future of Jerusalem. Today, as we approach the end of the season of the branch, we look ahead to that vision, in which the exiled high priest Joshua is plucked from the fire of suffering and dressed in new garments.

The Jerusalem Talmud says that Joshua is among the priests who cannot bear to leave the Temple as it burns. With Babylonian soldiers outside, the priests hide themselves within the holy place. Many die, but for whatever miracle or chance reason, Joshua survives. It becomes his task to carry out the Temple's legacy.

As the trees put on fresh garments, we notice some of them may no longer be with us. Not all have survived the cold of winter—or some may not have survived the heat of summer. Like the high priest Joshua, the plants and animals around us are survivors of great dangers, and so are we. As Tu b'Shevat, celebration of the renewal of plant life, comes upon us, we ask for continued strength, for the trees and for ourselves, so that we can live through another year of seasons.

The Good Treasure

The Eternal will open for you the bounteous store of the Holy One, the heavens, to provide rain for your land in season.
—DEUTERONOMY 28:12

When the Holy One wants to make branches on the earth and feed the living creatures, the Holy One opens the good treasures within the rain, and immediately the earth becomes pregnant and puts forth a branch of blessing.
—PIRKEI DE-RABBI ELIEZER 4

In Shevat, we are in the *yemot hageshamim,* the six months the Babylonian Talmud (Gittin 70b) names "the rainy season." Deuteronomy tells us that hiding in the rain are good treasures to sustain the living. With the help of the rain the earth makes life and puts forth green plants. *Pirkei de-Rabbi Eliezer* refers to these plants as a "*tzemach bracha,*" a "branch of blessing." In this season of rains and branches, blessing is all around us.

The word "*tzemach*" signals concealed goodness to come. That is why "Tzemach" is one name for the Messiah (*Lamentations Rabbah* 1:13), who represents the justice in the world that will one day be revealed. The "branch of blessing" is a beginning, and its full goodness will be revealed in the coming season.

According to the Babylonian Talmud, Rosh Hashanah 14a, Tu b'Shevat marks the moment when most of the rains have fallen. Now it is up to the earth to do her part and produce the blessed branch. As we end the season of fire within water, we pray for the success of life throughout the coming year.

The Second Coal

Then one of the seraphs flew over to me with a live coal, which he had taken from the altar with a pair of tongs. He touched it to my lips."
—Isaiah 6:6–7

In the month of Shevat, the Holy One throws down three burning coals to warm the earth. On the seventh of Shevat the first coal falls, to warm the air. On the fourteenth of the month the second falls, to warm the water in the trees. On that day the Arabs say: "Today water has entered the trees." On the twenty-third of Shevat, the third coal is thrown, to warm the soil.
—Hai Gaon[9]

This is the last day of the season of fire within water. As we learned on 7 Shevat, Hai Gaon retells the legend that at this season the Holy One throws down three coals to warm the world. On the 14th of Shevat, a coal falls into the water within the trees, and the sap begins to rise. This mythic event propels us out of the season of branches and into the season of sap. Fire within water, the elements of this season, is the heat inside the trees, a heat that will bring flowers and fruit to the world.

In the book of Isaiah, an angel uses a coal to open Isaiah's lips and purify them so that he may speak prophecy. Today, a coal opens the closed passages of the trees and cleanses them, preparing them for the trees' new year. We too prepare for the warmth of the sun to increase and spur us to greater action and growth.

We began this stage of the year in Tevet with the Festival of the Daughters, a night of Hanukkah when one generation celebrates with the next. On the 14th of Shevat, we prepare for the Festival of the Trees, when one ring of a tree trunk yields to another, and all the trees become a year older.

NOTES

1 Nancy Luena, *Celebrations of Light: A Year of Holidays around the World* (Athenaeum, 1988), pp. 21–22.

2 Yom-Tov Lewinsky, *The Book of Festivals/Sepher Moadim* (Agudat Oneg Shabbat, 1950–1957) 5, p. 286–287.

3 Howard Schwartz, *Tree of Souls: The Mythology of Judaism* (Oxford University Press, 2004), pp. 216–218.

4 Raphael Patai, *The Hebrew Goddess* (Wayne State University Press, 1990), pp. 250–251.

5 Adrienne Rich, "Prospective Immigrants Please Note," *Collected Early Poems: 1950–1970* (W.W. Norton and Company, 1993), p. 188.

6 http://www.ou.org/chagim/roshchodesh/tevet.

7 Greg Killian, "Calendars and Feasts," http://www.tckillian.com/greg/feasts.html.

8 Norman Cohen, *Voices from Genesis: Guiding Us Through the Stages of Life* (Jewish Lights, 1988), p.149.

9 Penina Adelman, ed., *Praise Her Works* (The Jewish Publication Society, 2005), p. 51.

10 Rebecca Alpert, "Rediscovering Tziporah," in *The Women's Torah Commentary*, Elyse Goldstein, ed. (Jewish Lights, 2000), p. 122.

11 A 9th-century Sage quoted in Priscilla Fishman's *Minor and Modern Festivals* (Leon Amiel Publishers, 1973), p. 64.

12 Ibid.

SEASON

Winter moving into spring

WIND

The east

HALF OF THE YEAR

The rains

ELEMENT

Earth within air

GATE

The earth

ANGEL

Uriel (wisdom)

DIVINE FACE

Tiferet (compassion and balance)

The Sap

15 SHEVAT TO 29 ADAR

A ladder stood on the ground,
and its head reached to heaven,
and messengers of God were going
up and down on it.

—GENESIS 28:12

The fourth movement of the year is flowing. The sap in the trees begins to rise, and life runs through all the veins of the trees. The blood of living creatures also begins to move faster as they awaken to seek food. Ice cracks and melts; water disperses over the land. In the Middle East and similar climates, trees blossom and flowers emerge. Though there may be still a chill on the earth, it is an invigorating cold, one that inspires us to move.

In nature, this is the season of air, when fresh winds blow, bringing the rebirth of spring. The sky clears and lightens. Just-opened buds work their magic on the wind. Within, this is the season of earth, when we connect to planting and harvest and ground ourselves in the rhythms of life. In Jewish mysticism, this is the time of *tiferet:* "balance, compassion, and beauty." *Tiferet* is the heart of the Tree of Life. *Tiferet* is also the Holy One, the compassionate father or counselor who listens to the hearts of all.

Tu b'Shevat, the full moon of Shevat and the new year of the trees, begins this season. Once, the 15th day of the month of Shevat was a tax date used in tithing the fruits of new trees. In Tzfat during the days of the kabbalists, Tu b'Shevat became a holiday, celebrated by a mystical seder or "ritual meal." The mystics who conceived the Tu b'Shevat seder imagined God as a tree, with divine light running like sap through its branches. They believed eating a simple fruit could release sparks of divine light into the world.[1]

The season moves on into Purim, a holiday of masks and disguises where truth ascends slowly, like a shoot, through many layers of ground. On Purim, everything is topsy-turvy. In the book of Esther, ritually recited on Purim, nothing is what it seems to be. Queen Esther, for example, is a Jew pretending not to be a Jew, married to a gentile, King Ahasuerus, who dislikes Jews and then learns to love them. Haman, the villain, seems invulnerable, yet is defeated with a single word. Jew flows into non-Jew, male flows into female, friend flows into enemy. Traditionally, Jews wear costumes on Purim to increase the sense of masquerade, and many engage in performances that make fun of sacred text and tradition. Like trees that transform their appearances with new leaves, Purim transforms us into something we thought we weren't—but it turns out we are!

Flowing wine is the symbol of the season, both the wine ritually drunk at Tu b'Shevat and the wine imbibed at Purim to bring us joy. This is a time of pouring ourselves into new shapes. What will we become? What have we not yet discovered about ourselves? We learn about all our faces and gradually begin to find our deepest truths. At this time of year, we peel off our own masks and those of the Divine, letting all that flows within us come to the surface. Soon the buds will burst open, and we too will open to the warmth of spring.

As Jews celebrate Tu b'Shevat, other cultures mark the season as well. Christians celebrate Candlemas or, in Mexico, Candelaria, to honor the Virgin Mary's purification. The Irish Celts celebrated Imbolc or "the feast of ewe's milk" at this season to honor the return of spring.[2] In China, the New Year begins at this time.[3] The Basant kite-flying holiday in Pakistan celebrates the coming of spring with play and merriment.[4] The Japanese Setsubun or Bean-Throwing Festival, marking the beginning of spring, also falls during these weeks.[5] The fragile newness of things invites us to feel awe at the miracle of life. This fourth phase of the calendar connects us to the Tree of Life by allowing us to explore the most tangible elements of the season, the earth, and ourselves.

The Tree of Life

Tu b'Shevat

And from the ground the Divine caused to grow every tree that was pleasing to the sight and good for food, and the Tree of Life was in the middle of the garden.
—GENESIS 2:9

At the hour that the Holy One created the first human being, the Holy One brought that being before all the trees in the Garden of Eden and said: "Behold the beauty and abundance of My works! All that I created, I created for you. Consider this and do not destroy or ruin My world, for if you ruin it, there will be no one after you to make it right."
—ECCLESIASTES RABBAH 7:28

The 15th of the month of Shevat, or Tu b'Shevat, is one of the four new years listed in the Babylonian Talmud (Rosh Hashanah 2a), the new year of trees. Tu b'Shevat was once a talmudic tax date, but 16th-century mystics in the city of Tzfat invented a Tu b'Shevat practice of eating fruit, drinking wine, and honoring the Divine as the Tree of Life.[6]

Isaac Luria invented the custom of drinking four cups of wine on Tu b'Shevat—white, white mixed with red, red mixed with white, and red. This wine can also represent the rising of the sap. The fruit of Tu b'Shevat is divided into fruit with rinds, representing earth and body (*assiyah*); fruit with pits, representing emotion (*yetzirah*); and fruit that is completely edible, representing mind (*beriyah*). (Some use the scent of fruit to represent essence, or *atzilut.*) In the 17th century, Nathan of Gaza, a mystic, created a Passover-like seder for Tu b'Shevat that included biblical and Rabbinic passages about trees.[7]

In modern Israel, Tu b'Shevat celebrates the fruits of the land: dates, figs, carobs, oranges, and other fruits of local trees. As the above midrash on Creation reminds us, the Tu b'Shevat seder has also become a way to remember the human responsibility to care for trees and all of nature. If we do not, there will be no one to repair our mistakes.

Asherah, Lady of the Tree of Life

Don't you see what they are doing in the towns of Judah and in the streets of Jerusalem? The children gather wood, the fathers build the fire, and the women knead dough, to make cakes for the Queen of Heaven....
—JEREMIAH 7:17–18

She is a Tree of Life to those who hold fast to her—this tree is the Lady, the Shekhinah.
—ZOHAR 1:27B

The Tree of Life, the Jewish symbol for the Torah and for the *Shekhinah,* is an image rooted in pre-Israelite history. The Tree of Life was once a symbol for Asherah, a Near Eastern goddess of love, fertility, and wisdom. According to ancient Israelite inscriptions, Asherah may once have been worshiped by the Hebrew people as a consort of God. Although Asherah worship disappeared as strict monotheism took hold, the spirit of the divine feminine remained. According to scholar Raphael Patai, Asherah is one of the origins of the image of the *Shekhinah,* the feminine Divine Presence.[8] The menorah and/or seven-branched candelabrum may come from this ancient Near Eastern image of the Tree of Life.

Why represent divinity as a tree? A tree, like the Divine, is a source of life not only for itself but for the creatures who live in it or eat its fruit. A tree has many branches, reminding us there are many pathways to holiness. The menorah calls us to see ourselves as one branch of the human spirit. When we reach out to others who share our thirst for life, peace, and justice, the sap of the Tree of Life runs through all of us.

The Psalms of the Birds

But the Israelites had marched through the sea on dry ground, the waters forming a wall for them on their right and their left. . . . Then Moses and the Israelites sang this song to the Holy One: I will sing to the Eternal.
—EXODUS 14:29, 15:1

Why does it say "on dry ground"? When an Israelite woman was walking through the sea, and her child was hungry, she only had to stretch out her hand, pluck an apple or a pomegranate from the sea, and give it to the child.
—EXODUS RABBAH 21:10

Tu b'Shevat often falls near parashah Be-shallah, the Torah portion that describes the splitting of the Sea of Reeds. One fantastical midrash (*Exodus Rabbah* 21:10) imagines that when God split the sea, fruit trees bloomed in the miraculous passage through the waters. Birds perched in the trees and sang to celebrate the freedom of the former slaves. These trees in the middle of the sea connect the holiday of Tu b'Shevat with the story of the Exodus.

Birds have also kept the songs of the Jewish people alive. Rabbi Debra Orenstein relates a story her grandfather told her: When King David, legendary author of the Psalms, came to believe that the Temple would be destroyed, he was afraid his psalms would be forgotten. He taught the psalms to the birds so that his words would not be lost.[9] (In Hebrew numerology, the word "nest" equals 150, the number of psalms in the Bible.)

One Eastern European Jewish custom, reportedly encouraged by Rabbi Judah Loew (the Maharal) of Prague, is to go out and feed birds on *Shabbat* Shirah, the "Sabbath of song," when the tale of the crossing of the sea is chanted. Jews do this in gratitude for the birds' acts of kindness to the Israelites and in recognition of the songs of praise that the birds sing every morning. The birds remind us that everything we do can be an act of praise.

Do Not Cut Down the Trees

When in your war against a city you have to besiege it a long time in order to capture it, you must not destroy its trees, wielding the ax against them. You may eat of them, but you must not cut them down. Are trees of the field human, to withdraw before you into the besieged city?
—DEUTERONOMY 20:19

When a fruit-bearing tree is cut down, its cry carries from one end of the world to the other, but we cannot hear the sound.
—PIRKEI DE-RABBI ELIEZER 34

In Deuteronomy we learn that when besieging a city we are not to cut down fruit trees to build siege works or to afflict the enemy. Trees should not be part of our wars with other humans; they are peaceful beings without defenses and are not to be destroyed without reason. This is both for the benefit of humans, who need living trees, and out of respect for the Holy One's creation. Later Jewish law expanded this idea to suggest that nothing—human, plant, or animal—be wasted for no reason. A mishnah (Sotah 1:7) claims that the truly righteous do not waste even a mustard seed.

Pirkei de-Rabbi Eliezer (34) puts forth the notion that trees cry out when they are cut down. Though we cannot hear them, trees suffer when they are destroyed, and their suffering diminishes the world. They make a sound just like the one a human soul makes when leaving the body.

In recent decades humans have decimated the tree population of the world as well as many other natural resources. We imperil our own survival though these wasteful actions. The season of Tu b'Shevat reminds us to take seriously the Rabbinic law against squandering the blessings of creation.

The Holy Apple Orchard

Is a person like the tree of the field?
—Deuteronomy 20:19

Certainly a person is like a tree of the field. A person is like a tree in the Holy Apple Orchard, the Shekhinah.
—Zohar II:60b

The Zohar depicts the *Shekhinah,* the immanent Divine dwelling in all things, in many ways: as a bride, as a mother bird, as the Torah. One way the Zohar imagines the *Shekhinah* is as an apple orchard: not a single tree but a gathering of trees. Each soul, the Zohar imagines, is a tree in the flowering orchard of the *Shekhinah.* At night, when we dream, we return to the orchard and renew our spirits. Even in winter, the inner orchard is in blossom.

This orchard is a radical concept, because it implies each of us is a cell in the Divine being. In fact, one mystical word for the *Shekhinah* is "the community of Israel"—the *Shekhinah* is a gathering of all of us. Shevat, the season of sap, reminds us we are not alone—we may be individuals, but we are also part of the apple orchard. We can act as part of a larger web of life.

The Birth of Asher

When Leah's maid Zilpah bore Jacob a second son, Leah declared, "What fortune!" meaning, "Women will deem me fortunate." So she named him Asher.
—GENESIS 30:12–13

Asher never in his life stayed anywhere but in a hotel.
—GENESIS RABBAH 71:10

According to the *Sefer Yetzirah* (5:2), the month of Shevat is the month of the tribe of Asher. Asher, son of Jacob and Zilpah, was born on this day of Shevat (*Midrash Tadshe*). Asher is the only one of the 13 children of Jacob who, in legend, is born in his tribal month. There is something rooted and centered about Asher. His name means "joy," and he is the exemplar of good fortune.

What is so fortunate about Asher? One playful midrash suggests that unlike his brothers, Asher and his kindred did not sleep in the wilderness while on journeys. Somehow, whenever they traveled, there was always a comfortable inn waiting. Through some mysterious luck (or good planning!) the tribe of Asher achieved an ease in life unknown to other family members.

Asher is like the first tree to bloom in the Land of Israel at this season or the first tree to develop hard brown buds in the winter months of parts of North America. What makes that tree in particular the one to burst forth, while the others are still dry and struggling? Some particular luck or divine grace touches it, and that is the tree to take our breath away with the first small bud or almond flower or apple blossom. We might well say of such a tree: "What fortune!"

The Tree of Marah

Then Moses caused Israel to set out from the Sea of Reeds. … they traveled three days in the wilderness and found no water. They came to Marah, but they could not drink the water of Marah because it was bitter; that is why it was called Marah. And the people grumbled … saying, "What shall we drink?" So he cried out to the Eternal, and the Eternal showed him a tree. He threw it into the water, and the water became sweet.
—EXODUS 15:22–25

What was the tree? Rabbi Joshua said it was a willow. Rabbi Natan said it was a bitter oleander. … There are those who say it was a fig or a pomegranate, but in any case, it was certainly a bitter tree Moses threw.
—MIDRASH TANHUMA, BE-SHALLAH 24

The Torah portions of this season tell of the Exodus, in preparation for the spring re-enactment of freedom from slavery. In one story, the Israelites come to a bitter spring called Marah. They are thirsty, but the water is impossible to drink. Moses cries out to the Eternal, and the Eternal shows him a tree. Moses throws a branch of the tree into the water and the water becomes sweet.

The Sages argue about what kind of tree has such healing power. They do agree that the tree had bitter wood. It was not the inherent sweetness of the tree but the Holy One's intervention that made the tree able to turn water sweet.

This story too is reminiscent of sap. The sap of the tree is sweet, not because of the taste of the wood itself, but because the tree is able to make sugar from the light it receives from its leaves. So too in Shevat the Holy One teaches us that only when we allow ourselves to take in the light can we bring sweetness to the world.

The Trees of Elim

And they came to Elim, where there were twelve springs of water and seventy palm trees, and they encamped there beside the water.
—Exodus 15:27

This teaches that Israel never camps except by water.
—Seder Olam 5

After the Israelites leave Egypt, they come to a mysterious place known as Elim. Elim has 12 springs of water, one for each tribe of Israel, and 70 palm trees, one for each of the elders of the people. The water and the trees are connected: Both symbolize the life force, that the Israelites experience now that they are free. They also represent Torah: Trees and water are both common metaphors for sacred text. Elim represents a community gathered around a common purpose, just as trees in the desert gather around a water source to grow.

This is the season of earth within air, and the fragrant trees of Elim remind us how the scent of trees can carry in the wind. Perhaps this scent greets the Israelites as they approach the oasis. Torah too is earth within air, the strength and permanence of trees, surrounded by ever-changing currents of human interpretation.

At Elim, the Israelites rest, and begin to expand their horizons. At the end of Shevat, as we prepare for spring, we too expand our horizons. Like the Israelites, we look for waters, physical and spiritual, to sustain us as we climb toward a new season.

The Final Coal

The Divine makes messengers of the winds, and servants of fiery flames.
—PSALMS 104:4

In the month of Shevat, the Holy One tosses down three burning coals to warm the earth. On the seventh of Shevat the first coal falls, to warm the air. On the fourteenth of the month the second falls, to warm the water in the trees. On that day the Arabs say: "Today water has entered the trees." On the twenty-third of Shevat, the third coal is thrown, to warm the soil.
—HAI GAON[10]

Today, the 23rd of Shevat, is the day the Eternal "throws a coal" to warm the earth. This is a mythic representation of the spring thaw, when the earth softens enough for easy planting. Although in some places the spring thaw will not come for a while and in other places the ground has been warm all winter, this date on the Hebrew calendar invites us to consider the thawing process. This is the season of *tiferet,* or compassion, and we may imagine how we might thaw ourselves as the earth thaws, opening to feeling and empathy.

In this season of earth within air, we note how the warming of the air rouses the earth. Beneath our feet, plants and animals awaken and act. Life begins to flow and ascend.

Three, in Jewish lore, is a sacred number representing completion. With the third coal, the Holy One sets spring in motion. Now there is no turning back. As Shevat ends, the earth loosens and opens to change.

The Horsemen of Shevat

On the twenty-fourth day of . . . Shevat, … the Eternal came to the prophet Zechariah. . . . In the night, I had a vision. I saw a man, mounted on a red horse, standing among the myrtles … and behind him were red, sorrel, and white horses. I asked, "What are those, my lord?" . . . The man who was standing among the myrtles … said, "These were sent out by the Eternal to roam the earth."
—Zechariah 1:7–8

Esther was called Hadassah (myrtle) because of her righteousness. Mordechai too was called a myrtle… . The scent of a myrtle is good but its taste is bitter; so too Esther and Mordechai were good for the Jews but bad for the nations that opposed them.
—Midrash Tehillim 22:3

On this day, Zechariah has a vision of mysterious figures on horses roaming the earth to learn the fates of the nations. The three colors of the horses—red, dappled, and white—may refer to the changing light of the sun as it rises. The figures on the horses discover the fate of Israel and seek to help.

The head of these mysterious figures stands "between the myrtles." *Midrash Tehillim* explains that the "man between the myrtles" is Mordechai of the Purim story, who brings up Esther (also called Hadassah, "myrtle.") He and Esther are both compared to the myrtle because, just as the myrtle is both fragrant and bitter, they are kind in some circumstances and fierce in others. They ride the horses of history, aiding their people at critical moments. Perhaps the three horses represent Mordechai, Esther, and the many others who help to move the Purim story forward.

Purim will arrive in less than a month. We can begin to prepare for Purim by recalling the qualities of Esther and Mordechai. We may do this by taking out myrtle branches saved from Sukkot and using them as spices during the *Havdalah* (end of Sabbath) ceremonies of this month, honoring the trees of Shevat and the heroes of Purim.

Rebekah at the Well

[Abraham's servant] had scarcely finished speaking, when Rebekah, who was born to Bethuel, the son of Milcah the wife of Abraham's brother Nahor, came out with her jar on her shoulder. The maiden was very beautiful, a virgin whom no man had known. She went down to the fountain, filled her jar, and came up.
—GENESIS 24:15–16

All women went down and drew water from the well, whereas for her the water ascended as soon as it saw her. The Holy One of Blessing said to her "You have provided a token for your descendants: as the water rose when it saw you, so it will be for your descendants. As soon as Miriam's well sees them, it will immediately rise."
—GENESIS RABBAH 60:5

Rebekah, the woman who is destined to marry Isaac, is a young woman living in the land of Haran. She comes out to the well to fetch water. Abraham's servant Eliezer is watching her. If she proves herself generous, he will ask her to marry Isaac, the son of Abraham, and become a matriarch of the tribe of Abraham and Sarah.

Rebekah is indeed kind and generous. She offers water to the stranger and all his animals. One midrash claims she also performs a miracle. As she goes down to the water of the well, one legend claims, the water rises up to meet her. It is as if Rebekah were the moon, creating a tide to pull the water upward. This gift symbolizes her connection to the *Shekhinah,* who is also represented by the moon (Babylonian Talmud, Sanhedrin 42a).

Rebekah is a Shevat heroine: She symbolizes the miracle of the trees, the gift of drawing water upward out of the ground. Because water moves toward her, we know she is a keeper of the flow of life. She shows kindness to others, allowing goodness to course through her into the world. So too we hope to be conduits for love—the sap of the tree of life.

Cedar Houses

Cedars are the beams
of our house,
cypresses the rafters.
—Song of Songs 1:17

In Tevet, Shevat, and Adar,
the Israelites in the wilderness
would cover their houses
with cedar wood.
—Otzar Midrashim: Arakhim 6

A midrash teaches that the Israelites, wandering in the wilderness, build new houses for each new season. In the spring, roofs are of glass to view the beauties of the season. In the summer, roofs are of marble, to cool the inhabitants within. In the autumn, roofs are of ivory. In the winter, roofs are made of cedar.

Why cedar? Possibly to keep the inhabitants warm, but also because cedar is a tree. While in other seasons they use mineral or animal products, in the season of Shevat, the Israelites roof their houses in wood to honor the trees. And there may be another reason as well. The *mishkan*, the house of the *Shekhinah*, contained a great deal of cedar wood. By roofing their houses in cedar, the Israelites turn their homes into small sanctuaries and recycle leftover wood.

The winter season of Tevet, Shevat, and Adar contains no pilgrimage festivals. Rather, it contains the holidays of Hanukkah, Tu b'Shevat, and Purim—minor holidays marked by home observance. These months fall during a time the Sages called *yemot hageshamim*, the "days of rain," when the sky dims and thoughts are turned inward. The cedar roofs of the Israelites teach us that, during times when we turn inward, we must make our homes and inner selves sanctuaries.

The Cedar That Hid Isaiah

Manasseh put so many innocent persons to death that he filled Jerusalem [with blood] from end to end.
—2 KINGS 21:16

King Manasseh's soldiers came and Isaiah fled from them. He fled to a cedar tree and it swallowed him, but his tzitzit *(ritual fringes) hung out. . . . They went to Manasseh and told him, and Manasseh said: "Cut down the tree." They cut down the tree until the blood flowed out.*
—JERUSALEM TALMUD, SANHEDRIN 51B

In Shevat we remember our duty to preserve human life is woven together with our duty to preserve the earth. This story of the prophet Isaiah's death makes the point. Manasseh, a descendant of David, is a corrupt king of Judah. Isaiah, a prophet, criticizes Manasseh, and Manasseh sends soldiers to kill him. Isaiah runs to a forest and asks a cedar tree to hide him. The cedar tree complies, but the ritual fringes on Isaiah's garments stick out, and the soldiers see him. Manasseh orders the tree cut down, and the tree and Isaiah perish together. It is as if the sap of the tree and the blood of the prophet were indistinguishable. Isaiah himself is a kind of tree, giving comfort and sustenance to the people until the moment of his death.

Isaiah, the most joyous of the prophets, sings often of the glory of trees, mountains, and vineyards, and it is a tree that shelters him in his time of need. So too trees shelter us, giving us fruit, paper, housing, even the air we breathe. Our lives and theirs are wound together. Isaiah teaches us of the need to resist tyrants who decimate life and invites us to ally with all life as we do so.

The Taste of Honey

Saul had laid an oath upon the troops: "Cursed be the man who eats any food until night falls and I take revenge upon my enemies." So none of the troops ate anything. Everybody came to a stack of beehives where some honey had spilled on the ground. When the troops came to the beehives and found the flow of honey there, no one put his hand to his mouth, for the troops feared the oath. Jonathan, however, had not heard his father adjure the troops. So he put out the stick he had with him, dipped it into the beehive of honey, and brought his hand back to his mouth, and his eyes lit up.
—1 SAMUEL 14:24–27

Honey is one-sixtieth of manna.
—BABYLONIAN TALMUD, BERAHOT 57B

In the *Sefer Yetzirah,* Shevat is the month of taste. One story of Jonathan, King Saul's son, shows him tasting honey even though his father has declared a fast. Saul threatens to kill Jonathan for violating the ban on food, but the troops save Jonathan from the king, reminding Saul that Jonathan, with the strength he gained from the honey, won a great victory for his father.

In many cultures, honey is a symbol of divine wisdom or the pleasures of Paradise. The Talmud tells us the taste of honey is an echo of the taste of manna, the heavenly food fed to the Israelites in the wilderness. Honey, like sap, is a liquid thickened by sugar; it has substance and yet it flows. Honey calls to mind the Torah, which is both "solid" and "liquid": It has a fixed text, yet changing meanings.

Saul denies his troops food while on an important mission, a foolish move for any leader. Denial for the sake of denial is a poor strategy. Jonathan, on the other hand, sustains himself and proves himself a wiser man than his father. We too look for ways to sustain ourselves with the flow of Shevat.

The East Wind

Then Moses held out his arm over the sea, and the Eternal drove back the sea with a strong east wind all that night, and turned the sea into dry ground.
—EXODUS 14:21

From the wind of the east light comes to the world.
—PIRKEI DE-RABBI ELIEZER 3

As we move closer to Nisan and the celebration of spring, we contemplate the east, the direction mystically associated with spring. An ancient legend says the east wind brings light to the world. This light is the light of the dawn; it is also the light of freedom. The east wind carries with it the freedom holidays of Purim and Passover, the spaces of the wilderness, the scent of softened earth, and the stirring of life.

The word "*shevat*" can mean "rod" or "staff." In the month of Shevat we read the story of how Moses stretches his staff over the Sea of Reeds. The Divine sends an east wind, the wind of light and freedom, to push back the waters of the sea so the Israelites can cross out of Egypt. In the latter days of Shevat, as we greet the east wind, we offer prayers that it will push back all that oppresses us and allow us to cross into liberty.

Conceiving Fruit

New Moon of Adar

Blessed shall be the fruit of your belly and the fruit of your land.
—DEUTERONOMY 28:4

Tree, tree, apple tree, apple tree, I come to you, a barren woman. I take the fruit you have conceived, and give up to you my affliction.
—TREE RITUAL OF NORTH AFRICAN JEWISH WOMEN[11]

We began Shevat with the Tree of Life, the cosmic web of sustenance and spiritual vitality, connecting all things with its branches. We end Shevat with another Tree of Life. In North Africa, Jewish women who wanted to conceive but were unable to do so would go and speak to a tree about their troubles. The women would ask the tree to take away their barrenness, then would pick a fruit from the tree and eat it in their marriage beds, hoping the fruit would bring new life.

The Torah itself refers to both human offspring and tree offspring as "fruit," suggesting our deep connection to the fruit of the earth. It may be this linguistic connection that gives rise to rituals like this one from North Africa. As Shevat ends, as trees awaken and seeds sprout, we pray for the success of the fruit: ours and the world's.

The Half Shekel

New Moon of Adar

When you take a census of the Israelite people according to their enrollment, each shall pay the Eternal a ransom for himself on being enrolled. . . . This is what everyone who is entered in the records shall pay: a half-shekel by the sanctuary weight.
—EXODUS 30:12–14

*Resh Lakish said: The Creator of the World knew Haman would pay money (*shekalim*) to convince Ahasuerus to give him permission to destroy the Jews. So the Holy One made the Jews give their* shekalim *first. This is why the announcement of the* shekalim *must be made on the first of Adar.*
—BABYLONIAN TALMUD, MEGILLAH 13B

Adar arrives with mystery and laughter, with secrets, masks, and revelations, with opposites and paradoxes. Shevat teaches us about the flowing of sap, and Adar teaches us how we too become fluid as we awaken into spring.

In temple times, a census tax of a half shekel for each Jewish citizen was due on the 1st of Nisan. The announcement that this payment was about to fall due was made on the 1st of Adar. Jews still read the Torah verses related to this custom on or near 1 Adar to observe the ritual of announcing the half-shekel tax.

The Talmud connects the half shekel to the arrival of Purim. Haman, the villain of Purim, bribes the king to lure him into signing a document condemning the Jews. The half-shekel donation is an ironic opposite: a "bribe" to the Ruler of Heaven to save the Jews from their oppressors. Why is the Jews' bribe more meritorious than Haman's bribe? Perhaps because each Jew gives a half shekel: One needs two donations to make a whole shekel. Haman's donation drives people apart, but the donation of the half shekel brings people together. Adar is a time when Jews come together to offer their individual gifts toward the common good.

2 ADAR

Increasing Joy

The month [was] transformed for them from one of grief and mourning to one of festive joy.
—Esther 9:22

When we enter Adar, we increase in joy.
—Babylonian Talmud, Ta'anit 29a

Adar has a double edge. In fact, Adar is sometimes a double month—sometimes a second Adar is included in the calendar as a leap month (see "Adar II: on p. 221). Adar is a month of anxiety, in which we tell a story of near destruction, and a month of merriment, when Jews celebrate their rescue with gifts, costumes, and laughter. In many climates Adar can be a gentle month or a month of fierce winds, rains, and snows.

The Sages tell us that merely entering the month of Adar can make us more joyous. Yet it is hard to imagine that we can be commanded to feel joy. What if we are sad in Adar? Are we violating the tradition?

The message of Adar is not to cover up our true feelings with forced merriment but to recognize the double edge that lies under all reality. Our lives flow through both good and bad times. The key to Adar is to know this and still to believe happiness is possible. In Adar, joy is a mask we put on to conceal pain, yet we also know the joy is real.

Welcoming the Temple

The house was finished on the third of the month of Adar. . . . The Israelites, the priests, and the Levites, and all the other exiles, celebrated the dedication of the House of the Divine with joy.
—Ezra 6:15

They made the mishkan *with delight and joy. . . . Rabbi Shmuel bar Nachman said: They finished the work of the* mishkan *during Tishrei, Heshvan, and Kislev, and it stayed folded up during Tevet, Shevat, and Adar, and they stood it up during the first of Nisan.*
—Midrash Tanhuma, Pekudei 11

The 3rd of Adar is the anniversary of the dedication of the Second Temple. This anniversary reminds us that the 1st of Nisan, when the Israelites dedicated their very first shrine to the Eternal, is not far away. The joy of Adar is connected to this joy of building a sacred space.

Yet in Adar, the *mishkan* has not yet unfolded. Like a leaf within a protective outer covering, it remains boxed up. Adar is a month of hiddenness, and in Adar the shrine is still hidden. So too in the book of Esther we read this month, no divine name is mentioned. The Divine is hidden away or covered over.

This holds a deeper teaching. Adar is the last month of the *yemot hageshamim*, the "days of rain"—the six months of the year when we turn inward to examine our spirits. Nisan begins the six months of the year known as *yemot hachamah* or "days of the sun"—the days when we examine ourselves as a collective. Adar, the month of the folded Tabernacle, is a month when the dwelling of the *Shekhinah* is still folded inside us, the way a seed or bulb's secrets are folded inside it. This may give us a deep joy and delight, or it may make us long for Nisan, when we will burst outward at last.

The Coin of Fire

This is what everyone who is entered in the records shall pay: a half-shekel by the sanctuary weight. . . . Everyone who is entered in the records, from the age of twenty years up, shall give the offering of the Eternal. The rich shall not pay more, and the poor shall not pay less.
—Exodus 30:14–15

Moshe could not understand the commandment of the half-shekel. The Holy One took out a coin of fire from beneath the heavenly throne and said: "This you shall give."
—Midrash Tanhuma, Ki Tissa 13

In Adar, we recall the half shekel the Israelites donated to the *mishkan*. Meanwhile, all around us nature is sharing its gifts in ever greater profusion. The motion of Adar is flowing, and gifts—from nature and from one another—keep abundance flowing from one spirit to another.

The interesting thing about the gift of the half shekel, though, is that it is not a free-will donation. Nor is it adjustable for poverty, as are many other sacred sacrifices. Everyone must give exactly the same. Why this sameness? Perhaps the half shekel, unlike most other gifts, teaches us our equality with one another. It represents the truth that each soul takes up the same amount of space in the treasury of the spirit.

In *Midrash Tanhuma,* Moses does not understand the gift of the half shekel. Perhaps he does not understand what a shekel is, or perhaps he does not see why the gift should not be more if one can afford more or less if one can afford less. The Holy One shows Moses a coin of fire from the divine treasury, and says: "Exactly like this." The half shekel is not just a coin, it is a flame. This shows us that each gift we give is like a fire warming the world.

The Lot Is Cast

In the first month, that is, the month of Nisan, in the twelfth year of King Ahasuerus, pur, *which means "the lot," was cast before Haman concerning every day and every month, [until it fell on] the twelfth month, the month of Adar.*
—Esther 3:7

When the lot fell on Adar, Haman rejoiced greatly, for he said: "The lot has fallen on the month that Moses died!" He did not know that was the month Moses died and also the month Moses was born.
—Babylonian Talmud, Megillah 13b

According to legend, Adar is the month Moses is born and dies (*Exodus Rabbah* 1:24; *Midrash Tanhuma, Va-ethannan* 6). One midrash connects Purim to the death of Moses. Haman, the adversary of the Jews in Persia, is casting lots, divining tools known as *pur,* to determine what month to exterminate the Jews. The lot falls on Adar. Haman is overjoyed. He thinks this month is ill omened for the Jews, as Moses died then. However, Haman does not know that Adar is also the month of Moses' birth.

Haman has made a classic spiritual mistake: He has looked at a two-sided coin and seen only one side. He gazes into his lots and sees death alone, instead of looking deeper and finding life. Adar, the two-sided month, pulls us away from Haman's single-minded, vindictive thoughts and reminds us always to look at both sides of a question.

Haman is like a number of classical ferocious winter figures in folklore throughout the world. Like a winter frost, he attempts to nip the spring buds before they open. Though he does not know it, fate is against him. Queen Esther, messenger of hope and of the spring, is on her way. Haman believes the season favors him, but he has already lost.

The Birth of Moses

A certain man of the house of Levi went and married a Levite woman. The woman conceived and bore a son, and when she saw how beautiful [lit. good] he was, she hid him for three months.
—EXODUS 2:1–2

The Sages say: At the hour Moses was born the whole house filled with light. We know this because the Torah says, "She saw that he was a good child," and it also says, "God saw the light, that it was good."
—EXODUS RABBAH 1:20

Today is the day before 7 Adar, the day Jochebed gives birth to her third child, Moses. When Moses is born, a great light fills the house. Yet his birth presents a terrible dilemma: Egyptian law dictates the child must be thrown into the Nile. Jochebed sees the light around the child, and knows he must be saved.

The light around Moses is like the light at the dawn of Creation. Perhaps the light indicates Moses is a special child, or perhaps the light arises from the creation of any new child. Because she perceives this light and sees its goodness, Jochebed hides her infant for three months. Her bravery is also an act of creation: Because she saves Moses, an entire people will be born during the Exodus.

Adar is a month of concealment. Perhaps this is why it is the month of Moses' birth: When just an infant, Moses is hidden away. So too Adar hides the light of the coming Exodus within its secretive days.

The Death of Moses

The Eternal said to [Moses], "This is the land of which I swore to Abraham, Isaac, and Jacob, 'I will assign it to your offspring.' I have let you see it with your own eyes, but you shall not cross there." So Moses the servant of the Eternal died there, in the land of Moab.
—DEUTERONOMY 34:4-5

The Eternal commanded Samael [the Angel of Death], "Go and get me Moses' soul." … A Divine voice said: "The time of your death is here." Moses said to the Divine: "Master of the Universe, remember when You showed Yourself to me in the bush? … Please do not hand me over to the Angel of Death!" A heavenly voice said to him: "Do not be afraid. I myself will see to you."
—DEUTERONOMY RABBAH 11:10

The 7th of Adar, the day of Moses' death, is one of the most poignant in the Jewish calendar. Moses does not die willingly: He argues and cajoles and begs to live. He is so committed to life that he asks to become a bird or animal rather than face death (*Deuteronomy Rabbah* 11:10). When the Angel of Death arrives, Moses beats him to a pulp. Moses pleads with the Divine: Don't you remember the special moments we had together? How can you allow me to die? In the end, the Holy One sends the Angel of Death away and promises Moses that no one but the Divine will take away Moses' soul. The Holy One ends Moses' life with a kiss, and weeps. In the kiss and the tears of the Divine we hear the echo of all grief and the mystery of all love. Moses could be any one of us.

Because no human is allowed to know where Moses is buried, the Holy One must bury him. In Eastern European custom, the *hevra kadisha,* the Jewish burial society holds a feast on the 7th of Adar to honor the yahrzeit of Moses.[12] This feast also honors the founder of all burial societies: the Holy One of Blessing, who buries Moses with gentleness and respect.

Old and New Growth

The Israelites bewailed Moses in the steppes of Moab for thirty days, and the period of wailing and mourning for Moses came to an end. Now Joshua son of Nun was filled with the spirit of wisdom because Moses had laid his hands upon him, and the Israelites heeded him, doing as the Eternal had commanded Moses.
—Deuteronomy 34:8–9

When Moses our teacher passed away to the Garden of Eden he said to Joshua, "Tell me your doubts." Joshua said: "Have I ever left you and gone to another place?" . . . Immediately, Joshua forgot three hundred laws, and seven hundred doubts were born in him, and the people wanted to kill him. The Holy One said: "It is impossible for me to tell you."
—Babylonian Talmud, Temurah 16a

In Deuteronomy, when Moses dies, Joshua ably takes over the prophetic and leadership functions of his predecessor. The Talmud imagines things somewhat differently. In the talmudic version of the story, Moses asks Joshua to reveal his doubts. Joshua replies indignantly that he has none. Yet after Moses dies, Joshua becomes confused. Doubt arises in him even though he has denied it.

Joshua's doubts are part of the natural course of grief, growth, and separation. Joshua cannot be Moses: He needs to differentiate himself from Moses and learn to be himself. He needs to have doubts about Moses' ideas and rules. He needs to have doubts about God. Because of these doubts, the people are angry with Joshua; but these doubts also may be why Joshua eventually becomes a good leader.

Outside, new plants are growing up through a layer of old leaves and branches toward the sun. They must break through the plants that nourished them in order to live. If they stay stuck beneath the layer of old leaves, they will never grow. We too must break out of old patterns. Our parents, teachers, and ancestors matter; but if we are to face the future, we must strike out on our own.

The Coming of Amalek

Remember what Amalek did to you on your journey, after you left Egypt—how, undeterred by fear of God, he surprised you on the march, when you were famished and weary, and cut down all the stragglers in your rear. Therefore, when the Eternal your God grants you safety from all your enemies around you, in the land that the Eternal your God is giving you as a hereditary portion, you shall blot out the memory of Amalek from under heaven. Do not forget!
—DEUTERONOMY 25:17–19

The glory of the Divine cannot appear in this world as long as Amalek exists.
—SEFAT EMET, VA-YISHLAH[13]

Every year before Purim, we read the commandment to wipe out Amalek. Amalek is a grandson of Esau. Amalek is a tribe that attacks the weakest members of the Israelites as they straggle out of Egypt. Amalek is also the ancestor of Haman, the villain of Purim.

Amalek is a symbol of wanton and selfish violence. We are warned to blot out Amalek—yet Amalek is a part of the human spirit, and lives within all of us. When we feel certain and confident, it is exactly then that Amalek arises to convince us that we have the right to harm others. The Hasidic thinker Rabbi Yehudah Leib Alter (the Sefat Emet), in describing the great force of the spirit of Amalek, tells us that the *Shekhinah*, the sacred life force, cannot enter the world when Amalek is present.

The processes of creation and destruction occur around us all the time, and both are necessary for our world to function. Wanton destruction is not part of this process: It devastates life and shakes our faith in humanity's goodness. We have the task of fighting Amalek: of refusing to allow our fellow human beings to act with cruelty. As we take on this responsibility, we learn to keep our own destructive impulses in balance.

Vashti Speaks

On the seventh day, when the king was merry with wine, he ordered . . . the seven eunuchs in attendance on King Ahasuerus to bring Queen Vashti before the king wearing a royal diadem, to display her beauty to the peoples and the officials, for she was a beautiful woman. But Queen Vashti refused to come at the king's command.
—ESTHER 1:10–12

The sages said
she had a tail,
that she was vain
and did not want the world
to see her shame. . . .

If Vashti were my guest,
I'd ask if I could touch.
It might be soft and thick
or dragon-scaled,
or tawny, lion-tufted.
It might be anything
wild, untamed.
—JILL HAMMER, "VASHTI'S TAIL"[14]

One of the first characters we meet in the Purim story is Vashti, the queen of Persia. Her husband, King Ahasuerus, orders her to come from the banquet she is hosting for the noblewomen of Persia and show herself before his officials. Jewish tradition adds that the king wants her to appear naked.

In one midrash, Vashti is ashamed to go in to the king not because of her modesty but because the angel Gabriel has given her a tail and she is embarrassed to be seen in public (Babylonian Talmud, Megillah 12b). This midrash displays the Talmud's discomfort with Vashti's rebellion against her husband. Yet Vashti's strength, her refusal to obey her husband's cruel wish, is an example for all people who face injustice. The poem "Vashti's Tail" imagines the tail as a sign of the queen's power and strength of purpose.

Vashti reminds us to speak up about injustice as soon as we perceive it. If we wait, it may be too late. Injustice is like a destructive weed that overruns a garden: If not pulled out, it grows and spreads until there is nothing else left.

Esther, the Morning Star

In the fortress Shushan lived a Jew by the name of Mordechai.... He was foster father to Hadassah—that is, Esther—his uncle's daughter, for she had neither father nor mother. The maiden was shapely and beautiful, and when her father and mother died, Mordechai adopted her as his own daughter. When the king's order and edict was proclaimed, and when many girls were assembled in the fortress . . . Esther too was taken into the king's palace.
—Esther 2:5–8

Just as the morning star at dawn comes little by little and then breaks forth quickly, so does the redemption brought by Esther to Israel.
—Midrash Shocher Tov 22

Esther, the heroine of Purim, is an orphan who is raised by her uncle. Her name, though, suggests that her story is more complex. Esther has the same name as Ishtar, goddess of the morning star and keeper of love and abundance. Like the goddess Ishtar (or Inanna), who enters the underworld and then leaves it,[15] Esther descends into a frightening place and emerges whole.

Esther represents a new dawn for her people. Coming at the end of winter, she is like the light of dawn, ending a period of fear and uncertainty. Esther's entry into the palace, though frightening for her, allows her to plead for her people when the king's minister, Haman, threatens them. So too the world's entry into night inevitably brings the morning.

As *Midrash Shocher Tov* tells us, the light of the morning star increases gradually. Similarly, the events of Esther's life lead slowly but inexorably toward her role in redemption. Esther's deliverance of the Jews happens not all at once, but slowly, over time. She is like the morning star appearing in the sky: a miracle of everyday experience.

Mordechai: The One Who Resists

All the king's courtiers in the palace gate knelt and bowed low to Haman . . . but Mordecai would not … bow low. Then the king's courtiers … said to Mordechai, "Why do you disobey the king's order?" . . . They told Haman, … in order to see whether Mordechai's resolve would prevail, for he had explained to them that he was a Jew. When Haman saw that Mordechai would not … bow low to him, Haman was filled with rage. . . . Haman plotted to do away with all the Jews.

—Esther 3:2–6

Haman said to the courtiers: "Tell him his ancestors bowed to my ancestors, for it says: 'Joseph and Rachel … bowed down [to Esau].'" Mordechai replied: "But Benjamin was not born."

—Esther Rabbah 7:8

Haman and Mordechai are enemies from the beginning. They engage in a battle of wills, just as nature goes through an apparent conflict as winter warms into summer. Mordechai is named for Marduk, the Persian god of war and order. Haman seems to represent disorder. Just as Marduk engages in battle with chaos, Mordechai resists Haman. Yet Haman and Mordechai not only represent natural forces, they also represent human ones.

Haman is a descendant of the mighty hunter Esau. Jacob, Rachel, Leah, and their family once bowed to Esau out of fear, but Rachel's son Benjamin was not yet born then. Mordechai, a proud descendant of Benjamin, refuses to succumb to fear and bow to Haman. In rage, Haman seeks to exterminate Mordechai and all the Jews. He promises the king the possessions of the Persian Jews, and the king agrees to Haman's plan. Haman and Mordechai, along with Esther and the king, face off in a palace drama that leads to a bloody battle between the two sides.

Mordechai represents the desire in us not to bow down to anyone. Haman symbolizes the desire in us for power over others. Sometimes the conflict between them flares up inside us. The battle of Mordechai and Haman teaches us to cherish our freedom yet be wary of our wish to rule others.

The Three Days

The Fast of Esther

Mordechai had this message delivered to Esther: "Do not imagine that you … will escape with your life by being in the king's palace. On the contrary, if you keep silent in this crisis, relief and deliverance will come to the Jews from another quarter, while you and your father's house will perish. … Perhaps you have attained to royal position for just such a crisis!"
—Esther 4:12–14

Live with your eyes wide open. Prepare yourself always to hear the voice that calls you to fulfill your mission. You are on this earth for a purpose, at least one. Meaning may not come like mine came … urgent and clear in the voice of Mordechai, a life or death choice, my people's fate in the balance.
—Tamara Cohen, *Praise Her Works*[16]

Today is the Fast of Esther, a remembrance of Esther's three-day fast in the story of Purim. This fast recalls an ancient symbol: the descent into darkness. In an ancient Sumerian myth, the goddess Inanna descends to the underworld, where she encounters her sister, the queen of death, and dies. After three days, her allies send help: Small holy creatures revive Inanna and lift her out of the underworld.[17] Esther has a similar three-day period of descent, after which she arises, reborn.

The king of Persia issues a decree that on the 14th of Adar all his citizens are to murder and pillage the Jews. When Esther's uncle, Mordechai, asks her to interfere, Esther demurs, saying the king will punish her for appearing without permission. Mordechai reminds Esther that she too may perish in the slaughter. He asks her to reflect that the saving of the Jews may be her destiny. Esther agrees to go to the king, but first she fasts.

When she emerges, Esther dresses in robes of royalty. She goes to the king, and he admits her with joy. Esther's three-day descent into the depths of her soul suggests the earth's descent into winter and its emergence, full of radiant life. Esther reminds us that we too have choices to make, even if they are not as dramatic as her own. We too have a destiny we must not flee out of fear.

Removing the Masks

Purim

The king . . . asked Esther at the wine feast, "What is your wish, Queen Esther? It shall be granted you. And what is your request? Even to half the kingdom, it shall be fulfilled." Queen Esther replied: "If Your Majesty will do me the favor, and if it pleases Your Majesty, let my life be granted me as my wish, and my people at my request. For we have been sold, my people and I, to be destroyed, massacred, and exterminated."
—Esther 7:2–4

What did the money issued by Mordechai and Esther look like? They had Mordechai on one side and Esther on the other [or: they had sackcloth and ashes on one side and a crown on the other].
—Esther Rabbah 10:12

Today is Purim. Jews read the book of Esther in the evening and morning, blotting out the name of Haman with merry noise and celebrating Mordechai and Esther (and sometimes Vashti too) with cheers. Costumes are worn as part of the celebration.

The costumes and masks we wear on Purim remind us of the masks in the Purim story. At the climax of the biblical story, Esther invites the king and Haman to a wine feast and begs the king to stop the massacre of the Jews. Esther unmasks three people. She unmasks herself as a Jew; she unmasks Haman as a villain; and she unmasks the king, who has callously and greedily agreed to allow Haman to kill the Jews so the king can get their property.

Purim unmasks all of us. It even unmasks the Jews in the story, who eagerly fall on their enemies once the king has given them permission. No one is immune from the truth about his or her own dark side.

In one midrash, Esther and Mordechai issue double-sided coins in honor of Purim, with a man on one side and a woman on the other, or with a sign of grief on one side and a sign of triumph on the other. Purim is like this coin, showing us two faces in every person and circumstance.

The Book of Wine

Shushan Purim

Mordechai left the king's presence in royal robes … with a magnificent crown of gold.… And the city of Shushan rang with joyous cries. The Jews enjoyed … happiness and honor. And in every province … when the king's command and decree arrived, there was gladness and joy among the Jews, a feast and a holiday.
—ESTHER 8:15–17

Rabbah said: "A person must get drunk on Purim until he does not know the difference between 'blessed is Mordechai' and 'cursed is Haman.' Rabbah and Rabbi Zeira had a Purim meal together. They got drunk, … Rabbah killed Rabbi Zeira, but Rabbah prayed … and he became alive.… The following year, Rabbah said to Rabbi Zeira, "Shall we have another Purim meal together?" Rabbi Zeira said, "We do not depend on miracles!"
—BABYLONIAN TALMUD, MEGILLAH 7B

Today, Shushan Purim is a kind of second Purim. This is the day Purim is celebrated in ancient walled cities like Shushan, Jerusalem, and Jaffa. For most of us, Shushan Purim is a chance to quietly reflect on Purim.

On Purim, in fulfillment of the biblical injunction to be joyful, we toss away restrictions. We make fun of Torah law and of one another; we dress in costumes that reveal our wilder side. We send gifts of food to one another through a third party, to make the giving more secretive and fun. We help the poor celebrate by making gifts to them as well. The symbol of all this chaos is flowing wine.

Yet the wine in Adar has a double edge. The story of a Sage who kills his friend at a Purim feast may be a Purim joke, yet it reveals discomfort. Drunkenness is dangerous. If one cannot tell the difference between Mordechai and Haman, what else is one likely to do? As we come out of winter into the warm sunlight, it is natural to want to celebrate. Wildness and release is necessary at this time. Yet our exuberance must be tempered by good sense: After all, as Rabbi Zeira says, we do not depend on miracles.

The Once and Future Purim

These days of Purim shall be observed at their proper time, as Mordechai the Jew—and now Queen Esther—has obligated them to do.
—Esther 9:31

All the holidays will be annulled in the future, but the celebration of Purim will never be nullified.
—Midrash Mishlei 9:2

As we leave behind the full moon and the holiday of Purim, we note that although Purim is a minor holiday, its mystical effect is among the greatest of the year. Perhaps this is why the joy and laughter of Purim spread through the whole month of Adar; the *Sefer Yetzirah* (5:10) teaches that Adar is the month of laughter. Purim, by turning everything upside down, teaches us the deepest truths of all. Purim is like the plow that turns the soil so seeds can grow or the sap that runs crazily up and down to give life to the tree.

This is why, one tradition tells us, Purim will never leave us. All other holidays will lose their meaning in the far-off messianic world of unity and peace, yet we will still need Purim for its silliness, its irreverence, its ability to unmask secrets and unseat self-righteous powers. Purim, like the April fool or like a jester in the divine court, awakens us through laughter and teaches us to know ourselves.

Listen in the wind for the laughter of this season. Do you hear the startlement, the self-mocking of all that is? Do you hear ice breaking up, animals awakening from dreams, flowers opening in surprise?

The Month of Offerings

The Eternal spoke to Moses, saying: "Tell the Israelite people to bring Me gifts; you shall accept gifts for Me from all the people whose hearts so move them."
—Exodus 25:1–2

You will find that everything the Divine made above, the Divine also made below. Not only that, but all that is below is more precious to the Divine than all that is above. How do we know? Because the Divine left what was above and went down to what was below.
—Exodus Rabbah 33:4

One of the principles of Jewish mysticism is "As above, so below." Each heavenly thing parallels an earthly thing. As there is a sacred center in heaven, so there is a sacred shrine on earth. As there is a *Shekhinah*, a Divine Presence, so there is a human community on earth to carry that presence.

In Adar, we read the Torah portions related to the building of the *mishkan*, the dwelling place for the Divine. This is appropriate because the new moon of the coming month, Nisan, is the anniversary of the shrine's completion. The Divine tells Moses to solicit gifts from all the Israelites to make this beautiful sacred space. But why is such a physical space necessary? Doesn't the Divine live everywhere?

Exodus Rabbah tells us that all things above have counterparts below in the physical world, and the Divine loves the physical world even more than the world of infinite reality. We know this because the Divine asks Moses for a physical dwelling place on earth, to share in our earthly existence and bring down blessing from above. The flow from above to below, and from below to above, is the most precious gift of this season.

The Red Heifer

Instruct the Israelite people to bring you a red cow, without blemish. . . . It shall be taken outside the camp and slaughtered. . . . Eleazer the priest shall take some of its blood … and sprinkle it … toward the front of the Tent of Meeting. The cow shall be burned in his sight . . . and the priest shall take cedar wood, hyssop, and crimson stuff and throw them into the fire consuming the cow.
—NUMBERS 19:1–6

Both the offering of the red heifer and the offering of Passover are called statutes. How can one know which is greater? … The red heifer is greater than the Passover offering, for those who eat the Passover must first engage in the offering of the red heifer.
—EXODUS RABBAH 19:2

In Adar we read the Torah verses regarding the red heifer. This heifer was burned to ash to create a substance that eliminated the impurity of death. Once this impurity was removed, it was permissible to enter the holy shrine. We read about the heifer in Adar to remind us that Jews once had to purify themselves at this season so they could make the Passover offering in the Temple. Of the two offerings, the red heifer is the more important, for it must come first.

The Sages of the Talmud, and later commentators, regard the red heifer as a mysterious law (see *Numbers Rabbah* 19:8). Why should the ashes of a red cow convey purity? One reason may be that the offering of a cow signifies life. The cow's red color resembles blood, which in the Bible represents life itself. The crimson thread, like an umbilical cord, represents our connection to birth at this spring season. Cedar represents the sacred space, which is built with cedar. And hyssop is used as a brush or sponge: a cleansing agent. The red heifer represents the purifying of life. Its ashes are used to wash away death in preparation for the spring festival of Passover.

Blessings over the Air

Fire and hail, snow and smoke, storm wind that executes the command of the Divine.
—PSALMS 148:8

If one examines these words, one notices they conclude with: "Praise the Divine, human beings, for His strength"—when one sees fire and hail and all the things that go on under the heavens, for their might is clear in many ways, large and small.
—MAIMONIDES, MISHNEH TORAH, HILKHOT YESODEI HA-TORAH 3:11

On Tu b'Shevat we entered the season of the air, of winds, breezes, and breath. The scholar Maimonides, commenting on the verse from Psalms, honors the activities of the air and the skies, for their power is an echo of divine power. Maimonides believes it is incumbent on us to be awed by the skies and to praise creation.

Maimonides writes: "Over winds that blow with force, and over lightning, and over thunder . . . and over light that appears in the air like stars falling or running from place to place, or over stars that appear with a tail, over each of these we say: 'Blessed is the One whose strength and power fill creation,' and if one wants one can say: 'Blessed is the One who makes creation'" (*Mishneh Torah, Hilkhot Berakhot* 10:14) These blessings allow us to express our thanks for the skies and winds above and around us.

The Rising of Istehar

When men began to increase on earth and daughters were born to them, the divine beings saw how beautiful the daughters of men were and took wives from among those that pleased them.
—GENESIS 6:1

Flying ineffable vowels
stretch across me.
If I learn them as words
I will return
to domesticity, to bliss,
to pitchers on the morning
table, children's voices
at the brim of sound. . . .
How will I know to leave them
when it's time?
—LINDA ZISQUIT,
"ISTEHAR RETURNING"[18]

In this season of air, we look to the skies for inspiration. The story of Esther, whose name means "star," brings to mind another star story. Jewish legend holds that one of the Pleiades was once a human woman, Istehar, a maiden who said no to an angel.

Before the Flood, angels are attracted to human women and begin to marry, seduce, or rape them. One of the angels, Shemhazai, pursues a woman called Istehar. Istehar is not interested in his advances, and she outsmarts the angel. She says she will give in to him if he teaches her the secret pronunciation of the divine name. Once Shemhazai complies, Istehar utters the name and flies into the sky, where the Holy One turns her into a star in the constellation of the Pleiades.[19]

The poet Linda Zisquit imagines Istehar, now a star in the heavens, struggling to learn a new divine name, one that will bring her home to familiar surroundings. Yet Istehar hesitates, wanting to preserve her freedom, to hover in the expanse of the skies. She wishes to return to the world, but only when she is ready. Istehar is that within us that resists the call of the mundane world, and lingers in the world of spirit.

The Tapestry of Naphtali

Naphtali's sons: Jahzeel, Guni, Jezer, and Shillem.
—GENESIS 46:24

They were called children of Naphtali for they wove (potlim) *on seventy-two cords the curtains for the Tabernacle.*
—EXODUS RABBAH 94:8

In the *Sefer Yetzirah,* Naphtali, the fleetest and most graceful son of Jacob, becomes the tribe linked with Adar. Adar, the month of many faces, is the month during which we prepare for the appearance of the *mishkan.* One midrash connects the name "Naphtali" with the work of the *mishkan,* saying that the children of Naphtali wove (*potlim,* similar to the root letters of the word "Naphtali") the sacred curtains.

The midrash goes on to tell us that the curtain is woven on 72 cords. This is significant, for 72 is the number of letters in the secret name of the Divine. The tribe of Naphtali holds the secret of weaving the sacred into the works of human hands. Naphtali shows us how the spirit and the natural world can be woven together into a single fabric. Adar, month of flowing, is also the month of mingling heaven and earth.

In Adar, Naphtali reminds us that creativity is sacred, for through our creative lives we touch the spirit of the Creator. The tribe of Naphtali is our guide as we learn to play with words, objects, and music to make new things. In Adar, month of laughter, we discover our inner artist can be a source of delight.

Deborah, Singer of Naphtali

Deliverance ceased, ceased in Israel, till you arose, O Deborah, arose, O mother, in Israel!… Awake, awake, O Deborah, awake, awake, strike up the chant! Arise, O Barak, take your captives, O son of Abinoam!
—JUDGES 5:7–12

Moses, David, and Deborah sang, and the spirit of holiness rested on them.
—MEKHILTA BE-SHALLAH 6

A midrash tells us that Deborah, the prophet and judge, was descended from the tribe of Naphtali (*Genesis Rabbah* 98:17). Deborah's name means "bee" and makes us think of honey and the flowing sap of this season. She is called *eishet lappidot*, a "woman of flames," and is credited with making wicks for the sanctuary lamps—so she reminds us of the lights of Hanukkah as well. Deborah, the flame woman, is our guide through the entire winter season.

Deborah summons the warrior Barak to defend Israel from its oppressors, the Midianites. She also prophesies that the enemy general Sisera will be killed by a woman. Later, Jael the Kenite lures the general into her tent. Deborah witnesses the battle of Barak and sings a victory song afterward to praise the bravery of her people and of Jael. In it, she refers to herself as "mother, in Israel." She also describes the grief of the mother of Sisera when her son fails to return. Deborah's song has a double edge; it contains the triumph of the victor but also sympathy for the defeated.

Deborah's song is a place where the *Shekhinah* rests. This is perhaps because the song encompasses all of Deborah's feelings, from anger to pride to empathy. Like Adar, the song of Deborah prepares us for every aspect of the human condition.

A Time to Build Up, and a Time to Tear Down

Moses … anointed the Tabernacle and all that was in it, thus consecrating them.… Moses said to Aaron and his sons: You shall not go outside the entrance of the Tent of Meeting for seven days, until … your period of ordination is completed. For your ordination will require seven days. . . . You shall remain at the entrance of the Tent of Meeting day and night for seven days, keeping the charge of the Eternal.
—Leviticus 8:10,31,33,35

All the seven days of the priests' ordination, Moses put up the Tabernacle each morning and anointed it and made offerings and took it down the same day. One day later, on the first of Nisan, he set it up and anointed it and did not take it down.
—Numbers Rabbah 12:15

Today is the day Moses began to ordain the priests to serve in the *mishkan*. The commentators find a contradiction: The Torah says the *mishkan* was set up on the 1st of Nisan, the eighth day of ordination (eight being the beginning of a new cycle). How could the *mishkan* have been set up seven days earlier for the priest's ordination?

The solution told in one midrash is that Moses did put up the *mishkan* on the 23rd of Adar and the following days, yet each night he took it down again. Only on the 1st of Nisan did Moses put up the *mishkan* and leave it up. Yet this presents another problem: The priests were ordered to remain in the *mishkan* overnight. How could Moses be putting up the *mishkan* and taking it down around them?

The midrash hints part of the ordination process is witnessing the creation and destruction of sacred space. All moments of holiness are finite. All are eventually dismantled. They must be replaced with new sacred moments. The task of the priests is not to fix the sacred in place, but to witness this constant motion. We too are priests and priestesses watching as the *mishkan* is built and unbuilt around us. We too are witnesses to the cosmic dance.

Through a Glass Darkly

When Jacob saw that there were food rations to be had in Egypt, he said to his sons, "Why do you keep looking at one another? Now I hear," he went on, "that there are rations to be had in Egypt. Go down and procure rations for us there, that we may live and not die."
—GENESIS 42:1–2

From the day Joseph was stolen the holy spirit vanished from Jacob. His hearing was not hearing and his seeing was not seeing. Why does it say "shever" *[corn, food] rather than another suitable word? Rather,* "shever" *should be read* "sever" *[hope]. Jacob saw through a dark mirror that his hope was in Egypt.*
—GENESIS RABBAH 91:6

The month of Adar now begins to turn toward Nisan, month of Passover. Adar is a cloaked messenger, hinting at the freedom of the Exodus. One might even say Adar is a mirror in which we see Nisan and Passover dimly reflected.

At a time of famine, Jacob sends his sons to buy food in Egypt, where they will meet their brother Joseph in disguise as an Egyptian lord. Jacob knows none of this, yet we are told Jacob sees "in a dark mirror" that his hope lies in Egypt. The mirror is dark indeed, for Jacob does not see the future enslavement of his children in Egypt. No doubt if he did he would avoid the place. Yet Jacob's vision in that dark mirror is true—after the enslavement, the Israelites will come out of Egypt a nation. Jacob's children must descend in order to ascend.

At this point in the year, the harvest is not ensured. We see the future of the seeds through a dark mirror. Yet we know the descent into the soil will bear fruit in the end, just as the descent into Egypt bears fruit. Adar's mirror, like Jacob's dark glass, helps us see the end of the Passover journey.

The Nile's Blood

And the Eternal said to Moses, "Say to Aaron: Take your rod and hold out your arm over the waters of Egypt—its rivers, its canals, its ponds, all its bodies of water—that they may turn to blood; there shall be blood throughout the land of Egypt, even in vessels of wood and stone."
—Exodus 7:19

Why were the waters not stricken through Moses? The Holy One said, "The waters guarded you when you were cast into the Nile. It is not just that they should now be afflicted through you."
—Exodus Rabbah 9:10

The spring equinox, which often falls at the very end of Adar or the very beginning of Nisan, is reputed to be the day the water in the Nile turned to blood.[20] This is why, some say, medieval Jews avoided drawing water on the spring equinox—because there is a drop of blood in the water on that day (*Shulchan Arukh, Yoreh De'ah* 116:5). Remembering the plague on the Nile at this time reminds us of the coming Passover festival.

The hidden drop of blood in the waters may refer to the new life flowing in the rivers and streams at this time of year. As life struggles to emerge, we refrain, symbolically, from drinking the waters that are its home. The spring equinox is a day when we honor the birthings all around us. The drop of blood also reminds us of the birth of the Israelites, who leave Egypt to become a new people.

This interpretation is supported by a midrash telling of Moses and the Nile. Aaron is the one to turn the Nile into blood, the midrash explains, because Moses has a special relationship with the Nile's waters. Since the waters protected him as an infant, he may not harm them. So too we, who are sustained by water at birth and throughout our lives, must take special care to protect the waters of the world.

Announcing the New Moon

The Eternal said to Moses and Aaron in the land of Egypt: This month shall mark for you the beginning of the months; it shall be the first of the months of the year for you.
—Exodus 12:1–2

The Holy One said to Israel: "In the past, the calendar was in My hands . . . but now I give it into your hands. If you say yes, then yes, and if you say no, then no. This is what it means: 'This month shall be for you.'"
—Exodus Rabbah 15:2

During the last week of Adar, on the *Shabbat* before the month of Nisan begins (a day called Shabbat ha-Hodesh, or the Sabbath of the New Moon), Jews read an additional Torah portion announcing the arrival of Nisan. These verses of Torah describe the moment, just before the Exodus, when the Holy One gives to the Hebrew people their own calendar. The Israelites are becoming a nation, and a nation defines itself partly by how it structures time. For Israel to leave Egypt, the Hebrew people need their own way of understanding the seasons.

What does it mean: "This month shall be for you"? The midrash above implies: "This month shall be determined by you. Whereas in the past the seasons were determined by the laws of creation, now you will decree when months begin and end and when festivals fall. You will take upon yourself the ordering of the natural world. Through this, you will develop an identity separate from every other nation."

At this season, when we move into the half year of peoplehood and community, we reaffirm our right and ability to abide by our own calendar and to understand the seasons in accordance with our own unique sensibility as a people. By reaffirming this truth, we prepare ourselves to enter Nisan.

The Freeing of the King

In the thirty-seventh year of the exile of King Jehoiachin of Judah, on the twenty-seventh day of the twelfth month, King Evil-merodach of Babylon, in the year he became king, took note of King Jehoiachin of Judah and released him from prison. He spoke kindly to him, and gave him a throne above those of the other kings who were with him in Babylon. His prison garments were removed, and he received regular rations by the king's favor for the rest of his life.

—2 KINGS 25:27–29

There was a synagogue called Shaf veYativ in Nehardea: that was a place where the Shekhinah *stayed always, for Yechoniah [another name for Jehoiachin] and the exiles built it with stones they brought from Jerusalem.*

—RASHI ON BABYLONIAN TALMUD, ROSH HASHANAH 24B

At the very end of the second book of Kings, we hear how King Jehoiachin (a name meaning "The Divine will establish") receives favor from the king of Babylon and leaves prison. A legend related by the commentator Rashi reveals that the king then founds a synagogue built with stones from Jerusalem. Like the Hebrews in Egypt, Jehoiachin remains true to his culture even while in exile. This special synagogue, even in later talmudic times, is a place regarded as the abode of the *Shekhinah.*

It is no accident that the king is freed on the 27th of Adar, three days before the 1st of Nisan. As we have learned during the Purim season, three days is a sacred time period that represents descent leading to ascent. The freeing of King Jehoiachin from prison is connected to the freeing of the Hebrews from slavery in Egypt. The freeing of the king also represents the coming of spring and the new life flowing through the world. So too Jehoiachin's rise represents the rebirth of Israel. At the end of Adar, we celebrate the freedom we feel coursing through our spirits.[21]

The Seraphim

The Divine will cover you with wings; you will find refuge under the wings of the Eternal.
—Psalms 91:4

The Holy One created human beings, and opposite them created spirits and demons and set the fear of them in humans, and were it not for the compassionate actions of the Holy One, the human creatures could not stand a single hour before the demons and spirits. What action did the Holy One take to rectify the situation? The Holy One decreed that every spring equinox seraphim would raise their heads up high, and spread their wings over the human beings.
—Otzar Midrashim: Hashem Behohmah, Yasad Aretz 6

The spring equinox generally falls at the end of Adar or the beginning of Nisan. The *Otzar Midrashim* imagines that heavenly creatures rise at this moment in the year to defend human beings from what invisibly attacks them: their demons. Perhaps these demons are creatures from the spirit world, or perhaps they are the inner sufferings of people. The demons represent slavery of all kinds, while the seraphim represent freedom. The wings of the seraphim shelter humanity from its afflictions.

One of the meanings for the word "seraph," or holy angel, is "fire." The other meaning is "sap." We can see the angels of Nisan as glowing, enlivening sap flowing through the limbs of the world, healing the living so that they are not plagued by demons. The seraphim arrive with the rising sap of the trees and the blooming of the flowers. They bring with them Passover, the festival of escape and liberation. The seraphim are a symbol of what spring can do to move us forward into freedom.

The Circle of Life

Now Abraham was a hundred years old when Isaac was born to him. Sarah said, "The Divine has brought me laughter. Everyone who hears will laugh with me." And she added, "Who would have said to Abraham that Sarah would suckle children? Yet I have borne a son in his old age."
—GENESIS 21:5–7

Abraham issued a coin. What was his coin? It had an old man and an old woman on one side and a young man and a young woman on the other.
—GENESIS RABBAH 39:11

We began Adar with a coin: the half shekel donation to the Temple, announced to the Israelite nation in Adar and due by the 1st of Nisan. We end Adar with another coin: the turning coin that represents new life. Adar, the month of flowing and shifting, now shifts into the 1st of Nisan, the new year of the spring.

On Passover will fall the anniversary of the birth of Isaac, son of Abraham and Sarah (Babylonian Talmud, Rosh Hashanah 11a). As we learned on the 1st of Tishrei, six months ago, Abraham and Sarah had given up on the possibility of having children. Yet Sarah conceived on Rosh Hashanah, and now, at the opposite point of the calendar, she gives birth to her son, Isaac, or "laughter." As she gives birth, she comments that everyone around her laughs at the extraordinary events of her life.

A midrash tells how Abraham issued a coin with an old man and woman on one side and a young man and woman on the other. This coin may represent Abraham and Sarah and Isaac and Rebekah, one generation yielding to another. Or both sides may represent Abraham and Sarah, who are old, yet become young and fruitful again. The two half coins of Abraham and Sarah show us the circle of life: old age and youth working together to bring abundance into the world.

NOTES

1 Ari Elon, Naomi Mara Hyman, and Arthur Waskow, *Trees, Earth, and Torah: A Tu b'Shevat Anthology* (Jewish Publication Society, 2000), pp. 115–152.

2 Karen Bellenir, ed., *Religious Holidays and Calendars: An Encyclopedic Handbook* (Omnigraphics, 1998), pp. 217–218.

3 Ibid., p. 183.

4 "Spring Is Near, But the Traditional Welcoming Kites of Lahore Are Grounded," *New York Times*, March 11, 2006, A7.

5 Ibid., p. 195.

6 Ari Elon, Naomi Mara Hyman, and Arthur Waskow, *Trees, Earth, and Torah: A Tu b'Shevat Anthology* (Jewish Publication Society, 2000), pp. 115–152.

7 Priscilla Fishman, *Minor and Modern Festivals* (Leon Amiel Publishers, 1973), pp. 65–66.

8 Raphael Patai, *The Hebrew Goddess* (Wayne State University Press, 1978), pp. 34–53.

9 Debra Orenstein, "Parashat Beshalach/Tu b'Shevat" in *The Jewish Journal of Greater Los Angeles*, Feb. 6, 2004.

10 Quoted in Pricilla Fishman, *Minor and Modern Festivals* (Leon Amiel Publishers, 1973), p. 64.

11 David Rouach, *Imma, ou, Rites, coutumes, et croyances chez la femme juive en Afrique du Nord* (Maisonneuve & Larose, 1990), pp. 87–88. Quote translated by Jill Hammer.

12 A. Sztejn and G. Wejsman, eds., *Pinkas Sochaczew,* (Jerusalem, 1962), p. 696.

13 Arthur Green, *The Language of Truth: The Torah Commentary of the Sefat Emet, Rabbi Yehudah Leib Alter of Ger* (Jewish Publication Society, 1998), p. 49

14 Jill Hammer, "Vashti's Tale," in *Voices Israel* (1995), 83.

15 Diane Wolkstein and Samuel Noah Kramer, *Inanna, Queen of Heaven and Earth: Her Stories and Hymns from Sumer* (Harper and Row, 1983), pp. 66–67.

16 Tamara Cohen, "Esther," in *Praise Her Works: Conversations with Biblical Women,* edited by Penina Adelman, (Jewish Publication Society, 2005), p. 193.

17 Diana Wolkstein, and Samuel Noah Kramer, *Inanna, Queen of Heaven and Earth: Her Stories and Hymns from Sumer* (Harper & Row, 1983), p. 61.

18 Linda Zisquit, *Ritual Bath* (Broken Moon Press, 1993), pp. 42–43.

19 Louis Ginzberg, *Legends of the Jews* (Jewish Publication Society, 1938), vol. 1, p. 149.

20 Machzor Vitry, cited in Ginzberg, *Legends of the Jews*, supplement 14 (Jewish Publication Society, 1938), vol. 6, p. 204, note 109.

21 My thanks to Dr. Diane Sharon for her analysis of Jehoiachin as a symbol of the Israelites.

Adar II: Leap Year

Adar II, or Adar Bet, is the Hebrew leap month of twenty-nine days. It is sometimes also called "Ve'adar" (literally "and Adar"). It is inserted after the first month of Adar seven times every nineteen years. In years when it appears, Adar II falls after Adar I and before the spring month of Nisan. A year containing a second Adar is called *me'uberet*—pregnant—as if Adar II is like an embryo in the belly of the year, making the whole year larger and more complex.

The function of Adar II is to keep the Hebrew calendar in sync with both the sun and the moon. Since a 12-month lunar year is shorter than a solar year by several days, the leap month must be inserted in certain years. This makes the calendar's lunar year longer, so it catches up with the solar year. This strategic adjustment makes sure all the months fall in their proper seasons.

In years when Adar II falls, it is possible to use the Adar meditations twice. Or, one might instead meditate on the 22 letters of the Hebrew alphabet and the seven levels of being: *guf (body)*, *nefesh* (life force of the body), *ruach* (emotional being), *neshamah* (mind and memory), *yechidah* (spiritual self), *chayah* (soul-root), and the e*in sof* (the Infinite).

Another possibility: Since Adar II is a month that is usually hidden, use the month to meditate on "hidden" characters in your life: obscure biblical characters, angelic forces, people you wish to call to mind, or hidden aspects of your own soul.

The Bud

1 NISAN TO 14 IYAR

SEASON
Spring

WIND
The east

HALF OF THE YEAR
The sun

ELEMENT
Earth within air

GATE
The earth and sea

ANGEL
Uriel (revelation)

DIVINE FACE
Tiferet (compassion and balance)

The buds appear on the earth,
the time of singing has come,
and the voice of the dove is
heard in our land.

—Song of Songs 2:12

The fifth motion of the year is emerging. In some regions of the world, leaves lean out of branches, buds unfurl from their casings, and red seeps into the landscape. The word "Nisan" itself means "bud." In the Middle East and similar climates, spring is already in full bloom, and the first harvest is about to come in. Spring is the moment when the hard-earned strength of the winter pours itself into foliage and flower. The *Shekhinah* has opened a door somewhere and flung it open. The days of sun have begun.

It is at this light-filled time of year that Jews celebrate the festival of Passover and relive the going out from Egypt. From the bitter taste of slavery to the wonder of the parting sea, we enter the experience of sudden freedom. Houses undergo a thorough cleaning, and for a week we change our diet as if to remind us that liberty requires the willingness to change. It is we ourselves who must rush out of Egypt on the full moon of the month of Nisan, we who must pass the story to our children. Liberation happens to us not once, but each year at this season.

Outside, this is the season of air, when fresh winds blow through the world. Yet inwardly, we are in the season of earth, the season when we are most grounded. At Passover, Jews relearn who we are, what our task in the world is. We remember we are part of a people. Looking around us in the spring, we remember we are part of the tribe of life. This is a different kind of rebirth than the one at Rosh Hashanah; this is a birth that draws us out of ourselves.

The Omer, the 49-day period beginning on the second night of Passover, celebrates the journey of the sprouting grain (Leviticus 23:15–17). Our ancestors reaped a sheaf on the first day of the Omer and baked bread on the last day, the transformation of life into life. In Jewish mystical tradition, each day of the Omer connects us to a mystical attribute of the Divine. As Nisan and Iyar unfold, we travel through all 49 of these attributes, collecting a spiritual harvest that will ground and nourish us.

Other cultures around the world recall rebirth, freedom, and sustenance at this season. In spring, the Babylonians celebrated the triumph of the god Marduk over the sea goddess of chaos, Tiamat.[1] In summer, in the ancient Middle East, this was the time of the sacred wedding of Inanna.[2] Persephone, the Greek goddess of the underworld, returned to the earth at this time of year to rejoin with her mother, Demeter, the earth.[3] Europeans once celebrated Eostre at the spring equinox, honoring the goddess of spring. The name of that festival gave rise to the English word "Easter," the Christian celebration of the resurrection of divinity, which also falls at this time of year.[4] Nowruz, the Iranian holiday of the spring equinox, includes housecleaning (similar to Passover housecleaning), seed sprouting, and the welcoming of the spirits of ancestors. The Igbo people of Nigeria celebrate their new year in the springtime, hiding their children in their houses to make certain that the old year does not sweep them away as it departs.

In Nisan, the warming earth embraces the rain and sun. We receive the first commandment of the Torah: to consider this season the rebirth of time itself. Spring unfolds. We honor the Divine Presence as She buds into Her full glory.

The Indwelling

The New Moon of Nisan

In the first month of the second year, on the first of the month, the Tabernacle was set up. . . . When Moses finished the work, the cloud covered the Tent of Meeting, and the Divine Presence filled the Tabernacle.
—Exodus 40:17,33–34

The Tabernacle represents the whole world. The altar represents the earth. The sacrifices on the altar represent the fruits of the earth. The twelve loaves of showbread represent the twelve months. The two pillars represent the sun and the moon. The washbasin of the priests represents the sea.
—Midrash Tadshe 2

This new moon is one of the four new years of the Jewish calendar, the new year of months. A minority opinion in the Babylonian Talmud (Rosh Hashanah 11a) claims the world was created on the 1st of Nisan. The 1st of Nisan celebrates the moon, the seasons, and time itself.

On this day, the *Shekhinah* descends into the Tabernacle, the *mishkan*, for the first time. The Israelites have built a traveling shrine for God. Now, as the air grows fragrant and trees blossom, the *Shekhinah*, the tangible glory of God, descends into the shrine the Israelites have made—just as the presence of life descends into the earth and makes it green again. Within the *mishkan*, the *Shekhinah* is like a bird in a nest, nestling at the center of the world to warm and shelter it.

The first chapter of *Midrash Tadshe* imagines the *mishkan* as a microcosm of the whole world: sun, moon, sea, and land. By creating a model of the world and inviting the Divine into it, the Israelites declare they want to be vessels for the Divine Presence. As Nisan begins, we too remember our desire to become dwelling places for the *Shekhinah*.

Miriam's Well

The Israelites arrived in a body at the wilderness of Zin on the first new moon.... Miriam died there and was buried there. The community was without water, and they joined against Moses and Aaron.
—NUMBERS 20:1–2

She was the one we followed, who knew each of us by name. Healing rose from her touch as drink from the deep, as song from her throat. She was the well. In our hearts we called her not Miriam, bitter sea, but Mayim, water.
—BARBARA HOLENDER, "MIRIAM'S WELL"[5]

A miraculous well follows Miriam, Moses' sister, in the wilderness and lodges in front of the *mishkan*. Trees and sweet-smelling fruit grow near the well, and it is a place of healing and comfort (*Song of Songs Rabbah* 4:14; *Midrash Tanhuma, Be-shallah* 21–22).[5] The poet Barbara Holender imagines Miriam herself is so redolent of water that the people hear water in her voice and drink it from her footprints. Miriam, who watches by the Nile and dances by the Reed Sea, is the embodiment of water.

In Exodus 40:1, on the 1st of Nisan, Miriam dies.[6] Today, perhaps, would be her burial in the wilderness. In the Torah, just after Miriam dies, the people complain they have no water to drink. Rabbinic interpreters conclude the well dried up when Miriam died (*Song of Songs Rabbah* 4:14). Only after Moses goes into the wilderness to search for it does the well reappear.

But the well is not gone. The Babylonian Talmud (Shabbat 35a) tells us the well can be found to this day in the waters of the Sea of Galilee. The Shulchan Arukh (*Orach Chayyim* 299:10) teaches that every Saturday night Miriam's well moves through all the waters of the world, bringing healing to those who are ill and suffering. In modern times, some place a cup of fresh water on the seder table in honor of Miriam.[7]

The New Year of Kings

A new king arose over Egypt who did not know Joseph. And he said to his people, "Look, the Israelite people are much too numerous for us. Let us deal shrewdly with them that they may not increase."
—EXODUS 1:8–9

The first of Nisan is the new year for kings and festivals… . A king who arose on the twenty-ninth of Adar, the next day on the first of Nisan we count him as having reigned a year. If he arose on the first of Nisan, we do not count him as having reigned a year until the next Nisan.
—BABYLONIAN TALMUD, ROSH HASHANAH 2A

In ancient Israel, the 1st of Nisan was the date on which a Hebrew king was considered to have reigned another year, regardless of what date he became king. Why this date? Perhaps because of its association with Passover. Passover is the feast of liberty, and any ruling authority must learn the importance of freedom. In these first days after the new year of kings, we consider the implications of our own sovereignty.

In Nisan, every person has a chance to become new, just as the world around us is becoming new. We become sovereign over our lives, just as kings become sovereign anew on this day. We can use that fresh start with courage, or we can use it with fear and suspicion. The example of the men who became Kings of Israel shows that we must step into the season of budding with courage and awareness.

The Blessing of Work

People go out to their work,
to their labor until evening.
—Psalms 104:23

At the time Abraham was going through Aram Naharaim and Aram-Nahor, he saw the people eating and drinking and having fun. "May there not be a portion for me in this land!" he exclaimed. When he came to the Ladder of Tyre, and he saw the people busy with weeding at weeding time and hoeing at hoeing time, he exclaimed, "May there be a portion for me in this land!" The Holy One said to him, "To your seed I will give this land."
—Genesis Rabbah 39:8

For observant Jews, the early days of Nisan are days for Passover cleaning. In the two weeks before Passover, all leaven is removed from the house, the kitchen is scoured, and all the rooms are swept and wiped down. This spring cleaning has a spiritual purpose. Some say *hametz*, "leaven," represents all the crumbs of old habits and bad behavior we must remove from ourselves to be free. Passover cleaning is a physical symbol of an interior process of emergence.

As Abraham searches for his new land, he watches the inhabitants of the different lands through which he passes. When he sees people celebrating all the time, he is disturbed. Why? Because sustenance requires work. Those who are disconnected from the land that feeds them may easily lose their sense of gratitude and humility. When Abraham finds a land where people work—not excessively, but in the right ways at the right times—he desires to live in that land.

We benefit from the work we do: sustaining ourselves and our families, caring for children and others who need us, creating art, refining ourselves and bringing justice to the world. We should not be ashamed of work—work is a part of who we are. Freedom is not the absence of work, but the gift of working in meaningful ways.

The Bitter Herbs

The Egyptians ruthlessly imposed upon the Israelites the various labors that they made them perform. Ruthlessly they made life bitter for them with harsh labor at mortar and bricks and with all sorts of tasks in the field.
—EXODUS 1:13

What does it mean, "with all sorts of tasks in the field"? After they would do hard work with bricks and mortar, they would come home to rest in the evening. An Egyptian would come and say, "Go and get me a vegetable from the garden! Chop down this tree for me! Fill this barrel full of water for me!"
—MIDRASH TANHUMA, VA-YETSE 9

Midrash Tanhuma gives us a vivid picture of a slave: someone who cannot rest, who must say yes to every task, who must go on producing and serving until he or she drops. Meanwhile, by seeking to avoid all work, the Egyptians become enslaved to their need for slaves. They are ruled by their own cruel whims. Both slaves and masters are in need of redemption.

Imagine millions of slaves feverishly digging up millions of vegetable gardens in response to their masters' whims. Before long, there would be no gardens, and no one to tend the soil. Slavery by its nature harms everything. In the spring season, when we work to plant and to harvest, we need to be reminded not to enslave ourselves or others. The bitter herb we harvest for our seder plate teaches us the bad taste of slavery.

Nisan reveals the divine face known as *tiferet*, or "compassionate balance." Embodying *tiferet* means being true to your heart and being kind to others. When we bring *tiferet* into the world, we are not slaves and we enslave no one. We can rest and work in proper measure.

The Righteous Women, Part 1

The more they were oppressed, the more they increased and spread out.
—EXODUS 1:12

Because of the merit of righteous women, Israel was redeemed from Egypt. What did the women do? At the time they would go out to draw water, the Holy One would bring them little fishes in their pitchers, so that they drew half water and half fish. They would bring these to their husbands and boil for them one pot of hot water and one pot of fish. They would feed them, … give them water to drink, and take them out to the hills to lie with them, as it is said: "For those of you who lie among the hills…." (Ps. 68:14) When they became pregnant, they went home to their houses.
—EXODUS RABBAH 1:12

It is said the Exodus happened because of righteous women. A midrash tells us these women are righteous because even among the miseries of slavery, they go on seducing their husbands. One of the teachings of Passover is that love and creativity are stronger than the forces that seek to suppress them.

Spring is the time of fecundity, when new life is conceived. We see this abundance in a story from *Exodus Rabbah:* The women's pitchers fill up so thickly with fish there is barely room for water. And the women themselves are fertile, lying with their husbands on the earth to conceive new children. In spite of their enslavement, they know their life force cannot be imprisoned. The husbands respond to this seduction with affection and new hope.

Although these loving pairs are oppressed nearly to death, they still feel desire. They reveal the true meaning of the buds of Nisan—the deep persistence of life against all odds. The greens of the Passover seder remind us of the hills in which the Hebrews lay and those who chose to be lovers, not slaves.

The Righteous Women, Part 2

The Hebrew women are not like the Egyptian women; they are vigorous. Before the midwife comes to them, they have given birth.
—EXODUS 1:19

When the time came for them to give birth, they went and gave birth in the field.... The Holy One of Blessing sent an angel ... to clean and care for them.... The Divine then provided for them two round nipples, one of oil and the other of honey.... [The] Egyptians ... wanted to kill them, but a miracle was done ... and they were swallowed into the earth.... When they grew up, they came in flocks to their homes.... When the Divine was revealed at the sea, these children recognized the Divine first, as it is said: "This is my God."
—EXODUS RABBAH 1:12

Today's midrash echoes the miraculous flowering of spring. The Hebrew women give birth to their children under apple trees, as if the children themselves were apples. The earth suckles the children by divine command. When the Egyptians attack, the earth swallows the children, protects them from the iron blade of the plow, and pushes them forth like sprouted seeds. The boys and girls return to their homes like flocks of lambs, another symbol of spring fertility. Because they have been suckled by the Divine, these young ones are the first to recognize the Holy One when, as the sea parts, the people encounter the Infinite.

This is the season when Jews recite blessings over flowering trees. As we approach Passover, we may be surrounded by blooming fruit trees or other flowering plants. The *haroset*, traditionally made of apples and other fruits, reminds us of the fruit trees under which the Hebrew women gave birth. It is a visible sign of the blossoming Nisan brings.

In Service to Life

The king of Egypt spoke to the Hebrew midwives … saying, "When you deliver the Hebrew women, look at the birthstool: if it is a boy, kill him; if it is a girl, let her live." The midwives, fearing the Divine, did not do as the king of Egypt had told them; they let the boys live… . The Divine dealt well with the midwives; and the people multiplied….

—EXODUS 1:15–22

"They let the boys live." … It was not enough for them simply to disobey Pharaoh's command. Rather, they went further, and did good deeds on the children's behalf. If the families of the children were poor, the midwives would go to the houses of the rich and bring food and water to the poor women….

—EXODUS RABBAH 1:15

The midwives Shiphrah and Puah embody the spirit of Nisan, for they serve the emergence of life. The Bible relates that when Pharaoh orders Shiphrah and Puah to kill male Hebrew babies to reduce the Israelite population, the women refuse, even at the risk of their own lives. A midrash adds that they do not merely resist Pharaoh's order. They actively fight to save the lives of children by reducing the effects of their poverty. Shiphrah and Puah encounter life at its most fragile and act to save life whenever it is in their power.

In *Exodus Rabbah* (1:13), Shiphrah and Puah are considered to be identical with Jochebed and Miriam, the mother and sister of Moses. Others believe Shiphrah and Puah are righteous Egyptian women. Rabbi Lynn Gottlieb has imagined Shiphrah is the mother of Jochebed, and a number of contemporary midrashim have adopted this reading.[9] Either way, these women have earned their place at the seder. The roasted egg on the seder plate represents their commitment to life.

The Serpent and the Tree of Life

The Eternal said to Moses and Aaron, "When Pharaoh speaks to you and says 'Produce your marvel,' you shall say to Aaron, 'Take your rod and cast it down before Pharaoh. It shall turn into a serpent.'" So Moses and Aaron came before Pharaoh and did just as the Eternal had commanded: Aaron cast down his rod … and it became a serpent. Then Pharaoh … summoned the wise men and the sorcerers … and they did the same with their spells; each cast down his rod, and they turned into serpents. But Aaron's rod swallowed their rods.
—EXODUS 6:1,7,8–12

A great miracle was done with the rod.… The miracle was that after Aaron's snake had turned back into a rod, it still swallowed the other snakes.
—MIDRASH TANHUMA, VA-YERA 3

As a man of 80, Moses returns to Egypt and teams up with his brother, Aaron, to free the Hebrew slaves from Pharaoh. The Divine has given Moses and Aaron a mysterious staff to help them in their task. This staff, created at the dawn of time, has been passed down since the days of Adam. When Aaron throws this staff down before Pharaoh, it becomes a snake. Pharaoh is not impressed by this: He commands his magicians to turn their staffs into snakes as well.

If a snake swallows other snakes, this is simply the way of the world, the greater attacking the smaller. So, instead, the snake turns back into a staff and then swallows the other snakes. Pharaoh's snakes have not been vanquished by a greater might, they have been reabsorbed into the Tree of Life—for this is what the wooden staff represents. The Divine teaches Pharaoh not of despotic power but of the oneness of all life.

Pharaoh continues to receive this lesson about the power of the life force. The plagues bring down blood and beasts and insects on Egypt to show Pharaoh his vulnerability to nature and his dependence on the proper workings of the earth. The plagues illustrate that Egyptians can suffer as well as create suffering; they too are part of the earth and its inhabitants. Each plague Moses and Aaron bring holds the message that all life is one, but Pharaoh cannot yet hear it.

The Taking of the Lamb

Speak to the … community of Israel and say that on the tenth of this month each … shall take a lamb to a family … keep watch over it until the fourteenth day of this month, and all the … Israelites shall slaughter it at twilight. They shall take some of the blood and put it on the two doorposts … of the houses in which they are to eat it. They shall eat the flesh … with unleavened bread and bitter herbs. . . . And the blood on the houses … shall be a sign for you.

—Exodus 12:3, 6–8,13

"It shall be a sign for you," and not a sign for others. From here we learn that they daubed the blood only on the inside of the house.

—Rashi on Exodus 12:13

Today, the 10th of Nisan, is the day Israelites take a lamb into their households. They will slaughter the lamb on the 14th of the month as a Passover sacrifice to the Eternal. This lamb offering represents gratitude for safety: After all, as plagues of frogs, hail, and disease rain down on Egypt, the Israelites remain safe in their houses. The lamb's stay in the house also represents the Egyptians who have oppressed the Israelites. By slaughtering the lamb, the Israelites break the hold of Egyptian terror. The bone on the seder plate (some now use a beet as a vegetarian alternative) represents the sacrifice of the lamb.

The blood of the lamb must be daubed on the doorposts. It appears to be a protective substance, warding off the Angel of Death. Yet Rashi tells us this blood is not a sign to keep away outside dangers. The blood is a sign on the inside, reminding the Israelites of their own power. The blood is a warning of the violence and danger in the world but also a promise of our ability to come together as a community.

The Coming of Elijah

Behold, I will send the prophet Elijah to you before the coming of the awesome, fearful day of the Eternal. He shall turn the hearts of parents to children, and the hearts of children to their parents.
—MALACHI 3:23–24

Rabbi Yosi said "I once was traveling on the road, and I went into a ruin to pray, one of those left from the destruction of Jerusalem. Elijah the prophet came and guarded the door for me until I was finished."
—BABYLONIAN TALMUD, BERAKHOT 3A

The Sabbath before Passover, which falls around this time, is known as Shabbat ha-Gadol, the Great Sabbath. It is traditional for a rabbi to give a weighty sermon on this day, often focusing on the laws of Passover. The name "Shabbat ha-Gadol" comes from the words of the prophet Malachi, read on this Sabbath: "I will send the prophet Elijah to you before the coming of the great and terrible day of the Eternal."

Elijah, the stern prophet of the books of Kings, becomes a spiritual guide in the Talmud. Unanswerable legal questions are left for Elijah to decide, and he often visits perplexed Sages to advise them (Babylonian Talmud, Avodah Zarah 36a; Babylonian Talmud, Menachot 45a). He also comes to every circumcision, every *Havdalah* (end of Sabbath) ceremony, and every Passover seder. Elijah sometimes appears to human beings as a beggar and does good deeds for them. In the midrash for today, Elijah accompanies a Sage on his journey and guards him as he prays.

On Passover, a special cup is set out for Elijah, and we open the door for him. What does the prophet Malachi mean when he says Elijah will turn the hearts of parents to children and the hearts of children to parents? It means Elijah will connect the generations across time, so that none is forgotten.

The Plague of Darkness

Then the Eternal said to Moses: "Hold out your arm toward the sky that there may be darkness upon the land of Egypt, a darkness that can be touched." Moses held out his arm toward the sky and thick darkness descended on all the land of Egypt for three days. People could not see one another, and for three days no one could get up from where he was, but all the Israelites enjoyed light in their dwellings.
—EXODUS 10:21–23

Where did the darkness come from? … Rabbi Judah said: From the darkness above. Rabbi Nehemiah said: From the darkness below. Rabbi Abdimi of Haifa said: The darkness was doubled and doubled again … yet wherever a Jew entered, light entered with that person.
—EXODUS RABBAH 14:2–3

We have already encountered the idea that three days is a symbol of descent into darkness. Three days before Passover, we remember the three days of darkness upon Egypt. During these three days of darkness, everything in Egypt stops. The mechanisms of slavery grind to a halt.

A midrash in *Exodus Rabbah* claims this is no ordinary darkness. It emerges from the voids of space, the treasuries of heaven, or the depths of the underworld. This is a darkness of the spirit, and traveling through such darkness is an initiation—it foreshadows change. As the Egyptians sit in darkness, they can no longer see the differences between themselves and the Hebrews. No one is looking at them and shaming them for their actions—even Pharaoh is invisible to others. Perhaps a few Egyptian hearts begin to open. The Hebrews, meanwhile, blessed with a light that follows them everywhere, learn to open themselves and trust.

In Nisan, in the season of earth within air, we remember the earth wrapped in darkness. This darkness is not just a plague; it teaches us to let down our boundaries. Under cover of night, without ordinary vision, we listen to one another's voices.

The Search for Leaven

Seven days you shall eat unleavened bread, and on the seventh day there shall be a festival to the Eternal. Throughout the seven days unleavened bread shall be eaten; no leavened bread shall be found with you, and no leaven shall be found in all your territory.
—Exodus 13:6–7

We do not search for hametz *before Pesach by the light of the moon or by the light of the sun, but rather we light candles to search for the* hametz. *In the same way, the Holy One will one day search Jerusalem with a candle … to root out the evil inclination.*
—Pesikta Rabbati 8:3

Tonight, just at the end of the 13th of Nisan is the search for leaven. Many Jews who observe Passover go through their houses, their way lit only by a candle, to scrape up little pieces of bread or cereal that have been left around the house. This ritual, called *bedikat hametz*, marks the end of the housecleaning for Passover and signals the beginning of the eight days when only matzah and other unleavened foods may be eaten.

Many commentators see yeast as a symbol of the evil inclination that we must remove from our lives.[10] Yeast also represents what is old, as yeast starters are passed down from generation to generation. We take the yeast out of our houses at Passover in the same way we take old habits out of our lives at Rosh Hashanah—to make room for something new. Matzah, bread made without yeast, symbolizes the freshness and unpredictability of the spring. The Israelites leave Egypt carrying matzah on their backs to show they are leaving the past behind. At the end of Passover, we will allow our bread to rise again, this time with new yeast and with a new future ahead.

The Tenth Plague

Fast of the Firstborn

Moses said, "Thus says the Eternal: Toward midnight I will go forth among the Egyptians, and every first-born in the land of Egypt shall die. And there shall be a loud cry in Egypt such as has never been or will ever be again."
—EXODUS 11:4–6

Pharaoh was in darkness, he and his servants, and there was a great cry through all Egypt.… . Pharaoh went running … through every marketplace, calling: "Where is Moses? Where does he live?" The Israelite children laughed at him and said: "Pharaoh! Where are you going?" He said; "I am seeking Moses!" The children would say, "Here he lives!" … and trick him, until finally Pharaoh stood before Moses and said: "Get up and get out from among my people."
—MIDRASH TANHUMA (BUBER), BO 19

Today, the day before Passover, some Jews observe the fast of the firstborn. Firstborn men (in some communities, all firstborn adults) have an obligation to fast in memory of the firstborn Egyptians slain in Egypt during the last of the Ten Plagues.

During this plague, legend tells, the Angel of Death moves through Egypt, killing all the firstborn. This final plague, terrifying in its effect, convinces Pharaoh to release his slaves. A midrash imagines a nightmare scene in which Pharaoh, like a dreamer who cannot wake up, tries to find Moses to tell him the Hebrews are free. Hebrew children misdirect him, and he roams the alleys of the royal city calling, "Moses, Moses," seeking the man he was only too willing to ignore days before.

Pharaoh has been living in a dream. He has believed he can escape suffering and cast it onto the Hebrew slaves. Now, having lost his own firstborn child, he sees Israelite children shouting at him. It is almost as if they were ghosts of the children he has killed. In his nightmare, Pharaoh dimly dreams the truth of his responsibility. During the fast of the firstborn, we dream this truth with Pharaoh.

The Telling

First Day of Passover

You shall explain to your child on that day, "It is because of what the Eternal did for me when I went free from Egypt." And this shall serve you as a sign upon your hand and as a reminder on your forehead … that with a mighty hand the Eternal freed you from Egypt.
—Exodus 13:8

Rabban Gamliel said: You must speak of three things to fulfill your obligation of telling: the Passover sacrifice, matzah, and maror. *In every generation, … a person must see himself or herself as if he or she went out of Egypt, as it says: "You shall explain to your child on that day: 'It is because of what the Eternal did for me.'"*
—Babylonian Talmud, Pesachim 116b

Today, according to the book of Exodus, the Israelites leave the slave huts of Egypt and begin walking toward the wilderness. We celebrate this event with a ritual called a seder. The Passover seder is the quintessential springtime ritual. In the season when all grows anew, Jews clean their houses, then gather around a festive meal to tell the tale of their ancestors—not as if it were history but as if it were their own story. Slavery and redemption come alive through midrash, invention, discussion, and play. The richly symbolic food on the table helps us embody our ancestors as they receive their freedom.

The Passover seder is most probably based on the Greek symposium, a meal at which learned men gathered to discuss philosophy.[11] Yet the seder is different. It gathers together the family, and it invites all generations to be present, from the Hebrew slaves to the prophet Elijah and the prophetess Miriam. At the seder, one does not talk about redemption; one lives redemption. The seder is a ritual of the renewal of life through sacred story. In the *Sefer Yetzirah,* Nisan is the month of speech. In the Jewish calendar, not only flowers emerge in the spring but words blossom as well.

The Counting of the Omer

Second Day of Passover

When you enter the land that I am giving to you and you reap its harvest, you shall bring the first sheaf of your harvest to the priest. … And from the day on which you bring the sheaf of elevation offering … you shall count off seven weeks. They must be complete: you must count until the day after the seventh week—fifty days; then you shall bring an offering of new grain to the Eternal.
—LEVITICUS 23:9,15–16

[On the second night of Passover] all the nearby villages would gather, so that the sheaf would be reaped with great pomp. The reaper would ask: "Shall I reap?" And they would respond: "Yes!" Three times the reaper would ask, and three times they would answer.
—BABYLONIAN TALMUD, MENACHOT 64B

The second seder, which Jews in the Diaspora celebrate on the second day of Passover, coincides with the beginning of the counting of the Omer. On this day, in temple times, the first barley sheaf would be cut and offered to the Divine in gratitude for the coming harvest. The people counted 49 days—called the counting of the Omer—and on the day after, they celebrated the holiday of Shavuot and brought two loaves of new grain as a gift to the Eternal.

Levi, son of Leah and Jacob, was born today. The ancestor of the priests is born on the day the barley harvest begins, showing that the true meaning of priesthood is service.

In later days, when the Temple no longer stood, Jews developed the practice of simply counting the 49 days between Passover and Shavuot. Jewish mystics believe each of these days represents a unique combination of seven divine attributes.[12] The first week of the Omer represents *hesed*, or "love." Today, the first day of the Omer, represents *hesed shebehesed*, or "love within love." The reaping of the barley and the sustaining of the people through the land's nourishment do indeed signify the essence of love.

Four Children

Third Day of Passover

When, in time to come, your children shall ask you, "What mean the decrees … that the Eternal … has enjoined upon you?" … you shall say to your children, "We were slaves … in Egypt and the Eternal freed us … with a mighty hand."
—Deuteronomy 6:20–21

The Bible speaks of four children: one wise, one wicked, one simple, and one who does not know how to ask. What does the wise child say? "What mean the … laws … that the Eternal … has enjoined upon you?" What does the wicked child say? "What do you mean by this rite?" What does the simple child say? "What does this mean?" And … the one who does not know how to ask? For that child, you must begin the story.
—Passover Haggadah

One of the powerful moments of the Passover seder is the discussion of the four children. Four times in the Torah, one is told to tell one's child about the Exodus, but each time the child's words and the parent's response are slightly different. In these verses, the tradition sees four archetypal children, reminding us that each of us learns differently. Some of us are guided by information while others are guided by feelings. Some of us long for order while others are rebellious. Some are quiet, waiting for an ear to listen to us. Like trees that need water and soil in different measure to bud, we too have unique needs. We discover our freedom as a people partly by understanding ourselves as individuals.

In Jewish mysticism, the second day of the Omer represents *gevurah shebehesed*, "strength or severity within love." In the Kabbalah, *gevurah* and *hesed* are opposites: one represents boundaries and limitations, whereas the other represents limitlessness. Yet today, we imagine the strength of adults loving and supporting children and helping them grow. Today we remember that even when we are different from one another—in attributes or age—we can nourish one another's freedom.

The Song of Songs

Fourth Day of Passover

My beloved spoke thus to me: "Arise, my darling; my fair one, come away! For now the winter is past, the rains are over and gone. The blossoms have appeared in the land, the time of pruning has come; the song of the turtledove is heard in our land."
—Song of Songs 2:10–12

The winter is over: this "winter" is the four hundred years of slavery decreed upon our ancestors. The rain is over and gone: this refers to slavery. … The buds appear on earth: what does this signify? This is Moses and Aaron. The time of pruning has come: It is time for Egypt to be pruned!
—Pesikta Rabbati 15:10

On the Sabbath of Passover, Jews read the Song of Songs. This biblical love song describes a loving couple surrounded by images of nature. The song is said to represent ideal human love or the courtship between Israel and the Divine or the love between the male and the female aspects of the Deity. Its images of figs and grapevine blossoms and gazelles evoke the spring, even as they evoke the "elopement" of Israel and the Divine during the Exodus.

Pesikta Rabbati compares the years of Israelite slavery to the winter, and the rains of autumn to slavery. The buds of Nisan are the redeemers of the people who arise to lead them into a new flowering. The Exodus, the birth of the people, and the spring, the birth of nature, flow together into an image of flowers opening in the sun. It is during Passover that Jews stop praying for rain and begin to pray for the gentle waters of the dew.

Today is the third day of the Omer—*tiferet shebehesed*. The word "*hesed*" is "love," and "*tiferet*" can mean "beauty, balance, compassion," or the "truth of the heart." The beauty of love is clearly the mood of the Song of Songs.

The Gathering of the Bones

Fifth Day of Passover

So Joseph made the children of Israel swear, saying: "When the Divine has taken notice of you, you shall carry up my bones from here." Joseph died at the age of one hundred and ten years, and he was … placed in a coffin in Egypt.
—GENESIS 50:25–26

The old woman began walking … quickly … and Moses followed behind. After a short while he realized that they were heading … towards the banks of the Nile. When they arrived, Serach waited until Moses stood at her side. … Serach said to Moses. "My voice is weak with age. And … your speech heavy. … [If] I help you find the words, you can make Joseph hear you. … The righteous of Israel are never deaf to the cries of their people.…
—MARC BREGMAN, "SERACH: THE RECOVERY OF JOSEPH'S BONES"[13]

For the Israelites to cross the sea and leave Egypt, they must fulfill a promise. Generations ago, their ancestors told Joseph they would carry his bones to Canaan. Yet, legend says, the people do not know where Joseph's bones lie. Only Serach daughter of Asher, an old woman, remembers where Joseph's coffin was sunk in the Nile. Her grandfather Jacob blessed her with extraordinarily long life, for she was the one who told him his son Joseph was alive while playing her harp.[14] Serach leads Moses to the place of Joseph's bones. Moses calls out to Joseph to arise, saying that the *Shekhinah* is waiting for him. The coffin with Joseph's bones gently floats to the surface (*Midrash Tanhuma, Be-shallah* 2).

Serach, like Passover itself, is a link among generations. Like the tree that sprouts anew in spring, she lives into the future so she can go on telling the truth of the past. One tale has it that she comes to a talmudic study house to reveal what the sea looked like as it parted (*Mekhilta Be-shallah, Petichta*). Today, the fourth day of the Omer, is linked to *netzach shebehesed:* "persistence that rises out of love," and we remember Serach's persistent voice on this day.

The Courage of Nahshon

Sixth Day of Passover

The Eternal said to Moses: "Why do you cry out to me? Tell the Israelites to go forward. Lift your rod and hold out your arm over the sea and split it, so that the Israelites may march into the sea on dry ground."
—Exodus 14:15–16

One tribe said, "I will not go first into the Sea," and another tribe said, "I will not go first into the sea." Nahshon ben Amminadab arose and went into the sea first.
—Babylonian Talmud, Sotah 37a

The Israelites flee Egypt, but Pharaoh, having regained his stubbornness, pursues them with an army. Today, the army catches up with them. As the Israelites reach the shore of the sea, we remember the moment the sea splits to allow the Israelites to pass through to the wilderness. In legend, the Israelites stand on the shore of the sea bickering about who should go in first. No one is willing to risk drowning to escape from the Egyptians.

Nahshon, son of Amminadab, is a prince of the tribe of Judah. While others argue, he leaps into the water. Because of his courage, the waters begin to part. The rest of the people follow Nahshon, crossing the Sea of Reeds to freedom. As a reward, Nahshon later becomes the first prince to offer gifts for the *mishkan*, the divine dwelling place. Nahshon reminds us that at Passover, the gate of the sea opens: the gate to time and eternity.

This fifth day of the Omer is *hod shebehesed*, the "glory of love" or the "prophecy of love." Nahshon, though his courage, shows others how to believe in the possibility of redemption. Like the buds that pick their time to open, Nahshon chooses the right moment to act. He too is a spirit of spring, teaching us to have courage as we burst outward into freedom.

The Songs of Angels

Seventh Day of Passover

The waters were split, and the Israelites went into the sea on dry ground, with the waters forming a wall for them on their right and on their left. The Egyptians came in pursuit after them into the sea, all of Pharaoh's horses, chariots, and horsemen. … Then the Eternal said to Moses, "Hold out your arm over the sea, that the waters may come back upon the Egyptians and upon their chariots and upon their horsemen." Moses held out his arm over the sea, and at daybreak the sea returned to its normal state.
—EXODUS 14:21–23,26–27

The angels of the heavenly court wanted to sing, but the Holy One said "My creatures are drowning in the sea and you want to sing songs?"
—BABYLONIAN TALMUD, MEGILLAH 10B

At Passover, the gate of the sea opens. We see the Divine not in the heavens or the earth, but in the waves. Today, according to Jewish tradition, the Israelites enter the Sea of Reeds and cross through an oceanic passage into their new life as a people. Nisan is a season of rebirth, and the parting of the sea is the birth of a new people. Just as the soil parts wondrously to allow the tiny shoot to emerge, the sea parts to let the new tendrils of Israelite nationhood emerge into the wilderness. As the people gather on the sea's far side, they sing a song of wonder and deliverance. Moses declaims poetry. Miriam dances. It is a moment of supreme joy.

In a well-known midrash, the angels are so delighted by the rescue of the Hebrews they want to sing praises. The Holy One instead commands the angels to sit silently. While the Israelites are entitled to be glad they are free of their oppressors, the angels must remember that the Egyptians too are creatures of the Holy One. Their death is a cause for sadness, not rejoicing.

Today, the sixth day of the Omer, is *yesod shebehesed:* "connection that rises out of love." The song at the sea teaches gratitude for our triumphs, but the angels' silence teaches us compassion even for our adversaries.

The Basket

Eighth Day of Passover

When [Moses' mother] could hide him no longer, she got a wicker basket for him and caulked it with bitumen and pitch. She put the child into it and placed it among the reeds by the bank of the Nile. And his sister stationed herself at a distance, to learn what would befall him.
—Exodus 2:3–4

She stood rocked by the spell
as by white steps of waves.
She leaned over the baby as
a vow, as command, as
redemption, as fate.
—Yocheved bat Miriam, "Miriam"[15]

This day of Passover is observed only in the Diaspora. Today we hearken back to the moment when a Hebrew slave and the daughter of a Pharaoh colluded to save Moses' life. Passover celebrates not only the rescue of a people but the saving of a single life.

In the Babylonian Talmud (Sotah 12b), on the 21st of Nisan, long before the Exodus, Pharaoh's daughter finds Moses floating on the Nile in a basket. Miriam bravely approaches her, offering to find a Hebrew wet nurse for the child. Pharaoh's daughter agrees, and so Moses' mother receives her child back into her arms.

In the poem by Israeli poet Yocheved bat Miriam, the young Miriam stands by the river. She leans over the basket where the child Moses floats, praying, willing that he be rescued. Her act of waiting is like a spell conjuring Moses to live. The moment by the Nile contains the whole Exodus in miniature: the drawing out of life through water.

Moses' name means "drawn out of the water," just as all life on earth comes from the water. Moses floating in his basket could be a single-celled organism. He represents all life, all potential for growth. Passover celebrates the Exodus; but underneath, it is a celebration of survival. Today is the seventh day of the Omer, and it truly is *malkhut shebehesed*, "the sovereignty of love."

Maimouna

The Divine further said to Abraham: "As for you, you and your offspring to come throughout the ages shall keep My covenant. Such shall be the covenant between Me and your offspring to follow which you shall keep; every male among you shall be circumcised. … And throughout the generations, every male among you shall be circumcised at the age of eight days."
—GENESIS 17:9–10,12

Isaac was born on Passover.
—ROSH HASHANAH 11A

For North African Jewry, the night after Passover is a celebration known as Maimouna. Some say it marks the yahrzeit of the father of Maimonides, while others say it means "protected by God" and is a time to offer prayers for the crops. Various fertility rituals are associated with Maimouna, from the Moroccan custom of displaying live fish in bowls (fish represent fertility) to the Libyan custom of baking a challah with an egg in the center.[16]

While there are no sources to indicate this, Maimouna rather neatly falls the evening after the anniversary of Isaac's circumcision. The Talmud suggests Isaac, the son of Abraham and Sarah, was born on Passover, and the last day of Passover would have been his circumcision. While the Bible does not record a feast in honor of Isaac's circumcision, Maimouna falls at the time when such a celebration would have occurred.

Circumcision, an ancient, difficult, and even incomprehensible rite, may well be a mark dedicating the fertility of Jewish men to the Divine. In spring, when fertility is crucial, we remember the first Jewish male child and the covenant with Abraham. Circumcision represents both the love within each generation and the enduring strength of the covenant.

The Life of Abel

The man knew his wife Eve and she conceived and bore Cain, saying: "I have gained a male child with the help of the Eternal." She then bore his brother Abel. Abel became a keeper of sheep, and Cain became a tiller of the ground. … When they were in the field, Cain set upon his brother Abel and killed him.
—GENESIS 4:1–2,8

Rabbi Eliezer and Rabbi Joshua disagree. Rabbi Eliezer says: The world was created in Tishrei. Rabbi Joshua says: In Nisan. He who says in Tishrei holds that Abel lived from Sukkot until Hanukkah. He who says in Nisan holds that Abel lived from Passover until Shavuot. In either case, all agree Abel was only in the world for fifty days.
—GENESIS RABBAH 22:4

Today the Israelites arrive at Marah, a place of bitter waters (*Seder Olam Rabbah* 5:2). We are now just over a week into the counting of the Omer. One ancient midrash cites Rabbi Joshua, who believes the 49 days of the Omer are the days of Abel's life. Abel is a shepherd, the second son of Adam and Eve. His brother, Cain, is a farmer. When the Divine prefers Abel's offering of animals to Cain's offering of grain, Cain becomes angry. He lures his brother into the field and kills him.

Rabbi Joshua imagines Abel has a mythically short life: Like a frail blossom, he is born, grows up, and dies in the course of seven weeks. Abel's name means "breath" or "emptiness." By viewing the days of the Omer as the days of Abel's life, we remind ourselves how fragile we are. We must make every day count, just as we count the days of the Omer, for we do not know how long we have. During the Omer, we turn toward the sea that represents the element of time and reflect on its power over us—and on our power over it.

Today is the ninth day of the Omer: *gevurah shebegevurah*, or "limits within limits." Abel functions within severe limits on his lifespan, yet his life is precious. We look at Abel and learn to number our days.

The Apple Blossoms

Like an apple tree among the trees of the forest, so is my beloved among the youths.
—Song of Songs 2:3

The apple tree is the Holy One of Blessing, more delightful and colorful than all other trees.
—Zohar I:85b

In this season, in many climates, apple trees fill with fragrant white flowers. The ancient legends of the Jews associated apple trees with Nisan and ordained that a special blessing be said over flowering trees in this month.[17] These trees are one of the most beautiful outward signs of spring. Today, the day the Israelites arrived at the tree-filled wilderness refuge of Elim (Ibn Ezra on Exodus 15:27), is a good moment to stop and consider the trees.

In Jewish mysticism, apple trees have a hidden meaning as well. In the Zohar (II:83b), apple trees can represent the Holy One, a compassionate masculine face of God, and the "holy apple orchard" is a name for the *Shekhinah,* the divine feminine. The apple blossoms, in their multiplicity and fecundity, remind us of the multiple names and faces we have for the Divine.

Today is the 10th day of the Omer, *tiferet shebegevurah*, which can be translated as "beauty within severity." The apple blossoms, which last for just a short time before falling, are the epitome of ephemeral beauty. Their beauty is limited by mortality, as is ours. Yet they seem even more beautiful because of this. The buds are a frail and short-lived house for the Divine, but a glorious one.

The Death of Joshua

Joshua son of Nun, the servant of the Eternal, died at the age of one hundred and ten years. They buried him on his own property, at Timnath-serah in the hill country of Ephraim.
—Joshua 24:29–30

Israel failed in doing loving-kindness to Joshua after his death. … The Land of Israel had been divided, and each piece of it was too much loved by its inhabitants. This one was involved with his field, and that one with her vineyard, and that one with his olive trees. Because of this, the Divine wanted to overthrow the world.
—Ecclesiastes Rabbah 7:4

Today, according to the ancient book *Megillat Ta'anit*, Joshua dies. This day was once commemorated as a minor fast day. Joshua, Moses' successor, is the leader with whom the Israelites cross the Jordan and settle in the land of Israel. In a way, his death is the culmination of the Exodus.

Moses' death is full of pathos: He desires the Land of Israel, yet may not enter. Joshua, on the other hand, is buried without fuss on his own property. We do not hear about his fight with the Angel of Death. The people do not mourn him for 30 days. A midrash claims the people do not mourn Joshua at all, because, it being springtime, each person is involved in tilling the land. Joshua's quiet death is in deep contrast to his life. A soldier who killed many, he dies at home in bed, almost unnoticed.

The Divine is angry at the people for not mourning Joshua. The message is clear: People are more important than any piece of land, even if it is growing season. This message, not fully realized by Joshua during his life, is finally transmitted through his death.

Today is the 11th day of the Omer, *netzach shebegevurah*, the "persistence of strength." It makes sense that we honor Joshua, the successor of Moses, on this day.

Eternal Mourning

Holocaust Memorial Day[18]

Now when Pharaoh let the people go, the Divine did not lead them [nacham] *by way of the land of the Philistines, although it was nearer, for the Divine said, "The people may have a change of heart when they see war, and return to Egypt." So the Divine led the people roundabout.*
—Exodus 13:17–18

"The Divine did not lead them" means "The Divine was not comforted." This is similar to a king whose children were captured and enslaved, and some of them died. The king went and saved the ones that were left. He rejoiced because of the children he had saved, but could not be comforted for those who had died.
—Exodus Rabbah 20:13

The 27th of Nisan is the date to honor all those who perished in the Holocaust. This date does not commemorate a specific event, though it is near the time when the Warsaw uprising began. It falls just after Passover, at a season when slavery ends and new life begins, as a sign that even in spring we do not leave the dead behind. It is the 12th day of the Omer: *hod shebegevurah*: the "receiving of brokenness."

The author of the midrash from *Exodus Rabbah* attempts to cope with grief. Rather than celebrating the end of slavery, this text dwells on the inconsolable sadness of the Infinite for those Hebrews who died in Egypt. This midrash does not and cannot explain why suffering happens or why the Divine does not rescue the oppressed. Indeed, the Holy One in the midrash is all too human, arriving much too late to save the murdered. This legend has no explanation for tragedy; rather, it expresses the feeling that the Eternal too grieves for what is lost. As Jews honor the memories of Holocaust victims and pledge to end unjust suffering, this midrash stands as a witness to the memory of those who died.

I Am First and I Am Last

Now Bezalel, son of Uri son of Hur, of the tribe of Judah, had made all that the Eternal had commanded Moses; at his side was Oholiab son of Ahisamach, of the tribe of Dan, carver and designer, and embroiderer in blue, purple, and crimson yarns….
—EXODUS 38:22–23

There is no greater tribe than Judah and none more lowly than Dan … of whom it is said: the sons of Dan: Hushim [he had only one tribal clan to his name]. The Holy One said: "Let Judah … partner with Dan, so that no one will despise him or lord it over him, for great and small are equal before the Omnipresent One. Bezalel came from Judah and Oholiab from Dan, yet one partnered with the other.
—EXODUS RABBAH 40:4

Nisan, according to the *Sefer Yetzirah* (5:2), is the month of Judah, the tribe of royalty. Naturally, the powerful Judah is assigned one of the most engaging and desirable months. Yet we find that in the work of the *mishkan*, Judah shares its power with the least of the tribes.

Bezalel and Oholiab are the chief artists of the *mishkan*. Bezalel comes from the prestigious tribe of Judah, while Oholiab comes from the small and humble tribe of Dan. Both work side by side to create the wonders of the *Shekhinah*'s dwelling place. The designs of Bezalel and Oholiab enhance one another. They teach us how great artistry and vision are not limited to one social class or condition.

The Holy One chose Bezalel and Oholiab from tribes with opposite social status. This is an important lesson in Nisan, a month of *tiferet* (balance). As a community, we may assign status or prestige, but we are still equal. Today is the 13th day of the Omer: *yesod shebegevurah*, the "foundation of strength." When we rely equally on the gifts of all, we build strength together.

The Strength of the Midwife

Has any people heard the voice of a god speaking out of a fire, as you have, and survived? Or has any god ventured to go and take for himself one nation from the midst of another by prodigious acts?
—DEUTERONOMY 4:33–34

Like one who pulls a fetus from the womb of a mother animal, the Divine took Israel out of Egypt.
—YALKUT SHIMONI 828

Nisan is the month of birth; and, as the midrashic collection *Yalkut Shimoni* notes, the Exodus is the almost literal birth of the people. The Divine is like a midwife, drawing the new infant from the depths. Yet the Divine is also a mother, pushing the people forth from Her womb.

How so? Biblical law ordains that a new mother stay away from the public sanctuary for 33 days in the case of a male child and 66 days in the case of a female child (Leviticus 12:3–5). Exactly halfway between these two numbers is the number "49." The counting of the 49 days of the Omer is the ritual seclusion of the Divine with Her (male and female) infant Israel in the wilderness. Sinai is the *mishkan*, the sanctuary, where both mother and child enter when their protective time together has come to an end.

Today, in one legend, is the day Jericho's walls fall down. The "falling of the walls" is an image of violence but also an image of birth. It reminds us of the moment Israel passes through the "walls" of Egypt to be reborn. This is the 14th day of the Omer, *malkhut shebegevurah*, which may be translated as "the *Shekhinah* of strength." On this day, we remember the birth of Israel out of Egypt and honor the Presence who delivers us from narrow places.

The Scrolls of Nisan

New Moon of Iyar

Pharaoh charged the taskmasters and foremen of the people, saying: "You shall no longer provide the people with straw for making bricks … let them go and gather straw for themselves. … Let heavier work be laid upon the men; let them keep at it and not pay attention to deceitful promises.
—Exodus 5:6–9

The people had in their hands scrolls with which they would delight each Sabbath, and these scrolls promised that one day the Holy One of Blessing would redeem them. Because they rested in this way each Sabbath, Pharaoh demanded their work be increased … so they would not be playing with these scrolls and reviving themselves every week.
—Exodus Rabbah 5:18

The *Shekhinah* may choose to reside in a sanctuary, as we learned on the 1st of Nisan. Yet the *Shekhinah,* for most of Jewish history, has resided in Torah, a portable shrine of words. During the 49 days between the festival of Passover and the festival of Shavuot is a journey from grain to bread: a journey from the raw material of a freed people to the refined unity of a nation with a vision. Torah, with all of its multiple interpretations, is that vision.

A midrash suggests the extraordinary idea that before Torah there is Torah. The slaves in Egypt have scrolls promising them redemption, a kind of proto-Torah. Pharaoh realizes the liberating effect this text has on the slaves and tries to take it away from them. Yet this proto-Torah is destined to blossom into a new Torah when the people reach Mount Sinai. The Torah will go on budding in every generation, producing new commentaries, ideas, and promises of redemption. On this 15th day of the Omer, *hesed shebetiferet*, or "love of truth," we go on searching for our people's truth.

I Am Adonai Your Healer

New Moon of Iyar

If you will heed the Eternal your God diligently, doing what is upright in the sight of the Eternal … then I will not bring upon you any of the diseases that I brought upon the Egyptians, for I am Adonai your healer.
—EXODUS 15:26–27

At this season the earth yields her produce and strengthens all the trees and plants. Fruits ripen, and all healing plants increase in power, for the earth puts strength into them at this time. … This is why the Hebrew letters of Iyar are the same as the first letters of the words "Ani Adonai Rofecha" *(I am Adonai your healer).*
—NACHMAN OF BRATZLAV, LIKUTEI MOHARAN I:277

Today is the new moon of the month of Iyar. Nachman of Bratzlav, the Hasidic master, notes that the letters of the word "Iyar" stand for the letters of the phrase "*ani adonai rofecha*," or "I am Adonai your healer." He recommended that healing herbs be harvested this month, when the earth is pouring strength into its emerging fruits.

Iyar is the month of wilderness, and the only month entirely filled with the counting of the Omer. This is a month to heal ourselves of what ails us—to free ourselves from the habits of mind we learned in our own Egypts. Each day of the Omer, with its divine attribute, allows us to work on reclaiming that attribute in our lives. In Iyar, month of healing, we use the power of the budding earth to strengthen ourselves.

This is the 16th day of the Omer: *gevurah shebetiferet*, which can mean "the strength of balance." Healing restores our bodies and spirits to balance. Even when we cannot heal a particular ailment physically, the energy of Iyar can help us find a place of strength within ourselves.

The Temple without Walls

Then Solomon began to build the house of the Eternal in Jerusalem on Mount Moriah, where the Eternal had appeared to his father David, at the place where David had designated, at the threshing floor of Ornan the Jebusite. He began to build on the second day of the second month.
—2 CHRONICLES 3:1

Rabbi Huna said in the name of Rabbi Yosi: Everyone helped Solomon to build the Temple, humans and spirits alike.
—EXODUS RABBAH 52:4

The first Iyar is a month of wandering for the Israelites. There is no Torah, no *mishkan*, no outward form to focus their spirituality. They are simply free. It is interesting that Solomon, when he builds his Temple, chooses the 2nd of Iyar to begin his work. Although the structure will have walls and a roof and specific rituals, it is still an embodiment of the wilderness of Iyar.

Solomon, in Jewish tradition, is a master of the otherworld (Babylonian Talmud, Sanhedrin 20b; Babylonian Talmud, Gittin 68a–b; *Exodus Rabbah* 52:4). When he builds the Temple, he summons not only human workers but also spirits to help with the work. This suggests the Temple is both a substantial and an insubstantial place. One can enter it and find oneself in the past with one's ancestors or in the future with one's descendants—in a heavenly palace, a cave in the underworld, or the wilderness.

So too one can enter any spiritual discipline—prayer, study, righteous deeds—and discover something new and unusual. In Jewish tradition there is a tension between *keva*, "ritual form," and *kavanah*, "spontaneous intention." Today, the 17th day of the Omer, is *tiferet shebetiferet*, the "heart within the heart": the outer *keva* and the inward *kavanah*.

The Grapevine

You plucked up a vine from Egypt.… You cleared a place for it, it took deep root and filled the land. The mountains were covered by its shade, mighty cedars by its boughs.
—Psalms 80:9–11

Why is Israel compared to a grapevine? Just as when a grapevine's owners want to make it more beautiful, they uproot it from one place and plant it in another place and it becomes more beautiful, so when the Holy One of Blessing wanted to make Israel known to the world, the Holy One uprooted them from Egypt and brought them to the wilderness, and there they began to flourish.
—Exodus Rabbah 44:1

To be uprooted is to be without moorings, uncomfortable, disoriented. Yet a midrash reminds us life emerges stronger after it is uprooted. The Hebrews, taken out of Egypt, become more abundant in their character, not only because they are free but because they have to cope with new and alien surroundings. Today, the 18th day of the Omer, *netzach shebetiferet*, can be understood to represent the "victory of the heart" in the face of new surroundings.

There is something strange about today's midrash. Why does it not say that the Holy One uprooted the Hebrews from Egypt and brought them to Israel? Why is the wilderness mentioned? Indeed, why are the biblical Hebrews not swooped up by eagles and carried to farms in the Jordan River valley? Instead, both the Bible and the midrash dwell on the wilderness experience: exile, wandering in a strange place.

Exile can be productive. Psychologically, when we face change, even positive change, we too become uprooted. We may feel confused or fearful. Yet losing our moorings can mean an opportunity to find more abundance in our lives. Like the grapevine, our new buds may be stronger because of our wilderness experience.

The Lament for Jonathan

Yom ha-Zikaron

How have the mighty fallen
in the thick of battle—
Jonathan, slain on your
heights! I grieve for you,
my brother Jonathan.
—2 SAMUEL 1:25–26

Great is peace, for no vessel can hold blessing but peace. … Great is peace, for it is weighted against everything, as it says in the morning prayers: The One who makes peace and creates everything.
—NUMBERS RABBAH 11:7

Today is Yom ha-Zikaron, the day the state of Israel remembers its fallen soldiers. Today is also the 19th day of the Omer, *hod shebetiferet*, the "beauty of compassion"; and today Israelis observe a moment of silent compassion for soldiers fallen in war.

In the Bible, King David wrote a lament for Jonathan, son of Saul and prince of Israel, who fell in battle against the enemies of his people. The lament, born of David's deep love for Jonathan, seems as poignant today as it must have in ancient times, for millennia later, men and women still die in wars.

Yet the Jewish tradition has developed a deep commitment to peace. The above midrash teaches: "No vessel can hold blessing but peace." Even a nation proud of its soldiers cannot be blessed without peace. Peace, like the harvest of the land, is a gift that comes only with hard labor.

Numbers Rabbah goes on to say that if peace and all creation were put into a scale, the two would weigh the same. We cannot enjoy the emerging beauty of the spring without serenity and safety. Nor can we enjoy the budding of children when they must know war. As Israel mourns the dead of its wars, we pray to be able to commit ourselves to the dialogue and hard work that bring peace.

Israel Independence Day

Yom ha-Atzmaut

The Eternal your God … will bring you together again from all the peoples where the Eternal your God has scattered you. Even if your outcasts are in the ends of the world, from there the Eternal your God will gather you in, from there the Holy One will fetch you.
—Deuteronomy 30:3–4

Our sages learned from this that the Shekhinah *is present with exiles, and when they are redeemed it is as if She is redeemed. … Great is the day of the exiles' ingathering and difficult, as if the Holy One of Blessing had to take each person by the hand and bring each person to his or her place.*
—Rashi on Deuteronomy 30:2

For many centuries after the exile of the Jews from Rome, Jews lived with a national consciousness but had nowhere to live as a self-governing people. While they found prosperity in some places, in others they found persecution and hatred. By the 20th century, Jews had become equal citizens of many countries, yet in the same century, one third of Jewry was wiped out in the Holocaust.

The State of Israel was founded on this day in 1948 by Jewish pioneers and immigrants during a territorial war between Arabs and Jews. Today Israel serves as a modern ingathering of exiles, welcoming persecuted Jews from Ethiopia and Russia, cultivating the ancient Jewish homeland, and successfully reinventing a language and culture. Yet Israel has had to struggle, both with implacable enemies and with its own shortcomings. The State of Israel is home to Palestinian Arabs, and they too need and deserve a secure homeland.

Rashi reminds us that the ingathering of exiles is difficult and painful. Yet as the midrash says, the *Shekhinah* cannot be redeemed until we end the pain of all exiles. Today is the 20th day of the Omer, *yesod shebetiferet*, or the "root of the heart." Today we root ourselves in the land, and also acknowledge the need of all people for peace.

Covenant of the Road

Then Naomi said: "Turn back, my daughters!" … They broke into weeping again, and Orpah kissed her mother-in-law farewell. But Ruth clung to her … "Do not urge me to leave you…. For wherever you go, I will go, … your people shall be my people, and your God my God." … When [Naomi] saw how determined she was to go with her, she ceased to argue with her. … They arrived in Bethlehem at the beginning of the barley harvest.
—Ruth 1:11,14–18,22

You will come to a border. Walk across it. You will arrive under the shelter of the wings of one who is not jealous, who is not a warrior or a punisher, but a being as naturally benign as nature in a year of good harvest.
—Alicia Ostriker, "The Redeeming of Ruth"[19]

Imagine a vast old tree with dry branches. It appears nearly dead throughout the winter. Then, in spring, green buds and tendrils appear near its base. It appears the old tree is not dead after all. Ruth is to Naomi what those green tendrils are to the old tree.

Naomi, an Israelite widow whose husband and sons have died, is returning to her old home in Bethlehem. She tells her widowed daughters-in-law, Orpah and Ruth, to return to their mothers' houses. They have no reason to follow a destitute woman to a strange land. Sensibly, Orpah heads for home. Yet Ruth is moved to cling to Naomi. In her love for Naomi, Ruth chooses a new spiritual home. The poet Alicia Ostriker imagines that Ruth finds a new deity in her newfound land, not a warrior but a harvester of the earth.

Ruth Rabbah (3:6) tells that Ruth and Naomi return to Bethlehem; and all through the Omer, Ruth supports Naomi by gleaning in the fields of barley for grain the reapers have dropped. Eventually Ruth marries Naomi's kinsman Boaz and becomes the mother of a child who will comfort Naomi in her old age.

On the 21st day of the Omer, *malkhut shebetiferet*, or the "triumph of compassion," we remember the love of Ruth and the sustaining power of the new grain.

Clothing of the Snail

Remember the long way that the Eternal your God has made you travel in the wilderness these past forty years. … The clothes upon you did not wear out, nor did your feet swell these forty years.
—DEUTERONOMY 8:1,4

The clouds of glory would rub against their clothes and clean them, just as clothes are pressed in a laundry. Their children—as they got bigger, their clothing would grow with them, just like the covering of a snail, which grows as the snail grows.
—RASHI ON DEUTERONOMY 8:4

It is astonishing to imagine the *Shekhinah* functioning as a laundress. Yet in the legends of the Sages, the wilderness is a miraculous place where surprising things happen. The clouds of Divine Presence rub up against clothes to wash out the dirt, and the clothes of children are like living things, growing like the bark of trees, or the house of a snail. The springtime wandering in the desert echoes the miracles and surprises of spring.

This midrash also hints that when we are truly on a journey, we are liable to grow without realizing it. We do not notice our clothes outgrowing us—we are focused on the goal. It may even seem to us that the things, people, and places around us are helping us arrive at our destination, just as the clouds help the Israelites along the hard roads of the desert with their helpful moisture. On the 22nd day of the Omer, *hesed shebenetzach*, or the "outpouring of persistence," we feel in ourselves the ability to persist on our journeys.

Healing at Elim

In the first weeks after they leave Egypt, the Israelites stop at a mysterious place called Elim, full of trees and springs of water. Elim is almost a physical embodiment of the spring, ripe with life and beauty. Though the Torah does not say so exactly, it is clear that Elim is a place meant to heal the Israelites of their emotional and physical wounds. Though they have left Egypt, they are still in need of healing.

The weeks of the Omer are our Elim: the time when we remember the attributes of the Divine and strive to embody those attributes. Each day of the Omer offers us a place to examine each aspect of ourselves that is hurt so we may heal it. If we are hurt in the area of *hesed* (love), this is the time to rediscover love. If we are hurt in the area of *netzach* (persistence), this is a time to build back our strength.

Today is the 23rd day of the Omer: *gevurah shebenetzach*, or the "pain within our persistence." Each *sefirah*, each "divine realm," presents us with healing for that pain, so that we can go on. So too, around us, the beauty of the spring invites us to heal, to identify with flowers and newborn creatures, to choose life. Like the Israelites at Elim, we use inner and outer beauty to heal ourselves.

Sustain me with raisin cakes, refresh me with apples, for I am faint with love.
—SONG OF SONGS 5:5

Just as a sick person hopes for healing, so the generation of Hebrews in Egypt hoped for redemption.
—SONG OF SONGS RABBAH 5:8

Healing the Stranger

When a stranger resides with you in your land, you shall not wrong him. The stranger who resides with you shall be to you as one of your citizens; you shall love him as yourself, for you were strangers in the land of Egypt.
—LEVITICUS 19:33–34

I came to speak to Pharaoh in Your name, for Your name is life and healing for all who walk the earth.
—MIDRASH TANHUMA VA-YERA 6

One of the principles of the Torah is that strangers are worthy of respect. One who lives in your community, yet is different from you, is entitled to the same support and care as a home-born citizen. The Israelites, having left a cruel Egypt, may not be feeling inclined toward empathy. Nevertheless, they are told to empathize with the stranger because of their own experience. They have been foreigners in a land that suspects and fears them—it is now their challenge not to treat others the same way. This is part of the healing of Iyar.

In one legend, Moses says to the Divine that he goes to speak to Pharaoh—a man who hates and fears strangers—in the name of the One who brings healing to all. He does not take the risk of speaking to Pharaoh merely to rescue one group of people. He takes that extraordinary risk because he feels called to do so by the Presence connecting the lives of all beings—the Presence before whom there are no strangers.

Today is the 24th day of the Omer: *tiferet shebenetzach*, or the "compassion of persistence." This is the day of trying to do the hardest thing: respect the other who is very different from us, yet very much the same. By doing this, we also learn to heal.

The Grief of the Omer

The Ark of the Divine was captured, and Eli's two sons … were slain. A Benjaminite ran from the battlefield and reached Shiloh the same day…. When he arrived, he found Eli … waiting beside the road. … The man entered the city to spread the news, and the whole city broke out into a cry. And when Eli heard the sound of the outcry and asked, "What is the meaning of this uproar?" the man rushed over to tell Eli. . . . When he mentioned the Ark of the Divine, Eli fell backward … and broke his neck and died.
—1 Samuel 4:11–18

On the 10th of Iyar Eli the priest died and his two sons, and the Ark of the Covenant was lost.
—Megillat Ta'anit, conclusion

Today is the halfway point between Passover and Shavuot. *Megillat Ta'anit*, an ancient record of Jewish sacred days, tells that on this day two priests, the sons of Eli, took the Ark of the Covenant into battle with them, believing it would help the Israelite army achieve victory. Instead, the Ark was captured. Enemy soldiers killed Eli's sons, Eli died of grief, and that same day Eli's daughter-in-law, wife of Phinehas, died in childbirth.

In talmudic tradition, the seven weeks of the Omer are a time of mourning. This is why many Jews abstain from weddings and other celebrations during the Omer period. The Babylonian Talmud (Yevamot 62b) claims that during these days Rabbi Akiva's students were stricken with plague, because they quarreled with one another over their religious disagreements, and did not treat one another with respect.

Like Rabbi Akiva's students, Hophni and Phinehas use sacred things to engage in violent conflict. The result is disastrous. This 25th day of the Omer, *netzach shebenetzach*, or the "essence of eternity," is a day for keeping the sacred free from human quarrels.

Knowers of Times

The people of the tribe of Issachar were wise regarding matters of time, to know what Israel should do.
—1 Chronicles 12:33

What does it mean, "matters of time"? Rabbi Tanhuma said: They understood the seasons. Rabbi Yosi bar Ketzari explains: They knew how to intercalate the year.
—Genesis Rabbah 72:5

In the *Sefer Yetzirah,* Iyar is the month of the tribe of Issachar, a tribe renowned for its Torah scholarship. The Bible refers to the Issacharites as "*yodei vinah l'itim*" or "knowers of the wisdom of time." One Rabbinic opinion says Issacharites had a special understanding of the seasons—they knew about the shifting of light across time. Another opinion says they knew the specifics of the Jewish calendar and how to keep it aligned with the moon and sun.

This 26th day of the Omer is connected to *hod shebenetzach*, or the "receiving of eternity." Time is the vessel of eternity, unfolding from the first moment the universe came into being. This day is a day to do the work of the Issacharites by learning more about time and the ways it affects us.

Today, Israel is still camped at Elim, the oasis of 12 springs and 70 palm trees. The palm trees, some say, represent the scholars and judges of the people: posts often filled by the Issacharites (*Midrash Tanhuma, Naso* 14). As we learn about time, we honor the Sages of our people who created the Jewish calendar.

The Month of Radiance

In the month of Ziv, that is, the second month....
—1 Kings 6:1

Why was that month called Ziv? Because in it was the radiance of the world, in which the plants and trees are known.
—Jerusalem Talmud, Rosh Hashanah 6a

Before the Babylonian exile in the 6th century B.C.E., the month of Iyar was called Ziv, a name that means "radiance." The word "Iyar" is not very different: Many believe it comes from a root meaning "light." The Jerusalem Talmud describes Ziv/Iyar as a month of light, when the beauty of the natural world is revealed to us most deeply. The light of this month is like a kind of halo, beneath which everything seems greener. Iyar holds within it the *ziv ha'olam*, the "radiance of the world," the life force.

This 27th day of the Omer is related to *yesod shebenetzach,* the "connectedness of eternity." On this day we reflect on the stubbornness of life, a persistence we see bursting out of the trees and being born in infant creatures all around us. This day of Iyar is sacred to the life force and is a time to bless life for its vigor and variety. *Malkhut shebenetzach* can also mean "the *Shekhinah* residing in eternity." As we observe the vitality of the life force, we see the intricate workings of holiness.

The Fruits of the Sun

Of Joseph he said:
Blessed of the Eternal
be his land
With the bounty of dew
from heaven
And of the deep that
crouches below,
With the bounteous
yield of the sun,
And the bounteous crop
of the moons.
—DEUTERONOMY 33:13–14

One who really wants to
taste a fig, let that person
turn to the east, as it is said:
"With the bounteous yield
of the sun."
—BABYLONIAN TALMUD, YOMA 83B

The direction of the spring season is east: toward the sun. A talmudic tradition claims the sun side of the tree, the eastern side, produces the sweetest fruits. Direct exposure to the sun brings out the fruit's sugars and ripens them to perfection. So too the "eastern side" of the year is the spring, ripening all things to their fullest sweetness.

Perhaps this is what Moses means when he blesses the tribe of Joseph with "the bounteous yield of the sun." The crops of spring can be called the sun's harvest, for it is the sun's growing light and heat that produces them. Moses' blessing also speaks of the crop of the moons, reminding us that different fruits and produce ripen in different months of the year. We are blessed that our harvest does not come all at once, but in stages, so we can enjoy different foods at different seasons.

As the bees and winds fertilize the buds of Nisan, our thoughts turn toward the fruit that will come. This 28th day of the Omer is *malkhut shebenetzach*, or the "eternity of the earth." Today we witness the fruits thriving in the ever-radiant light of the sun.

Night at Elim

Pesach Sheini

When any of you or your posterity who are defiled by a corpse, or are on a long journey would offer a Passover sacrifice to the Eternal, they shall offer it in the second month, on the fourteenth day of the month, at twilight.
—Numbers 9:10–11

Why did the Holy One create the world in Nisan and not in Iyar? Because when the Holy One wanted to create the world, He said to the angel of darkness: "Go away, for I desire to create the world with light." . . . The angel of darkness asked: "And after you create light, what will you create then?" He said to him: "Darkness."
—Pesikta Rabbati 20:2

This is the Israelites' last night at the lush oasis of Elim before they face the challenges of the desert (Babylonian Talmud, Shabbat 87b; *Seder Olam* 5). Elim, like the *mishkan*, is a holy sanctuary: precious, but limited. The Israelites now must leave this place of comfort. No doubt the desert night seems very dark to them.

A midrash from *Pesikta Rabbati* follows the opinion that the world was created on the 1st of Nisan. The Divine warns the angel of darkness to stay away from Nisan, for the Holy One desires to fill the world with light. Cleverly, the angel reminds the Holy One that after light must come darkness, just as after Nisan must come Iyar.

Iyar is light itself, yet within it is the darkness of struggle, wandering, and mystery. It is the month of healing, which requires facing both the darkness and the light in our lives.

This 29th day of the Omer reveals *hesed shebehod*, or the "giving of prophecy." It is also Pesach Sheini, "second Passover," when journeyers, or those who have become ritually impure, are permitted to make the Passover sacrifice (Numbers 9:1–12). These physical and ritual journeyers remind us of the journey we too must make in Iyar.

NOTES

1 Henri Frankfort, *Kingship and the Gods: A Study of Ancient Near Eastern Religion as the Integration of Society and Nature,* (University of Chicago Press, 1978). See also Julye Bidland, *The Akitu Festival: Religious Continuity and Royal Legitimation in Mesopotamia* (Gorgias Press, 2002). See also, Michael Jordan, *Myths of the World: A Thematic Encyclopedia* (Kyle Cathie, 1993), pp. 42–43.

2 Diane Wolkstein and Samuel Noah Kramer, *Queen of Heaven and Earth: Her Stories and Hymns from Sumer,* (Harper and Row, 1983), p. 173.

3 James George Frazer, *The Golden Bough* (Touchstone, 1995), pp. 456–462. See also, Jordan, *Myths of the World*, pp. 241–242.

4 Jakob Grimm, *Teutonic Mythology* (George Bell and Sons, 1883), pp. 289–291.

5 Barabara Holender, "Miriam's Well," in *All the Women Followed Her*, edited by Rebecca Schwartz (Rikudei Miriam Press, 2002), p. 37.

6 Louis Ginzberg, *Legends of the Jews*, (The Jewish Publication Society, 1938), vol. 1, p. 53.

7 However, the *Megillat Ta'anit,* a talmudic source, places her death on 10 Nisan.

8 Tamara Cohen, ed., *The Journey Continues: The Ma'yan Passover Haggadah* (Ma'ya: The Jewish Women's Project, 2002), pp. 29–30.

9 Lynn Gottlieb, *She Who Dwells Within: A Feminist Vision of a Renewed Judaism* (HarperSanFrancisco, 1995), p. 107.

10 Rabbi Yehudah Leib Alter of Ger, in Green, *Language of Truth: The Torah Commentary of the Sefat Emet* (Jewish Publication Society, 1998), p. 390.

11 Siegfried Stein, "The Influence of Symposium Literature on the Literary Form of the Pesah Haggadah," *Journal of Jewish Studies,* 8 (1957) pp. 13–44.

12 See Arthur Waskow, *Seasons Of Our Joy: A Modern Guide to the Jewish Holidays* (Beacon Press, 1991), p. 165–184.

13 Marc Bregman, "Serach: the Recovery of Joseph's Bones," in *The Journal of Contemporary Midrash*, p. 16.

14 Louis Ginzberg, *Legends of the Jews* (Jewish Publication Society, 1938), vol. 2, 115–116.

15 Yocheved Bat Miriam, "Miriam," in *And Rachel Stole the Idols: The Emergence of Modern Hebrew Women's Writing*, Wendy I. Zierler, translator (Wayne State University Press, 2004), pp. 104–105.

16 Lesli Koppelman Ross, "Maimouna; A Post-Passover Celebration," http://www.myjewishlearning.com (accessed Feb. 1, 2006).

17 *Siddur Sim Shalom: A Prayer book for Shabbat, Festivals, and Weekdays*, Jules Harlow ed. (Rabbinical Assembly, 1989), p. 710.

18 The date of this memorial day is changed in some years so that it does not fall before, after, or on *Shabbat*.

19 Alicia Ostricker, "The Redeeming of Ruth," in *Nakedness of the Fathers: Biblical Visions* (Rutgers University Press, 1994), p.171.

The Leaf

15 IYAR TO 30 SIVAN

SEASON
Spring shading into summer

WIND
The south

HALF OF THE YEAR
The sun

ELEMENT
Water within fire

GATE
The sea/the heavens

ANGEL
Raphael (healing)

DIVINE FACE
Hesed (Love)

I saw a tree of great height in the midst of the earth. The tree grew and became mighty. Its top reached to heaven, and it could be seen from all the ends of the earth. Its leaves were beautiful and its fruit abundant, and there was food for all in it.

—Daniel 4:7–9

The sixth movement of the year is increase. Leaves multiply on the trees, grapes multiply on the vine, plants and animals bear offspring and multiply over the earth. Late spring and early summer may bring us days of green plenty. Or they may bring us scorching heat, when trees and all living things must use their multiple resources to wrest water and nutrients from the wind and soil. This is a season of consuming, when life must feed itself to fullness.

At this time of year Jews celebrate holidays of Revelation: the wisdom that comes from the meeting between the human and the Eternal. The biblical festival of Shavuot, both a harvest and a celebration of the Revelation at Sinai, falls on the 6th of Sivan, at the end of the seven weeks of the Omer. Shavuot is often portrayed as a wedding between God and Israel or between Israel and the Torah (Zohar I:18a). As creatures everywhere seek mates, Israel seeks its divine mate. The Torah may be said to be their wedding contract—or the Torah may even be said to be their offspring, the fruit that comes of covenant and union.

Shavuot is preceded by another holiday of revelation. Lag b'Omer, the 18th of the month of Iyar and the 33rd day of the Omer, is a minor holiday from the talmudic period, falling three weeks before Shavuot. Legend holds that on that day the Holy One revealed to Rabbi Shimon bar Yochai the secrets contained in the Zohar (III:296b), thus joining heaven and earth. Traditionally, we spend Lag b'Omer in nature, engaging in physical activities and building bonfires.

Both Shavuot and Lag b'Omer are associated with the awesome forces of nature: thunder, fire, and the passionate joining of one being with another. This is the season of fire and water, the outer fire of the sun's heat and the inner rain of Torah as it falls on the human heart. The burning mountain of Sinai beneath the thick cloud of the Divine Presence evokes this same swirling image of mist and flame.

How does Revelation fit in with the season of increase? Interpretation of Torah is by nature multiple. There are always two or more ways to view the meaning of any sacred text. All of these views, according to Rabbinic midrash, are part of the divine Revelation (*Midrash Tanhuma, Shemot* 25; *Exodus Rabbah* 28:4). In Jewish lore, Torah is called a Tree of Life, and, as the writer Alicia Ostriker points out, this means it must grow to stay alive. This growth is midrash—the Jewish process of always seeking new meaning in sacred texts. As the life around us multiplies and increases, Jews delve into texts full of multiplicity, seeking to create new midrash in every generation. Through our coming together to learn, we give the Torah new life. The Jewish holidays of Revelation mirror the growing season itself.

Jews are, of course, not alone in celebrating the season of abundance. The Romans also celebrated the flowering of earth on May 1, with the Floralia or flower festival.[1] Beltane, a Celtic holiday of revelry and sensuality that also fell on May 1, was and is celebrated like Lag b'Omer, with bonfires and with a sacred marriage between heaven and earth represented by the maypole.[2] On the same day, Germans celebrate the coming of spring with Walpurgisnacht. The Mayan rain dance and the Iroquois corn-planting festival celebrate fertility at this season.[3] In modern times, May Day is a secular celebration of the productivity of work.

The late spring connects us to *hesed*: the divine flow of love and abundance. We revel in our power to add to the world through work, through art, through interpretation, through fertility. We are all leaves on the Tree of Life, part of the vast multiplicity that is Revelation.

The Search for New Bread

Setting out from Elim, the whole Israelite community came to the wilderness of Sin, which is between Elim and Sinai, on the fifteenth day of the second month after their departure from the land of Egypt. In the wilderness, the whole Israelite community grumbled against Moses and Aaron. The Israelites said to them, "If only we had died by the hand of the Eternal in the land of Egypt, when we sat by the fleshpots, when we ate our fill of bread! For you have brought up out into this wilderness to starve this whole congregation to death."
—Exodus 16:1–3

The day of the encampment is specifically mentioned because on that day, the provisions they brought from Egypt ended, and they needed the manna.
—Rashi on Exodus 16:1

On this day, the Israelites run out of matzah. While in the wilderness, they have been living on the bread they baked in Egypt, and now even the crumbs are gone. Immediately, they despair, crying out to Moses and Aaron that they are hungry. Only after they complain does the Divine send manna to feed them.

Under this story lies the truth that the Israelites are still eating the bread of their affliction long after their suffering is over. We know this to be a psychological truth: The pain of trauma does not quickly go away. Often, we continue blindly, responding to our pain for a long time until our options run out and we feel trapped. Then and only then are we ready to receive a new revelation about our lives.

This is also true in nature. A creature will keep coming to a food source even after the food is gone, until it learns that it must seek new sustenance. Today is the 30th day of the Omer, *gevurah shebehesed*, or the "strength of receiving." In this season of increase, we learn to be hungry for new kinds of sustenance.

The Quail

The Eternal spoke to Moses: "I have heard the grumbling of the Israelites. Speak to them and say: By evening you shall eat flesh, and in the morning you shall have your fill of bread, and you shall know that I the Eternal am your God." In the evening, quail appeared and covered the camp.
—EXODUS 16:11–13

In accordance with "Let there be a firmament," the Holy One made the cloud of the Divine above them by day. In accordance with "Let the waters be gathered," the Holy One had Moses hold out his arm and split the sea. . . . In accordance with "Let the waters bring forth . . . birds that fly above the earth," in the wilderness quail appeared at evening.
—OTZAR MIDRASHIM: PINCHAS BEN YAIR 5

In response to the Israelites' hunger in the wilderness, the Divine sends quail to fly over the Israelite camp, then thud to earth to feed the starving people. In one legend, these quail represent the new world that comes to be as the freed Israelites wander. Each of the freed slaves' experiences is like a day of Creation. The pillar of cloud is the sky, the splitting of the sea evokes the creation of oceans, the manna represents the trees, the quail represents the birds, and the glowing face of Moses represents humans, made in the divine image.

For the Israelites to move on in the wilderness, they must see the earth as a newly created place. The narrowness of Egypt can no longer be their reality. Each miracle of the Exodus, in this reading, is an attempt to give the Israelites new eyes to see the world.

We too, in the growing light of the season, try to find new eyes to see the natural world. Today, the 31st day of the Omer, is *tiferet shebehesed*, the "beauty of receiving." As we take in the wonders of life, we ourselves become the Israelites receiving their daily miracles.

The Serpent's Secret

Now the serpent … said to the woman: "Did God really say, You shall not eat of every tree of the garden?" The woman replied, … "It is only about the fruit of the tree in the middle of the garden that the Divine said, 'You shall not eat of it … lest you die.'" And the serpent said …: "You are not going to die, but … as soon as you eat of it your eyes will be opened, and you will become like the Divine, knowing good and evil."
—GENESIS 3:1–4

In the second month, on the seventeenth day, the serpent came and … said to the woman: "Has God commanded you, saying: 'You shall not eat of every tree of the garden?'"
—JUBILEES 3:17

The shrewd serpent who convinces Eve to eat from the Tree of Knowledge is the first biblical revealer. In Jubilees (3:17), the serpent approaches Eve on the 17th of Iyar and tells her that if she eats from the tree she will not die but will become divine, knowing everything.

What knowledge do Eve and Adam receive from the fruit? Is it sexuality they discover or the power of rational thought? Does their new wisdom make them like God? Do they eventually die of it? The text leaves the questions unanswered, and we are left to guess at the secret of the serpent's words.

Today is the 32nd day of the Omer, *netzach shebehesed*, or the "eternity of receiving." As we prepare to receive Torah, it is appropriate to consider whether all revelation has a little of the serpent in it and we are meant to have doubts. It is partly our willingness to question that allows us to navigate in a confusing world.

The Fall of Manna

Lag b'Omer

In the morning there was a fall of dew about the camp. When the fall of dew lifted, there over the surface of the wilderness lay a fine and flaky substance, fine as the frost on the ground. When the Israelites saw it, they asked one another: "What is it?" for they did not know what it was. Moses said to them: "This is the bread which the Divine has given you to eat."
—Exodus 16:13–15

"The taste of the manna was as a cake baked with oil." Rabbi Avuha said: Do not read "leshad" *(cake) but* "shad" *(breast). As an infant tastes many flavors in the breast, so Israel found many flavors in the manna.*
—Babylonian Talmud, Yoma 75a

The 18th of Iyar, the 33rd day of the Omer, is Lag b'Omer. ("*Lag*" is a combination of Hebrew letters adding to 33.) This holiday comes in April or May, at a time when spring is in full bloom. Jews celebrate Lag b'Omer with bonfires, dancing, archery contests, haircutting, and often with weddings because this is one of the rare days of the Omer when weddings are permitted.

Tradition holds this was the day a plague on the students of Rabbi Akiva ended (Babylonian Talmud, Yevamot 62b). In one legend (Zohar III:296b), it was the day the Sage Shimon bar Yochai revealed the Zohar as he lay dying. Many Jews still make a pilgrimage to bar Yochai's grave in Meron on this day. They light bonfires to represent the sun, which did not set until the Sage was finished with his revelation.

Although *Seder Olam* (5) claims the manna fell on the 15th of Iyar, the Hatam Sofer (an 18th-century German rabbi) believes that it is today that the manna first falls from heaven. Manna was said to have many tastes, just as Torah sounds somewhat different to all who hear it. The fall of manna, compared to milk from the divine breast, represents the feeding of heavenly wisdom to earthly creatures. On the day of *hod shebehesed*, "prophecy within prophecy," we honor the many revelations of Lag b'Omer.

The Pruning of the Trees

When you enter the land and plant any tree for food, you shall regard its fruit as forbidden. Three years it shall be forbidden for you, not to be eaten. In the fourth year all its fruit shall be set aside for jubilation before the Eternal, and only in the fifth year may you use its fruit.
—Leviticus 19:23–24

Rabbi Shimon and Rabbi Eliezer hid in a cave. A miracle happened, and a carob tree and a well of water sprang up for them.
—Babylonian Talmud, Shabbat 33b

On Lag b'Omer, some Jews participate in the custom of *upsherin*, or "cutting the hair" of three-year-old boys.[4] This custom comes from the idea that people are related to trees, as it says: "The human is a tree of the field" (Deuteronomy 20:19). Just as the fruit of young trees is set aside to return to the earth, the hair of young children is set aside. This custom generally applies to boys, but some families apply it to girls as well.[5] The hair, once cut, is thrown into the Lag b'Omer bonfire. The bonfire consumes trees, and they rise up as smoke. Meanwhile, the hopes of the human "trees"—the children—are also sent up to heaven in the bonfire's smoke.

Lag b'Omer also honors scholars who studied Torah when the Roman authorities forbade it on pain of death. When a Roman arrest order forced Rabbi Shimon and his son to flee into the wilderness, a well of water and a carob tree miraculously provided for all their needs. We see the ever-replenished carob tree in the children who come to Meron every year to the fires of Shimon bar Yochai. The young children whose hair is cut at Meron represent *yesod shebehod*, the root of beauty, the 34th day of the Omer.

The Rising of the Cloud

In the second year, on the twentieth day of the second month, the cloud lifted from the Tabernacle of the Pact, and the Israelites set out on their journeys from the wilderness of Sinai. The cloud came to rest in the wilderness of Paran.
—NUMBERS 10:11

The Holy One said to Moses: "Write down the journeys that the Israelites journeyed in the wilderness, so that they will know how many miracles I did for them on every single journey."
—MIDRASH TANHUMA, MAS'EI 1

We are now in the countdown to Sinai. Yet this text about the 20th of Iyar reminds us that just under a year after the Sinai Revelation, the Israelites must set out on yet more journeys. Sinai is not the end of the story; it is one stage in a series of revelations. Even the journey itself is a revelation.

In the book of Numbers, the lands of the wilderness through which the Israelites travel are very specifically noted. *Midrash Tanhuma* imagines the Holy One asking Moses to write down the stages of the journeys so everyone will know how many miracles happened at each one. One might think this is because the Holy One has an ego and wants the people to know how they have been coddled. Or perhaps the Holy One wants to encourage the faith of the people.

Perhaps the point of remembering the miracles on each journey is that each journey is important, no matter how insignificant it appears. A short, safe journey between two points many be just as good a teacher as is a journey with vast difficulties and extraordinary wonders. This midrash reminds us to pay attention to all of our travels, not just the ones labeled "revelation." This 35th day of the Omer, *malkhut shebehesed*, celebrates the totality of revelation: the small as well as the great.

The Blessing over Manna

And the Israelites ate manna forty years, until they came to a settled land; they ate the manna until they came to the border of the land of Canaan.
—Exodus 16:35

Moses established for the Israelites the blessing "who feeds all things" in the hour that the manna came down for them, while Joshua established the blessing "for the land and for the food" when the people entered the Land of Israel.
—Babylonian Talmud, Berakhot 48b

The Jewish grace after finishing a meal is quite long and complex, and contains a number of different blessings. The first of these blessings ends "Blessed are You, Eternal, Who feeds all things." This blessing thanks the Holy One for giving food to each creature and for sustaining human beings with grain and all the other foods we eat.

The origin of this blessing is obscure, but talmudic legend imagines that Moses wrote it while the manna was falling in white flakes from the sky. The blessing over ordinary food, this legend implies, is really a blessing over the miraculous food that nourished the Israelites in the wilderness. This tradition hints that all food is an extraordinary gift. The food cycle itself is one of the wonders of life on earth.

The second blessing in the grace after meals, the Talmud relates, is written by Joshua when the Israelites enter the Land, and it ends "Blessed are You, Eternal, for the land and for the food." This blessing reminds us how much we depend on the earth itself for our lives. On this 36th day of the Omer, we remember that 36, in Jewish tradition, is double the numerical value of the word "life." We honor *hesed shebeyesod*, the "abundance at the foundation of the world." Today we remember how life feeds life.

The Sabbath (*Shabbat*) Meal

On the sixth day they gathered double the amount of food [lechem mishneh], *two omers for each, and when all the chieftains of the community came and told Moses, he said to them: … "Tomorrow is a day of rest, a holy Sabbath of the Eternal. … Six days you shall gather [manna]; on the seventh day, the Sabbath, there will be none."*
EXODUS 16:22–30

"Lechem mishneh" means "lechem meshuneh," *"different bread," because on an ordinary day one omer of manna per person fell while on a Friday two omers per person fell, and also because every day the smell of the manna carried, and on* Shabbat *more so. Every day the manna had a golden shine, and on* Shabbat *even more so.*
—MEKHILTA BE-SHALLAH

In *Seder Olam* (8), today is the first *Shabbat* after the Israelites begin to receive manna. On the day before, a Friday, two portions of manna fall, so that no Israelites need gather food on *Shabbat*. Normally manna goes bad after a day, but on the *Shabbat* the manna stays fresh. In fact, a midrash relates that on the *Shabbat* the day-old manna becomes even more golden and fragrant. The mistrustful Israelites try to look for manna on the *Shabbat*, but there is none: *Shabbat* is a day of rest for all.

Traditional Friday night and Saturday meals do have a golden shine to them, as they are not pressured by work, phone calls, or the need to be somewhere else. The food we eat on *Shabbat* is like manna: We prepare it beforehand so that *Shabbat* itself is a day for enjoyment. We share the food with guests so they too can taste the delights of the *Shabbat*. On this 37th day of the Omer, *gevurah shebeyesod,* or the "strength of connection," we remember to connect with one another and with the earth's abundance through *Shabbat* hospitality.

The Endless Torah

Would you discover the mystery of the Divine? Would you discover the limit of the Almighty? Higher than heaven—what can you do? Deeper than Sheol—what can you know? Its measure is longer than the earth and broader than the sea.
—Job 11:7–9

Why was Torah given in the wilderness? This teaches that if you do not make yourself as free as the wilderness, you will not merit the words of Torah. And as the wilderness has no end, so too Torah has no end, as it says, "Its measure is longer than the earth and broader than the sea."
—Pesikta de-Rav Kahana 12:20

As the Israelites move through the wilderness, they empty themselves of slavery, as a balloon shooting through the air empties itself of wind. They become open to something different, though that something has not yet manifested itself. The Torah they receive is not yet a Torah of words. It is a Torah of silence, of sky. It is a Torah of freedom.

Pesikta de-Rav Kahana teaches that the people must receive this Torah of wilderness before they are prepared to receive a Torah of words. Torah received by slaves becomes just another rule laid down by a master. For Torah to be a covenant between heaven and earth, it must be received by people free to think for themselves. Torah, as the midrash says, is not limited by its ink borders. It has no end, as the sea has no end. Its words grow anew, like leaves on trees. As long as we explore our covenant with the Infinite, Torah continues to expand. It is ever moving, like the horizon in the distance.

This 38th day of the Omer is *tiferet shebeyesod*, the "truth and compassion at the root of things." This is the Torah we hope to find as we freely engage the world.

Proclaim Liberty throughout the Land

You shall hallow the fiftieth year. You shall proclaim release throughout the land for all its inhabitants. It shall be a jubilee for you: each of you shall return to your holding and each of you shall return to your family.
—LEVITICUS 25:10–12

Why is the word "jubilee" added? To teach you that it is to be proclaimed even outside the Land of Israel.
—BABYLONIAN TALMUD, ROSH HASHANAH 9B

Though Iyar is a month of farming the land, in the Torah portions we read at this season, we learn of the custom of the jubilee, when the land becomes wilderness once more. Any land bought by an individual returns to its original tribal owners. Any Israelite who has been held as a slave is freed. All debts are forgiven. How extraordinary it would be, what an upheaval, if in modern times the world declared a jubilee even once, freed its slaves, cancelled its debts, and returned land to peoples from whom it had been taken.

The 49 days of the Omer are, in a way, a reminder of the 49 years until the jubilee. Shavuot, the 50th day, is a kind of jubilee, when Israel is freed of its slavery and prepares to return to its ancestral land. Shavuot's connection to the jubilee reminds us that accepting the Torah means accepting the challenges and responsibilities of freedom and offering freedom to others as well.

This 39th day of the Omer is *netzach shebeyesod*, which means "eternal rootedness" and "eternal connection." On this day, we celebrate one another's roots in the earth. We dedicate ourselves to the dignity and freedom of all.

Eating Like the Wild Beasts

That fiftieth year shall be a jubilee for you: you shall not sow, neither shall you reap the aftergrowth or harvest the untrimmed vines, for it is a jubilee. It shall be holy to you, you may only eat the growth direct from the field.
—LEVITICUS 25:11–12

From that which grows in the field by itself, you may eat.
—NACHMANIDES ON LEVITICUS 25:12

In the Torah portion of Be-har, read at this season, we learn that in the 50th year of the Israelite calendar, the jubilee year, one may not sow or harvest in the way humans normally cultivate the ground. One may eat only what grows naturally or what is left over from previous years of planting. This custom has two benefits. First, it lets the earth rest from the ravages of farming and recover its strength. Second, it reminds people that the earth does not yield infinitely.

The human experience in the jubilee year is one of wilderness, just as our experience of Iyar is one of wilderness. By breaking from the cycle of seedtime and harvest, we remember the experiences of our ancestors before they were attached to a particular piece of land. We are even able to identify with the experiences of animals, who must forage without planting. Jubilee has the potential to teach us new and resourceful ways of living and gives us empathy with other peoples and forms of life.

In modern times, we have lost the date of the jubilee. Yet in this season, we remember how our ancestors practiced kindness to the earth by abstaining from cultivating land. On this 40th day of the Omer, *hod shebeyesod*, or the "humility of our roots," we remember our origins in the wilderness.

The Name of Multiplicity

There came out among the Israelites one whose mother was Israelite and whose father was Egyptian. And a fight broke out in the camp between that son of an Israelite woman and a certain Israelite. The son of the Israelite woman pronounced the Name in blasphemy, and he was brought to Moses. Now his mother's name was Shelomith daughter of Dibri of the tribe of Dan.
—Leviticus 24:10–11

Rabbi Hiyya said: He came to pitch his tent with the tribe of Dan, but they told him that Israelites can only march with the banners of their fathers, not their mothers. He took them to court in front of Moses, and lost, and got up and cursed.
—Leviticus Rabbah 32:3

It is not always easy to accept what is different. Sometimes we react to multiplicity with fear and rejection. One of the stories we read in the Torah this month is of Shelomith bat Dibri and her son. Shelomith's son is half Israelite. A midrash tells that when he attempts to join his mother's tribe, they reject him on the grounds that his father is not an Israelite. Of course, the man has no other tribe to march with on the wilderness journey. Isolated and shamed, Shelomith's son is so angry that he curses using the divine Name. Moses orders him killed.

This story, by focusing on the angry actions of the outcast, does not acknowledge the violence of the tribe that rejects him. By blaming the outsider, Moses takes no responsibility for the tribe's narrow view of the situation. Yet there is a remedy for this vicious circle, and it is hidden in the story. The name of the outcast's mother, Shelomith bat Dibri, means "peace, daughter of speech." By speaking with those who are different from us, by listening to those who have been rejected, we come to know peace. If Moses had truly listened to Shelomith's son, the outcome might have been different.

This 41st day of the Omer is the day of *yesod shebeyesod*, or the "root of connection." Today we look for the ways connection and dialogue can bring peace to the world.

The Names of Healing

She went on until she came to the man of God on Mount Carmel. … He arose and followed her. … Elisha came into the house and there was the boy, laid out dead on his couch. He went in, shut the door behind the two of them, and prayed to the Eternal. Then he mounted the couch and placed himself over the child. He put his mouth on its mouth, his eyes on its eyes, and his hands on its hands…. And the body of the child became warm.
—2 Kings 4:25–34

He wrote on him the ineffable Name, composed of seventy-two names. . . . Elisha named the child Habakkuk. By the names his spirit was returned to him and by the letters his limbs were remade.
—Zohar I:7b

In Iyar, the month of healing, we remember the Shunammite woman from the book of 2 Kings. This dignified, wealthy woman builds a room for the prophet Elisha in her home. As a reward, Elisha prays for her to have a son. Years later, the boy becomes ill and dies. The mother puts him in the prophet's bed, goes to the prophet Elisha, and pleads with him to restore her son. Elisha prays for the child, and he revives. The child grows up to become a prophet himself.

In the Zohar, Elisha uses the 72 names of God to resurrect the Shunammite woman's son. The 72 names of God, like different medicinal leaves or herbs, each add their own measure of goodness to the ill child. Then Elisha gives the child a new name: Habakkuk, "embrace." This name embodies the love of the child's parents. In Jewish tradition, a new name can also be medicine for an illness of the body or soul (Babylonian Talmud, Rosh Hashanah 16b; Shulchan Arukh, *Yoreh De'ah* 335:10).

On this 42nd day of the Omer, we meditate on *malkhut shebeyesod*, the "wholeness of connection." Through our names, we embrace the Divine and one another.

The Calling of Samuel

Young Samuel was in the service of the Eternal under Eli. … the Eternal called: "Samuel!" Samuel rose and went to Eli and said: "Here I am, you called me." . . . Then Eli understood that the Eternal was calling the boy. And Eli said to Samuel, "Go lie down. If you are called again, say, 'Speak, Eternal, for Your servant is listening.'" And Samuel went to his place and lay down. The Eternal came, and stood there, and called as before: "Samuel, Samuel!"

—1 SAMUEL 3:1–10

We have seen that Moses and Samuel are considered equal. . . . Come and see the difference between them: Moses would enter before the Holy One and listen to the divine word, but with Samuel, the Holy One came to him.

—EXODUS RABBAH 16:4

According to *Megillat Ta'anit* (2), today marks the anniversary of the death of Samuel, the last judge of Israel. Samuel becomes a leader as a young man. His mother, Hannah, dedicates him to the service of the Divine in gratitude for her conception (1 Samuel 1). As a young boy, Samuel serves under the high priest Eli. When his first divine call comes, he thinks his teacher, Eli, is calling him. Only after several calls does Samuel understand he hears a divine voice.

Not all revelations are obvious. Sometimes it is a small voice, a wind rustling through leaves or an inner whisper, that calls to us. Sometimes we need someone else to help us recognize our calling. We are woken up from sleep and struggle to respond.

This is the 43rd day of the Omer, the day of *hesed shebemalkhut*, or the "flowing of the Divine Presence." Today, like Samuel, we stand before a still, small voice, trying to understand its message.

The Coming of Jethro

Jethro, priest of Midian, Moses' father-in-law, heard all that the Divine had done for Moses and for Israel ..., how the Eternal had brought Israel out from Egypt. So Jethro, Moses' father-in-law, took Zipporah, Moses' wife, after she had been sent home, and her two sons. . . . Jethro brought Moses' sons and wife to him in the wilderness, where he was encamped at the mountain of God.
—Exodus 18:1–5

Jethro reproved Moses when he saw him sitting and judging Israel all day. He said: "Why are you sitting alone? This is foolishness! It is not just me who thinks this. The Holy One of Blessing shares my opinion." And so it says: "Moses took the advice of his father-in-law and did everything he said."
—Exodus Rabbah 27:6

As Sivan begins, the Hebrew people arrive at the foot of Mount Sinai. As they make camp, they receive a visitor: Jethro, a priest of the land of Midian, father to Moses' wife Zipporah. Jethro has brought Zipporah and Moses' sons with him from Midian. Moses and his family are reunited, and Jethro becomes Moses' adviser.

Jethro notices Moses is working himself to death judging disputes between Israelites. Concerned, Jethro suggests a system of courts, so Moses need decide only large matters, while others judge small matters. It is noteworthy that Jethro, a priest of another religion, helps Moses set up the system that later develops into the Rabbinic courts. In today's midrash, Jethro is confident of his own connection to the Infinite. He tells Moses that the Holy One of Blessing concurs with Jethro's opinion: Moses should not make the people wait around all day because he thinks he is the only one who can help them. Moses must delegate.

In this season, when we observe the multiplicity and interdependence of nature, we remember we too are not islands. Strangers and foreigners may have great wisdom to teach us. On this 44th day of the Omer, *gevurah shebemalkhut*, or "limits within sovereignty," we balance our sense of self-rule with our knowledge that we need to ask for help from others.

The New Moon of Apples

New Moon of Sivan

On the third new moon after the Israelites had gone forth from the land of Egypt, on that very day, they entered the wilderness of Sinai.
—Exodus 19:1

Sinai is compared to an apple tree, for just as an apple tree gives fruit in Sivan, so the Torah was given in Sivan. . . . Why not a nut or another tree? With all other trees, their way is to give forth leaves first and fruits second, the apple tree gives its fruits first and then puts forth leaves. So Israel agreed to do the commandments even before it heard them.
—Song of Songs Rabbah 8:3

The entire month of Sivan is filled with the perfume of the Torah. The Torah says that on the third new moon, the new moon of the month of Sivan, the people of Israel enter the desert of Sinai, where they will receive the Torah from the Eternal. Sivan promises the ripening of fruit: the fruit of the trees blossoming at this season and the fruit of Torah.

At Sinai, Israel is compared to the apple tree. As the apple tree bears fruit before it makes leaves (at least in the imagination of the midrash), Israel too does things backward, by agreeing to do good and righteous deeds before being told what deeds will be required of them. Sivan, in the *Sefer Yetzirah* (5:7), is the month of motion. In Sivan, we feel the command to act, even before we reflect on how hard those actions might be to carry out. So too the apple tree begins to blossom before it knows what the season will bring.

Today, the 45th day of the Omer, is *tiferet shebemalkhut*, or the "beauty of the *Shekhinah*." The *Shekhinah*'s beauty shines in us—and it shines even more radiantly when we, like the Israelites of the wilderness, engage in acts of love.

The Covenant with Creation

And the Divine saw all that had been made, and found it very good. And there was evening and there was morning, the sixth day.
—Genesis 1:31

Why, on the sixth and last day of Creation, does it say "the sixth day" [instead of a "sixth day"]? To show the Divine made a stipulation with the world that it would exist only if Israel would accept the Torah. Thus, "the" [the numerical equivalent for the word "the" is five] for the five books of the Torah, and "sixth" for the sixth day of Sivan.
—Rashi on Genesis 1:31

The Israelites begin to prepare for the giving of the Torah in Sivan. Yet a legend says the world has been preparing for the giving of the Torah since Creation. Rashi teaches that the Divine made a deal with the world: Its existence would depend on the acceptance of Torah.

Two lessons stem from this teaching. The first is that Jewish tradition is inextricably entwined with the natural world. The world of nature inspires the stories and laws of the Torah, and Torah influences the way we understand nature. The second lesson is that the survival of the world does indeed depend on whether we, and all peoples, are willing to act as stewards of life and of the planet on which we live. Creation does depend on Torah, and Torah depends on Creation. Perhaps this is why we receive Torah when spring moves into summer, when creation is in full swing.

The 2nd of Sivan is a day of recognizing our holiness: "On the second day of Sivan the Divine said to them: You shall be a people of priests and a holy nation" (Babylonian Talmud, Shabbat 86b). It is the 46th day of the Omer, or *netzach shebemalkhut*, the "endurance of the kingdom." Today we commit to the holy task of preserving Creation.

Boundary Making

And the Eternal said to Moses, "Go to the people and warn them to stay pure today and tomorrow. Let them wash their clothes. Let them be ready for the third day, for on the third day the Eternal will come down, in the sight of all the people, on Mount Sinai. You shall set bounds for the people round about, saying, 'Beware of going up the mountain or touching the border of it.'"
—Exodus 19:10–12

On the third of Sivan Moses gave them the mitzvah of boundary making.
—Babylonian Talmud, Shabbat 86b

Spring is a time when forms of life crowd into one another, and leaves overlap on the trees. Yet within the abundance of spring are many boundaries. Creatures, organisms, even individual cells need boundaries to survive, to keep nutrients in and invaders out. Without boundaries, life could not exist.

The Eternal instructs Moses to set a boundary around Mount Sinai. The boundary is a matter of practical safety, as Sinai is steaming and smoking like a volcano. It is also a matter of spiritual wisdom. The covenant at Sinai, like the skin of a cell, will make the Israelites into a separate entity, with its own norms, ideals, and needs. The line around Sinai teaches the importance of setting limits.

Yet boundaries must also be permeable, just as the line around Sinai gives way to admit Moses. Only by allowing its borders to open can an organism feed or give birth. To let in is just as important a function as to keep out. On this 47th day of the Omer, *hod shebemalkhut*, or "restraint and wholeness," we remember our need for both limits and limitlessness.

The Third Day

On the third day, as morning dawned, there was thunder, and lightning, and a dense cloud upon the mountain, and a very loud blast of the horn, and all the people who were in the camp trembled. Moses led the people out of the camp toward the Divine, and they took their places at the foot of the mountain. Now Mount Sinai was all in smoke, for the Eternal had come down upon it in fire.
—EXODUS 19:16–17

The three first letters of the word ashan *[smoke]*—ayin, shin, *and* nun—*refer to* olam, shanah, *and* nefesh, *or world, year, and soul.*
—SHNEUR ZALMAN OF LYADY (THE ALTER REBBE)

According to Shneur Zalman of Lyady, the founder of Chabad Hasidism, the experience of Sinai—the experience of meeting the sacred—unifies the three dimensions of the universe. These three dimensions are place, time, and consciousness or spirit. Jewish mystics refer to these dimensions as *olam*, *shanah*, and *nefesh*—world, year, and soul (*Sefer Yetzirah* 3:3). The "third day" of waiting for Revelation may be a reference to these three qualities of existence.

Each of us experiences place, time, and soul. Yet it is not easy to bring these three dimensions together, to become completely aware of who we are, when we are, and where we are. In the moments when we are completely present and centered, we experience a kind of inner knowing. We are able to hear the voices of past and future calling across the generations.

Today is the 48th day of the Omer—*yesod shebemalkhut*, or the "foundation of the world." Today we deeply root ourselves in space, time, and soul and connect to the fiery smoke of Mount Sinai.

The Silence before Speech

The Eternal spoke those words—those and no more—to your whole congregation at the mountain, with a mighty voice out of the fire and the dense clouds.
—Deuteronomy 5:19

When the Holy One of Blessing gave the Torah, no bird chirped, no bull bellowed, no angel flew, no seraph uttered "holy." The sea did not move a single wave, and humans made no sound. The world was silent and still, and the Eternal said, "I am the Infinite your God." This is why it says: those words and no more.
—Exodus Rabbah 29:9

There is a moment, sometimes at evening, sometimes before a thunderstorm, when nature is still. The multiplicity of life's voices gives way to a quiet that reminds us of the moment before Creation. Jewish tradition imagines such a moment before Sinai: a time of stillness and wordlessness, as if the world were emptying itself so that it may receive the mystery of Revelation.

This is the last day of the Omer, day 49, the culmination of seven weeks of counting. We began the Omer with a grain of barley; we end it with a risen loaf of bread. Somewhere along the line, a transformation has occurred. We began with *hesed shebehesed*, a promise of "love and generosity." This final day of the Omer is *malkhut shebemalkhut*, the *Shekhinah* within the fabric of Creation, the Torah within the world, the yeast within the bread, the "fullness of life within the earth." On this day we take a moment of silence to experience the wonder of our multiplicity and wholeness. At evening, Shavuot will begin.

The Voice of the Bride

First Day of Shavuot

I am the Eternal your God,
who brought you out of the land of Egypt, the house of bondage.
You shall have no other gods besides Me.
—Exodus 20:2–3

Come, O beloved,
to meet the bride.
—Shlomo ha-Levi Alkabetz, "Lekhah Dodi"

If Passover is like a birth, Shavuot is like a marriage, and the Revelation at Sinai is a wedding between heaven and earth. On the first night of Shavuot, some Jews have the custom of staying up until dawn to study. This all-night study session is called the *Tikun leil Shavuot*, the "repair of Shavuot eve." Those who study the Torah that night are like bridesmaids waiting up with the bride on the night before she marries. In the morning, the participants in the *tikun* "accompany the bride to the *huppah*"—they pray at dawn, and read the story of Revelation (Zohar I:8a).

On the morning of Shavuot, in Yemenite and some other Jewish cultures, a wedding contract is read before the Torah service. In some synagogues, the bride is the Torah, the groom is Israel, and the Holy One gives away the bride. Another tradition says the *Shekhinah* is the bride, the Holy One is the groom, and the wedding brings the immanent and transcendent parts of the Divine together.[6]

Shavuot, the harvest of first fruits, celebrates the union of sky and earth. We imagine Torah falling to earth to make our ethical and mythic imaginations fertile for yet another year. We decorate our synagogues and homes with flowers and greens to bring new fertility and creativity into our lives.

The Voice of Thunder

Second Day of Shavuot

Now Mount Sinai was all in smoke, for the Divine had come down on it in fire, the smoke rose like the smoke of a kiln, and the whole mountain trembled violently. The blare of the horn grew louder and louder. As Moses spoke, the Divine answered him in thunder [lit. with a voice].
—Exodus 19:18–19

The voice reached each Israelite according to his or her ability to hear. The elderly heard according to their strengths, and the young according to their strengths, the children according to their strengths, the women according to their strengths. Moses too heard according to his strengths, for it says: Moses spoke, and the Divine answered him with a voice.
—Midrash Tanhuma, Shemot 21

The festival of Shavuot celebrates the offering of bread on the Temple altar as well as the Revelation of Torah at Mount Sinai. The celebration of bread and the celebration of Revelation are similar in theme. The Jewish blessing over bread thanks God for bringing bread from the earth, yet the Divine is only part of the process. Human beings must harvest the grain; winnow it and grind it; use the flour to make loaves, kneading the dough and baking the bread. So too Revelation is unfinished until humans become part of the process.

Midrash Tanhuma shares the surprising midrash that at Sinai, each person heard something different. Each heard the holy voice according to his or her strengths and weaknesses. One imagines Sinai as a little like a United Nations meeting, with each person receiving a simultaneous translation into the language of his or her own heart.

According to the Babylonain Talmud (Sotah 12a), today, the second day of Shavuot, is also the day Moses is conceived in his mother's womb. The conception of the Torah and the conception of the human who brings Torah fall at the same time. It is as if each is a womb for the other. Torah and the human heart are like flour and yeast, combining to make spiritual sustenance.

Ruth's Harvest

Isru Hag: Day after Shavuot

Ruth the Moabite said to Naomi, "I would like to go to the fields and glean among the ears of grain, behind someone who may show me kindness." … She came and gleaned in a field, behind the reapers; and, as luck would have it, it was the piece of land belonging to Boaz. … Boaz said to Ruth: "Listen to me, daughter. Don't go to glean in another field."… She answered: "You are most kind, my lord, to comfort me and to speak gently to your maidservant, though I am not so much as one of your maidservants."
—Ruth 2:2–3

Boaz said to Ruth: "God forbid! You are not like one of the maid-servants [amahot], *but like one of the matriarchs* [imahot]."
—Ruth Rabbah 5:5

The Book of Ruth is read on Shavuot. Though there is no fire or thunder in her story, Ruth represents the covenant, for she chooses to be part of the Israelite nation out of her love for her mother-in-law, Naomi. In this story, the growing and harvesting of grain is a sign of love. Ruth gathers grain to feed Naomi and Ruth in turn is fed by Boaz, a local landowner who admires her courage. On Shavuot, as the loaves of grain are offered, we too are like Ruth. We have come to glean in the fields of Torah, and often we find many more grains of insight than we expected.

Like the wedding of Sinai, Ruth's story also ends with a wedding. Boaz marries Ruth after she approaches him on a threshing floor and asks him to spread his wings over her. Boaz plays the role of the Holy One, wedding Ruth after her long journey. He symbolizes the abundance of the summer Shavuot season. Ruth, having been received under the *Shekhinah*'s wings, becomes the great-grandmother of David, the ancestor of the Messiah. Ruth is indeed one of the Matriarchs, sustaining the people with the grain of summer.

The Death of David

David slept with his fathers, and he was buried in the city of David. The length of David's reign over Israel was forty years.
—1 KINGS 2:10

David said before the Holy One: "Tell me when I will die"…. The Holy One said, … "You will die on Shabbat." *Every* Shabbat, *he would … study all day, and the Angel of Death could do nothing…. David had a garden behind his house. The Angel of Death climbed into a tree and shook it. David went out to see what all the noise was about. When he went down the steps …, a step broke under him, and he was distracted from his thoughts of study. He died and was taken away to the world to come.*
—BABYLONIAN TALMUD, SHABBAT 30A–B

Legend holds that King David, the singer of psalms and the ruler of Israel, dies on Shavuot (Jerusalem Talmud, Hagigah 12a). The day of David's death is also a *Shabbat* afternoon. David knows he is destined to die on *Shabbat*, and so he spends every *Shabbat* in the study of Torah so the Angel of Death will not be able to interrupt. But the angel tricks him by shaking a tree and distracting him from Torah long enough to take away his soul.

This story tells us a great deal about the season. David, by studying Torah constantly, enters the world of eternity. The power of Torah extends his life and rejuvenates his soul. He cannot be taken away from his sacred work. The Angel of Death, by climbing a tree and shaking it, reminds David that he is part of the natural world as well. He is frail and mortal. He must die like all other creatures.

In fact, David contains within himself both mortality and immortality. Though David dies, the Jewish people still sing: "King David lives forever." David represents the two aspects of humanity we confront at Sinai: the eternal and the earthly, the cyclical and the transcendent.

The Waves of the Sea

His hands are waves of gold,
inlaid with beryl.
—Song of Songs 5:14

"His hands are waves of gold"—As in between each large wave in the sea there are small waves, so between each word of the commandments are all its details and interpretations.
—Song of Songs Rabbah 5:20

At Passover, the Israelites pass through the sea. All through the counting of the Omer, the gate of the sea, the gate of time, has been open. During the Omer, holiness is primarily experienced through the counting of days. On Shavuot, the gate of the sky opens, and holiness is primarily experienced through the heavens and though prayer. This sky gate will remain open until Sukkot, when the gate of the earth will open once more.

Before leaving the sea, though, we receive Torah, and Torah itself is like a sea. It is wide, deep, endless, and multiple, containing many secrets. A midrash comments on a difficult verse in the Song of Songs concerning waves, by telling us the Torah is like the ocean. Each of its words have many smaller, perhaps even invisible, notions and ideas between them. As we ride the waves of Torah beneath the bright heavens of summer, we remember how many of its truths have yet to be discovered.

We have now entered the season of water within fire. The Torah, given in fire, holds life-giving water within, if we are able to reach it.

The Fragrance of Sinai

His cheeks are like beds of spices, banks of perfume; his lips are like lilies, they drip flowing myrrh.
—Song of Songs 5:13

With every word that went out of the mouth of the Divine Power, the world was filled with the fragrance of spices. When the fragrance of one word had filled the world, the Holy One brought out wind from the divine treasuries, and scattered the first fragrance, so the second one could bloom. This is why it says in the Song of Songs, "His lips are like roses." Do not read "roses" [shoshanim] *but "changing"* [sheshonim].
—Babylonian Talmud, Shabbat 88b

The *Sefer Yetzirah* (5:7) tells us that Sivan is the month of movement, and this month we move with and in Torah. The changing currents of Torah are imagined as water but also as wind. Torah, like the breezes of summer, carries fragrance to us, and each word has its own fragrance. When all the scent has been wrung from that word, a wind comes along and blows the scent away, and a new wind arrives with a new word on its wings.

The midrashim about it suggest Torah is a current of motion as much as it is a series of words. In this season, we try to capture its motion, to let some of its words flow alongside our present reality. To move with Torah, we must be willing to change course, to be surprised.

The fragrances in the midrash from the Talmud also help us become more sensitive to the changes in the air. In Sivan, we watch the movement of seasons. When the delicate fragrance of spring vanishes, the ripe scent of summer will not be far behind.

The Burning Bush

Now Moses, tending the flock of his father-in-law Jethro, the priest of Midian, drove the flock into the wilderness, and came to Horeb, the mountain of the Divine. An angel of the Eternal appeared to him in a blazing fire out of a bush. He gazed, and there was a bush all aflame, yet the bush was not consumed.
—Exodus 3:1–2

Moses saw the bush burning with fire, and the fire did not devour the bush, and the bush did not quench the fire—yet no bush grows in the earth unless there is water beneath it. And Moses was greatly astonished in his heart.
—Pirkei de-Rabbi Eliezer 39

Before the Exodus, as a shepherd in Midian, Moses sees a small bush flaming, yet the flame does not burn up the bush. A midrash goes on to say that Moses is astonished, because he knows that where there are plants there must be water. Yet within the bush, fire and water coexist: The fire does not harm the bush, and the water beneath the bush does not quench the fire. Moses sees the mystery of fire and water together.

The story of the burning bush is tied to Shavuot because, according to Jewish lore, both Moses' witnessing of the bush and the Revelation at Sinai happen on the same mountain (*Pirkei de-Rabbi Eliezer* 40). Moses' meditation on fire and water teaches us about the season. As the weeks move into summer, the sun's heat will scorch the earth. Yet the waters of the earth will quench the thirst of plants, animals, and humans. The story of the burning bush tells of a miracle outside nature, yet it also speaks of a daily miracle: the coexistence of heat and coolness, sun and water.

Going Up the Mountain

The Eternal said to Moses, "Come up to me on the mountain and wait there, and I will give you the stone tablets with the teachings and commandments which I have inscribed to instruct them." So Moses and his attendant Joshua arose, and Moses ascended the mountain of the Divine.
—Exodus 24:12–13

Manna came down to Joshua there, and it fell on his limbs, and he would take it from his limbs and eat it.
—Mekhilta Be-shallah 4:3

In *Seder Olam* (6), Moses ascends the mountain on the seventh day after the Revelation at Sinai—today. He leaves the people and vanishes inside the cloud at the top of the mountain, taking only Joshua with him. While Moses receives the Torah for 40 days, Joshua waits on the mountain.

A midrash imagines Joshua is sustained by manna while he waits for Moses halfway up the mountain. Unlike the rest of the people, who go out to gather manna each day, the manna comes to Joshua. He is fed like a child, without effort. So too, as we enter summer, there may be a moment when nature's abundance seems like the fall of manna for Joshua—effortless and endless.

Mountains, in many traditions, are places of spiritual retreat. Joshua's solitary retreat on the mountain feeds him in multiple ways, preparing him to lead the people. We too may seek retreat or rest at this time of year, to take in the gifts of the summer.

Under the Mountain

Israel encamped there in front of [lit. under] the mountain.
—EXODUS 19:2

Miriam looked, and saw in the mountain a wrinkled brown stone like an eyelid. As Miriam watched, the eyelid opened. The stone wrinkled and lifted as if pulled by a muscle, and behind it was a door into the heart of the mountain. . . . "What is this place?" Miriam asked. "You are in the hollow of the mountain," the old woman said. "Inside the words. The stone tablets your brother will receive—if he broke them open, this is what he would find."
—JILL HAMMER, "MIRIAM, UNDER THE MOUNTAIN"[7]

There is a legend (*Midrash Tanhuma, Noah* 3) that when the Israelites stand at Sinai, the Divine lifts up the mountain and holds it over their heads. If they do not accept the Torah, the Holy One threatens, the mountain will fall on them and bury them. This somewhat bitter midrash is, perhaps, the Sages' way of saying they do not feel they have a choice about accepting the Torah.

But what if the Holy One lifted up Mount Sinai so that the Israelites could see inside the mountain? Today's midrash imagines that while Moses is on top of the mountain, receiving the stone tablets of Torah, Miriam is underneath the mountain, looking at the inside of the Torah. Like sap on the inside of the trunk of a tree, the spirit of Torah flows unseen within its limbs.[8]

Genesis Rabbah (34:11) tells that when half of Sivan is over, the wheat harvest is over. Today, half of Sivan is over. As we move away from Shavuot and the harvest of Torah, we begin to look inside ourselves as a people. The coming months of Tammuz and Av are months of heat, hardship, and self-reflection. Yet through these difficult journeys we will enter Torah even more deeply. In the season of water within fire, we look for the cooling streams that flow from within.

The Birth of Judah

She conceived again and bore a son, and declared, "This time I will praise the Eternal." Therefore she named him Judah.
—Genesis 29:35

Leah grasped the spindle of praise, and from her were born masters of praise: Judah, David, and Daniel.
—Genesis Rabbah 71:5

According to the *Midrash Tadshe,* Judah, fourth son of Leah and Jacob, is born today. When her first three children are born, Leah uses their names to reflect on her sadness that Jacob does not love her. Reuben, Simeon, and Levi are all named for Leah's grief. Judah, however, is named for praise. Leah does not say why she praises: She simply chooses to praise.

Judah himself becomes gifted at praise. In Hebrew, the word "praise" (*hodaya*) also has the sense of "acknowledgment." When Judah's daughter-in-law Tamar accuses him of wrongdoing, he admits to his faults. When speaking before the grand vizier of Egypt (who is really Judah's brother Joseph), Judah is able to acknowledge how much his father, Jacob, has suffered from losing Joseph. Because of his gift of self-awareness, Judah becomes the ancestor of King David.

In Sivan, surrounded by the growing light of the sun, we emulate the overflowing praise of Leah, who found reason for joy even though she lived a difficult life. As we praise, we may find our hearts more open, so that we are more able to look inward as Judah did. This full moon of the month of Sivan brings us the gifts of outer and inner sight.

The Month of Zebulun

Of Zebulun he said: Rejoice, Zebulun, in your journeys, and Issachar in your tents!
—DEUTERONOMY 33:18

Issachar sat and studied Torah, and Zebulun went out on the sea, and brought back and put food in the mouth of Issachar.
—GENESIS RABBAH 72:5

In the *Sefer Yetzirah*, Sivan is the month of the tribe of Zebulun. On the surface this is strange because generally Issachar is considered to be the tribe of Torah, whereas Zebulun is the tribe of business and everyday life. Why not make Issachar the tribe of Sivan, month of Revelation?

Yet without Zebulun, there could be no Issachar. In the Ethics of the Fathers (Pirkei Avot 3:17) our Sages say: "If there is no flour, there is no Torah." Torah must be met through action in the real world. Issachar is a farmer, never leaving his plot of land. He is a student of Torah, forever studying. Zebulun is a journeyer on the sea, braving the risks of travel and bringing new things from afar. His reward is just as great as Issachar, who stays on his own land and farms his plot in quietness. Zebulun teaches us that learning is gained through doing and all wisdom must have real-life application and purpose.

Many of us are kinesthetic learners: We learn better by doing than by seeing or hearing. Those of us who are like Zebulun will feel more alive if we journey, try new things, and take on the world. Those of us who are more like Issachar will benefit from the knowledge the Zebuluns in our lives bring back to us.

The Grounding of Noah's Ark

In the seventh month, on the seventeenth day of the month, the ark came to rest on the mountains of Ararat.
—Genesis 8:4

The seventh month—this is Sivan, the seventh month since Kislev, when the rains ended.
—Rashi on Genesis 8:4

On this day of the Jewish calendar, Noah's ark is said to have run aground on Mount Ararat. Sinai and Ararat are similar in their spiritual power, yet they are opposites as well. Both Sinai and Ararat are peaks, bringing earth and heaven together. Both are places where the Divine makes a covenant with humans: the covenant with Noah on Ararat, and the covenant with the Israelites on Sinai. However, Sinai is a dangerous place. Fires burn there, and bounds are set around it so unwary human beings do not touch it and die. Ararat, on the other hand, is the only safe place in a literal sea of danger. Sinai is a challenge; Ararat is a relief.

We are in the half year of the *yemot hachamah*, the "days of the sun," when we concentrate on our connection to the larger whole. Both Sinai and Ararat offer us models for how to do this. Sinai shows us how frightening yet inspiring it can be to be part of something larger than oneself. Ararat shows us how comforting and soothing it can be. Both things are true: Covenant offers awe as well as security.

In some parts of the world, summer is a time of abundant water, fruit, and growth. In others, summer brings days of drought, heat, and dying plants. Like the covenant, summer has a double edge, depending on where one stands. As we greet summer, we honor the twin peaks of Ararat and Sinai.

The New Year of Fruit

The Eternal spoke to Moses, saying: Speak to Aaron and say to him, "When you mount the lamps, let the seven lamps give light at the front of the lampstand." Aaron did so; he mounted the lamps at the front of the lampstand, as the Eternal had commanded Moses.
—NUMBERS 8:1–3

Shavuot is also a new year, for then the world is judged regarding the fruits of the trees.
—BABYLONIAN TALMUD, MEGILLAH 31B

A passage in the Talmud indicates Shavuot is the season when the *Shekhinah* determines how much fruit there will be in the coming year. There is some sense to this notion, for at this time the trees do most of their growing and blooming. The Shavuot season, when the first fruits are offered, is the moment when we reflect on how much fruit we hope will grow in the coming year.

During this week of the calendar, not long after the Shavuot festival, we read from the Torah the story of how the sacred menorah was made to light the shrine of the Israelite people. The lamp was made in the shape of a tree with seven branches. Aaron was supposed to light the seven lamps, as if the tree were bearing fruit of light.

The menorah we discover in the Torah is the same image as the fruit trees we hope will prosper on the earth. All year round, a symbol of the fruit trees resides in our houses of worship, reminding us of our need to carefully husband and harvest the land's abundance. In the Shavuot season, we eat the ripe fruit of summer and hold in our minds the invisible fruit of the future.

The Gifting of the Elders

Then the Eternal said to Moses, "Gather for me seventy of Israel's elders of whom you have experience as elders and officers of the people, and bring them to the Tent of Meeting and let them take their place there with you. I will come down and speak with you there, and I will draw upon the spirit that is upon you and put it upon them; they shall share the burden of the people with you, and you shall not bear it alone."
—NUMBERS 11:16–17

To what is this similar? To a candle that was burning, and one lit from it many other candles, yet the light of its flame did not diminish. So too Moses gave of his spirit and lost nothing of his own.
—NUMBERS RABBAH 15:19

In late Sivan, we begin to move toward Tammuz, the season of falling flowers. The sun tires us as we labor in the heat. So too in the wilderness story, Moses becomes weary of his task as leader, prophet, and nursemaid of the people. He complains to the Divine, "Did I give birth to this people that I have to carry them through the desert?" The Divine decides to assign 70 elders the task of prophesying, so that Moses will not feel alone.

It was around this time of year that the Divine put some of Moses' spirit onto the elders (Babylonian Talmud, Ta'anit 29a; *Yalkut Shimoni*, *Be-ha'alotekha* 738). The season of multiplicity, when many creatures mate and reproduce and when the many leaves of the trees create nourishment from the sun, is a good moment to notice we are not alone.

Further, this abundant season is a time to remember we can give away without being diminished ourselves. As the midrash in *Numbers Rabbah* tells us, Moses was able to place his spirit upon the elders without losing any of his own ability. The story reminds us we too can give away love, generosity, compassion, and wisdom without losing anything. In the season of *hesed*, "pure love," we scatter our spirit like pollen over the earth.

Eldad and Medad

Two men, one named Eldad and the other Medad, had remained in camp. … A youth ran out and told Moses, … "Eldad and Medad are acting the prophet in the camp!" And Joshua … said, "My lord Moses, restrain them!" But Moses said to him, "… Would that all the people of the Eternal were prophets!"
—NUMBERS 11:26–29

Eldad and Medad … were humble and said, "We are not worthy to be among the elders." Because they were humble, they were found to be greater than all the elders. … Eldad and Medad made prophecies about that which would happen at the end of forty years. … Some said they prophesied Moses would die and Joshua would lead the people into the Land of Israel.
—NUMBERS RABBAH 15:19

Eldad and Medad, of whom we read at this time of year, receive the gift of prophecy from Moses and become prophets themselves. Even though they are not among the elders chosen to be prophets, they begin to utter oracles. Joshua is upset by this apparent flouting of Moses' authority, but Moses insists that he wishes all the people were prophets.

In *Numbers Rabbah,* it is because Eldad and Medad are humble and do not want to take their place among the elders that they are given the gift of inner sight. Their gift is even greater than that of the other elders—even greater than that of Moses. It is they who first prophesy Moses will die in the wilderness and that Joshua will finish the task of leading the people into the land.

This sad note moves us into the summer months of Tammuz and Av, months of exile and waning light. Eldad and Medad, whose names come from a root meaning "love," make the people aware of the eventual loss of Moses. These humble prophets remind us of the turning circle of life and help us face the changes ahead.

Zipporah Lights a Candle

While they were in Hazeroth, Miriam and Aaron spoke against Moses because of the Cushite woman he had married: "He married a Cushite woman!"
—NUMBERS 12:1–2

When the elders were appointed, all Israel lit candles for them and rejoiced in them. Miriam saw the candles burning and said to Zipporah: "What is going on with these candles?" Zipporah explained, and Miriam said: "How fortunate are the wives of these men, that they see how their husbands have risen to high estate!" Zipporah said: "Woe to them, for now they will no longer join with their wives."
—YALKUT SHIMONI, BE-HA'ALOTEKHA 738

In Numbers (12), Miriam and Aaron complain about Moses because Moses has married a Cushite, or Ethiopian, woman. While this incident may refer to a second marriage, most commentators identify Moses' wife, Zipporah, with this unnamed Cushite woman. Some say "Cushite" refers to an unusually beautiful woman (Rashi on Numbers 12:2).

At a candlelighting ceremony for the elders who have been invested with Moses' spirit, Miriam opines that their wives must be very happy. Zipporah curtly replies that, on the contrary, their wives will now be miserable, for their husbands will no longer make love to them. It appears that because the Divine is always speaking to him, Moses does not find it proper to engage in sexual intercourse with his wife. Miriam is indignant about this injustice and complains to Moses that it is not right.

As we move toward the summer solstice, when the sun's light will decrease, we begin to examine themes of loss and separation. Indeed, it is on this day that Zipporah is said to express her loss of love and intimacy (Babylonian Talmud, Ta'anit 29a). Miriam responds that connection and love are necessary to life. Holiness need not mean withdrawal from human intimacy.

The Casting out of Miriam

As the cloud withdrew from the Tent, there was Miriam stricken with snow-white scales! When Aaron turned toward Miriam, he saw that she was stricken with scales. And Aaron said to Moses, "… Let her not be as one dead who emerges from his mother's womb with half his flesh eaten away." So Moses cried out to the Eternal, saying, "O Divine One, pray heal her!" But the Eternal said to Moses: "If her father spat in her face, would she not bear her shame for seven days? Let her be shut out of camp seven days, and then … readmitted."
—NUMBERS 12:10–14

My reward:
HE has turned against me,
Whiteness of skin,
Shielded from sun and friends
With no one to listen
To my prophecy.
—NAOMI GRAETZ,
"MIRIAM THE BITTER"[9]

In the wilderness, Miriam and her brother Aaron challenge the leadership of their brother, Moses. "Has the Divine not spoken also through us?" they ask. Because Miriam tries to claim authority alongside Moses, the Divine strikes her with *tzara'at* (a biblical skin ailment sometimes translated as "leprosy"). Only she, not Aaron, is stricken. She faces humiliation and illness as Aaron pleads for her. The Holy One rejects her as if she were a spurned daughter.

Miriam, a woman prophet, tries to gain legitimate power and is punished with exile. As Naomi Graetz writes, though Miriam is a true prophet, outside the camp there is no one to listen to her—only blowing sand. She is shut up out of the light of the sun, just as women have been shut away so that no one will see them.

The Babylonian Talmud, Ta'anit 29a, claims that today Miriam is sent outside the camp. At the season of the summer solstice, Miriam is the sun whose light wanes. Yet those of us who listen to Miriam's voice know she cannot be shut away forever. At midsummer, when according to legend Miriam's well returns to the people, Miriam's prophecy will once again enlighten us.

The Great Miriam Sit-Down Strike

So Miriam was shut out of
camp seven days, and the
people did not march on until
Miriam was readmitted.
—NUMBERS 12:15

Miriam the leprous,
Miriam the hag
Miriam the cackling one
What did I have but a voice,
to announce liberty
No magic tricks, no miracles,
no history, no stick
or stone of law. You who
believe that God
speaks only through Moses,
bury me in the desert
I curse you with drought
I curse you with spiritual dryness
But you who remember my music
you will feel me under
your footsoles
like cool ground water
under porous stone—
Follow me, follow my drum.
—ALICIA OSTRIKER,
"THE SONGS OF MIRIAM"[10]

The Bible notes that Miriam is shut out of the camp for seven days, as punishment for her spiritual rebellion. Today is the second day of her exile. The people do not move on until Miriam returns to the camp. The storyteller Arthur Strimling points out that the text does not say Moses commands the people to wait for Miriam. The people wait of their own accord, knowing they cannot go on without Miriam's gifts of water and healing song. Strimling calls this action "The Great Miriam Sit-Down Strike."

The poet Alicia Ostriker imagines that Miriam curses those who would leave her behind in the desert. The poet calls on those who remember and cherish Miriam's music to follow the rhythm of her drum through the wilderness. In Ostriker's vision, Miriam's voice, though not codified or sanctified like the voice of Moses, is a voice that offers true guidance as we make the journey of the spirit. Today we remember the drum of Miriam and listen to it sounding like a heartbeat, even from its place of exile. We hear it as the heart of the earth, guiding us toward life. Miriam, the water within fire, the well beneath the blazing sun, opens to us the soul of Sivan.

Houses of Glass

When a prophet of the Eternal arises among you, I make myself known to that person in a vision.
—NUMBERS 12:6

In Tevet, Shevat, and Adar the Israelites in the wilderness would cover their houses with cedar wood. In Nisan, Iyar, and Sivan they would cover their houses with panes of glass. In Tammuz, Av, and Elul they would cover them with marble, and in Tishrei, Heshvan, and Kislev they would cover them with ivory.
—OTZAR MIDRASHIM: ARAKHIM 6

Today is the third day of Miriam's exile. As the end of Sivan approaches, we consider the legend that in each season of the year the Israelites of the wilderness built their houses from a different material. In Nisan, Iyar, and Sivan, the people built their houses out of glass, perhaps so that they could see the bright light of the spring and summer.

Perhaps, as she dwells in the desert during her exile, Miriam too lives in a glass house. She opens herself to the elements and seeks new vision, in spite of her community's rejection. Maybe the Eternal comes to her—not a punitive deity, but a clear, translucent divinity that allows her to see clearly, without illusions. It may be that Miriam returns from the desert with a greater revelation than she had before she left.

At this season, we too try to live in glass houses. We look out into the world, trying not to put up too many barriers between us and the universe. We recognize that like Miriam, we are vulnerable to pain, rejection, and doubt. In spite of this vulnerability, we seek to be open. Beneath the summer sky, we wait for the dreams and visions that come when we wait to receive them.

Green Garments

[The wild ass] roams the hills for his pasture, and searches for any green thing.
—Job 39:8

The colors correspond to the four seasons of the year. From Tishrei to Tevet [autumn], the days are like the color blue, so blue is worn. From Tevet to Nisan, snow comes down, so white garments are worn. From Nisan to Tammuz, the green sea is calm enough to sail upon, so the garments worn are green, and from Tammuz to Tishrei, fruits are ripe and red, so the garments are red.
—Beit ha-Midrash 5:39

In Nisan, we left Egypt through a passage in the sea; and through Nisan, Iyar, and Sivan, we counted the 49 days of the Omer that represent the sea of time. In Sivan, we remembered the receiving of the Torah, which is compared to a sea and its waves. Now, in Sivan, we remember Miriam and the well of water that followed her through the wilderness. It is no wonder that legend says the Israelites wore green during this season to represent the sea.

Green also represents the living plants of summer. Today is Miriam's fourth day in exile. We imagine her looking outside her tent for something green, something growing that will give her hope. Perhaps she searches for healing herbs or greens she can cook for her dinner. Even though stricken with a deathly disease, perhaps Miriam wears green as she goes out to look for life.

In Sivan, we too search for green in our lives, looking for signs of life in our everyday comings and goings. We remember the waters of the sea and the rivers of Torah. We remember the camp of Miriam, where a green shoot sprouts up to comfort her in her exile and remind her of her undefeatable spirit.

The Meaning of *Tzara'at*

Moses spoke up and said: "What if they do not believe me and do not listen to me, but say: 'The Eternal did not appear to you'?" . . . The Eternal said to him…: "Put your hand into your bosom." He put his hand into his bosom; and when he took it out, his hand was encrusted with snowy scales! And the Eternal said: "Put your hand back into your bosom." He put his hand back into his bosom; and when he took it out of his bosom, there it was again like the rest of his body.
—Exodus 4:1,6–7

Because of an evil tongue, people are smitten with tzara'at.
—Midrash Tanhuma, Tsav 13

Today is Miriam's fifth day outside the camp. She is nearing the end of the exile imposed on her because she rebelled against Moses. Some claim Miriam is punished with *tzara'at* (a biblical disease that whitens skin) because she gossiped about Moses, complaining about the way he conducted his role as leader (Rashi on Numbers 12:10). This interpretation comes from the Rabbinic belief that *tzara'at* is a punishment for *lashon ha-ra,* or "evil speech" about someone else.

It is interesting to recall that Moses too was once smitten with *tzara'at*. When the Divine appeared to Moses at the burning bush, Moses expressed worry that the people would not believe him. As a sign, the Holy One showed Moses how to make his hand white and then make it normal again. This sign was to convince the Israelites and the Egyptians that Moses' prophecy was true.

Why this sign? Perhaps Moses was being warned not to think badly of the Hebrews and doubt their faith (a kind of evil speech). Or perhaps *tzara'at* is itself a sign of revelation. This disease, which causes white skin, simulates death, and its cure may represent rebirth. Both Moses and Miriam are reborn as prophets. In Sivan, month of Revelation, we too seek this skill of truth telling.

The Life of Aaron

Then Miriam the prophetess, sister of Aaron, took a timbrel in her hand.
—Exodus 15:20

Why was she called Aaron's sister? Was she not the sister of both Moses and Aaron? Rather, because Aaron gave his life for her, she is called Aaron's sister.
—Genesis Rabbah 80:10

Today is Miriam's sixth day in the wilderness. Perhaps her thoughts are turning toward home, and toward the brothers she has left behind. How does she feel about seeing Moses and Aaron again? Moses is the occasion for her exile, and Aaron, although he pleads for Miriam, does not share her punishment for speaking against Moses.

A midrash in *Genesis Rabbah* imagines that the Torah calls Miriam "Aaron's sister" because Aaron is willing to risk his life for her by asking Moses to heal her of her illness. Yet one could as easily say Aaron is called "Miriam's brother" because she shields him, bearing a difficult punishment that should have been Aaron's as well.

In one sense, we can imagine Miriam as our sister the earth, stricken with diseases because of our actions, though we may blame her for her malfunctions. Though we ourselves are not immediately victims of the pesticides and pollutants we pour into the soil and water, if we do not plead on the earth's behalf as Aaron pleaded for Miriam, we will soon share her maladies.

Though we never see the reconciliation of Miriam, Moses, and Aaron, we can hope that they find a way to resolve their power struggle and become close siblings again.

Miriam Returns

On the seventh day, the priest shall examine [the leper]. . . . If the affection has faded and has not spread on the skin, the priest shall pronounce him clean. It is a rash; that person shall wash his clothes, and he shall be clean.
—LEVITICUS 13:6

The Holy One did a great honor for Miriam at that moment, and said: "I will be her priest. I shut her out . . . and I will bring her in."
—BABYLONIAN TALMUD, ZEVACHIM 102A

We are told in the Babylonian Talmud (Taa'nit 29a) that this is Miriam's last day in exile. What ceremony does she encounter as she re-enters the camp? We might imagine people gathering to greet her and bring her to her tent. Or we might imagine the well of Miriam following her from the wilderness into the camp and taking up its usual place in front of the sacred shrine.

The Talmud imagines Miriam must go through the priestly ceremony instituted to cleanse lepers. However, neither Aaron nor his sons can conduct this ceremony because they are Miriam's relatives. Only the Holy One is available to be Miriam's priest and perform the ceremony, releasing her back into the community.

This image of the Divine as high priest is uncomfortable: It sets God up as a religious official, reminding us that Miriam, unlike her brothers, is not allowed to serve as a priest. She may only receive the ministrations of one. Ultimately the Talmud's imagination traps Miriam in a powerless state. Yet there is something moving about imagining the Holy One donning priestly garments, taking Miriam by the hand, and bringing her into the camp. Perhaps, after seven days under the stars, Miriam has new dreams to share. We end Sivan as we began, by contemplating the messages passed between heaven and earth.

The Departure of the Spies

Rosh Hodesh Tammuz

The Eternal spoke to Moses, saying, "Send men to scout the land of Canaan, which I am giving to the Israelite people; send one man from each of their ancestral tribes, each one a chieftain among them." So Moses, by the command of the Eternal, sent them out from the wilderness of Paran, all the men being leaders of the Israelites.
—Numbers 13:1–3

On the twenty-ninth of Sivan, Moses sent the spies.
—Babylonian Talmud, Ta'anit 29b

According to the Talmud, today Moses appoints 12 spies to view the Land of Israel and bring back some of its fruit for the people to see. Why 12 rather than one? Perhaps because they each will have their own viewpoint on how the land appears.

We know from the Torah that when the spies return, they will have widely differing reports. A few will be eager to enter the land, while many others will be fearful of the country's mighty inhabitants. The spies represent the fragmentation of perspective. At Sinai, the people have the same vision in spite of their individual views. In the wilderness of Paran, the spies, who are leaders of the people, show how different and opposed the people's visions can be.

In nature, the tree's needs may be opposite to the tent caterpillar's, and the minnow does not have the same perspective as the shark. Multiple opposing views are part of life on earth. Yet part of what it means to be human is to be able to hear the view of someone who opposes you. This is why humans can be peacemakers. Like leaves on a tree, we can be different and still work toward a common goal.

The Journey of the Spies

Swing the sickle, for the crop is ripe; come and tread, for the winepress is full, the vats are overflowing!
—Joel 4:13

The redemption of Israel is compared to four things: the harvest, the grape harvest, spices, and a birthing woman. A harvest, because if a field is reaped not in its time even the straw in it will not be good.... The grape harvest, because if grapes are gathered before their time even their vinegar will not be good.... Spices, because if the spices are gathered when they are soft and moist, their smell will not carry.... A birthing woman, because if she gives birth to her child not in its time it will not live....
—Song of Songs Rabbah 8:14

As Sivan ends, we move into deep summer, the season of harvest. Today is the spies' first day living off the Land of Israel. We began the season of the leaf with the manna; now we end it with gratitude for the grapes on the vine and the grains of wheat in the husk.

Before the last of the harvest is gathered in, there will be hot days, maybe drought. The summer of the Jewish calendar is tinged with sadness and anxiety. National tragedies are remembered at this time, as are personal failings. Summertime is not an easy time—its light has a scythe's edge, cutting away our illusions and leaving us vulnerable.

A midrash compares redemption to four kinds of harvest: grain, grapes, spices, and children. Each of these precious fruits must be gathered in at the right time, or else not gathered in at all. As we traverse the month of Tammuz, we remember that everything must happen in its proper time. A dry, hot summer may bring discomfort, yet it helps the fruits ripen. So too the coming months, if we attend to them, will help ripen our spirits.

NOTES

1 Pliny the Elder, *Natural History XVIII*, trans. H. Rackman (London: Harvard University Press, 2000), p. 286.

2 James Frazer, *The Golden Bough* (Touchstone, 1995), pp. 716–719. See also Ronald Hutton, *The Stations of the Sun* (Oxford, 1966), pp. 218–225.

3 http://www.wheel of the year.com/2003/nativeamerican.htm (accessed March 7, 2006).

4 Priscilla Fishman, *Minor and Modern Festivals* (Leon Amiel, 1973), pp. 24–26.

5 Arthur Waskow, *Seasons of Our Joy: A Modern Guide to the Jewish Holidays* (Beacon Press, 1991), p. 179.

6 Philip Goodman, *The Shavuot Anthology* (Jewish Publication Society, 1992), pp. 99–101.

7 Jill Hammer, "Miriam Under the Mountain," in *Sisters at Sinai: New Tales of Biblical Woman* (The Jewish Publication Society, 2001), p. 130.

8 My thanks to Rabbi Michael Bernstein for his image of the hollow Mount Sinai.

9 Naomi Graetz, "Miriam the Bitter," in *All The Women Followed Her* (Ridukei Miriam Press, 2002), p. 37.

10 Alicia Ostriker, "The Songs of Miriam," in *Thirteenth Moon* (1993) Vol. II, nos. 1 and 2.

The Flower

1 TAMMUZ TO 14 AV

SEASON
Summer

WIND
The south

HALF OF THE YEAR
The sun

ELEMENT
Water within fire

GATE
The sky

ANGEL
Michael
(love and covenant)

DIVINE FACE
Hesed (love)

Man born of woman is short of days, and fed with trouble. He blossoms like a flower and withers, and vanishes, like a shadow.

—Job 14:1–2

The seventh movement of the year is falling. In midsummer in the northeast United States, the blossoms on the fruit trees drop in white showers to the ground, and the roses come to their overabundant bloom. The sun's heat wilts leaves and dries up streams. In the Southwest, the heat blooms into almost unbearable temperatures. In the Middle East, this is a parched season, when the sun is overbearing and the remaining crop is under threat. All over the world, the crop may fail during summer from locusts, drought, or terrible rainstorms. For life to continue, it must traverse these days of light and threat.

The flower symbolizes all that is beautiful but ephemeral. In the Jewish calendar, this season of the year is a time of mourning for loss. From Revelation at the height of Sinai, we now come to the reality of human suffering. In Tammuz, first of the summer months, we remember exile. On the 17th of Tammuz, Jews fast to recall the day Jerusalem's walls fell to Rome. This day begins three weeks of mourning, when traditional Jews avoid music and celebration. We reflect on how violence continues to wound us, and we try to understand the apparent absence of the Divine in the world. In these days of the sun, we turn outward to be witnesses to the past and the present.

In Av we descend deeper into exile. On the 9th of Av we mark the destruction of the First Temple by Babylonian invaders and the destruction of the Second Temple by Roman forces. We also remember the Jewish zealots who out of hatred burned one another's supplies while the Romans were advancing. On the 9th of Av, mystic legends claim, the *Shekhinah* went into exile, wandering with her children through all the lands of the world (Babylonian Talmud, Rosh Hashanah 31a).

The sadness of this season mirrors a grief older than history. For human creatures to live, the harvest must be sacrificed. What grows must die. What lives must eat other living things to stay alive. This season asks an eternal question about the cycle of life:

What suffering can we prevent? What must we struggle to accept? Many other peoples have asked these questions at the height of summer. The Celts and the Sumerians, for example, mourned the death of the god of the grain at this time, imagining he had gone to the underworld to regenerate himself as the new seed.[1] The Sun Dance celebrated by the Sioux and other Native American tribes, held at the summer solstice, symbolizes death and rebirth.[2]

Yet this is also the season of *hesed*, of "grace." For many of us, these are days of light and joy, when we spend most of our time outdoors, enjoying the gifts of the earth. The south is the direction of blessing (*Numbers Rabbah* 3:12), and summer's harvest is a blessing for the world. For those of us in colder climates, the summer weather is especially precious, giving us a sense of play and freedom.

Outwardly, this is a season of fire, when cities and crops are scourged by heat. Yet inwardly, this is the water season, the time when fruits begin to fill with juice. Water is our role model, calling us to cry out our grief and quench one another's thirst for comfort. Summer teaches us love of life and pity for the falling flower. We pour out our hearts before the Divine Presence, so that we may prepare ourselves for the rebirth that will come in autumn.

Joseph in the Pit

New Moon of Tammuz

Next he brought me to the entrance of the north gate of the house of the Eternal, and there sat the women bewailing Tammuz.
—Ezekiel 8:14

On the first of Tammuz Joseph was born.
—Midrash Yalkut Shemot 1

The month of Tammuz is named for the Sumerian god Tammuz, a young shepherd who marries the goddess Inanna. Inanna descends to the underworld on a journey, and her husband, Tammuz, forgets about her. When Inanna returns, she condemns Tammuz to take her place in the underworld. Only through the kindness of Tammuz's sister Geshtinanna, who agrees to share his fate, is Tammuz freed from the realm of death for six months of every year. Tammuz represents the grain cut down in service to human life.[3]

The prophet Ezekiel complains of Israelite women mourning the death of Tammuz at the gates of the Temple. Yet the mourning for Tammuz allowed women to express the poignancy of the harvest and the mortality of human beings.

The 1st of Tammuz is the anniversary of the birth of Joseph, son of Jacob. Joseph, like the Tammuz of the myth, goes down into the underworld. His brothers throw him into a pit, and then he is sold into slavery. Yet each time he descends, Joseph rises again. In the end, he saves his family from famine, just as the grain harvest saves the people from hunger. Joseph reminds us the circle completes itself and growth comes again.

Exile from Eden

So the Divine Presence banished him from the garden of Eden, to till the soil from which he was taken. The Holy One drove the man out, and stationed east of the garden of Eden the cherubim and the fiery ever-turning sword, to guard the way to the Tree of Life.
—GENESIS 3:23–24

During the new moon of the fourth month Adam and his wife went out of the garden of Eden and made their home in the land of Elda, the land that they were created from. And Adam called his wife Eve.
—JUBILEES 3:32–33

In the book of Jubilees (3:32–33), Adam and Eve leave Eden on the 1st of Tammuz for their new existence as mortals. Eden, the first garden of human beings, fades like an early flower. At the season when Jews recall their various exiles throughout history, it is powerful to re-imagine today as the the first full day of this archetypal exile. Did Adam and Eve mourn their garden? Explore their new harsh land? Build a house? Tell one another their story?

The exile of Adam and Eve recalls the experiences of our families in exile: Jewish families expelled from Spain, Russian immigrants pouring into Israel and the United States, Ethiopian Jews leaving for the Promised Land. Exile brings suffering and sorrow, yet much of the Talmud and the Bible, as well as volumes of law, prayer, fiction, and poetry, have been written in exile. The falling flower can be what allows the fruit to grow.

The book of Jubilees tells that Adam and Eve establish a home in the land "from which the *adam* was taken." They choose to live on the soil that created them. Wherever we go, we are still part of the earth.

Sun, Stand Still

When the Eternal routed the Amorites before the Israelites, Joshua addressed the Eternal; he said in the presence of the Israelites: "Stand still, O sun, at Gibeon, O moon, in the valley of Aijalon! And the sun stood still and the moon halted."
—JOSHUA 10:12–13

The sun said to Joshua: "You are asking me to be still?" "Yes," Joshua said. "Who, then, will sing the praises of the Holy One?" the sun asked. Joshua replied: "If you will agree to be quiet, I will sing the praises of the Holy One."
—MIDRASH TANHUMA (BUBER), AHAREI MOT 4

As the Israelite nation enters the land of Canaan, Joshua, warrior disciple of Moses, leads the Israelites in battle against the Amorites. The people need more light, and so Joshua prays for the sun and moon to stand still. The Divine causes the sun to remain in its noontime place while Israel defeats its enemy. *Seder Olam* (11) relates that this incident occurred on the 3rd of Tammuz, at the height of summer.

In one humorous midrash, the sun is irritated at being asked to stop in its tracks. The sun reminds Joshua that it is only doing its job and that Joshua is interfering with the sun's praise of the Divine. Joshua reassures the sun that he will stand in the sun's place and praise the Divine himself.

At the season in the Jewish calendar when we feel ourselves the most fragile, the story of Joshua reminds us that, though we are flowers that fade, we are as worthy as the sun to offer praise before the Holy One.

Moses Strikes the Rock

Moses and Aaron assembled the congregation in front of the rock, and he said to them: "… shall we get water for you out of this rock?" And Moses … struck the rock twice with his rod. Out came copious water.… But the Eternal said to Moses and Aaron, "Because you did not trust Me enough to affirm My sanctity … therefore you shall not lead this congregation into the land that I have given them."

—NUMBERS 20:10–12

Standing between the Rock and the hateful mob, he can bear it no longer. … he taunts … "Shall we get water for you out of this rock?"… His hand rises. … The rod crashes down. Sea splits. Blood gushes. Copious water—Miriam's water—pours forth.

—RIVKAH WALTON, "THE ROCK"[4]

In many Jewish legends, we hear of the well that follows Miriam through the wilderness, giving water to the people. After Miriam dies, the well dries up, and the people are thirsty. The Holy One tells Moses to speak to a rock and ask it for water. Instead, Moses strikes the rock twice in anger. The Divine decrees Moses will die in the wilderness. The *Machzor Vitry,*[4] an early medieval work, tells us Jews in Europe refrained from drawing water on the summer solstice, because on that day Moses was punished for striking the rock.

The midrashist Rivkah Walton connects Moses' anger at the rock to his anger at Pharaoh, at the overseer he killed, even at Miriam for dying. Moses seeks the waters of Miriam's well, but he is not able to truly grieve for his sister. It is his understandable rage at his loss that prevents him from moving onward into the new land. The splitting of the rock allows grief to finally move within him—and within us.

The Vision of Ezekiel

On the fifth day of the fourth month … I saw visions of God. … I looked, and lo … a huge cloud and flashing fire, surrounded by a radiance … in the center of the fire, a gleam as of amber. In the center of it were also the figures of four creatures. … Each of them had a human face, … the face of a lion on the right, … the face of an ox on the left, and … the face of an eagle at the back.
—EZEKIEL 1:1,4–5,10

Rabbi Levi said: to show the praise and might of the Holy One, that in Tammuz they were blemished and in Tammuz the Holy One's kindness returned to them.
—BATEI MIDRASHOT 2, 13:2

On this day of the year Ezekiel, an exiled prophet, received his mysterious vision of the heavenly chariot. A midrash above wonders why Ezekiel receives this vision in Tammuz, a month of "ill omen" when the walls of Jerusalem were breached. The answer is that the Holy One chooses to send compassion to the people at the same season that they were exiled. Tammuz contains both suffering and its remedy, *hesed*.

The creatures Ezekiel sees in his vision have four faces: a human, a lion, a bull, and an eagle. In Jewish mystical tradition these faces represent the "petals" or facets of existence—four worlds, four elements, and four directions—all of which join within the human spirit. Tammuz brings together the many directions of the soul: grief, anger, and the potential for rejoicing.

The Flowering Staff

Moses spoke thus to the Israelites. Their chieftains gave him a staff ... twelve staffs in all. Among these staffs was that of Aaron. Moses deposited the staffs before the Eternal ... Moses entered the Tent of the Pact and there the staff of Aaron of the house of Levi ... had brought forth sprouts, produced blossoms, and borne almonds. Moses then brought out all the staffs from before the Eternal to all the Israelites; each identified and recovered his staff.
—NUMBERS 17:21–24

God commanded them to take staves, for in the future God will reveal to each person how he or she will come to his or her rightful portion, and will no longer wish for the portion of his or her neighbor.
—MEI HASHILOACH ON NUMBERS 17:14

In the season of the flower, we remember the flowering staff of Aaron, which we read in the Torah during Tammuz. According to the book of Numbers, the people doubted Aaron's leadership as priest. The Divine suggested a test: Each tribal leader would place a staff in the *mishkan*. The staff that flowered would indicate the true high priest. Aaron's staff flowered and bore fruit; like the summer among the seasons, Aaron's staff was the one that brought forth life in plenty.

This tale of the priesthood's intrinsic superiority is troubling to those of us who are suspicious of hereditary or social hierarchy. This may be why the Hasidic commentator Rabbi Mordechai Yosef of Isbitza, known as the Mei haShiloach, chooses to read this text in a radical way. In his reading, the blossoming of the staff indicates not that Aaron is more important than the other tribal leaders, but that each individual has a unique and precious destiny. Each staff, he says, flowers in its own way. Though we may be gifted and wounded in different areas, all of us have a valued place in this world. In a mystical sense, all our staffs blossom.

Tempering the Sun

The Divine placed in the heavens a tent for the sun, and he is like a bridegroom coming forth from his huppah.
—PSALMS 19:5

The sphere of the sun has a sheath, as it is written: "The Divine has placed a tent for the sun." A pool of water is before it. At the hour the sun rises, the Holy One tempers its strength so that it will not go out and burn up the world.
—GENESIS ṚABBAH 6:6

Psalm 19:5 imagines the sun bursting out of the tent of night like a bridegroom running from his *huppah* after a wedding. It is surprising that Rabbinic legend uses this happy image to remind us of the dangers of the sun. In one midrash, God puts the sun in a protective covering or canopy to keep the world safe from its fires. When the sun comes out at dawn, God plunges it into a pool of water to cool it. One might imagine the fog on the hills at dawn is steam from this divine lake, after the sun has been thrust into its depths.

The legend reiterates how this summer season encompasses both the sun's fire and the freshness of cool water. In the Jewish mystical tradition, fire represents severity and judgment, whereas water represents love and generosity. The tale of the sun's immersion suggests both fire and water are needed to sustain the world. In Tammuz, we temper our own fires with the water of reflection and stillness so that we too do not burn up the world with our heat.

The Marble Ceiling

King David said: "I have spared no effort to lay up for the House of my God … every kind of precious stone, and much marble.
—1 CHRONICLES 29:1–2

In Tevet, Shevat, and Adar the Israelites in the wilderness would cover their houses with cedar wood. In Nisan, Iyar, and Sivan they would cover their houses with panes of glass. In Tammuz, Av, and Elul they would cover them with marble, and in Tishrei, Heshvan, and Kislev they would cover them with ivory.
—OTZAR MIDRASHIM: ARAKHIM 6

We have learned how in each season the wandering Israelites would construct roofs of a new material. Each of these building materials comes from a different source: marble from stones within the earth, cedar from a tree, ivory from an animal, and glass from the labors of humans. These four substances correspond to the four levels of being mentioned by the kabbalists and Hasidim: the *domemim* (stones), the *tzmachim* (plants), the *chayot* (animals), and the *b'nai adam* (human beings).[6]

Tammuz, in this midrash, is the season of marble. Marble feels grand and permanent. Some of the world's most prominent buildings are made of marble. Yet marble, in Jewish lore, is resonant of the Temple, razed to the ground in Av. Summer, with its short-lived insects and flowers, teaches us that all things are transitory, even the marble buildings we put up for our glory. This is the deeper meaning of the tribes' constantly changing houses.

The Breach in the Walls

King Nebuchadrezzar moved against Jerusalem with his whole army. … By the ninth day of the fourth month [9 Tammuz], the famine had become acute in the city. … Then the city was breached. All the soldiers fled; they left the city by night through the gate between the double walls, which is near the king's garden… . But the Chaldean troops pursued the king, and they overtook Zedekiah in the steppes of Jericho, as his entire force left him and scattered.
—Jeremiah 52:4–8

The fast of the fourth month: this is the ninth of Tammuz, for on it the city was broken, as it is written: "By the ninth day of the fourth month the famine had become acute in the city."
—Babylonian Talmud, Rosh Hashanah 18b

As the first exile of the Jews begins, the Judean king and his soldiers flee Jerusalem, leaving it to face the Babylonians alone. Eventually, the soldiers abandon the king, who is taken captive. This abandonment takes place on 9 Tammuz.

We all fear being abandoned. Human beings are vulnerable when alone. The 9th of Tammuz is a day to remember the abandonment of King Zedekiah, yet perhaps also a day to remember our own aloneness. All of us have moments when we feel cast out or left behind. At those moments, we can try to find reserves of strength within, but we can also try to reach out, believing that we are not truly alone.

No Shadows

In *Genesis Rabbah,* the summer solstice is the moment when the sun stands still, shining equally on everything, so that nothing has a shadow. Everything is clear in the light of the sun. The sun warms all things, yet also takes away the shadows where we hide. It is as if the eye of heaven peered at us without blinking.

[The sun's] rising place is at one end of heaven and his circuit reaches the other; nothing escapes his heat.
—PSALMS 19:8

On the first day of the solstice of Tammuz, no creature has a shadow, for it is written: "Nothing is hidden from the sun's heat" [Ps. 19:7.]
—GENESIS RABBAH 6:6

In the *Sefer Yetzirah* (5:8), Tammuz is the month of sight, the month when vision is greatest. Tammuz teaches us to look at ourselves without distortion, arrogance, or self-hatred. Leaving behind our shadows means leaving behind our attempts to be someone we are not. Only then can we blossom. The light of summer draws us out of our hiding places and into a clearer vision of ourselves.

The Mouth of the Donkey

When the ass now saw the angel of the Eternal, she lay down under Balaam. Balaam was furious and beat the ass with his stick. Then the Eternal opened the ass's mouth and she said to Balaam: "What have I done to you that you have beaten me these three times?"
—NUMBERS 22:27–28

Ten things were created on the evening of the Sabbath of Creation at twilight and these are they: The mouth of the earth, the mouth of the well [of Miriam], the mouth of the donkey, the rainbow, the manna, the staff [of Moses], the shamir [a magical worm that cut the stones for Solomon's Temple], the writing [of the Torah], the writing tool, the tablets.
—ETHICS OF THE FATHERS (PIRKEI AVOT) 5:8

In Tammuz we read the story of Balaam, a non-Israelite prophet. King Balak of Midian sends for Balaam and asks him to curse the Israelites. Balaam consults the Divine, who instructs him not to comply. Balak is insistent (and wealthy). When his messengers ask Balaam a second time, Balaam inquires of the Divine a second time and is instructed to go with the men.

On his way to Midian, Balaam is confronted by an angel he cannot see. Only his she-donkey can see the spirit being. Three times she tries to avoid it, and three times Balaam beats her for going off the path. Finally, the donkey chastises Balaam for beating her. The angel too chides Balaam, saying the donkey has saved his life. Balaam continues on his journey and finds himself unable to curse Israel: Rather, he blesses the people.

The donkey is comic relief, showing Balaam is not as spiritually aware as he thinks he is. The donkey also represents our instincts. Inwardly, Balaam knows he should not go with Balak's messengers, but it takes his "donkey" (that is, his guts) to tell him. In the *Sefer Yetzirah* (5:8), Tammuz is associated with the gut or the intestine as well as with the gift of sight. Balaam's donkey reminds us that we should trust our guts, our deepest intuitions, when searching for the truth.

The Blessing of Balaam

How fair are your tents,
O Jacob,
Your dwellings, O Israel!
Like palm-groves that
stretch out,
Like gardens beside
a river,
Like aloes planted
by the Eternal,
Like cedars beside the water.
—NUMBERS 24:5–6

How fair are your tents:
because the doorways of the
tents did not face one another.
—RASHI ON NUMBERS 24:5

One of the blessings Balaam speaks over Israel echoes with summer pleasures: gardens, tall trees, cool water, and beautiful tent dwellings. Why this particular blessing? One midrash says the tents of Israel had doorways that faced away from one another. Israel blossomed in the wilderness because even the way they built their houses was kind.

This legend partly refers to sexual modesty: With doors that do not face one another, no one can catch a stranger in the act of getting dressed! The story also emphasizes the value of respecting someone else's privacy. According to the *Sefer Yetzirah* (5:8), Tammuz is the month of sight. When we use our sight, we are not to seek out the shame of our fellow human beings. In Tammuz, as we pursue the gifts of spiritual sight, we also learn not to gawk at others.

The Throne of the Divine

For the Eternal Divine
is sun and shield.
—PSALMS 84:1

Rabbi Chanina said: "In the future the Eternal will reveal His glory to everyone in the world, and will send down a throne into the middle of the sky. The throne will move from the place where the sun shines in summer to the place where the sun shines in winter." Rabbi Chanina the Elder countered, "How can the Eternal reveal His glory? Is it not written, 'A human may not see Me and live'? How can you say: The Divine will reveal the glorious Presence to everyone?" He answered "Is it not written: 'The Divine is a sun and a shield, and bestows grace and glory' "?
—MIDRASH TANHUMA, SHOFETIM 9

In Tammuz, the month of sight, we dance with the idea of seeing God. This is the month when, while on Mount Sinai, Moses sees the divine back, but not the divine face (Exodus 33:23). It is also the month when the Israelites build the Golden Calf as a depiction of the Divine (Exodus 32). The notion of seeing, or not seeing, what is infinite weaves through the month of Tammuz like a thread.

Rabbi Chanina makes an outrageous claim. In the messianic future, he says, the Divine will sit in a throne in the sky and move from place to place as the seasons change, just as the sun does now. Rabbi Chanina's elder, also called Chanina, is shocked. He reminds the younger Chanina it is forbidden and even impossible to see the Divine. The younger Chanina responds with a prooftext linking the Holy One with the sun.

One Chanina has a desire to see the Divine in nature, to look at God's face. The other Chanina wants God to remain a mystery. The tension between these two desires ultimately causes the Israelites to build an elaborate, beautiful—yet empty—holy Temple.

The Flowering of Life

Writhe and scream, fair Zion, like a woman in labor. For now you must leave the city and dwell in the country, and you will reach Babylon.
—MICAH 4:10

We call [for a woman in labor] a midwife from anywhere, even if it is a midwife who is giving birth, and we profane the Sabbath for her. We light her a bonfire even if it is the season of Tammuz.
—JERUSALEM TALMUD, SHABBAT 65B

In Jewish law, the birthing woman is entitled to special protections, because her life is in danger. The Jerusalem Talmud tells us we may call a midwife to travel on *Shabbat* so that she may help the woman in labor, even though travel is normally forbidden on *Shabbat*. Even if the woman in labor is herself a midwife, we still call a midwife because the birthing mother needs aid in spite of her expertise. We light a bonfire, though fire is prohibited on the Sabbath, so that the midwife can see to arrive. We light the bonfire even if it is summer (that is, the month of Tammuz) and the sky is light quite late in the evening. All this goes to show how awesome and dangerous the process of birth is and how strong the need is to preserve life.

The word for "midwife" is "*hakhamah,*" wise woman. The prophet Jeremiah uses the same word for a woman who wails at a funeral. Tammuz teaches us about the extreme ends of life: birth and death, both contained in the flower that falls. The *hakhamah* who watches over us at this time is the *Shekhinah,* the Divine Presence who is both mourner and midwife. In Tammuz, the fire of the summer sun lights Her way.

Borrowed Light

*Day to day pours out words,
night to night proclaims
the news.*
—PSALMS 19:3

"Day to day pours out": This refers to the four seasons. On the day of the spring equinox and the day of the autumn equinox, the day and the night are equal. From the day of the spring equinox up until the summer solstice, the day borrows time from the night. From the summer solstice until the autumn equinox, the day gives up time to the night. From the autumn equinox until the winter solstice, the night borrows from the day, and from the winter solstice until the spring equinox, the night gives up time to the day … they borrow from one another in trust and give to one another in trust.
—MIDRASH TEHILLIM 19:10

The full moon of Tammuz may hang in a brilliant night sky crinkled by warm breezes, yet the nights begin to grow perceptibly longer. It is just past the summer solstice: time, in the conception of today's midrash, to pay back the light we have borrowed all spring.

Midrash Tehillim points out what good lenders and borrowers the seasons are. Every bit of light the summer borrows, it will pay back as autumn approaches. Every bit of darkness the winter borrows, it will give back come spring. Unlike human debtors and lenders, who often quarrel, the seasons always lend fairly and pay back on time.

There are many ways we divide our days—sleeping and waking, work and amusement, outside and inside, spiritual concerns and secular ones, taking care of self versus taking care of others. The seasons remind us to live in balance. When we get out of balance, when we borrow time from one crucial activity to give to another, we will eventually need to pay back the days.

Violence in God's Name

When the people saw that Moses was so long in coming down from the mountain, the people gathered against Aaron and said to him: "Come, make us a god who shall go before us, for that man Moses, who brought us from the land of Egypt, we do not know what has happened to him."
—EXODUS 32:1

In that hour Hur [Moses' nephew] stood against them, saying: "Stiff-necked ones, don't you remember what miracles the Holy One did for you?" They rose against him and killed him.
—EXODUS RABBAH 41:7

The 16th of Tammuz is the day before Moses comes down from Mount Sinai with the stone tablets. Moses has been absent for 40 days. The people become restless and angry. According to some Jewish commentators, the people have counted differently than Moses. They are convinced 40 days have already passed. They ask Aaron, Moses' brother, to make them a symbol of the Divine they can see and touch—perhaps to replace Moses, who has served as the emissary of God. Aaron makes the people a Golden Calf.

According to one midrash, Hur, an Israelite leader, is the son of Caleb and Miriam (Babylonian Talmud, Sotah 11b). Hur objects to the calf, saying the people are ungrateful to the Divine. In anger, a mob attacks Hur and kills him. Aaron, terrified, does what the mob wants in order to save his life.

Violence in the name of religion is one of the world's great scourges. In this legend, the Israelites kill those who do not agree with their newfound religious practices. Yet in the Bible, it is Moses and the Levites who kill those who have built the Golden Calf, showing their own unwillingness to tolerate a spiritual practice that angers them. In Tammuz and Av, we seek peace among religious traditions as well as nations and individuals.

The Walls of Jerusalem Shatter

The Fact of the 17th of Tammuz

Moses hurled the tablets from his hands and shattered them at the foot of the mountain.
—Exodus 32:19

Five things befell our ancestors on the 17th of Tammuz… . The walls were broken. The eternal offering was ended. The city was laid open to invasion. Apostamos burned the Torah and put up an image in the Temple.
—Babylonian Talmud, Ta'anit 26a–b

The 17th of Tammuz is a fast day from sunup to sundown. Many traditional Jews abstain from food, drink, and other pleasurable activities on this day, a day of devastation in ancient Jerusalem. The Talmud also tells us it was the day on which Moses, angry with the Israelites for building the Golden Calf, broke the stone tablets on which the commandments were written. All that is deemed eternal breaks and falls on the 17th of Tammuz. This day begins a period of mourning known as the Three Weeks, 21 days culminating with the fast of the 9th of Av.

The broken walls of Jerusalem, the defiled Temple, and the broken tablets all represent something the people held sacred, now shattered through violence and mistrust. Yet there remains the hope of repair. In Jewish mysticism, repair is our primary work in the world: to put back together the shattered pieces into a whole.

Broken Tablets

There was nothing in the Ark but the two tablets of stone which Moses placed there.
—1 KINGS 8:9

Be kind to an elder who has forgotten his or her learning because of trouble, as it is said: Both the tablets and the broken tablets were placed in the Ark.
—BABYLONIAN TALMUD, BERAKHOT 8B

Legend has it that the pieces of the tablets Moses smashed were later put in the Ark along with the whole tablets he carved later. The keeping of the broken tablets instructs us not to disparage one who through old age or illness has lost his or her knowledge. Individual gifts must be respected even if they have been diminished by time.

These broken tablets seem of a piece with the broken stems, dried flowers, and smashed fruits we find outside at this season. Though they have lost their freshness, they are still symbols of life. It is because they have labored to grow that they now seem faded. So too humans who are broken or withered have lived through many things and have Torah to teach us simply because of who they are. Like the broken tablets, they deserve a holy place among us.

The Face

The Eternal came down [to Moses] in a cloud; the Infinite stood with him there, and proclaimed the name Eternal… "The Eternal, the Eternal is compassionate and gracious, slow to anger, abounding in kindness and faithfulness …."
—EXODUS 34:5–7

Moses our teacher saw the Divine face only once and then forgot. He did not desire to see the wilderness, not even the Promised Land, only the face of God. He struck the rock in his longing fury, went up to Mount Sinai and came down again, broke the two tablets of the covenant, made a Golden Calf, searched in fire and smoke, but could only remember the mighty hand of God and the outstretched arm, never the face…."
—YEHUDA AMICHAI, "MOSES OUR TEACHER SAW THE FACE OF GOD"[7]

According to *Seder Olam* (6), this is the day Moses returns to Sinai to plead for compassion for the people after they have built the Golden Calf. Perhaps Moses has now recognized the human need for an image of the Divine, for he asks the Eternal to show him the divine face. The Holy One of Blessing hides Moses in a cleft and passes before him, proclaiming attributes of compassion. Moses sees the Holy One's "back," not the face.

What is meant by the "face" of the Divine? Can God have a face? Or does the face signify some intimate contact humans can long for but never have? Israeli master poet Yehuda Amichai imagines that Moses spends his entire life searching for a glimpse of this face, never finding it until the moment of his death. We too may long for a face-to-face encounter with the author of the universe, and be frustrated in that longing.

In Amichai's poem, Moses makes a composite sketch of the Divine, using his memories of the burning bush and of the face of Pharaoh's daughter peering at him in his basket on the Nile. We too build our image of the Divine face from the compassion and wonder we encounter in the world. In Tammuz, the month of seeing, we grapple with what we can and cannot see.

The Flowering of Redemption

I will be to Israel like dew and it shall blossom like the lily.
—Hosea 14:6–7

The Holy One of Blessing said to Israel: "Just as this lily flowers with its heart upward, when you do teshuvah *before me (repentance), your heart will be directed upward like this lily."*
—Midrash Tehillim 44:4

Whenever we see brokenness in the world, we must consider our own role in it. When we see forests being destroyed, we must consider how our own purchases bring about that depredation. When we see conflicts in our own personal life, we are required to examine ourselves to determine our role in those conflicts. We are not obligated to blame ourselves for everything around us that goes wrong, only to make a fair and open assessment of our actions and try to change our behavior where necessary. This is *teshuvah*, or "returning to the circle of life." Through *teshuvah* we come to understand how all things are connected.

The lily is rooted downward yet grows upward. *Teshuvah* (as opposed to self-flagellation) helps us feel more grounded and more able to rise: It makes us graceful, like the lily. Through this spiritual practice, we become the bridge between heaven and earth.

The Month of Esau

Isaac pleaded with the Eternal on behalf of his wife, for she was barren, and the Eternal responded to his plea, and his wife Rebekah conceived. But the children struggled in her womb, and she said: "If so, why do I exist?" She went to inquire of the Eternal, and the Eternal answered her: "Two nations are in your womb, two separate peoples shall issue from your body."
—GENESIS 25:21–23

Esau said: "Bless me too, father." But Isaac refused. "Father, if you have not reserved a blessing for me, I shall leave."
—GAVRIEL MICCIO, "AND JACOB WEPT"[8]

There is a tradition that the twins Jacob and Esau divide up the months between them. Jacob, ancestor of the Jews, receives the months of Nisan and Iyar, when the Exodus and the Revelation at Sinai occur, and Esau receives the months of Tammuz and Av, when tragedies befall the Jewish people (Zohar II:78b).

The modern midrash of Gavriel Miccio has no parallel in the Bible. In Genesis, Jacob steals his father's, (Isaac's) blessing. A few minutes later, Isaac's elder son, Esau, comes in and asks for a blessing, yet Isaac says he has none. Esau weeps and pleads and finally receives an inferior, secondary blessing from his father.

The Esau of this midrash does not settle for an inferior blessing. Tricked by his brother and rejected by his father, he leaves home and makes his own way in the world. In the season of exile, Esau is not an enemy but a teacher; he shows us how to respond to cruelty and indifference by reasserting the human right to dignity.

Both brothers are necessary in their respective seasons. Esau represents self-reliance, a need we face in Tammuz and Av when we confront upheaval and destruction. Jacob represents vision and blessing, the gifts of Nisan and Iyar, months of redemption and revelation.

The Flowering of the Peoples

The righteous bloom like a date-palm, they thrive like a cedar in Lebanon. Planted in the house of the Eternal, they flower in the courts of the Divine. In old age they still produce fruit, they are full of sap and freshness.
—Psalms 92:13–15

"Planted in the house of the Eternal"—this refers to Abraham, whom the Holy One of Blessing planted in the Land of Israel. "They flower in the courts of the Divine"—this refers to Ishmael. "In old age they still produce fruit"—this refers to Isaac. "They are full of sap and freshness"—this refers to the children of Keturah.
—Yalkut Tehillim 848

Many verses of Psalms speak of righteous people as being like summer plants: lush, fragrant, vigorous, and fertile. In *Yalkut Tehillim*, the verses in Psalms refer to the members of Abraham's family: his eldest son, Ishmael, son of Hagar; his next son, Isaac, son of Sarah; and his children by a third wife, Keturah. Each child has his or her own unique fragrance.

The midrash has global implications as well. In Rabbinic tradition, Abraham's children are symbolic of different nations: the Jewish people, the Arab peoples, the peoples of Asia. Different peoples are like different trees, each with distinct flowers and fruits. In Tammuz, in the abundance of summer, we strive to appreciate all the songs of creation.

Summer and Exile

The green figs form on the fig tree; the vines in blossom give off fragrance. Arise, my darling; my fair one, come away.
—SONG OF SONGS 2:13

The Holy One said: "If I exile them in the winter they will suffer in the frost and cold, but if I exile them in the summer, even if they walk on roads and highways they will come to no harm… . If I exile them in the winter there will be no grapes on the vine and no figs on the fig tree, but if I exile them in summer, there will be grapes on the vine and figs on the fig tree."
—LAMENTATIONS RABBAH 1:42

Lamentations Rabbah imagines the Holy One carefully choosing in what season to bring exile upon the Jews. The Holy One picks summer, so that the roads will be dry and there will be fruits to pick while the Jews are walking. Even exile, the legend implies, can come with a hint of grace.

This kind of divine providence may not be how we look at the world, certainly not in the face of tragedy. Yet sometimes the timing of events can prove astonishing. Sometimes we feel that we have been given an opportunity at precisely the right moment. We lose a job and another one offers itself instantly, or we miss a train and meet an old friend we have not seen in years. These coincidences (or noncoincidences) are part of the mystery of living. As the summer passes, we contemplate the opportunities that appear out of nowhere to guide us farther on our path.

The Almond Blossom

The almond tree may blossom … and the caper bush may bud again, but the human being sets out for the eternal abode, with mourners all around in the street.
—ECCLESIASTES 12:5

Rabbi Eliezer said: What does the almond tree mean? From the time it begins to flower until the time it finishes is twenty-one days; so too, from the seventeenth of Tammuz until the ninth of Av is twenty-one days.
—LAMENTATIONS RABBAH, PROLOGUE 23

Rabbi Eliezer suggests that the almond tree mentioned by Ecclesiastes refers to the Three Weeks between the 17th of Tammuz and the 9th of Av. Just as the almond tree blooms for 21 days, so too the mourning for the tragedies of the Jewish people lasts 21 days.

This is a strange analogy. What has a period of national mourning got to do with beautiful almond blossoms? Perhaps Rabbi Eliezer is reminding us that tragedy, like the ephemeral blossoms, will not have a lasting effect on Israel, that we will be able to find *joie de vivre* even after our suffering. Or perhaps he is suggesting that when we mourn someone or something we have lost, we remember not only its tragic end but also its beauty. We still have our memories and experiences. Rabbi Eliezer teaches us not to let loss obliterate the joy we have felt in the presence of loved ones. He teaches us how to mourn and also how to celebrate life.

The Call of the Behemoth

Mine is every animal of the forest, and the Beast of a Thousand Mountains.
—PSALMS 50:10

The Divine created wild and tame beasts, and created lions and leopards and bears to prey on them. If the great Divine had not made a merciful decree, the wild and tame beasts could not stand against the lions and leopards and bears. What was the decree? The Divine One created Behemoth of the Thousand Mountains, and each season of Tammuz the Behemoth lifts her head and roars a roar that reaches every inhabited place. The animals hear this cry and a fear falls on the lions and leopards … for an entire year, and were it not for this cry, no animal could survive against its predators.
—OTZAR MIDRASHIM: HASHEM BEHOHMAH, YASAD ARETZ, 6

During the Three Weeks we remember the drastic consequences when humans prey on one another. The image of Jerusalem's walls crumbling reminds us of all helpless citizens of cities and nations conquered by greed and violence. We think of ourselves as higher than the beasts, yet humans attack one another.

At this time, the Behemoth cries from the Thousand Mountains. The Behemoth, a mythical beast, roars this great cry to frighten the predators. For an entire year, the predators, shaken by the Behemoth's roar, are intimidated and ashamed, and they dare not devour all the animals of the earth.

As civilized beings, we hope principles of civilization—justice, peace, mutual respect—will act like the Behemoth's roar among humans, intimidating and shaming those who would engage in arrogant and selfish violence. In Tammuz, we each rededicate ourselves to becoming part of the Behemoth's roar, part of the societal commitment to mutual trust and peace.

Reuben and Repentance

While Israel stayed in that land, Reuben went and lay with Bilhah, his father's concubine, and Israel found out.
—GENESIS 35:22

The Holy One of Blessing said to Reuben: "No one has ever repented after sinning before Me, and you are the first to repent. By your life, your descendant will come forth first to urge repentance." Whom does this mean? Hosea, who said: "Return, Israel, to the Eternal your God."
—GENESIS RABBAH 84:19

According to the *Sefer Yetzirah,* Tammuz is the month of sight and the month of the tribe of Reuben. Reuben's name means: "See! A son!" We can also read Reuben's name to mean "see between" or distinguish.[7] Tammuz is a month for discernment, for careful seeing.

In Jewish legend, Reuben, son of Jacob and Leah, is the first to embark on the journey of change, *teshuvah*. As a young man, Reuben is intimate with Bilhah, one of his father's concubines. We do not know whether Reuben approaches Bilhah out of love or lust or out of anger at his father; perhaps Reuben's deed is a political act to usurp his father's power. *Genesis Rabbah* tells us Reuben regrets his actions and fasts and prays to ask for forgiveness. Because he does this, the Divine honors Reuben as the first human being to engage in *teshuvah,* and grants him a descendant, the prophet Hosea, who will call others to repent.

In Tammuz, we take Reuben as our model and begin to look for what must change. Just as flowers must fall to make room for fruit, some things must fall in us to make room for *teshuvah*.

Reuben and Regret

When Reuben returned to the pit and saw that Joseph was not in the pit, he rent his clothes. Returning to his brothers, he said: "The boy is gone! Now what am I to do?" Then they took Joseph's tunic, slaughtered a kid, and dipped the tunic in the blood.
—GENESIS 37:29–31

Reuben returned to the pit. Where had he been? Rabbi Elazar said: He was with his sackcloth and fasting, and when he finished he went and looked in the pit.
—GENESIS RABBAH 84:19

As we learned on the 26th of Tammuz, Reuben, son of Jacob and Leah, is a master of repentance. However, at some moments, his concern about the past keeps him from acting in the present. When Joseph comes to visit his brothers, the jealous men plot to kill him and throw his body in a dry cistern. Reuben, thinking quickly, convinces the brothers to throw Joseph alive into the pit, hoping that he will be able to rescue Joseph later.

After this quick save, Reuben mysteriously disappears. A midrash in *Genesis Rabbah* says he has gone to pray for forgiveness for his former sins. While he is gone, the brothers sell Joseph to the slave traders. Reuben comes back and is distraught with grief and regret, but it is too late. Joseph is gone.

In midrash, Reuben's good deed toward Joseph is referred to as a flower—a thing of beauty, but one that does not last (*Song of Songs Rabbah* on 7:14). Reuben, occupied with his old sins, misses a chance to save his young brother. We too cannot afford to obsess about the past, if we wish to act fully in the present.

Reuben and Rain

On the south, the standard of the division of Reuben, troop by troop.
—NUMBERS 2:10

From the south come the dews and rains of blessing, and in the south camped the tribe of Reuben, who was a master of return. On his behalf the Holy One sends blessing to the world.
—NUMBERS RABBAH 3:12

In the Northern Hemisphere, we associate summer with the south, for the sun tends toward the south at this season. The summer is also commonly associated with fire. Yet the inner secret of the month of Tammuz is water: the water of rain stored in the ground and the water of tears.

On the march through the wilderness, each Israelite tribe is assigned a space. The tribe of Reuben marches in the south. One tradition holds the south contains the blessings of water. Why is the tribe of Reuben honored with the distinction of camping in the direction of water? Rain, in the Rabbinic conception, is bestowed on the world because of those who do *teshuvah*. Reuben, as we have learned, is a master of repentance, and so his tribe is honored with overseeing the blessings of rain.

Numbers Rabbah contains a wonderful and probably unintended nod to modern science. Rain may not, in the scientific conception, depend on repentance, but it certainly depends on return! The water cycle, by which water returns from air to land to sea and back again, allows us to drink and to water our crops. The return of water, like the return of human beings to their best selves, sustains life.

Phinehas and Peace

Just then, one of the Israelites came and brought a Midianite woman over to his companions, in the sight of Moses and the whole Israelite community who were weeping at the entrance of the Tent of Meeting. When Phinehas, son of Eleazar son of Aaron the priest, saw this, he left the assembly and, taking a spear in his hand, he followed the Israelite into the chamber and stabbed both of them, the Israelite and the woman, through the belly.
—NUMBERS 25:6–8

Had Phinehas been brought before us for trial, we would have said to him: "The law may permit it, but we do not follow that law!"
—BABYLONIAN TALMUD, SANHEDRIN 82A

As we near the end of Tammuz, month of sun and light, we uncover some of the most difficult stories of our people. In Tammuz we read the story of Phinehas. Phinehas, grandson of Aaron, is a zealous man. Phinehas punishes an Israelite man, Zimri, for having sex with a foreign woman, Cozbi, by stabbing the couple to death. The Holy One responds by making a pact with Phinehas and giving him "a covenant of peace."

Jewish commentators show some discomfort with this shady story. The Talmud declares no one should emulate Phinehas's actions, saying: "That may be the law, but if so, we do not follow it!" They use their sight, their judgment—not the fixed rule—to determine Phinehas's actions are wrong.

Some modern commentators, such as Zalman Schachter-Shalomi, have sought to reinterpret the story of Phinehas, suggesting the Divine seeks not to reward Phinehas for violence, but to turn him aside from it by offering him the chance to become a peacemaker.[8] The Torah calls the covenant of Phinehas "a covenant of peace." In the heat of summer, we cool our own zealotry by exploring the paths of peace.

Alternate Reading

The Red Heifer Revisited

Instruct the Israelite people to bring you a red cow, pure, without blemish… . It shall be taken outside the camp and slaughtered… . The priest shall wash his garments and bathe his body in water; after that the priest may re-enter the camp, but he shall be unclean until evening. One who touches a corpse shall be unclean for seven days. That one shall cleanse with the ashes in the third day and the seventh day, and then be clean.
—NUMBERS 19:2–12

Red represents gevurah *[judgment or severity]. "Pure" represents tempered judgment. "Without blemish" refers to the* Shekhinah.
—ZOHAR V:180B

The month of Tammuz recalls the circle of the grain and the circle of life. We end Tammuz by returning to that circle through one of the Torah stories read during this season. In Numbers 19, the Torah describes the ritual slaughter of a red cow with no blemish and the burning of the cow together with cedar wood, hyssop, and red thread. The ashes of this cow are mixed with water and used as part of a seven-day ritual to purify people who have come in contact with death. However, all those involved in the making or administering of the water become impure. There is an inexplicable paradox: The ashes make the pure impure and the impure pure.

In biblical myth, impurity (*tumah*) is associated with forces of mortality and forces of fertility (childbirth, menstruation, seminal emission, and death). Purity (*tahara*) is tied to immortal forces (the Temple, the priests). The heifer's ashes make the impure pure and the pure impure because these ashes represent change: They bring life into death and allow death to return to life. The one who receives the sprinkling after a death allows himself or herself to accept change and re-enter the flow of life. Like Tammuz, the heifer is a symbol of life and death, reminding us the falling flowers and the brightness of the summer sun are only one phase in a larger circle of the seasons.[1]

The Death of Aaron

New Moon of Av

Take Aaron and his son Eleazar and bring them up on Mount Hor. Strip Aaron of his vestments and put them on his son Eleazar. Then Aaron shall be gathered unto the dead.
—Numbers 20:25

When Moses, Aaron, and Aaron's son Eleazar reached the top of the mountain, a cave opened to them. In it they found a lit lamp and a couch.... Aaron removed his garments ... and Eleazar put them on.... Moses said to Aaron: "My brother, arise and lie on the couch." ... "Stretch out your arms." ... "Shut your eyes." ... "Close your mouth." ... The Shekhinah *came down and kissed him, and his soul left him. ... The Holy One commanded: "Go now." As Moses and Eleazar left, the cave sealed itself.*
—Midrash Yalkut, Hukkat 764

In Rabbinic legend, Aaron has the perfect death. Aaron's family accompanies him as he dies. Aaron performs a ritual to give the priesthood to his son. His brother comforts him as his soul passes from his body. Last, the *Shekhinah* gives him a kiss, taking him painlessly from the world.

Moses and Eleazar act in accordance with Jewish law, which says we must provide the dead with *hesed shel emet*, "true and generous kindness." In Jewish tradition, the *hevra kadisha*, the Jewish burial society, dresses the dead person in garments like those of the high priest. In this way, we honor the body returning to the earth.

Accepting the earth as our spiritual teacher means accepting death as part of our existence. Yet our tradition demands we not resign ourselves to needless suffering. On the new moon of Av, we honor the mystery of death, and we recommit to the task of the living: to be a disciple of Aaron, a lover and pursuer of peace.

The Mothers of the High Priests

The towns that you assign to the Levites shall comprise the six cities of refuge that you are to designate for a manslayer to flee to. … he must remain inside his city of refuge until the death of the high priest.
—NUMBERS 35:6,28

The mothers of the high priests would send food and clothing to all those interned in the cities of refuge for manslaughter, so that they would not pray for the death of their sons.
—BABYLONIAN TALMUD, MAKKOT 11A

In Av we read the Torah portion concerning the cities of refuge. Cities of refuge were a place for those who had killed accidentally, a safe zone where no one could seek revenge on them. While these cities were not open as havens to deliberate murderers, they provided safety to those who had committed manslaughter. However, those who took refuge in these cities were not allowed to leave. Only the death of the high priest symbolically atoned for their unintentional crimes and freed them to go back to their home communities.

The Talmud suggests: Would not all the intentional killers pray for the high priest's death so that they could go home? The Talmud imagines the high priest's mother makes care packages for all the manslaughters in the levitical cities, so that they pray for the well-being of her son even though with his death they will be released from confinement.

The actions of the high priests' mothers remind us that sometimes we benefit when others suffer. We may receive an organ from someone who died. We may be saved from an accident while someone else is harmed. Although it is natural to feel relieved at being spared ourselves, the high priests' mothers remind us not to extinguish our empathy for others.

The Clouds of Glory Disappear

You, O Eternal, appear in plain sight when Your cloud rests over them and when You go before them in a pillar of cloud by day and in a pillar of fire by night.
—Numbers 14:14

When Aaron died, the clouds of glory ceased, as it is written, "When the Canaanite, king of Arad heard." What did he hear? That Aaron had died and the clouds of glory were gone.
—Babylonian Talmud, Ta'anit 9a

In traditional Jewish practice, one does not do laundry or buy clothes or swim during the nine days before Tisha b'Av. These actions are comforting: They give us a sense of freshness and newness. By failing to do them, we put ourselves in the mindset of those who are living in chaotic times, when things are not safe or predictable.

In Jewish legend, this time is the season when the clouds of glory, which surround the Israelite people on their journey through the wilderness, vanish because of the death of Aaron. As Miriam's well follows the people because of Miriam, the clouds of glory follow the people because of Aaron, and now they disappear. The people, who felt protected and enclosed, now feel exposed to the elements. Other nations perceive them as more vulnerable and begin making war on them.

This legend shows how vulnerable nations are at times of upheaval when leaders die or are overthrown. Yet it is also a metaphor for how we feel when we become aware of the trouble going on in our world: We may feel naked and unprotected, unsure of how to go forward. The beginning of Av, with its restrictions and lamentations, symbolizes a collective loss of innocence, an awareness of the dangers of being.

Between the Narrow Places

Judah has gone into exile because of misery and harsh oppression; when she settled among the nations, she found no rest. All her pursuers overtook her in the narrow places.
—LAMENTATIONS 1:3

In the narrow places: between the days of the seventeenth of Tammuz and the ninth of Av, when Keteb Meriri is present… . Rabbi Abba bar Kahana said: Keteb (a demon) walks through the larger part of the midday… . It does not walk in sun or shade but in the borderline between shadow and sun.
—LAMENTATIONS RABBAH 3:29

The Three Weeks between the 17th of Tammuz and the 9th of Av are sometimes know as *bein ha-meitzarim*, meaning "between the narrow places." It is as if we walk a long corridor through these 21 days, and only afterward do we find ourselves in a wider place.

The Sages imagined that a demon called Keteb-Meriri walked about at this season. They advised against staying in the sun or in direct moonlight because of Keteb-Meriri. Rabbi Samuel bar Nachmani even asked that schoolchildren be dismissed during the hottest hours of the day during these weeks, leading one to believe that Keteb-Meriri is a name for the lassitude we feel when we are hot in the summer! Yet notice that the demon does not walk in light or in darkness but on the line between them. Keteb-Meriri symbolizes the crossing of a boundary. It is at moments of transition that we feel vulnerable: when we move from one life stage to another or when our lives are in flux. Av is the month of transition par excellence, reminding us to take care of our hearts and spirits as we walk through changes in our lives.

5 AV

Lament of the Maiden

The maidens of Jerusalem have bowed their heads to the ground. My eyes are spent with tears, my heart is in tumult, my being melts away over the ruin of my poor people.
—LAMENTATIONS 2:10–11

Even when the gate of prayer is locked, the gate of tears is open.
—BABYLONIAN TALMUD, BAVA METZI'A 59A

The book of Lamentations, the main text of Tisha b'Av, depicts the wounded Israelite nation as a weeping maiden. This maiden represents the land of Zion as well as the women of the land of Judah who suffered during the exile. The image also calls to mind the *Shekhinah,* the Divine Presence, who often appears as a woman weeping over the exile of Her people.

After great loss, we may be too stunned or saddened or angry to pray, or our thoughts and beliefs may not permit us to pray. The Talmud tells us that at those moments, we must turn to the gate of tears. Tears have power: They allow us to express the inexpressible, to ask for comfort even when we cannot imagine being comforted. Tisha b'Av, the season of tears, is not a time to be avoided: Like all other seasons, it has a lesson we must learn in order to become fully human. The season of the flower is the season when we learn how to mourn. Through mourning, we learn how to heal.

In the season of water within fire, we conduct a special kind of alchemy. We turn the fire of our pain into the water of tears. These tears, like all forms of water, create change. When the gate of the past has closed behind us, our tears may allow us to open the gate of the future.

Journey of the *Shekhinah*

A voice cries in the wilderness:
"Make way for the Eternal!"
—ISAIAH 40:3

The Shekhinah *made ten journeys: from the Ark to the cherub, from the cherub to the other cherub, from that cherub to the threshold, from the threshold to the courtyard, from the courtyard to the altar, from the altar to the roof, from the roof to the wall, from the wall to the city, and from the city to the mountain, and from the mountain to the wilderness. From the wilderness, She arose and sat in Her place.*
—BABYLONIAN TALMUD, ROSH HASHANAH 31A

The Talmud tells of the *Shekhinah* darting furtively from one sacred item to the next until She finally makes it into the wilderness. We may imagine Her being chased away from Her home by the evil forces in the world. From another angle, perhaps She is trying to escape. Perhaps She wants to be in the wilderness, where all is unpredictable, where there is silence and a sense of waiting. The midrash implies that the *Shekhinah*'s place can be reached, not from the Ark or the altar or the city, but only from the wilderness.

Summer is a time when many of us go into the wilds for a time (we call this a vacation). Outside ordinary time and space, we can be open to voices we would not hear otherwise. Often what we need in our lives is not the Presence in the Temple, but the Presence in the wilderness: the Being we discover in still and empty places.

Rachel Pleads for Her Children

A cry is heard in Ramah: Rachel weeping for her children.... Thus said the Eternal, Restrain your voice from weeping, your eyes from shedding tears, for ... your children shall return to their country.
—Jeremiah 31:15–17

Rachel said: "Master of the World, You know that Jacob loved me ... yet my father decided to exchange me with my sister. I had compassion on my sister that she not be shamed.... I got under their bed, and when he spoke with her, she was silent and I answered him, so that he would not recognize my sister's voice.... And if I was not jealous of my rival, You, who are the living, enduring, and merciful king, how can you exile my children?..."
—Lamentations Rabbah, Prologue 24

The Talmud imagines that the exile to Babylon is the result of a spiritual crisis. The Holy One is angry with the people for worshiping other gods and sends them into exile. The patriarchs plead for the people's redemption without success. Rachel, however, does not plead. Instead, she reminds the Eternal of how she planned to marry Jacob, yet helped her elder sister, Leah, marry him instead. Caught between her love for her sister and her love for her future husband, Rachel chooses to protect her vulnerable sister. She even hides under the bed so that Jacob will hear Rachel's voice while he lies with Leah. "If I can overcome my jealousy for rivals," Rachel says to the Holy One, "why can't you?" Shamed, the Eternal promises to redeem the people.

Like Rachel, we teach by example. If we want children, citizens, and earthdwellers to do justice, we must model that justice ourselves. Rachel shows us how our small deeds can lead to powerful results.

Abraham's Prayer

Abraham came forward and said: "Will You sweep away the innocent along with the guilty? … Far be it from You … to bring death upon the innocent as well as the guilty, so that innocent and guilty fare alike. Shall not the Judge of all the earth do justly?"
—Genesis 18:23–25

Rabbi Ukba said: On the night of the ninth of Av … Abraham entered the Holy of Holies. … Abraham said: … Where are my children? The Holy One said …: They sinned and I exiled them. Abraham asked: Were there no righteous among them? The Holy One replied: They have given it up, and even more than that, they have taken pleasure in one another's downfall.
—Lamentations Rabbah 1:20

In this season of *hesed*, of "love," we remember the exemplar of *hesed:* Abraham. On the evening of Tisha b'Av (tonight), Abraham finds his way to the spot where the Holy of Holies will one day stand. The Holy One reveals the future exile. Abraham argues for Jerusalem just as he did for Sodom, pleading that some of the people must be innocent. The final word of the Holy One is that the people have taken pleasure in one another's downfall, and this is why they cannot be redeemed.

Traditional Jewish theology sees the destruction of Jerusalem as a punishment for the people's sins. We may not choose to see the destruction of cities as a reflection of the morality of those who live there. Yet it is important to note that the Sages blamed the people of Jerusalem not for ritual sins but for hating one another without cause. They were right: When we hate one another without cause, we endanger ourselves and our civilizations.

Tisha b'Av

What can have happened to you that you have gone, all of you, up on the roofs?
—Isaiah 22:1

When the First Temple was destroyed, all the young men, the flowers of the priesthood, gathered in crowds, carrying the keys to the Temple. They went up to the roof of the Temple and said before the Divine: "Keeper of the world! We have not been faithful keepers. Let us return the keys to you." And they threw the keys toward heaven. A hand came forth from the sky and took the keys from them, and they were gathered up into the light.
—Babylonian Talmud, Ta'anit 29a

A legend of Tisha b'Av tells that when the Temple was about to be destroyed, the keepers of the keys of the Temple, called "flowers of the priesthood," gathered on the roof of the sacred shrine and threw the keys toward heaven rather than give them to the enemy. A hand stretched forth and took the keys, and so the Temple passed back into the realm of mystery. Its physical form could be destroyed, but its spiritual existence could never be erased. Today, as Jews fast, chant sad poems and songs, and recite the book of Lamentations, we remember the keys to our spiritual home, vanished into the sky.

Tisha b'Av comes during the time of year when the gates of the skies are open and the winds of the south bring blessing. The ritual of returning the keys is a sign that receiving blessings can also mean letting them go. Even the *Shekhinah* must let go of the Temple when war ravages it and enter the wilderness. On Tisha b'Av, we follow Her into the unknown, hoping She holds the keys to open new blessings to us.

The Birth of Issachar

Issachar is a strong-boned ass, crouching among the sheepfolds. When he saw how good was rest, and how pleasant was the country, he bent his shoulder to the burden.
—Genesis 49:14–15

Just as the bones of a donkey can be clearly seen, so Issachar's studies were clear to him.
—Genesis Rabbah 72:5

This day is the birthday of Issachar, son of Jacob and Leah (*Yalkut Shimoni Shemot* 162). Issachar is known as the ancestor of Torah scholars and those who are wise in the ways of the calendar (*Targum Yonatan, Genesis* 46:13). Things are visible to him that are not visible to others. He looks at the bones of Torah and sees them clearly, just as the skeleton of a bony donkey can be seen by all.

There is a reason Issachar's birth is honored today. Issachar, with his ability to see the bones of the matter, is the antidote to the 9th of Av. After the fires that burn Jerusalem, we need Issachar's spirit of insight and hard work to rebuild. Not only does Issachar understand learning but he understands the benefits of peace and of living simply upon the earth. He directs us toward what is vital to our renewal.

The Sages compare Torah to water, and Issachar's gentle Torah is the water we throw on the fires of Tisha b'Av. With the patience and energy of this sacred ancestor, we begin to rebuild. We heal from our wounds and prepare to be reborn into a year of joy. With Tisha b'Av past, we prepare to eat the spiritual fruit of the summer season.

The Birth of the Messiah

Then shall maidens dance gaily, young men and old alike. I will turn their mourning to joy; I will comfort them and cheer them in their grief.
—Jeremiah 31:13

Abaye said: Joy will come to us on Tisha b'Av, for in the future the Holy One will make that day a holiday, as it is said: "I will turn your mourning to joy."
—Pesikta Rabbati 28:4

It is said that Elijah the Prophet visits every birth to see if that child will be the Messiah. Some stories say that child will be born on Tisha b'Av. Others say the Messiah will herald redemption on Tisha b'Av (*Pesikta Rabbati* 28:3). The Sage Abaye says in the future Tisha b'Av will no longer be a time of mourning but a holiday.

The Jewish calendar is a circle, in which we move from planting to harvest, from freedom and rejoicing to revelation to mourning and back again. From this perspective, mourning and joy are part of the same continuum of human experience. Yet the Jewish calendar is not only a circle: It is also a line of history, moving toward redemption.

To say that the Messiah will come on Tisha b'Av is to bring the line and circle together, to say that though we accept suffering and death, along with life and joy, as part of the world, we work toward a future that lightens our burdens and increases our well-being. In these latter days of Av, we keep in mind the possibility that each of our lives, though finite and bound by time and nature, may lead to a future day when mourning turns into dancing.

Doubling Comfort

Comfort, oh comfort My people, says your God.
—Isaiah 40:1

Why does it say: "Comfort, oh comfort My people?" Because it said [in Lamentations]: "She weeps, she weeps in the night," twice, the Holy One said: Now I will comfort you twice: "Comfort, oh comfort My people."
—Pesikta Rabbati 30:2

In a few days we will come to the 15th of Av, or Tu b'Av, a festival of dance, love, and harvest. It is a minor holiday, yet a very important hinge of the Jewish year. Like Tu b'Shevat and Lag b'Omer, Tu b'Av comes as a perceptible shift in climate happens: Summer begins to move toward autumn. It also comes with a perceptible shift in the mood of the Jewish calendar; from meditating on death, we move to waiting for rebirth. While we have not yet come to the new year, one might say that at this season, the Jewish year doubles back on itself.

This is the season of *hesed*, "love," and the haftarah read the *Shabbat* after Tisha b'Av is the first of seven prophetic readings of comfort. This haftarah from Isaiah begins: "Comfort, oh comfort My people." This doubling of the word "comfort" echoes the doubling of grief in the book of Lamentations. It is as if we had tied off a double knot of emotion: Sorrow is balanced by comfort. Summer is a time of journeying, and the seven *haftarot* of consolation are like lamps along the road as we travel toward home.

Between Two Lions

What a lioness was your mother among the lions! Crouching between lions she raised her cubs.
—EZEKIEL 19:2–3

The Shekhinah, *though she is fallen, is strong like a lion and a lioness.*
—ZOHAR I:237B

The astrological sign of Av is the lion (*Sefer Yetzirah* 5:4), and the lion is also the sacred animal of this summer season. In Jewish sources the lion has a double edge. In the Bible and elsewhere, the lion is a symbol for the brutal enemy. The lion or lioness is also a symbol for Israel, for Jerusalem, and even for the Holy One. In a passage from the Zohar, the *Shekhinah,* mother and protector of Israel, has the strength of both lion and lioness.

In this season of lions, we move from grieving as victims to claiming our own lion selves: We are proud beings who will not bow to evil. At the middle of the month of Av, the month of the lion, we face both halves of our existence—the part of us constrained by past events and the part of us free to discover the future.

The Flowering Bones

And Moses took with him the bones of Joseph, who had exacted an oath from the children of Israel, saying, "The Divine will be sure to take notice of you: then you shall carry up my bones from here with you."
—EXODUS 13:19

Become a dreamer like me. Come here to gather up my bones. Carry them like a compass of vision through the long years of the desert.
—JUDITH SCHMIDT, "JOSEPH'S BONES"[11]

We began the season of the flower with Joseph, and we end with Joseph. Throughout their wandering in the wilderness, the Israelites carry the coffin with Joseph's bones, not setting it down until they enter the Land of Israel. Throughout the 40 years of wandering, the bones whisper to the Israelites of their distant past and their still-unimagined future. Then the bones are planted in the land as if they were seeds, to bring new life to the people as they build a new home.

The midrashist Judith Schmidt imagines Joseph's bones calling to her, asking her to come and gather up their wisdom. The bones remind her there will be troubled times ahead and offer her their dreams to help her on her journey. Schmidt's poem suggests that all of us carry the bones of our ancestors as guides and witnesses.

The story of Joseph's bones leads us to the theme of late summer: the descent into the grave and the rising to new life. Isaiah (66:14) states: "Your bones will flower like new grass." Surely this verse must refer to Joseph. The flowering bones of Joseph help us move closer to the fruit of the harvest and the seed of the new year.

NOTES

1 Michael Jordan, *Myths of the World: A Thematic Encyclopedia* (Kyle Cathie, 1993) pp. 224–225.

2 Karen Bellenir, ed., *Religious Holidays and Calendars: An Encyclopedic Handbook* (Omnigraphics, 1998), p. 206.

3 Diane Wolkstein and Samuel Noah Kramer, *Inanna, Queen of Heaven and Earth: Her Stories and Hymns from Sumer* (Harper and Row, 1983), pp. 167–168.

4 Rivkah Walton, "The Rock," in *Living Text: The Journal of Contemporary Midrash* 1 (1997), p. 22.

5 *Machzor Vitry*, supplement 14, cited in Louis Ginzberg, *Legends of the Jews* (Jewish Publication Society, 1938), vol. 6, p. 204, no. 109.

6 Gershon Winkler, *Magic of the Ordinary: Recovering the Shamanic in Judaism* (North Atlantic Books, 2003), p. 202.

7 Yehuda Amichai, *Patuach Sagur Patuach*, quote translated by Jill Hammer (Schocken Press, 1998), p. 29.

8 Gavriel Miccio, "And Jacob Wept," in *Living Text: The Journal of Contemporary Midrash* 2 (1997), p. 42.

9 The author wishes to thank Rabbi Reuven Barkan for his translation of "Reuven" as "one who sees between."

10 Zalman Schachter-Shalomi, sermon given at Elat Chayyim Retreat Center, Summer 2000.

11 Judith Schmidt, "Joseph's Bones," in *Living Text: The Journal of Contemporary Midrash* 4 (1998), p. 18.

The Fruit

15 AV TO 29 ELUL

SEASON
Summer shading into autumn

WIND
The west

HALF OF THE YEAR
The sun

ELEMENT
Air within earth

GATE
The sky

ANGEL
Raphael (healing)

DIVINE FACE
Shekhinah/The Presence

They shall build houses and dwell in them, they shall plant vineyards and enjoy their fruit . . . and like the days of a tree shall be the days of My people

—Isaiah 65:21–22

Born from a seed, the tree bears seed. The land spends itself to create what will thrive next spring. Fruit swells to bursting. Humans, animals, and birds harvest the grains, nuts, and berries of the land. Plants begin to fade, their life concentrated on a single point: the new kernel, pulsing with stored-up life. We too know the journey will continue past the present moment. We turn from one year to the next. We use the growth of past seasons to sustain a new one.

The Jewish calendar now wends its way toward the new year. This eighth segment of the calendar begins with Tu b'Av, the obscure and mysterious talmudic holiday of dancing, love, and rebirth. The 15th of Av falls six days after Tisha b'Av, the day of mourning for the destruction of the Temple. This full moon of late summer represents the spiral of life rising out of death, union rising out of brokenness, planting rising out of harvest. In the Jewish calendar, Av is the month of the hinge, when death turns on itself and becomes birth once more. This is a time of healing, of rediscovering the miracle of being human. The *Shekhinah* is closest to us at this time: From Tu b'Av on, Her mourning turns to dancing.

From Av we move to the month of Elul, when Jews blow the shofar each day to signal the season of return has begun. The 25th of Elul, according to legend, is the date of the making of the earth and heaven. Seven days later, the 1st of Tishrei marks the new year and the anniversary of humankind's creation.

For many peoples, this is the time of midharvest. Lammas (August 1) in the Celtic and Christian calendars and Second Planting (August 1) in the American calendar mark thanksgiving for the grain as well as a time to begin one more cycle of planting and harvest before the cold arrives.[1] Lammas is also a festival of death and rebirth, like Tu b'Av.[2] In Japan, the Bon Festival is a season to celebrate with family and honor one's ancestors.[3] In North America, Hopi kachinas appear to pray for the cold weather to arrive so that the water in the earth will be replenished.[4]

The gate of the heavens is open, but we are in a new season of earth and air. We stretch ourselves between body and spirit, between sky and earth. Physically, this is the time when we eat from the fruit of the ground. Spiritually, this is the season of breath, the time of the shofar blowing, the dance of the spirit and the breath. We are still in the days of the sun, the days when we focus on the outer world, but soon the days of rain will come, the days of inner growth. Rich with the fruits of the year, we prepare to be winnowed down to a single seed: the new beginning of our lives.

The Grape Harvest

Tu b'Av

"The annual feast of the Eternal is now being held in Shiloh ... the girls of Shiloh [come] out to join the dances."
—JUDGES 21:19,21

Rabbi Shimon ben Gamliel said: The Israelites had no greater holidays than the fifteenth of Av and the Day of Atonement, on which occasions the maidens of Israel used to go out in white garments, borrowed so as not to put to shame one who didn't have a white garment. These garments were dipped in a ritual bath to purify them, and in them the maidens of Israel would go out and dance in the vineyards. The men would go there, and the maidens would say: "Young man, lift up your eyes and see what you will choose."
—BABYLONIAN TALMUD, TA'ANIT 31A

Today is Tu b'Av, the 15th of Av, a dancing festival when women go out to the fields wearing borrowed white clothing, so that none would know who was rich and who was poor. They would dance and celebrate the grape harvest. Men would go to that field to find wives. Tu b'Av was a holiday of love in which dance partners chose a life together. Coming six days after the 9th of Av, Tu b'Av contains the remedy for exile: joining together in love, without shaming anyone. The women purify their garments like priestesses as they oversee this crucial movement from death to life.

In legend, 40 days before the conception of a new person, God decrees who that person's life partner will be (Babylonian Talmud, Mo'ed Katan 18b). The *B'nei Yissaschar*, a commentary by Tzvi Elimelekh Shapira, demonstrates that Tu b'Av falls 40 days before the legendary date of Creation (the 25th of Elul). This is the moment when God becomes betrothed to Israel. Arthur Waskow teaches that the full moon of Av is the day when the Holy One makes a promise of marriage to the whole world.[5] Today we celebrate the Infinite's joining with the finite earth.

The Day of Rebirth

Remember the long way that the Eternal your God has made you travel in the wilderness these past forty years....
—Deuteronomy 8:2

On every eve of the 9th of Av Moses would send through the camp and announce: "Go out to dig graves." They would dig graves and sleep in them. In the morning he would send and say: "Separate the dead from the living." They would arise and find their number diminished. In the fortieth year, they did this but found themselves undiminished. They said: "we must have made a mistake in counting." They did the same thing on the tenth, eleventh, twelfth, thirteenth, and fourteenth, but still no one died. When the moon was full, they said: "The Holy One has annulled the decree." So they made the fifteenth a holiday.
—Lamentations Rabbah, Prologue 13

All this week, we contemplate the deeper meaning of Tu b'Av, the full moon of Av. According to a midrash, Tisha b'Av is the day the Holy One decrees the Israelites will wander 40 years in the wilderness until a whole generation dies off. In one legend, every year on the anniversary of God's decree of wandering, each person digs his or her own grave and lies down in it to sleep. In the morning, some arise and some do not. The people bury those who have died and keep moving. There is a shamanic aspect to this midrash, for shamans are often initiated through a symbolic death. Each Israelite must bury himself or herself in the earth and contemplate death, year after year.

In the 40th year of wandering, the Israelites perform their ritual on Tisha b'Av, but in the morning no one has died. They try again and again, thinking they have mistaken the date, but still no one dies. When the full moon appears, the people realize everyone now alive will enter the land. They establish the 15th of Av as a festival of celebration and rebirth. At the time of Tu b'Av we too begin our journey toward life, leaving behind all that has died in us. The full moon of Av paves the way for the coming of the new year.

Breaking the Circle

The fire on the altar shall be kept burning, not to go out; every morning the priest shall feed wood to it.
—LEVITICUS 6:5

Rabbi Eliezer the Elder says: From the fifteenth of Av onward the sun's strength wanes, and everyone stopped felling trees for the altar then, because the wood would not dry. Rabbi Menashya says: They called it the Day of the Breaking of the Axe. From this day forward those who add to study will add to life, but those who take away from study will take away from life.
—BABYLONIAN TALMUD, TA'ANIT 30B

At this point in the year, we are halfway between summer and autumn. The sun's waning at this time of year echoes the feeling of exile. Yet the ending of the summer contains its own beginning: Autumn and winter will come, with spring not far behind.

One of the many explanations for the ancient festival of Tu b'Av is that it was the day when those who chopped wood for the temple altar would cease because the wet wood would not have time to dry before the rains fell. The day was known as "The Breaking of the Axe," *Yom Shever Magal*. The Talmud seems to imply that this day marks the season to reduce one's outward activity and turn inward toward study, in preparation for the days of rain, the introspective half of the year that will begin in Tishrei.

This phrase "*Shever Magal*" also means "The Breaking of the Circle." The circle of life, having spun around from seed to fruit, is nearing its end. Yet it is important for us to remember we are not trapped by the circle. No matter what the season of the year or of our lives, we are always able to begin in a different way.

Returning to the Self

This is what the Eternal has commanded concerning the daughters of Zelophehad: Every daughter among the Israelite tribes who inherits a share of land must marry someone from a clan of her father's tribe, in order that every Israelite may keep his ancestral share.
—NUMBERS 36:6,8

What occurred on the fifteenth of Av? Rabbi Judah said in the name of Rabbi Samuel: That was the day when the tribes were given permission to intermarry.
—BABYLONIAN TALMUD, TA'ANIT 30B

The five daughters of Zelophehad, Israelite women in the wilderness, negotiated with Moses and with the Holy One the right to inherit their father's property. However, they were obligated to marry men of their own tribe. If one of them married a man of another tribe, his children would inherit the land and it would be lost to the daughter's tribe. To keep the patriarchal tribal structure intact, the daughters were constrained in their marriage choices. On Tu b'Av, the tribes permitted daughters who were heirs to marry whomever they chose, no matter who would inherit their land eventually.

What does this teach us about the season? The myths of the spring and summer are national ones: the Exodus, the Revelation at Sinai, the destruction of the Temple. Now, as we approach the new year, we move into a more individual mode, when we concern ourselves with our own souls. The daughters of Zelophehad are asked to marry to support the perceived national interest. At this season, later women heirs are freed to follow their own hearts. So too we are now freed to focus inward.

Crossing Boundaries

[Jeroboam] stationed at Bethel the priests of the shrines that he had appointed to sacrifice to the calves he had made. And Jeroboam established a festival on the fifteenth day of the eighth month, in imitation of the festival in Judah.
—1 Kings 12:32

Ulla said: Tu b'Av is the day when Hosea ben Elah took away the guards placed on the roads by King Jeroboam son of Nebat to keep the Israelites from making the pilgrimages to Jerusalem. He said: "Let them make pilgrimage to any shrine they want."
—Babylonian Talmud, Ta'anit 30b–31a

One Tu b'Av legend hearkens back to the days when the Israelites broke into two monarchies: Judah in the south and Israel in the north. The Temple, the central place of worship, was in the south, so the king of the north, Jeroboam, built his own shrines with their own religious cult. According to the Talmud, Jeroboam forbade those who wished to make pilgrimage to the Temple from doing so. On Tu b'Av, legend has it, Jeroboam's successor allowed the people to offer the fruit of their harvests in any way they wished, a success for religious freedom if not for national unity.

In many of the Tu b'Av stories, a single communal destiny gives way to individual destinies: A circle dance gives rise to many couples; a law that decreed one fate for all becomes the freedom to make choices. This teaches us to balance the collective with the unique and personal. The season of fruit is one of communal gratitude for the harvest, yet each seed must soon make its way alone into the earth, as another cycle of seasons gets under way.

Red Clothing

Gold, silver, and copper, blue, purple, and crimson yarns.
—EXODUS 35:5–6

Gold symbolizes Rosh Hashanah, silver is Yom Kippur, copper is Sukkot, blue is Passover, purple is Shavuot, and crimson is for Tu b'Av, for the daughters of Israel would wear silk dresses on that day.
—ZOHAR II:135A

A midrash from the Zohar takes the colors of the materials of the Tabernacle and invites us to imagine each color as a holiday. Blue is for Passover because it is the color of faith (the color of heaven and of the sea), silver is for the garments of Yom Kippur, and so forth. But why red for Tu b'Av? Because the garments of Israelite dancing women were white, the color of Tu b'Av would seem to be white, not red.

The midrashic collection *Beit ha-Midrash* (5:39) tells that the Israelites once wore four colors to honor the four seasons: from Tishrei to Tevet they wore blue for the sky, from Tevet to Nisan, they wore white for the snow, from Nisan to Tammuz, they wore green for the sea, and from Tammuz to Tishrei they wore red, for the ripe fruit. Perhaps the white garments of Tu b'Av are called "red" by the Zohar because they are stained with the red grapes that mark the passage of time. We are at the very middle of the red season: the season of red earth, the season of fruit flesh, the season of coursing blood. Red is a messy color, and it invites us to get messy as we investigate life at its fullest.

The Remarriage of Caleb and Miriam

When Azuvah died,
Caleb married Efrat,
who bore him Hur.
—1 CHRONICLES 2:19

Azuvah is Miriam, and why was she called Azuvah? Because everyone abandoned her. … "Azuvah died": When she was ill, everyone treated her as if she was dead, and even Caleb left her. "Caleb married Efrat": This is also Miriam. She was called Efrat because Israel was fruitful and multiplied because of her. Why does it say: "Caleb married Efrat"? When she was healed, he acted as if he were marrying her, carrying her in a litter, out of his vast joy in her.
—EXODUS RABBAH 1:17

On this last day of the week of Tu b'Av, we consider one final story. As we learned in the season of the leaf, the prophet Miriam is afflicted in the last days of Sivan, and sent outside the camp for seven days. In midrash, Caleb, one of the friends of Moses, is Miriam's husband. Caleb, we are told, abandons Miriam during her ordeal.

On the 29th of Sivan, Miriam returns to camp. On the 1st of Tammuz, Caleb leaves to reconnoiter the land of Canaan (thus avoiding an argument with his wife). He returns on the 8th of Av, a week before Tu b'Av. Caleb repents and returns to Miriam after she is healed and conducts a new wedding ceremony, perhaps today. Miriam no doubt has anger at Caleb, but she chooses to reconcile with him and heal their marriage. Miriam and Caleb come to one another not out of innocence but out of forgiveness, regret, and knowledge of one another. The joyful days of Av are not days of naïveté but days of true awareness.

The late summer can be unforgiving, drying us out or oversoaking us in storms. Miriam and Caleb bring compassion to this season, reminding us that our relationships have the potential for repair. Their wedding echoes the relationship of humans with the Eternal: often broken, yet on the mend.

The Source

A river issues from Eden
to water the garden.
—GENESIS 2:10

This river is a stream of the ever-flowing spring that waters the garden of Eden, and this stream of the holy spring is called "Av." Rabbi Abba said: Eden is called Av.
—ZOHAR II:90A

The word "Av" means "father" and can also mean "origin" or "source." In the Zohar, the "father" refers to the first divine face that came out of the unknowable mystery. In the *Sefer ha-Bahir*, and later in the mystic Isaac Luria's teachings, the Divine must contract to make space to create.[6] Av, with its sadness and its rites of rebirth, provides an empty space where the new year can create itself. Av is like Eden: a time outside time.

Today is 36 days before the day of Rosh Hashanah, and 36 is twice 18, which in Jewish lore symbolizes life. Perhaps today represents not only life but the source of life, the mystery that gives rise to everything we see. The number 36 is the fruit that is father to the seed.

Today is also the 22nd of the month. In Jewish tradition the letter representing "two" is *beit*, the first letter of the word "*bereshit*" (creation). Today reflects the *beit* of *beit*, the "creation of Creation."

Ripening the Fruit

Blessed shall you be in the city and blessed shall you be in the field. Blessed shall be the fruit of your belly and the fruit of your land.
—DEUTERONOMY 28:3–4

In Tammuz, Av, and Elul, the sun travels over inhabited places, to ripen the fruits.
—BABYLONIAN TALMUD, PESACHIM 94B

The Talmud tells us Tammuz, Av, and Elul are the season of fruit ripening, when the sun pours into figs and oranges, making them sweet. The harvest may contain loss, yet it also contains peaches, plums, and cherries and many other fruits to tempt the palate and nourish the body. In this season, according to legend, the sun makes a special effort to travel over places where humans live to ripen the harvest.

In Tammuz, our spiritual fruits were not yet ready. Now, in the latter half of Av, we return from our meditations to eat summer fruit and take in the spirit of blessing. We read the book of Deuteronomy, which speaks of blessing on the land and its inhabitants. After a long spiritual journey, we are ready to enjoy the benefits of our labor.

The fruit of the spirit always prepares us for another journey. At this season, we not only devour the fruit but begin to notice the seeds, the hints of the future that will guide us toward the new year.

The Father and the Mother

*Honor your father and your mother (*kabed et avikha ve'et imekha*).*
—Exodus 20:12

Rabbi Eliezer related the words "honor your father"' to the Holy One, "honor your mother" to the community of Israel, and the "et" *in between to the* Shekhinah. *Rabbi Judah said that "father" and "mother" refer to every facet of the Divine, and the* "et" *refers to everything above and everything below.*
—Zohar II:90a

In the Zohar, two Sages disagree about the esoteric meaning of the commandment "Honor your father and your mother." One rabbi says that the "father" is the Divine, the "mother" is the human community, and the *"et"* (which has no meaning in English but marks a direct object) refers to the *Shekhinah,* the feminine Divine Presence. That is, God and the human community are both sources of life, like a father and mother. What brings us together is the *Shekhinah,* the Divine embodied in the world. Through the world, the Divine and the human come together to make life. This is one message of Av.

The other rabbi's view is equally beautiful. He sees the different faces of the Divine as masculine and feminine, mother and father, appearing in different ways to meet the needs of human beings. The *"et"* is the world. The world brings the many facets of the Divine together to act as one. The world gives the Divine a reason to act in a unified way. This too is the message of Av.

The Month of Hearing

If you will hear the commands that I give you today, to love the Eternal and work for the Eternal with all your heart and spirit, I will give your land rain in its season, autumn rain in its time and spring rain in its time, and you will gather in grain and wine and oil.
—DEUTERONOMY 11:13–14

When Reuben died, they gave the leadership [of the Hebrews in Egypt] to Simeon.
—NUMBERS RABBAH 13:8

In the *Sefer Yetzirah,* Reuben is the tribe of Tammuz and Simeon the tribe of Av. Sight is associated with Reuben, and hearing with Simeon. If one reads today's midrash mystically, one sees that Reuben's leadership, the leadership of sight, gives way to Av's leadership, the leadership of Simeon, the hearing one.

Yet Simeon is famous for not hearing. When his sister, Dinah, is raped, he does not listen to her. Instead, he and his brother Levi massacre not only the perpetrator but an entire town. When Simeon's brother Joseph cries out, again Simeon does not listen. He plots to kill Joseph and aids in selling him into slavery. Yet when Reuben dies, Simeon is appointed as head of the tribes, presumably because he finally has learned how to listen.

We too take a long time to learn to hear. The Torah portions of this season—Ekev and Re'eh—warn us that when our harvest is good, when our troubles are past, and when all looks like clear sailing, we become satisfied and are no longer open to change or growth. Like Simeon, we must learn to hear again. Our ears must always be trying to hear what the world is telling us.

Preparing to Listen

If you will hear the commands that I give you today, to love the Eternal and work for the Eternal with all your heart and spirit.
—Deuteronomy 11:13

I might think, if I were an Israelite in the wilderness, that I should only study laws pertaining to those outside the land, such as offerings and tithes. Where do I learn I must study laws pertaining to dwellers inside the land, like the offering of the barley sheaf? From these words: "Hear them and do them faithfully."
—Sifrei, Ekev 5

In these last days of Av, we wait for the shofar to blow on the 1st day of Elul, the coming month. Outwardly, this is the season of earth, the season when the trees and the plants feed us fruit. Inwardly, this is the season of air, the season of empty space, when we wait for new breath to enter us. In this time of listening, we open our ears to anticipated sounds.

What does the command to listen mean? *Sifrei* answers that it means we should not study only those laws that pertain to our immediate situation. We should also seek to study laws and texts for their own sake, even if we do not yet know when and how we will practice them. We must be open to the possibility of a future we do not anticipate.

The Season of Earth

The Eternal your God is bringing you into a good land, ... a land of olive trees and honey, a land where you may eat food without stint, where you will lack nothing.
—DEUTERONOMY 8:7–8

The radiance [of the Divine] ... manifests its power and ability in the element of the earth in an immense manifestation, in more enormous strength than elements transcending [the earth], even the hosts of heaven. For they do not have it in their power and ability constantly to bring forth something from nothing, like the element of earth which constantly makes grow something from nothing—these are the plants and trees—from the creative power it possesses, which is Ayin *[Divine void] and spiritual.*
—SHNEUR ZALMAN OF LYADY (THE ALTER REBBE), OR HOZEIR

In this season of earth, as we reap the harvest, we become aware of the land's power to sustain us. In Hasidic thought, the earth has particular spiritual gifts that no other physical entity possesses: Like the Divine, the earth is able to create, to bring forth grasses and trees and all manner of plant life. Though the earth does not exactly create something from nothing, its ability to nurture life is the most necessary blessing we receive.

Reb Shneur Zalman, the founder of Hasidism, believed the earth's power to give life existed because the earth was the "lowest" form of being. All the divine light that radiated into the world pooled and gathered in the earth before it was reflected back toward the divine realms. In Shneur Zalman's vision, the earth is at the very bottom of the waterfall of heavenly radiance, and so the "splash" of holy light leaps higher from the earth than from any other place.[7]

Tithing the Fruit

You shall set aside every year a tenth part [asor te'aser] *of all the yield of your sowing that is brought from the field.*
—DEUTERONOMY 14:26

The wealthy of the Land of Israel, what is their merit? That they give tithes, as it is said, "asor te'aser"—asor *is spelled like* ashir, *"wealthy." They are wealthy in order that they may tithe.*
—BABYLONIAN TALMUD, *SHABBAT* 119A

At this season of fruiting we read in the Torah about how we are to treat the produce we take from the field. We are to give some of it to the priests (that is, dedicate it to sacred purposes) and some of it must be given to the poor and the stranger, people who have no families to support them. Some of it we are to consume ourselves, joyfully, on the harvest festival of Sukkot. The bounty of the harvest is to be consumed in multiple ways.

We work hard to get abundance for ourselves, and it is hard to give it away. Yet the Talmud reminds us there is no great merit in keeping everything we have. Rather, we get merit from sharing what we have, whether that is labor, love, creativity, or wealth. From our perspective, what we have is ours, but from a larger perspective, what we have is a temporary gift from the universe. It is meant to be given back.

The seeds we planted at the new year, physical and spiritual, are coming to fruition. That they bear fruit for us is perhaps to be expected. The mystery is that they bear fruit not only for us, but for everyone we touch.

Not Looking Back

When you reap the harvest in your field and overlook a sheaf in the field, do not turn back to get it; it shall go to the stranger, the fatherless, and the widow, that the Eternal your God may bless you in your undertakings. When you beat down the fruit of your olive trees, do not go over them again; that shall go to the stranger, the fatherless, and the widow. … Always remember you were a slave in the land of Egypt. Therefore do I enjoin you to do this commandment.
—Deuteronomy 24:19–22

If it is behind you, that is forgetting, if it is in front of you, that is not forgetting.
—Rashi on Deuteronomy 24:19

A biblical law states that when one is harvesting and leaves behind some of the fruit, one must not return to retrieve what was forgotten. The poor and others with few resources are entitled to those leavings, and they may search or "glean" for them in any field. Though sadly we no longer practice this Torah law, it has a deep spiritual message. First, it guards us against greed. We cannot gather up all the blessing in the world and keep it for ourselves. Second, it reminds us not to look back. It is easy to disregard the goodness in our lives and remember the opportunities we missed. This text asks us to value what we have.

Rashi adds to the text that although we must not return to pick up what has been dropped behind us, what is in front of us is available to us for harvest. As we move into Elul, we look at what is in front of us: the new year's opportunities for change.

The Last Day of Mourning

Rosh Hodesh Elul

The whole community knew that Aaron had breathed his last. All the house of Israel bewailed Aaron thirty days.
—NUMBERS 20:29

When Moses and Aaron's son Eleazar came down from the mountain, the people asked; "Where is Aaron?" Moses and Eleazar said: "He is dead." They said: "We saw Aaron defeat the Angel of Death during the incident of Korah! How could the Angel of Death harm him? Bring him to us or we will stone you!" Moses prayed: "Master of the World, remove doubt from us!" The Holy One of Blessing opened the cave and showed Aaron's body to everyone.
—NUMBERS RABBAH 19:20

We began Av with Aaron and end with him. The Torah tells us the Israelites mourned Aaron, the high priest, for 30 days after his death. Today, the 30th of Av, would have been the last day of his mourning period. From this we derive the Jewish custom of *sheloshim*—intensely mourning a dead person for 30 days, after which formal mourning lessens.

A midrash tells that when Aaron died, the Israelites, who had loved him greatly, refused to believe he was gone. They demanded proof. The Holy One opened the cave of Aaron's burial so everyone could see. This allowed the people to confront their loss and move on.

Sorrow does not vanish because of the needs of others or even because of our own wishes. We need help to process it before we can move beyond it. The wailing sound of the shofar on this last day of Av encompasses the mourning of Av—and the celebration of Tishrei. The sounding of the ram's horn is a formal ritual, like *sheloshim*, helping us transition from grief to joy.

The Ram's Horn

New Moon of Elul/New Year of the Animals

You give to beasts their food, and to the young ravens when they cry.
—PSALMS 147:9

The first of Elul is the tithe for animals.
—BABYLONIAN TALMUD, ROSH HASHANAH 2A

In Elul, we blow the ram's horn as a call to examine our ways in preparation for the new year. In the Talmud, the 1st of Elul is also the new year of the animals, the day on which each animal was counted a year older (this was important in order to determine which animals had to be tithed). The 15th of Shevat, the new year for trees, became a mystical holiday known as Tu b'Shevat (see 15 Shevat). The 1st of Elul, though, never became a special holiday.

Yet why not? The *Perek Shirah* tells us that each animal has a song to sing to the Divine:

> Raven says: God gives food to the raven when its young cry. . . . Frog says: Blessed is the name of the Divine majesty forever. … Lion says: The Infinite goes out like a warrior. … Snake says: The Infinite lifts those who are fallen, and straightens those who are bent.

Rabbi Lynn Gottlieb and others have called for reinventing the 1st of Elul as a holiday honoring animals, just as Tu b'Shevat celebrates trees.[8] On the 1st of Elul, we can imagine geese and hummingbirds flying unerringly thousands of miles. We can learn from the animal kingdom about the returning instinct.

The Remaking of the Tablets

The Eternal said to Moses: "Carve two tablets of stone like the first, and I will inscribe upon the tablets the words that were on the first tablets, which you shattered."
—Exodus 34:1

Moses began to feel sorry he had broken the stone tablets, but God comforted him and said: "Do not be sad about the first tablets. They only contained the Ten Commandments. Now I will give you halakhah, *midrash, and legends."*
—Exodus Rabbah 46:1

At the beginning of Elul Moses ascends Sinai to get the new tablets of divine law after having broken the first ones (*Midrash Tanhuma*, *Ki Tissa* 31; *Pirkei de-Rabbi Eliezer* 35). These tablets, though they contain the same words, are different. Though the Holy One carved the first tablets, it is Moses' job to carve the second. The second tablets are a human-Divine collaboration.

A second difference, mentioned in *Exodus Rabbah,* is even more powerful. The first tablets contained only the written text of the Torah. The second tablets somehow mystically contain all the future commentaries of the Jewish people. The first tablets were fixed; the second will grow as the people grow. Midrash, the process of interpretation, begins with the second tablets. Midrash harvests new wisdom in each succeeding commentary on the Torah.

The first Torah is like fire: It burns brightly, yet it is extinguished when Moses throws it to the ground. The second Torah is like air: It is contained not only in stone but in the words of the Sages and in our own creative works. It can never be extinguished. So too, in Elul, one of the two months dedicated to Torah study by the Sages of the Talmud, we learn to grow, and to speak fresh words of Torah.[9]

The Shofar

Blow the shofar on the new moon, on the full moon for our feast day, for it is a law for Israel.
—Psalms 81:4

Three things preceded the creation of the world: water, wind, and fire. The water conceived and gave birth to darkness. The fire conceived and gave birth to light. The wind conceived and gave birth to wisdom.
—Exodus Rabbah 15:22

The shofar, the ram's horn, has been used to announce Jewish feast days for millennia. The shofar may symbolize the Holy One's compassion on Isaac: After the Divine commands Abraham to sacrifice his son Isaac, an angel stays his hand, and Abraham, seeing a ram caught in a thicket, sacrifices it instead. Some say the shofar represents Sarah's cries of grief when she learned how her son, Isaac, nearly died (*Targum Yonatan* on Genesis 22:20). Others say the shofar represents the cries of the mother of Sisera, an enemy general, whose son was killed in battle, and so it teaches us empathy with our foes.
The shofar holds the sound of tears and laughter, of compassion and despair, of creation and redemption.

The shofar represents the hollow womb of the new year that births us and the fragile, finite breath within us. An ancient midrash tells that even before Creation, the Divine creates fire, water, and wind to aid in the task of making the world (*Exodus Rabbah* 15:22). Each gives birth to a different entity. While fire and water both give birth to physical entities (light and darkness), wind gives birth to a spiritual entity: wisdom. Now, in the season before Creation, we call on the wind of the shofar to birth wisdom in us.

The King Is in the Field

The Divine ascends amid blasts of the ram's horn, the Eternal, amid the voice of the shofar. Sing to the Divine, sing! Sing to the king, sing! For the Divine is king of the earth.
—PSALMS 47:6–7

Before a king enters a city, the residents of the city go out to greet him and welcome him in the field. Anyone who wants can approach him and greet him, and he receives everyone kindly, with a pleasant demeanor toward everyone.
—SHNEUR ZALMAN OF LYADY (THE ALTER REBBE), LIKUTEI TORAH 5

Near Eastern peoples blew the ram's horn at the coronation of the king. With the shofar blast, we acclaim the Infinite as our sovereign, rather than any human power. Rosh Hashanah, in a sense, is an annual coronation feast, and Elul marks the festivities leading up to the coronation.

Hasidic thinkers say of this season that the king is in the field. Shneur Zalman, founder of Hasidism, writes of a king who prepares to enter a city. The city dwellers greet the king in the fields near the city; and because the setting is informal, they can approach the king and speak freely. Elul is like that too; in the days before the coronation, the Divine is in the field, available for our prayers, requests, and questions.

We can also imagine the phrase "the king is in the field" more literally to mean that the king is *in* the field. Elul, the last of the summer months, is a time to go out into nature and commune with the holiness of the land.

The West Wind

[O]n the fifth day of the sixth month the hand of the Eternal Divine fell upon me. As I looked, there was a figure that had the appearance of fire.… He stretched out the form of a hand, and took me by the hair of my head. A wind lifted me up between heaven and earth, and brought me to Jerusalem in visions of the Divine.
—EZEKIEL 8:1–5

From the wind of the west come the treasures of hail and snow and heat and cold and rain.
—PIRKEI DE-RABBI ELIEZER 3

On the 5th of Elul, Ezekiel has a vision of the things Israel has done to enrage God. What is striking about the vision is that Ezekiel flies to Jerusalem on the wind, lifted by some unknown and mysterious spirit. A creature of earth, his prophetic gift lifts him into the air so that he may learn secrets.

In some areas of the world, this late summer season is a time of thunderstorms and gusting winds. The electricity of the storms is powerful and sometimes frightening. The west wind, in Jewish lore, is the wind of storms, bringing rain, hail, cold, and heat. When the west wind comes to us in Elul, it brings with it deep emotions: guilt, hopes, and fears, the need to reconcile and the need to stay angry. Like Ezekiel, we are blown about, reliving our memories. Yet if we ride the wind, we may come to a place of wisdom and peace.

The west wind of Elul rises from the shofar and carries us into the storm. It is the breath of the *Shekhinah,* moving us to places we do not know. In the center of that storm, we will discover what we need in the coming season.

6 ELUL

I Am My Beloved's and My Beloved Is Mine

My beloved is mine and I am his, who browses among the lilies.
—Song of Songs 2:16

The community of Israel said before the Holy One, "You be a deity to me and I will be a people to You."
—Psalms Rabbah 23:1

It has often been noted that the word "Elul" is an acronym for the phrase "*Ani ledodi vedodi li,*" meaning "I am my beloved's and my beloved is mine." Elul is a kind of annual honeymoon between divine and human. Elul represents the unconditional love, not of starry-eyed lovers who have not learned each other's faults, but of mature mates who have gone through good and bad together.

Elul is not a time to cover up our flaws but rather a time to put them in a proper context as part of a complicated journey through life. Elul encourages us to view ourselves as loved enough to be vulnerable and honest in facing ourselves.

In Elul, we tell others we have offended that we are sorry. This is not only a good way to improve our characters. It is also a way of spreading the love of Elul. When we apologize, we let people know we find them worthy of dignity. By offering them the chance to forgive, we offer them the possibility of giving and receiving love: the mystery of Elul.

Amram Remarries Yocheved

A certain man of the house of Levi went and married a Levite woman. The woman conceived and bore a son. When she saw how beautiful he was, she hid him three months.
—Exodus 2:1–2

It should not say that he married her but rather that he returned to her … but it means that he made a litter for her, and Aaron and Miriam danced before her, and the angels sang: "A happy mother of children!"
—Babylonian Talmud, Sotah 12b

The Talmud tells that Pharaoh has threatened to kill all male Hebrew children and Amram does not want to see any of his sons killed. He separates from his wife, and all the other Israelite men do the same. His young daughter, Miriam, chastises him: "Your decree is worse than Pharaoh's. He decreed against the boys, but you will end the lives of the girls as well."[10] Amram listens to his daughter. Today, Amram of the tribe of Levi remarries his wife, Jochebed. Six months from today is 7 Adar, the day Moses will be born.

We expect to hear that Moses is conceived after Amram returns to Jochebed. However, the Talmud (Sotah 12a) tells us Jochebed is already pregnant, having conceived around Shavuot. The Egyptians, who think Jochebed conceived her child on the night of the return, do not expect Moses to be born for another three months, and so Jochebed has three months to care for her child before she must put him in a basket on the Nile. Therefore the text says: "She hid him three months."

This remarriage has a teaching for us too. We may think when we change something in ourselves, we are starting from scratch. However, if we make the commitment to change, we may find that forces within us have been conspiring to help us all along. The change we hope to begin may be growing already.

The Psalm for Elul

The Eternal is my light and my help: whom should I fear? The Eternal is the stronghold of my life: whom should I dread? … One thing I ask of the Eternal, only that do I seek: to live in the house of the Eternal all the days of my life… [and] shelter me in a Divine sukkah on an evil day [and] grant me the protection of the tent of the Infinite.

—PSALMS 27:1,4–5

Rabbi Levi said: The Holy One intended each summer month to have a festival. Therefore Nisan contains Passover, Iyar contains the second Passover, and Sivan contains Shavuot. But then came the incident of the Golden Calf, and because of it the holidays of the three months Tammuz, Av, and Elul were annulled. Rosh Hashanah corresponds to Tammuz, the great fast of Yom Kippur corresponds to Av, and the seven days of Sukkot correspond to Elul.

—PESIKTA RABBATI 4:2

Each day during Elul traditional Jews recite Psalm 27, the psalm for the Days of Awe. According to tradition, the words of the psalm, "my light" and "my salvation," refer to Rosh Hashanah and to Yom Kippur. The reference in the psalm to the divine sukkah refers to Sukkot, when we live in booths. By reciting the psalm, we prepare for the festivals.[11]

Pesikta Rabbati suggests Rosh Hashanah, Yom Kippur, and Sukkot are linked to Tammuz, Av, and Elul, months without major holidays. On Rosh Hashanah, we acknowledge the year's turning as the days grow shorter; this hearkens back to Tammuz, the height of summer, when the days grow shorter. On Yom Kippur, we speak of the Holy of Holies; this recalls the mourning for the Temple in Av. On Sukkot, we celebrate the harvest; this is reminiscent of Elul, the month of fruit. As we say the psalm for the autumn festivals, we also call to mind the gifts of summer.

The Birth of Dan

Today, the 9th of Elul, marks one month since the 9th of Av. Bilhah, Rachel's maid and Jacob's concubine, gives birth to her son Dan on this day (*Midrash Tadshe*). Bilhah becomes Jacob's concubine because Rachel, who desires offspring greatly yet has despaired of having biological children, hopes Bilhah will bear in Rachel's name. The birth of Dan is a renewal of hope for Rachel.

Bilhah conceived and bore Jacob a son. Rachel said: "The Divine has vindicated me; indeed, the Divine has heeded my plea and given me a son." Therefore she named him Dan.
—GENESIS 30:5–6

Because of the merit of Dan, Rachel was remembered.
—GENESIS RABBAH 73:4

It is telling that this birth occurs one month after Tisha b'Av. On Tisha b'Av, Rachel plays the part of the sorrowing mother whose children are in exile. Now, in Elul, Rachel once again becomes a mother of joyful children—and not only her own children but the children of others as well. In Elul, Rachel is the fruitful mother whose children are brought to her like the harvest brought in from the field. Bilhah, who bears a child to give Rachel hope, represents the hope we share with one another at this season. *Genesis Rabbah* relates how because Rachel and Bilhah act to preserve life, Rachel later merits to give birth to Joseph. Like the earth, Rachel embodies the urge to create.

The Raven

At the end of forty days, Noah opened the window of the ark that he had made and sent out the raven; it went to and fro until the waters had dried up from the earth.
—GENESIS 8:6

The dog that had been watching Abel's sheep came and guarded his body from the animals of the field and the birds of the sky. Adam and Eve came and sat by the body … but they did not know what to do. A raven whose friend had died said: "I will show the humans what to do." He took his friend and … buried him before the eyes of the humans. Adam said" "I will do the same…." He took his son's body and buried him in the earth.
—PIRKEI DE-RABBI ELIEZER 21

In this month, Noah sends the raven and the dove to find land. The dove, the second to go out, returns with an olive branch, and then flies away. Yet the raven, the first to go out, flies back and forth, and never returns to the ark. This is regarded by the Sages as very bad behavior. The raven is sulking, they say, because Noah has endangered him even though the raven is the only male left of his species (*Genesis Rabbah* 33:5). The raven has a point, of course: Noah did endanger the raven species without thinking.

In fact, the raven is one of our first teachers. When Abel, son of Adam and Eve, is killed by his brother, Cain, his parents do not know how to proceed. They have never buried anyone. The raven shows them how to bury a dead body and return it to the earth. Meanwhile, the dog shows loyalty to Abel and gives him protection even after his death. The raven and the dog together show human beings how to treat the dead with dignity, how to be even more human.

It is traditional to visit graves of loved ones during Elul as we reflect on the new year. As we do so, we thank the raven and the dog for the lesson we have learned from them.

Elijah and the Ravens

The word of the Eternal came to Elijah: "Leave this place, turn eastward, and go into hiding by the wadi Cherith, which is east of the Jordan. You will drink from the wadi, and I have commanded the ravens to feed you there." He proceeded to do as the Eternal had bidden: He went, and he stayed by the Wadi Cherith, which is east of the Jordan. The ravens brought him bread and meat every morning and every evening, and he drank from the wadi.
—1 KINGS 17:2–6

Leah said [when Gad was born]: "Fortune has come! The good luck of the house has come, the good luck of the world has come, for Elijah has come."
—GENESIS RABBAH 71:9

Jewish sources disagree about what tribe Elijah hails from, but many conclude he is of the tribe of Gad. In the *Sefer Yetzirah,* Gad is the tribe corresponding to Elul. In Elul, when the raven left the ark, we remember how ravens fed Elijah.

Elijah is not afraid to confront the powerful. He is even willing to confront the king when he feels the king has done wrong. In the story in 1 Kings, the king is angry because Elijah has withheld the rain. The Holy One tells Elijah to flee to a wadi, a riverbed that would normally hold no food for a human being. Ravens bring Elijah bread and meat. He stays in that secure oasis until he moves on into the wilderness to receive wisdom from the Divine.

There are moments when we need to change our lives, even if that means going beyond everything we know. Sometimes, like Elijah, speaking truth means leaving all that has supported us and kept us in place. This is why Elul, the month of change, is the month of Elijah. Elijah shows us how to walk into the wilderness even when it seems impossible. When we do, Elijah's ravens may arrive to feed us.

The Month of Study

Let not this Book of the Teaching cease from your lips, but recite it day and night.
—JOSHUA 1:8

There were two sittings of Israel where they would meditate on Torah night and day. Twice a year, in Adar and Elul, all Israel would gather and engage in the battle of Torah until the word of the Creator was established.
—MIDRASH TANHUMA, NOAH 3

In talmudic lore, Elul and Adar were months when Jews would gather together to study Torah in special *yeshivot,* or "sitting places." Their method was to study in pairs, with each person bringing prooftexts and arguments to one another. Both Elul and Adar are before harvest festivals (Passover and Sukkot). The tradition of Torah study during these months reminds us to gather in the fruit of Torah as well as the fruit of the earth.

One reason it is difficult to discuss the hard moments we have had with others is that we are afraid of conflict, of being accused, or of being misunderstood. The mode of study practiced in Elul, in which two study partners must listen carefully to one another's positions while holding to their own points of view, trains us in how to have respectful conflict with one another. *Hevruta* study teaches us how to state our case, and how to listen carefully to another side. The Torah study of Elul helps us approach the new year with a courageous heart, able to confront and be confronted by those we have hurt or those who have hurt us.

The Month of Deeds

The Eternal your God has blessed you in all your undertakings. The Holy One has watched over your wanderings through this great wilderness.
—DEUTERONOMY 2:7

Rabbi Yaakov said: I might have thought if I sat and did nothing, I would still be blessed, so the Torah says: "in all your undertakings."
—MIDRASH TEHILLIM 23:3

The *Sefer Yetzirah* (5:8) tells us that Elul is the month of *ma'aseh*, of "deeds." The last month before the new year, Elul reminds us that to be blessed, we must act in the world. The simple message of Elul is that the produce will not come in if we do not bring it in. The Hebrew root for "to be willing" is "*yud-alef-lamed*," a very similar combination of letters to Elul. Elul is fundamentally about willingness: to work, to remember, to forgive, to act, to change.

In talmudic language, *ma'aseh* can also mean "story." (This is where the Yiddish word "*meise*," or "story" comes from.) In Elul, not only do we act but we construct a story about our actions. Part of the work of Elul is to reunderstand and reinvent ourselves. Rabbi Joseph Soloveitchik wrote in *Halakhic Man* that *teshuvah*, "return or repentance," is the greatest form of creativity, because through it we make ourselves into entirely new people.[12] In that sense, even our inner work is the work of Creation.

Attacks from Within

Israel now sent messengers to Sichon king of the Amorites, saying: "Let me pass through your country. We will not turn off into fields or vineyards, and we will not drink water from wells. We will follow the king's highway until we have crossed your territory." But Sichon would not let Israel pass through his territory. Sichon gathered all his people and went out against Israel in the wilderness. He came to Jahaz and engaged Israel in battle. But Israel put them to the sword.
—NUMBERS 21:21–24

There are those who say: The war of Sichon was fought in Elul.
—NUMBERS RABBAH 19:32

Most of the month of Elul concerns gathering in the fruit of the field. A midrash in *Numbers Rabbah* says the opposite: In Elul, the wandering Israelites want to pass through a land without harvesting its fruit. They ask a foreign nation, the Amorites, to allow them to pass through, promising they will take nothing. Instead of honoring their request, the king of the Amorites, Sihon, goes to battle with them, at a place called Jahaz, meaning "divided" or "broken."

One way to interpret the Torah is to read it as a dreamscape. In one sense, the characters all refer to us, just as in a dream all the people we meet represent one of our characteristics. Using this strategy, we may read both the Israelites and Sichon of the Amorites as aspects of ourselves. The Israelites represent our own desire to do good. Sichon symbolizes our mistrust, our fear of others. It is the Sichon within us that attacks us in Elul, saying we do not dare to change, for fear of being hurt by others. We call on the Infinite to help us fend off these attacks.

David and Bathsheba

David said to Nathan: "I stand guilty before the Eternal." And Nathan replied to David: "The Eternal has remitted your sin; you shall not die. However, since you have spurned … the Eternal through this deed, even the child about to be born to you shall die."
—2 Samuel 12:13–14

Can you really stumble onto the ways of God through pools of blood? At this crossroad, will the soft songs from my pious days be any help?… There must be songs steeped in more truth than my sins.
—Jacob Glatstein, "Abishag"[13]

On the full moon of Elul, the moon of late summer, David summons Bathsheba, the wife of one of his soldiers, to the palace so that he may make love with her (Zohar I:8b). Bathsheba becomes pregnant. In an effort to conceal his wrongdoing, David orders Bathsheba's husband, Uriah, killed. The prophet Nathan accuses David and tells him the Eternal will punish him for his sin. David repents of what he has done and receives forbearance from the Divine. On Yom Kippur, David receives this remission of sin. By imagining this event transpiring on Yom Kippur, the midrash invites us to see ourselves as David, who sins, repents, and is forgiven.

The poet Jacob Glatstein imagines David, at the end of his life, mourning his bloody actions and wishing for absolution. In the poem, David considers the psalms he has written, and does not find them good enough to balance the harm he has done. Yet David, in spite of the ways he has missed the mark, is still a psalmist. He goes on looking for songs "steeped in truth."

As the High Holy Days approach, we find ourselves at a crossroads. Carried by the music of the penitential season, we set off down the road, following songs that will lead us to better lives.

Bathsheba Speaks

The Eternal afflicted the child that Uriah's wife had borne to David, and it became critically ill. … On the seventh day, the child died….
—2 SAMUEL 12:15,18

What kind of a man's reasoning could maintain that taking the life of the child I had so yearned for could be punishment for the murderer of my husband? "It was David's son too," you say. Yes, but David had many sons; this was my only one. And what of the innocent child?
—SAVINA TEUBAL, "BAT-SHEVA"[14]

As we have learned, the Zohar states that the middle of Elul is the season when David has the husband of Bathsheba killed so that he can marry her himself. David hopes this surreptitious murder will conceal the fact that he impregnated Bathsheba while she was married. Nathan the prophet predicts that the Divine will punish David for his actions by killing Bathsheba's child.

The Bible focuses on David's regret and grief during these events. However, the midrashist Savina Teubal raises different questions. She imagines Bathsheba was raped (a plausible reading of the text) and that the king forced both the death of her husband and a marriage on her. How is the death of Bathsheba's child a just act? Are we to imagine a loving and righteous deity imposing such a brutal and unfair penalty?

The arrival of the High Holy Days brings up our feelings about the notion of the Divine as judge. Like Bathsheba in Teubal's midrash, we may reject the thought that we are judged and punished at this season. Yet we still may be able to find the new year a period of reflection and increased awareness of how we act in the world. Like Bathsheba, we may use the new year to speak our truth about what offends our sense of justice.

Noah Sends the Dove

At the end of forty days, Noah opened the window of the ark that he had made and sent out the raven; it went to and fro until the waters had dried up from the earth. Then he sent out the dove to see whether the waters had decreased from the surface of the ground, but the dove could not find a resting place for its foot, and returned to him to the ark, for there was water all over the earth. So putting out his hand, he took it into the ark with him.
—GENESIS 8:6–9

The Holy One of Blessing said: "Just as the dove brought light to the world [by bringing news of dry land], so you, who are compared to a dove in Scripture, brought olive oil and lighted a lamp before me."
—MIDRASH TANHUMA, TETSAVVEH 5

According to tradition, on the 17th of Elul Noah sends the dove from the ark to look for dry land (Rashi on Genesis 8:5). Patiently, the dove searches a first time, then a second time, before it finds an olive tree from which to pluck a branch. In today's midrash, the Holy One tells the Jewish people they are like the dove, for just as the dove brought an olive branch to Noah to let the world know that the Flood was over, so Israel kindled olive oil in the Temple as an act of service to the Divine.

We too need faith, patience, and presence to gather up all the teachings of Elul. Change does not come easily but must be tried over and over, just as the dove was sent out of the ark several times before it could fly away. We can do as the dove does, trying again and again to find new life, even while the floodwaters are on the earth.

The Letter of Creation

In the beginning the Divine created sky and earth.
—Genesis 1:1

Why was the world created with the letter beit *(for* bereshit, *"in the beginning")? Just as the* bet *is closed on all its sides but open at its front, so you have no permission to ask what is above and what is below, what is before or what is after, except from the day of Creation forward. . . . Why was the world created with a* beit? *To teach you that there are two worlds, this world and the world to come. Why with a* beit? *Because* beit *begins* bracha, *the word for blessing.*
—Genesis Rabbah 1:10

In Rabbinic lore, Elul is the month the world was created (*Leviticus Rabbah* 29:1). Reflecting on the harvest makes us wonder about the seed hidden in the fruit, invisible yet potent. Reflecting on ourselves causes us to ask where we came from and why we are here.

According to *Genesis Rabbah,* the first letter of the Torah, *beit*, purports to answer the question of why that letter was chosen from among all Hebrew letters to begin the Torah. Yet the midrash asks far more questions than it answers. Why do we not know what happened before Creation? Why are we not supposed to ask? What would we find out if we did ask? What is the world to come? How is it different from our world? Is it real? How do we get there? What is the blessing hidden in Creation?

With these questions, we begin to awaken to how much we do not know. This may confuse us or depress us. It may fill us with a desire to find out. Or we may be filled with a sense of peace as we contemplate the unknown. In Elul, as we return to the beginning, we prepare to face the mystery: the closed sides of the letter *beit*, the doors we have not yet opened.

King David and the Frog

Sing to the Eternal a new song,
sing to the Eternal, all the earth!
—PSALMS 96:1

In the hour King David finished the book of Psalms, his head swelled and he said before the Holy One of Blessing: "Is there a creature in Your world that has sung more songs of praise to You than I?" In that hour a frog came and said to him; "David, do not get a swelled head! I recite more songs of praise than you, and not only that, but from each song I sing Solomon will make three hundred parables."
—PEREK SHIRAH, INTRODUCTION

When King David finishes creating the psalms, he is filled with pride, believing he is the most prolific sacred singer that ever lived. A small frog meets him at this moment and reminds him that she sings sacred songs every day. King Solomon, who in Jewish myth can understand the voices of animals, will write 300 parables about her songs. Presumably this statement restores David to a more balanced sense of his place in the world.

Perhaps Elul, the month of the new year of animals, is meant to remind us of this story. In Elul, we sing many extra praises in our preparations for the new year. We spend time reflecting and probing our deeds. Elul's focus on Creation helps us put our own grand dramas in perspective, reminding us that a frog singing a joyous song also contributes to the sanctity of the world. This realization may be humbling, but it also allows us to laugh at ourselves.

Solomon's Palanquin

King Solomon made him a palanquin
of wood from Lebanon.
He made its posts of silver,
its back of gold,
its seat of purple wool.
Within, it was decked with love
by maidens of Jerusalem.
—Song of Songs 3:9–10

"He made a palanquin"—this is the world, which is made like a kind of canopy. "King Solomon"—this is the Holy One of Blessing, who made peace between fire and water, mixed them up together and made the sky, as it is said: "The Divine called the firmament Sky" (shamayim)*—that is,* eish *(fire) and* mayim *(water). "Wood from Lebanon"—this means that the world was begun at the place where the Temple would be built. "Its pillars are made of silver"—this is the sky, for it rivals all the works of Creation. "Its back is gold"—this is the earth, raising up fruits of the ground and fruits of the trees whose color is like gold. As gold is made of many shades and colors, the fruits of the earth are many colors, some green and some red. "Its seat of purple wool"—this is the sun in the sky, riding in its chariot. "The inside was inlaid with love"—after the work of Creation was completed, Adam and Eve were made to rule over all.*
—Numbers Rabbah 12:4

In *Numbers Rabbah,* the palanquin of Solomon in the love poems of the Song of Songs is the world, with its astonishing sky, its bright sun, and its variety of fruits. The last line of the midrash tells that the world was made with love for humans to enjoy. The question the midrash asks is: Will we notice the grand chariot in which we are riding?

The World within the Womb

Who set [the world's] cornerstone
When the morning stars sang together,
And all the divine beings shouted for joy? Who closed the sea behind doors
When it gushed forth out of the womb?.
—JOB 38:6–8

When the Holy One began to create the world, the Holy One made it as a child grows within its mother. Just as the fetus in its mother's womb starts at the navel and spreads out this way and that way to the four sides, so too the Holy One made the world, making the foundation stone first and from it spreading out the world. It is called the foundation stone for from it the Holy One began to create the world.
—MIDRASH TANHUMA, PEKUDEI 3

Midrash Tanhuma tells that the Holy One creates the world just as a fetus grows in the womb—starting with a small point that will grow outward into a vast, complex entity. The world is not fixed in place like the beams of a house but continues to grow, like a living creature.

The tale invites us to imagine that in Elul, the *Shekhinah* is pregnant with the world. From a single dot, the universe begins to spread out like a growing embryo. What was once divine matter becomes fish and stars and human beings. We, the creatures of the world, are the fruit of the first Creation.

Creation is still unfolding, outside us and inside us. In this season we re-enter the womb of Elul to be remade. We remember we are part of Creation, and it is in our nature to grow.

The Thought of Creation

You have made everything with wisdom.
—PSALMS 104:24

In the hour that the thought of Creation arose in the mind of the Holy One, all the worlds were conceived in a single thought, and within this thought the world was created, as it is said: "You have made everything with wisdom." This thought, which was wisdom, created this world and the upper world together.
—ZOHAR II:20A

The year now comes close to the 25th of Elul, the anniversary of Creation. The Zohar tells us that—although Genesis describes it as a seven-day process—Creation actually occurred in a single thought. The rest of Creation was an unfolding of that instantaneous vision.

This midrash on a verse in Psalms suggests the world of the spirit and the world of physical reality are intimately linked. This means legend and life are always in dialogue. The sacred stories we tell throughout the year are a commentary on the world we live in, and the details of our mundane lives are part of an unfolding sacred story. We may think of the spirit and the body as separate entities, but the challenge of our tradition is to view them as one.

Soon we will tell the story of the Creation of the world. While we may not see Creation itself unfolding before our eyes, our challenge will be to look at the ripened fruit in our hands and see in it a newly created world.

The Dove Returns

The dove came back to him toward evening, and there in its bill was a plucked-off olive leaf! Then Noah knew that the waters had decreased on the earth. He waited still another seven days and again sent out the dove from the ark, and it did not return to him anymore.
—Genesis 8:11–12

The dove said before the Holy One of Blessing: "Master of the universe, may my food be as bitter as an olive from Your hand, but may it not be from the hand of flesh and blood, though it is as sweet as honey."
—Babylonian Talmud, Eruvin 18b

Seven days after the dove leaves the ark on the 17th of Elul, it returns to Noah with an olive branch in its beak. The dove with its olive branch symbolizes a new creation of the world following the Flood. Noah accepts this olive branch with caring and love.

Why does the dove pick an olive branch as the fruit of its search? A talmudic midrash indicates the dove sends a message through its choice. She indicates she does not ever want to depend on others for sustenance but only on the Divine. So too we ask not to be unhealthily dependent on people, old habits, or worn-out self-concepts.

The dove discovers fresh earth after the Flood of Noah. We too seek solid earth to stand on as we move into the future. At this hopeful season, we may wish to take the dove's olive branch as a promise we will find a place to send down roots.

The Four Corners of the Universe

When the Divine began to create heaven and earth—the earth being unformed and void, with darkness over the surface of the deep, and a Divine wind sweeping over the face of the water….
—Genesis 1:1–2

How did the Holy One of Blessing create the world? Rabbi Yochanan said: The Eternal took two balls, one of fire and one of snow … and from these the world was created. Rabbi Chanina said: four balls, for the four winds of heaven. Rabbi Hama said: six, four for the four winds, one for above and one for below. Hadrian asked …, "How did the Holy One … create the world?" … [Rabbi Joshua] … said to him: Stretch out your hand to east, west, north, and south. Even so was the work of Creation before the Eternal.
—Genesis Rabbah 10:3

According to *Leviticus Rabbah* (29:1), the 25th of Elul is the date on which the world was created. In Genesis, the Divine speaks to create the world, uttering the word "light." We hear rather than see God's actions. Yet according to Rabbi Yochanan, even before this the Holy One makes the world by combining opposites: fire and water, cold and heat. According to Rabbi Chanina, God creates the world out of the four directions. According to Rabbi Hama, God works in six directions, just as we wave the *lulav* in six directions. Finally, Rabbi Joshua imagines God in a small room, stretching out a hand to gather north and south, east and west, into a coherent world.

Imagine a great being wearing a tallit, a "prayer shawl," of light. The being calls fire and water, female and male, strength and love, eternity and finitude into a single circle of Creation. Beckoning to the four directions, the being invents dimensional space. Gesturing upward and downward, the being creates heaven and earth. Finally, the being begins a rhythm: the motion of time. Then the Holy One, maker of all the worlds, rests in silence, and the Sabbath begins.

The Creation of Light

The Divine said: "Let there be light," and there was light. The Divine saw that the light was good, and the Divine separated the light from the darkness. The Divine called the light Day, and the darkness the Divine called Night. And there was evening and there was morning, a first day.
—GENESIS 1:3–5

Long before the sun cast a shadow/before the Word was spoken/that brought the heavens/and the earth/into being/a flame emerged/from a single/unseen/point/and from the center of this flame/sparks of light sprang forth/concealed in shells/that set sail everywhere/above/and below/like a fleet of ships/each carrying its cargo/of light.
—HOWARD SCHWARTZ,
"GATHERING THE SPARKS"[15]

Today, five days before the new year, is the birthday of light (*Leviticus Rabbah* 29:1). In Genesis, light is the first noun the Divine speaks; it is created even before the sun. The light signals that, formed out of chaos and void, Creation is to be a place of radiance.

In the mysticism of Isaac Luria, light is the essence of the Divine, stored up in sacred vessels at the dawn of all things. At Creation the vessels of light break, and the light is scattered all over the world. It is up to us to gather up the sparks and rebuild the vessels of light. Howard Schwartz retells this beautiful legend, imagining the vessels of light as ships sailing on the sea of existence and alighting on the shores of the earth to discharge their glowing cargo.

Dividing the Waters

The Divine said: "Let there be an expanse in the midst of the water, that it may separate water from water." The Divine made the expanse, and it separated the water which was below the expanse from the water which was above the expanse. And it was so. The Holy One called the expanse Sky. And there was evening and there was morning, a second day.
—Genesis 1:6–8

On the second day, the Divine said: "Let there be an expanse in the midst of the water, and let it divide between water and water." And the Divine performed over the waters a havdalah *(separation), as it is said: "that it may separate water from water."*
—Midrash Tanhuma, Pekudei 2

Havdalah, meaning "distinction," is a ceremony Jews make to end the Sabbath. With blessings over wine, spices, light, and difference itself, *Havdalah* helps make the transition from the Sabbath to the week. It is a ceremony of liminality. The prophet Elijah is said to attend *Havdalah,*[16] and the waters of Miriam's well are said to move through the world at that time (Shulchan Aruch, *Orach Chayyim* 299:10).

On the second day of Creation, the Divine divides sky from sea. To make the world, the Divine creates many differences: light and dark, sky and sea, male and female, human and animal. *Midrash Tanhuma* claims the Divine took note not only of the creations but of differences themselves and blessed them with *Havdalah*, the ceremony of transition.

When we truly respect Creation, we value difference. Light and dark are important stages of growth and rest. Male and female together are needed to build the world and to create life. We need trees to breathe, and they need us. All creation is as intertwined as rain and sea.

The Creation of Trees

The Divine said, "Let the water below be gathered into one area, that the dry land may appear." And it was so. The Divine called the dry land Earth, and the gathering of waters the Divine called Seas. The Divine saw that this was good. And the Divine said: "Let the earth sprout vegetation: seed-bearing plants, fruit trees of every kind on earth that bear fruit with the seed in it." And the Divine saw that this was good.
—GENESIS 1:9–12

All trees speak with one another. All trees speak with other creatures. All trees were created for the delight of other creatures.
—GENESIS RABBAH 13:2

Those of us who are raised around trees are used to a certain whispering in the leaves. For those of us who grow up where trees dry out in the autumn, the leaves' rustlings grow particularly intense at this time of year. In the imagination of one midrash, the trees actually are speaking, to one another and to us.

On the third day of Creation, the Divine creates plants and trees. A midrash in *Genesis Rabbah* focuses not on the things trees do for us by giving fruit, wood, sap, and medicines but on their companionship. The aliveness of trees feels like friendship to us. We celebrate the plants that are our companions on earth.

Some plants will grow all winter. Some plants have died down to a bulb, yet they will come to life again in spring. Some seeds have been torn away by the wind to distant places. At the new year, we may feel like any one of these plants. In that sense as well, the plants are our companions, showing us the way to renew ourselves.

The Luminaries

The Divine said: "Let there be lights in the expanse of the sky to separate day from night: they shall be as signs for the set times—the days and the years; and they shall serve as lights in the expanse of the sky to shine upon the earth." And it was so. The Divine made the two great lights, the greater light to dominate the day and the lesser light to dominate the night, and the stars.
—Genesis 1:14–16

Rabbi Yochanan taught: Only the wheel of the sun was created to give light. If so, why was the moon created? For seasons, so that we might renew by her countings the new moons and the years.
—Genesis Rabbah 6:1

On the fourth day of Creation, the Torah records that the Divine made sun, moon, and stars to illuminate the earth. Rabbi Yochanan wonders why, given that we have the sun to warm us and light our days, we also need the moon. His answer is that the moon's sacred purpose is to help us measure our days. The four-week cycle of the moon allows us to break up our time into smaller units, to measure in months and half months. This day of Creation is not only about light but also about time.

On Rosh Hashanah, the new moon of Tishrei, we will celebrate our ability to reckon time. As Jews, we connect to the history of our people by counting the new moon of autumn as our new year—just as our people have done for millennia. We reflect on our past and our future. This too honors time. The sun, moon, and stars are our helpers in this process of numbering our days.

The Sixth Day

And the Divine said: "Let us make the human in our image."
—GENESIS 1:26

There are twelve hours in the day. In the first hour the earth was made. In the second hour, it became a human form. In the third hour, its limbs were stretched out. In the fourth hour a soul was hurled into it. In the fifth hour it stood on its legs. In the sixth hour, Adam gave names to all the animals. In the seventh hour, he married Eve. In the eighth hour they went into bed and Eve conceived twins. In the ninth hour they were commanded not to eat the fruit. In the tenth hour they ate, in the eleventh hour their fate was decided, and in the twelfth hour they left the garden and went away.
—BABYLONIAN TALMUD, SANHEDRIN 31B

As we began the season with the creation of new life, so we end with the creation of new life. The Torah tells that in the last two days of Creation, all the animate beings are made: fish, birds, land animals, and humans. This evening, Rosh Hashanah will mark the legendary anniversary of the creation of human beings.

A midrash from the Talmud telescopes our lives into 12 hours: we are made in the womb, we are born, we learn to walk, we discover the wonder of the world, we seek companionship, we make families, we make choices and mistakes, we die. We enter the garden and we leave it in the blink of an eye. Time passes quickly. We are caught up in the unfolding days of the world. Yet we can be awake and open—we can embrace those days.

The calendar has come around to its beginning. Creation is upon us. Entering the autumn, we receive breath and light as if for the first time. With each passing moment, the tree of days will grow.

NOTES

1 From a lecture by Donna Henes, August 1, 2004.

2 Ronald Hutton, *Stations of the Sun* (Oxford, 1966), p. 330.

3 Nancy Luena, *Celebrations of Light: A Year of Holidays Around the World* (Atheneum, 1988), pp. 19–20.

4 Patricia Telesco, *365 Goddess* (HarperSanFrancisco, 1998).

5 In his article "The Cosmic Origins of *Tu B'Av*," http://shalomctr.org/node/252.

6 Arthur Green, *A Guide to the Zohar* (Stanford University Press, 2004), pp. xxii–xxiii.

7 The author wishes to thank Rabbi David Seidenberg for his teaching on this passage by Shneur Zalman of Lyady.

8 Lynn Gottlieb, *She Who Dwells Within: A Feminist Vision of a Renewed Judaism* (HarperSanFrancisco, 1995), p. 188.

9 *Midrash Tanhuma*, Noah 3.

10 *Exodus Rabbah* 1:19.

11 From a lecture by Rabbi Adina Lewittes, September 1995.

12 Joseph Soloveitchik, *Halakhic Man* (Jewish Publication Society, 1983), p. 99 ff. See also David Cooper, *God Is a Verb: Kabbalah and the Practice of Mystical Judaism* (Riverhead Books, 1997), pp. 28–29.

13 Jacob Glatstein, "Abishag," translated from the Yiddish by Richard J. Fein, in *Modern Poems on the Bible: An Anthology*, David Curzon, ed. (Jewish Publication Society, 1994), p. 210.

14 Savina Teubal, "Bat-Sheva," in *Praise Her Works: Conversations with Biblical Women*, Penina Adelman, ed. (Jewish Publication Society, 2005), p. 111.

15 Howard Schwartz, "Gathering the Sparks," in *Voices Within the Ark: The Modern Jewish Poets*, Howard Schwartz and Anthony Rudoff, eds. (Pushcart Press, 1980), p. 636.

16 Nosson Sherman, *The Rabbinical Council of America Edition of the Artscroll Siddur: Weekday, Sabbath, and Festivals* (Mesorah Publications, 1984), pp. 627–629.

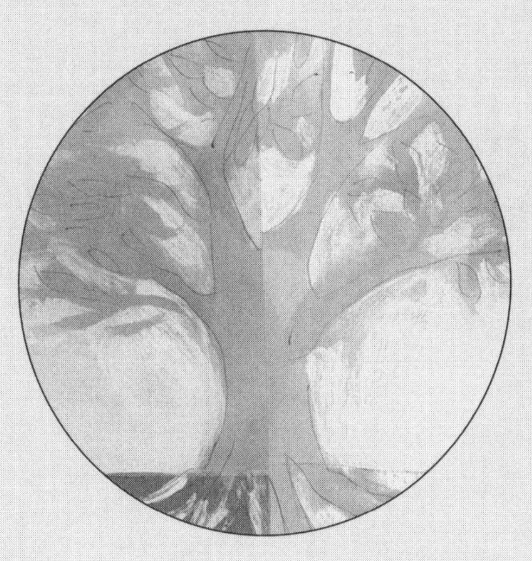

Solstices and Equinoxes

Humans have marked the turning points of the solar seasons for thousands of years. Ancient traditions from the Celts to the Mayans created elaborate stone "calendars" that marked the solstices and equinoxes. The Western calendar still remembers them as the first days of spring, summer, winter, and fall. The Jewish calendar, by contrast, is largely lunar. There are only a few indications today that Jews might once have celebrated these solar dates as sacred, though they are clearly named in the Talmud: *Tekufat Nisan*, the spring equinox; *Tekufat Tammuz*, the summer solstice; *Tekufat Tishrei*, the autumn equinox; and *Tekufat Tevet*, the winter solstice (Babylonian Talmud, Berakhot 59b; Babylonian Talmud, Shabbat 53a; Babylonian Talmud, Eruvin 56a).

However, several ancient hints point to the possibility that these four turning points might once have been sacred days for Jews. A number of medieval Jewish legends also attribute special power to these days. Creating a Jewish practice of the seasons might include new kinds of celebrations for these days, including blessings for the changing seasons and *kavanot* (prayerful intentions) for crossing from one time to another.

Such creative inventions might be based on very old traditions. The book of Jubilees, for example, a pretalmudic Jewish work of the 2nd century B.C.E., proposes an alternate solar calendar instead of the later-accepted lunar one. The text names the "first" days of Tishrei, Tevet, Nisan, and Tammuz as feasts of remembrance. Noah, according to Jubilees (7), established these four days as festivals in memory of events at the time of the Flood. Because the calendar of the book of Jubilees is solar, these days appear to represent the solar equinoxes of autumn and spring and the solar solstices of winter and summer.[1] While the solar calendar proposed by the author of Jubilees never became a mainstream Jewish calendar, it is interesting to wonder how widespread the author's ideas might have been and where they came from.

Significantly later, the Babylonian Talmud (Rosh Hashanah 2a) records that there are four new years. What are the four new years? The material that follows is confusing: There is considerable debate about what these new years are and when, though the Rabbis propose separate new years for trees, plants, animals, humans, and so forth. One theory, suggested to me by Rabbi Mordecai Schwartz and noted by other scholars,[2] is that these "four new years" once referred to the four solar transitions of the year, the equinoxes and solstices. In the talmudic passage, two of the mentioned new years, the 1st of Tishrei and the 1st of Nisan, do indeed fall close to the autumn and spring equinoxes, while another (the 15th of Shevat) seems to fall halfway between the winter solstice and the spring equinox. In discussing whether the new year of an *etrog* falls on the 15th of Shevat, the Talmud records the question "Shevat according to the *tekufah* (season) or Shevat according to the month?" This might lead us to believe that, at least in one way of looking at things, the 15th of Shevat was a solar rather than a lunar date (what the Celts called a cross-quarter day, a midpoint between solstice and equinox).

In the Babylonian Talmud (Berakhot 59b), we are told: "One who sees the sun in her *tekufah*, or the moon in her power, or the stars in their orbits, recites: 'Blessed is the one who makes Creation' (*baruch oseh vereshit*)." Abaye tells us this blessing is recited only every 28 years, when the spring equinox falls so that the sun is in the same place it was on the day of Creation. (This seems to fit with the Rabbinic opinion that the world was created in spring, not in autumn; Babylonian Talmud, Rosh Hashanah 11a.) However, the plain meaning of the statement is that there is a blessing over the sun on each equinox and solstice, one we do not use today but might adopt for use.

Pirkei de-Rabbi Eliezer, a Rabbinic work, tells of the teaching of *tekufot* to Adam and Eve as part of divine wisdom. *Pirkei de-Rabbi Eliezer* (7) also notes the combination of lunar and solar elements in the Jewish calendar. The passage explains that Rabbinic authorities inserted leap months in the calendar "for the sake of the trees, for the sake of the grasses, and for the sake of the *tekufot*," meaning that the lunar calendar had to be balanced with the cycles of planting and harvest and with the cycles of the solar year. Though the Rabbinic calendar was largely lunar, the Rabbis did indeed prefer that the winter solstice of Tevet fell in Tevet and the summer solstice of Tammuz fell in Tammuz. This was one of the reasons for the elaborate system of "long" and "short" months and leap months, which balanced the lunar calendar with the solar year. This implies a continued interest in the solar seasons from the point of view of Jewish sacred time.

Medieval traditions about the *tekufot* seem to have emphasized the eerie qualities of the solstices and equinoxes. The *Machzor Vitry* (13th century, France) indicates that frightening biblical events such as the plague of blood happened at the four seasonal transitions, and claims that there is blood in the water on these days.[3] Medieval authorities such as Moses Isserles (the Rema, 16th century, Germany) record that some Jews refrained from drawing water on solstices and equinoxes (Shulchan Arukh, *Yoreh De'ah* 116:5). This is a rare report of an actual Jewish practice related to the changes of the solar seasons. The idea that changes of the seasons had harmful side effects changes the valence of but does not negate the power of these days.

The *Otzar Midrashim* (*Hashem Behohmah, Yasad Aretz* 6) mentions an equally interesting and more positive midrash in which giant mythical beings and animals roar on each of the four seasonal dates. These roars compel the demons and wild creatures of the world to restrain themselves so that order prevails and life continues. Thus they encourage all beings to praise the compassion of the Divine. This midrash suggests that the solstices and equinoxes have both frightening and life-preserving qualities.

Contemporary Jews who feel connected to the solar year might use these ancient and medieval legends and practices as the basis for new seasonal rituals. *Midrash Tanhuma* (Korah 10) tells us that the chieftains of Moses were selected partly because they knew how to calculate and observe the *tekufot*. We can claim the wisdom of these mythic ancestors by learning ways to use the four seasons as a spiritual practice.

LEGENDS OF THE SEASONS

Spring equinox	*The triumph of life*
Summer solstice	*Loss and abundance*
Autumn equinox	*The link between earth and heaven*
Winter solstice	*The search for light*

Spring Equinox:

- Jubilees (6:25) records the 1st of Nisan as the day the Divine commanded Noah to build an ark and the day Noah opened the ark and saw dry land and was able to leave.
- *Seder Olam* (11:1), a work from talmudic times, relates that the new moon of Nisan, the day the Holy One gives the calendar to Moses in preparation for the first celebration of Passover, is also the spring equinox.
- The ancient midrashic collection *Pesikta Rabbati* (15:17), on the other hand, suggests the day of the Exodus was the spring equinox.
- In the *Machzor Vitry,* the spring equinox is the day the first plague, the plague of blood, falls upon Egypt.
- In *Otzar Midrashim* (*Hashem Behohmah, Yasad Aretz* 6), the spring equinox is the day when human beings receive protection from demons and evil spirits. On that day, the seraphim "lift up their heads to heaven, and the fear of them falls upon the demons and spirits, and the seraphim shelter human beings beneath their wings to hide them from the demons."
- The Purim holiday falls near the spring equinox. Its heroine, Esther, reveals herself as a Jew to save her people.

These tales associate the spring equinox with freedom (Noah leaving the ark, the Hebrews leaving Egypt), with divine protection from oppression or danger (entering the ark, the rising of the seraphim), and with life (the rebirth of the earth in the days of Noah, the blood in the Nile). In spring, the young plants bursting forth from the ground need protection and room to grow, and we ask this blessing for ourselves as well.

Summer Solstice:

- In Jubilees (6:26), in the story of Noah's Flood, the summer solstice is the day the mouths of the great abyss are closed, so that water ceases pouring onto the earth.
- Jubilees (3:32) also names the summer solstice as the day the Divine exiles Adam and Eve from Eden. This is the day the animals lose their power of speech.
- In *Seder Olam* (11:1), we learn that the day the sun stood still so that Joshua's warriors could win the battle of Gibeon was the summer solstice.
- In *Genesis Rabbah* (6:6), we learn that "on the summer solstice no creature has a shadow."
- In the *Machzor Vitry*, the summer solstice is the day Moses strikes a rock in anger while seeking water for the people. The Eternal tells Moses he will never enter the Land of Israel as a result of his actions.
- In *Otzar Midrashim (Hashem Behohmah, Yasad Aretz* 6), the summer solstice is the day animals receive protection from their predators. On that day "the Holy One puts strength in the Behemoth and it becomes strong and raises its head and cries out, and its voice extends through all the settled land, and the wild animals hear and are afraid."

In Jewish tradition, the summer solstice carries with it themes of closure (the mouth of the deep, the garden of Eden), exile (Adam and Eve, Moses), and loss (the animals' loss of speech), yet also the benevolence of nature and the Divine (the appearance of the water from the rock, the saving of the small animals, and the standing still of the sun). We meditate on grief, yet also on the world's abundance. Summer solstice is a day of paradox: maximum light but also a turn toward darkness.

Autumn Equinox:

- Jubilees (6:26), in its story of the Flood, records the autumn equinox as the day the floodwaters begin to descend back into the depths, so that the earth can be fruitful once again.
- On the autumn equinox, Abraham sits up all night to observe the stars, to forecast the rains of the coming season (Jubilees 12:16).
- In the *Machzor Vitry*, the autumn equinox is the day Abraham nearly sacrifices Isaac on Mount Moriah, before the Divine stays his hand. Because of his act, Abraham is blessed that his seed will be as the stars in the sky.
- According to the Babylonian Talmud (Rosh Hashanah 10b), Sarah, Rachel, and Hannah all conceive on the 1st of Tishrei, a date close to the autumn equinox (and possibly meant as the autumn equinox itself).
- In *Otzar Midrashim (Hashem Behohmah, Yasad Aretz* 6), the autumn equinox is the season of the *ziz*, when birds receive protection from their predators. "On the autumn equinox, the Holy One gives strength to the *ziz* and it becomes strong, and it lifts its head and flaps its wings and sends forth its voice, so that fear of it falls on the vulture and the osprey from one year to the next."

The autumn equinox seems related to the skies (birds), the stars (the blessing of Abraham), and the rains (as told in Jubilees). Yet it is also related to fertility (the matriarchs) and to the renewal of life. In many climates, autumn is a season of harvest and of rain. Perhaps the autumn equinox is the time of reforging the link between earth and heaven—a link necessary for life to continue.

Winter Solstice:

- In Jubilees (7), in the days of Noah, the winter solstice is the day the peaks of the mountains become visible after the floodwaters recede.
- In the Babylonian Talmud (Avodah Zarah 8a), Adam and Eve become frightened as the winter solstice approaches, thinking the shortening of the days is a punishment. They fast for eight days. On the winter solstice, when the light grows, they celebrate for eight days.
- In the *Machzor Vitry*, the winter solstice is the day Jephthah, a chieftain of Israel, sacrifices his daughter in fulfillment of a foolish battle vow. She has been bewailing her fate on the hills for two months.
- *Otzar Midrashim (Hashem Bechochmah, Yasad Aretz* 6), tells that on the winter solstice, Leviathan protects the creatures of the sea from their predators: "On every winter solstice he lifts his head and makes himself great, and blows in the water, and roils the sea, and makes all the fish in the ocean afraid." Leviathan is a creature known for being God's playmate (Babylonian Talmud, Avodah Zarah 3b) and a wise teacher of human beings (*Otzar Midrashim Alphabet of Ben Sira* 17). His eyes, according to the Talmud, flash in the deep (Bava Batra 74b).

The winter solstice seems to have to do with sight, or the lack thereof. Mountains become visible to Noah, and the patterns of nature become visible to Adam and Eve. Leviathan is associated with inner sight. Jephthah, on the other hand, is blind to his own wrongdoings. On the winter solstice, the sun's light begins to become stronger, and we too consider how to strengthen our vision.

A PRAYER FOR MARKING THE CHANGES IN SEASONS (*Havdalat ha-Tekufah*)

This blessing may be recited over a cup of wine on the day of the equinox or solstice. This prayer also may be recited along with a blessing over a scent related to the season, for example, flowers for spring, fruit for summer, leaves for fall, and pine boughs for winter. It is based on the following texts:

- The *Havdalah* ceremony dividing *Shabbat* from the weekday.
- The blessing over equinoxes and solstices found in the Babylonian Talmud (Berakhot 59b).
- The traditional evening prayer marking the transition between day and night.
- The Torah text in which the Holy One promises Noah that the seasons will continue as long as the earth endures (Genesis 8:22).
- The blessing over the abundance of years found in the daily *Amidah* prayer (recited in the feminine to honor the *Shekhinah*, the immanent Divine Presence).

Baruch ata Adonai Eloheinu melekh ha'-olam borei peri ha'gafen.

Blessed are You, Adonai, our Divinity who guides the world, creator of the fruit of the vine.

Beruchah at Shekhinah Eloheinu ruach ha'-olam, boreit isvei (atzei) vesamim.

Blessed are You, *Shekhinah,* our Divinity who embodies the world, who creates fragrant plants and grasses (or: fragrant trees).

Baruch ata Adonai Eloheinu melekh ha'-olam, oseh vereishit, asher bit'vunah meshaneh itim umachalif et hazemanim. Od kol yemei ha'aretz zera vekatzir vekor vechom vekayitz vechoref veyom velailah lo yishbotu. Beruchah at Shekhinah, mevarechet hashanim.

Blessed are you, Adonai, our Divinity who guides the world, who makes Creation, whose wisdom changes the times and turns the seasons. As long as the days of the earth endure, planting and harvest, cold and heart, summer and winter, day and night shall not cease. Blessed are You, Divine Presence, who blesses the years.

INTENTIONS FOR THE SEASONAL TRANSITIONS (*Kavanot la-Tekufot*)

For the Spring Equinox:

Arise, my beloved, my fair one, come away, for now the winter is past, the rains are over and gone, the blossoms appear in the land, the time of singing has come, and the song of the dove is heard in our land.
—Song of Songs 2:10–12

For the Summer Solstice:

A day is coming that burns like a furnace. . . . I will shine upon you who revere the name of the Infinite a sun of righteousness, with healing in Her wings.
—Malachi 3:19–20 (adapted)

For the Autumn Equinox:

May it be Your will that it be a year of rain and dew, a year of favor, a year of blessing, and a year of abundance . . . and please do not listen to the prayers of those who pray that there be no rain!
—Leviticus Rabbah 20:44

For the Winter Solstice:

We are grateful before You, Eternal One, for You have brought us from darkness to light.
—Midrash Bereshit 68:11[5]

NOTES

1 Crawford Howell Toy and Kaufmann Kohler, "Book of Jubilees," *Jewish Encyclopedia* (Funk and Wagall, 1906)

2 Cf. Crawford Howell Toy and Kaufmann Kohler, "Book of Jubilees," *Jewish Encyclopedia*.

3 *Machzor Vitry*, supplement 14, cited in Louis Ginzberg, *Legends of the Jews* (Jewish Publication Society, 1938), v. 6, p. 204, n. 109.

4 From the prayer of the high priest on Yom Kippur.

5 From the prayer for dawn.

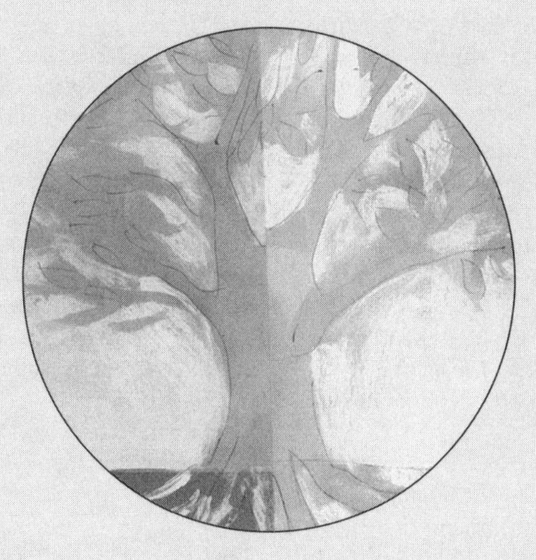

The author gratefully acknowledges permission to reprint excerpts from the following:

"Rediscovering Tziporah," by Rebecca Alpert, in *The Women's Torah Commentary,* edited by Elyse Goldstein, reprinted with permission from Jewish Lights Publishing, P.O. Box 237, Woodstock, VT 05091, *www.jewishlights.com.*

"Yocheved," by Penina Adelman, in *Praise Her Works: Conversations with Biblical Women,* edited by Penina Adelman, reprinted with permission from The Jewish Publication Society.

"Miriam," by Yocheved Bat Miriam, translated by Wendy Zierler, in *And Rachel Stole the Idols: The Emergence of Modern Hebrew Women's Writing,* edited by Wendy I. Zierler, reprinted with permission from Wayne State University Press.

"Serach: The Recovery of Joseph's Bones," by Marc Bregman, in *Living Text: The Journal of Contemporary Midrash* 4 (1998), reprinted with permission from the author.

Excerpt from *Voices from Genesis: Guiding Us Through the Stages of Life* by Norman Cohen, reprinted with permission from Jewish Lights Publishing, P.O. Box 237, Woodstock, VT 05091, *www.jewishlights.com.*

"Esther," by Tamara Cohen, in *Praise Her Works: Conversations with Biblical Women*, edited by Penina Adelman, reprinted with permission from The Jewish Publication Society.

The View from Jacob's Ladder: One Hundred Midrashim, by David Curzon, reprinted with permission from The Jewish Publication Society.
"Jephthah's Daughter," by Enid Dame, in *Living Text: The Journal of Contemporary Midrash* 5 (1999), reprinted with permission from Donald Lev.

From Jerusalem to the Edge of Heaven, by Ari Elon, reprinted with permission from The Jewish Publication Society.

"Abishag," by Jacob Glatstein, in *Modern Poems on the Bible: An Anthology*, edited by David Curzon, translated from the Yiddish by Richard J. Fein and reprinted with permission from The Jewish Publication Society.

"The Dark Rays of the Moon: Yom Kippur Katan as Preparation for Rosh Chodesh," by Shefa Gold, in *Celebrating the New Moon: A Rosh Chodesh Anthology*, edited by Susan Berrin, reprinted with permission from the author.

"Miriam the Bitter," by Naomi Graetz, in *All the Women Followed Her*, edited by Rebecca Schwartz, reprinted with permission from the author.

The Language of Truth: The Torah Commentary of the Sefat Emet, Rabbi Yehudah Leib Alter of Ger, by Arthur Green, reprinted with permission from The Jewish Publication Society.

Excerpt from *Sisters at Sinai: New Tales of Biblical Women*, by Jill Hammer, reprinted with permission from The Jewish Publication Society.

"Vashti's Tail," by Jill Hammer, in *Voices Israel*, reprinted with permission from the author.

"Miriam's Well," by Barbara Holender, in *All the Women Followed Her*, edited by Rebecca Schwartz, and reprinted with permission from Rikudei Miriam Press.

"Davar Acher," by Naomi Hyman, in *Biblical Women in the Midrash: A Sourcebook*, reprinted with permission from Jason Aronson.

"And Jacob Wept," by Gavriel Miccio, in *Living Text: The Journal of Contemporary Midrash* 2 (1997), reprinted with permission from the author.

"Marriage Certificate for Shavuot," by Israel Najara, in *The Shavuot Anthology*, reprinted with permission from The Jewish Publication Society.

"The Redeeming of Ruth," by Alicia Ostriker, revised from an earlier essay in *Reading Ruth*, eds. Judith Kates and Gail Twersky Reimer, reprinted with permission from the author.

"The Songs of Miriam," by Alicia Ostriker, in *Thirteenth Moon* 11 (1993) nos. 1 and 2, reprinted with permission from the author.

"In Search of Dreamers," by Debra Judith Robbins, in *The Women's Torah Commentary*, edited by Elyse Goldstein, and reprinted with permission from Jewish Lights Publishing, P.O. Box 237, Woodstock, VT 05091, *www.jewishlights.com*.

"Rachel and Leah: A Thousand and One Nights of Love," in *Biblical Women Unbound*, by Norma Rosen, reprinted with permission from The Jewish Publication Society.

A Prayer for the Earth: The Story of Naamah, Noah's Wife, by Sandy Eisenberg Sasso, reprinted with permission from Jewish Lights Publishing, P.O. Box 237, Woodstock, VT 05091, *www.jewishlights.com*.

"Joseph's Bones," by Judith Schmidt, in *Living Text: The Journal of Contemporary Midrash* 4 (1998), reprinted with permission from the author.

"Gathering the Sparks," by Howard Schwartz, in *Voices within the Ark: The Modern Jewish Poets*, edited by Howard Schwartz and Anthony Rudolf, reprinted with permission from the author.

"Bat-Sheva," by Savina Teubal, in *Praise Her Works: Conversations with Biblical Women*, edited by Penina Adelman, reprinted with permission from The Jewish Publication Society.

"The Rock," by Rivkah Walton, in *Living Text: The Journal of Contemporary Midrash* 1, (1996), reprinted with permission from the author.

Agnon, S. Y. *Present at Sinai: The Giving of the Law.* Schocken Press, 1959.

Amichai, Yehuda. *Patuach Sagur Patuach.* Schocken Press, 1998.

Angell, Carole. *Celebrations Around the World: A Multicultural Handbook.* Fulcrum, 1996.

Bellenir, Karen, ed. *Religious Holidays and Calendars: An Encyclopedic Handbook.* Omnigraphics, 1998.

Bialik, Hayim Nachman, and Yehoshua Hana Ravnizky. *The Book of Legends/Sefer haAggadah.* Schocken Books, 1992.

Bidland, Julye. *The Akitu Festival: Religious Continuity and Royal Legitimation in Mesopotamia.* Gorgias Press, 2002.

Cardin, Nina Beth. *Out of the Depths I Call to You: A Book of Prayers for the Married Jewish Woman.* Jason Aronson, 1991.

Charles, R. H. *Book of Jubilees.* A. and C. Black, 1902.

Chasida, Yisrael Yitzchak. *Otzar Ishi haTanakh.* Ya'ir Giat, 1995.

Cohen, Tamara, ed. *The Journey Continues: The Ma'yan Passover Haggadah.* Ma'yan: The Jewish Women's Project of the Jewish Community Center in Manhattan, 2002.

Crawford, Howell Toy, and Kohler Kaufmann. "Book of Jubilees." In *The Jewish Encyclopedia.* Funk and Wagnalls, 1906.

Davidson, Gustav. *A Dictionary of Angels, Including the Fallen Ones.* Free Press, 1994.

Edwards, Betsalel Philip. *Living Waters, The Mei haShiloach: A Commentary on the Torah of Rabbi Mordechai Yosef of Isbitza.* Jason Aronson, 2001.

Eisenstein, J. D. *Otzar Midrashim.* Judah David, 1915.

Elon, Ari. *From Jerusalem to the Edge of Heaven.* The Jewish Publication Society, 1996.

Elon, Ari, Naomi Mara Hyman, and Arthur Waskow. *Trees, Earth, and Torah: A Tu b'Shevat Anthology.* The Jewish Publication Society, 2000.

Encyclopaedia Judaica. Keter Publishing House, 1971.

Enkin, Jane. "Soul Candles." http://www.telshemesh.org/tishrei/soul_candles.html (accessed September 2005).

Fishman, Priscilla. *Minor and Modern Festivals.* Leon Amiel Publishers, 1973.

Frankfort, Henri. *Kingship and the Gods: A Study of Ancient Near Eastern Religion as the Integration of Society and Nature.* University of Chicago Press, 1978.

Frazer, James, *The Golden Bough.* Touchstone, 1995.

Ginzberg, Louis. *Legends of the Jews.* The Jewish Publication Society, 1938.

Goodman, Philip. *The Sukkot/Simchat Torah Anthology.* Jewish Publication Society, 1998.

Gottlieb, Lynn. *She Who Dwells Within: A Feminist Vision of a Renewed Judaism.* HarperSanFrancisco, 1995.

Green, Arthur. *A Guide to the Zohar*. Stanford University Press, 2004.

———. *The Language of Truth: The Torah Commentary of the Sefat Emet, Rabbi Yehudah Leib Alter of Ger.* The Jewish Publication Society, 1998.

Greenleigh, John, and Rosalind Rosoff Beimler. *The Days of the Dead: Mexico's Communion with the Departed.* Pomegranate Communications, 1998.

Harlow, Jules, ed. *Siddur Sim Shalom: A Prayerbook for Shabbat, Festivals, and Weekdays.* Rabbinical Assembly, 1989.

Hutton, Ronald. *The Stations of the Sun: A History of the Ritual Year in Britain*. Oxford University Press, 1996.

Jellinek, A. *Beit haMidrash.* Bamberger and Wahrman, 1938.

Jordan, Michael. *Myths of the World: A Thematic Encyclopedia*. Kyle Cathie, 1993.

Kaplan, Aryeh. *Sefer Yetzirah: The Book of Creation in Theory and Practice.* Weiser Books, 1997.

Killian, Greg. "Calendars and Feasts." http://www.tckillian.com/greg/feasts.html (accessed February 2005).

Leff, Boruch. "The Mystical White Snow." http://ww.aish.com/spirituality/kabbala101/The_Mystical_White_Snow.asp (accessed January 2005).

Lewinsky, Yom-Tov. *The Book of Festivals/Sefer haMoadim.* Agudat Oneg Shabbat, 1950–1957.

Luena, Nancy. *Celebrations of Light: A Year of Holidays around the World.* Athenaeum, 1988.

Marmorstein, A. "Midrash Avkir." *Devir* 1 (1923): 137–39.

Midrash Rabbah. Translated by H. Freedman. Soncino Press, 1983.

Orenstein, Debra. "Parashat Beshalach/Tu b'Shevat." In *The Jewish Journal of Greater Los Angeles*, February 6, 2004.

Page Two, Inc. "2003 Native American-Meso American-Hispanic Holidays." http://www.wheeloftheyear.com/2003/nativeamerican.htm (accessed March 2006).

Patai, Raphael. *The Hebrew Goddess.* Wayne State University Press, 1990.

Pliny the Elder. *Natural History*. Translated by H. Rackman. Harvard University Press, 2000.

Ribner, Melinda. *Kabbalah Month by Month: A Year of Spiritual Practice and Personal Transformation.* Jossey-Bass, 2002.

Rich, Adrienne. *Collected Early Poems: 1950–1970.* W. W. Norton and Company, 1993.

Rouach, David. *Imma, ou, Rites, coutumes, et croyances chez la femme juive en Afrique du Nord.* Maisonneuve & Larose, 1990.

Savedow, Steve. *Sepher Rezial haMelach/The Book of the Angel Rezial.* York Beach, 2000.

Scherman, Nosson, ed. *The Rabbinical Council of America Edition of the Artscroll Siddur: Weekday, Sabbath, and Festivals.* Mesorah Publications, 1984.

Schwartz, Howard. *Tree of Souls: The Mythology of Judaism.* Oxford University Press, 2004.

Soloveitchik, Joseph. *Halakhic Man.* The Jewish Publication Society, 1983.

Starhawk. *The Spiral Dance: A Rebirth of the Ancient Religion of the Great Goddess* (Special 20th Anniversary Edition). HarperSanFrancisco, 1999.

Stein, Siegfried. "The Influence of Symposium Literature on the Literary Form of the Pesah Haggadah." *Journal of Jewish Studies* 8, 1957.

Sztejn, A. and G. Wejsman, eds. *Pinkas Sochaczew.* Translated by Jerrold Landau. Jerusalem, 1962.

Telesco, Patricia. *365 Goddess.* HarperSanFrancisco, 1998.

Vilnay, Ze'ev. *Kol Agadot Eretz Yisrael.* Hotzaat haSafer, 1929.

Waskow, Arthur. "The Cosmic Origins of Tu b'Av." http://www.shalomctr.org/node/252 (accessed August, 2005).

———. *Seasons of Our Joy: A Modern Guide to the Jewish Holidays.* Beacon Press, 1991.

Wertheimer, Shlomo A. *Batei Midrashot.* Ktav vaSefer, 1968.

Winkler, Gershon. *Magic of the Ordinary: Recovering the Shamanic in Judaism.* North Atlantic Books, 2003.

Wolkstein, Diane, and Samuel Noah Kramer. *Inanna, Queen of Heaven and Earth: Her Stories and Hymns from Sumer.* Harper & Row, 1983.